TV Living

TV Living presents the findings of a British Film Institute project in which 500 participants completed detailed questionnaire-diaries over a five-year period, writing some three and a half million words on their lives, their television watching, and the relationship between the two.

David Gauntlett and Annette Hill use this extensive survey to explore some of the most fundamental questions in media and cultural studies, focusing on issues of gender, identity, the impact of new technologies, and the impact of viewers' own changing ideas and experiences. Opening up new areas of debate, the study sheds new light on audiences and their responses to issues such as sex and violence on television. The structure of the study enables the authors to track individual respondents' changing attitudes to new media as they experience life changes of their own.

Each chapter addresses a major contemporary theme in media studies: how families negotiate viewing choices, the impact of new technologies such as video, satellite and cable, how young people make the transition from children's TV to 'adult' programming, viewers' often guilty or ambivalent feelings about watching television, and audience responses to representations of women, disability, and violence. A unique study of contemporary TV audience behaviour and attitudes, *TV Living* offers a fascinating insight into the complex relationship between mass media and people's lives today.

David Gauntlett is Lecturer in Social Communications at the Institute of Communications Studies, University of Leeds. He is the author of *Moving Experiences: Understanding Television's Influences and Effects*, and *Video Critical: Children, The Environment and Media Power*, and edits the website www.theory.org.uk. **Annette Hill** is Senior Lecturer in Mass Media at the Centre for Communication and Information Studies, University of Westminster. She is the author of *Shocking Entertainment: Viewer Response to Violent Movies*, and is editor of the journal *Framework*.

Both David Gauntlett and Annette Hill are Research Fellows at the British Film Institute.

TV Living

Television, culture and everyday life

David Gauntlett and Annette Hill

Published in association with the British Film Institute

London and New York

First published 1999
by Routledge
11 New Fetter Lane, London EC4P 4EE

Simultaneously published in the USA and Canada
by Routledge
29 West 35th Street, New York, NY 10001

Routledge Ltd is a Taylor & Francis Group company

©1999 David Gauntlett and Annette Hill

Typeset in Palatino by Routledge
Printed and bound in Great Britain by MPG Books Ltd, Bodmin

British Library Cataloguing in Publication Data
A catalogue record for this book is available from the British Library

Library of Congress Cataloguing in Publication Data
TV Living: television, culture and everyday life/David Gauntlett and
Annette Hill.
Includes bibliographical references and index.
1. Television viewers – Great Britain – Attitudes. 2. Television – Social
aspects – Great Britain. I. HIll, Annette. II. Title.
PN1992.55.G38   1999   98–50244
302.23'45'0941–dc21   CIP

ISBN 0–415–18485–1 (hbk)
ISBN 0–415–18486–X (pbk)

For Susan and Don, for putting up with us, with love

Contents

Preface

This study has its origins in the BFI's *One Day in the Life of Television* project, which drew together the whole TV industry, and asked ordinary viewers about their experience of television on one day, 1 November 1988. This record of television, its makers and its audience was made at a point just before the immense changes which accompanied the introduction of satellite television in Britain. Some 20,000 members of the audience took part, and their contributions were reflected in the book edited by Sean Day-Lewis. So important seemed to be the changes underway in our television-viewing possibilities at that time that the BFI decided to embark on a longitudinal study with a small proportion of the original diarists. So was born the five-year Audience Tracking Study, and it is data from this project which forms the basis of this book.

The green light for the study was given by David Docherty, then Head of Research at the Broadcasting Standards Council, who believed that such a study was timely and provided the initial funding. The Council's (now Broadcasting Standards Commission) grant helped fund data collection for five years with Andrea Millwood Hargrave continuing to support the project when she took over the research role at the BSC. We would like to thank the members of the Audience Tracking Study advisory group, Jay Blumler, David Docherty, Andrea Millwood Hargrave and Roger Silverstone, for their advice and encouragement particularly during the design and development of the study.

For the financial support for this book we would like to thank the following institutions: Channel Four Television, the Independent Television Commission, Carlton Television and the BBC. We are particularly grateful for the enthusiasm and advice of Hugh Johnson, Bob Towler, Tony Hopewell-Smith and Robin McCron.

Thanks are also due to staff at the BFI, who during their careers there have made great contributions to this study: Jacintha Cusack for her invaluable assistance in the administration of the project and the storage of the data; Duncan Petrie, who was there at the beginning and co-edited the first book on the study, *Television and the Household*; and Alison Preston, who gave advice on diary design and had a special interest in the news.

We are particularly grateful to the writers, David Gauntlett and Annette Hill, who have managed to steer their way through the three and a half million words accumulated between 1991 and 1996 and have written so accessibly and interestingly about the role of television in people's everyday lives. They have been ably assisted by the research assistant at the BFI, Rob Turnock, who developed a method for finding a way through the data and who has advised at every stage of the process.

Finally we would like to thank the 450-plus television viewers who have stayed with us for so long, completing and returning their diaries over five years, and without whose generous and continued support this project would have been impossible.

Richard Paterson and Janet Willis
The British Film Institute

Acknowledgements

We would like to thank the BFI in general, and Janet Willis and Richard Paterson in particular, for inviting us to work on this project, and for their interest and support throughout. Janet Willis deserves an additional special mention for her fundamental role in the design and operation of the entire BFI Audience Tracking Study – along with Duncan Petrie. We extend a big thank you to Rob Turnock for his dedication and commitment to the project, and for the enormous amount of time and effort he put into reading the diaries and transforming them into a user-friendly format: you were invaluable. Many thanks to Rebecca Barden at Routledge for all of her enthusiasm and support. We are grateful to all of this project's sponsors, and particularly thank Andrea Millwood Hargrave of the BSC, Bob Towler of the ITC, Hugh Johnson of Channel Four, Tony Hopewell-Smith, and Robin McCron, for their interest in the work.

David would like to thank David Morrison for facilitating the original contact with the BFI, and Phil Taylor for his professional support whilst I have been working on the project. Graham Roberts has been a lovely and supportive colleague and friend. Justin Charlesworth and Andrew Thorpe again provided valuable practical help with shelving the diaries, and with software problems. Many thanks to Helen O'Nions, who assisted with further manipulation of the data, and had some useful reflections on the diaries. Thank you once again to the *Communications Theory* and *Media, Gender and Identity* students with whom I have discussed ideas, in particular Jenny Wood, Amy Bush, James McComas and Dave Miller; and Dyfrig Jones, who did some extra data excavation. Most of all I would like to thank Annette, for agreeing to join me in the ocean of diaries, and for being such an excellent companion as we struggled to haul some meaningful material out of the overwhelming amount of data.

Annette, in turn, would like to thank David for his encouragement and support, and for his ability to always say the right thing, and to always find a way through the maze. I would also like to thank my colleagues at CCIS for their advice and encouragement in the final stages of this research.

Annette extends special love and thanks to Don Butler, who cooks a mean chilli every night of the week. David's love and gratitude goes to Susan Giblin, a sparkly star, who (thankfully) doesn't.

Chapter 1

Introduction

Most of us carry television with us throughout our lives – albeit not, at the time of writing, literally. As children, the authors of this book had toys based on TV favourites, and we still struggle to fit paperwork on our desks without disturbing the plastic Dalek (pull back, trundles forward) and the die-cast metal Starship Enterprise (with alarming photon torpedoes). Sipping coffee from an *EastEnders* mug, we contemplate the books we have read and the different ways of looking at things we have acquired because of some TV series. At the age of 10 one of our favourite publications was the BBC book *Points of View* – based on the long-running show which airs viewers' letters about BBC programmes – published in 1981 (£1.50), and edited by its then presenter, the genial Barry Took. Since it involves people writing about television, it has some chilling similarities to this book, although we hope that our analysis is rather more sociological. Nevertheless, Took's book cuts straight to many of the same issues, with children often providing some of the best quotes. Ten-year-old Helen Steel, for example, provided this insight into family life around the television set:

> I like everything just like my Dad, even if he does not like the thing he still watches it. Mam says the box rules our life but i think thats stupid.

Similarly, Jonathan Chamberlain of Derby, aged 8, was beginning to get to grips with issues of sex and violence:

> My brother and I think Star Trek tonight was a waste of time. Grown ups kissing each other and saying sloppy things ugh it was dreadful. Please give us more fighting.

Perhaps the most refreshing letter was this acute methodological critique, from an anonymous child, and quoted here in full:

> Dear barry took. Why Do you get letters off people.

We know this feeling.

Like many other British viewers we also acquired a vague idea of what longitudinal social studies were about as we encountered programmes like *28 Up* and, seven years later, *35 Up*. These were part of a TV project which stems back to May 1964, when ITV broadcast a programme made by the *World in Action* documentary unit entitled *Seven Up*, which presented a group of fourteen 7-year-olds who were supposed to represent a cross-section of British children. Every seven years since then, update programmes have followed the group through their lives, with eleven of them still participating in 1998's *42 Up*. Its creator, Tim Hewat, was an Australian who had come to Britain and felt that it was 'fascinating, and appalling, the way class seemed to stamp someone's life from very early on', and he has described the programmes – directed by film-maker Michael Apted since 1970 – as 'the most remarkable documentary series in the history of television' (O'Hagan 1998). As the follow-up programmes had not been a part of *Seven Up*'s original design, the sample is not ideal. Its political emphasis on class differences meant that the fourteen included a comical trio of posh boys who could name the Cambridge colleges which they would attend, and only four girls (which Apted, who put the sample together as a researcher on the first show, now regrets).

Nevertheless, the sequence of programmes is a fascinating sociological resource. Like this study, they provide no really simple and straightforward conclusions, but reflect interestingly upon class in modern Britain (often but not always confirming the original suspicion that class would circumscribe the participants' destinies). The participants often convey sadness and regrets as they examine their lives, although they were generally satisfied with 'their lot', and are everyday yet remarkable examples of how people adjust to what life deals them. Through the unpredictable course of their lives, we also see their search for a place of *belonging* – a search which is only occasionally mucked up by the curse of being reluctant minor TV stars.

Taken together, the *Points of View* book and the *Seven Up* programmes represent the popular and rather more simple versions of what the BFI Audience Tracking Study, the major research project discussed in this book, was engaged in. Unlike *Points of View*, the respondents were meant to be reasonably representative, and were systematically asked to write about their lives as well as their media use and opinions, in an open diary-questionnaire, three times a year. Unlike *Seven Up*, our project covered five years – but involved around five hundred people. But just as the *Seven Up* documentaries managed to convey something of the richness and variety of the lives of different individuals in the course of relatively short TV programmes, we hope that we have also captured some of the detail and texture of the lives of our diarists, even though condensing all of that material into the confines of one book was, frankly, a struggle.

The method used in the present study, although conducted here on an unusually large scale, is not entirely new. In his account of the development of the BBC Audience Research Unit, Robert Silvey (1974) has noted that, at first, broadcasters did not feel any need to seek out their audience's attitudes and feelings. For ten years the BBC ignored the issue of audience research entirely: 'When anyone suggested that [the Corporation] was out of touch with its public, it would point to its postbag. Listeners had not waited to be asked their opinions; they had volunteered them' (1974: 28). Silvey was hired by the BBC in 1936 to set up a unit which would establish a more systematic approach to the study of BBC listeners. Silvey conducted large-scale, quantitative, longitudinal research, seeing the audience as 'customers' at the 'department store' called the BBC (Ang 1991: 142). In 1937, when Silvey decided to find out more about listeners for light entertainment radio programmes, he arranged for an announcement on the radio and in the *Radio Times*, the TV listings magazine published by the BBC, calling for volunteers for the study: 47,000 listeners offered their services. Throughout the second world war, the Audience Research Unit supplied important information to the BBC, and began to develop a picture of what the audience themselves liked and loathed about their radio broadcasts. Scannell and Cardiff (1991) note that Mass Observation's survey on the occasion of the 1937 Coronation recorded people's actions and feelings throughout the day as they listened, from their own homes, to the king being crowned. Mass observation was also used throughout the war as a means to judge the opinion of the people (Curran and Seaton 1997: 131). This early form of market research can be seen to share some similarities with survey and focus group research used today to judge the opinion of the people. There are also some similarities between mass observation and the BFI Audience Tracking Study, which also used diaries to ascertain the relationship between media and everyday life. However, before we consider the BFI study, we should take a look at the development of ethnographic audience research, a type of research which has influenced our approach to audiences and everyday life.

STUDYING TELEVISION AND EVERYDAY LIFE

In Morley's footsteps

No study of television, the household and everyday life could get away with ignoring David Morley's work in this area, if only because he was one of the first to do qualitative research in the domestic TV-watching environment, which means that his relatively small-scale *Family Television* study (1986) has been much-discussed – not least of all by Morley himself (whose 1992 book *Television, Audiences and Cultural Studies* recycles, but also engagingly and critically discusses, the same material). 'My own interests,' Morley explained, 'have increasingly come to focus on the *how* of television watching – in the sense of understanding how the process of television viewing is done as an activity' (1992: 133). Rather than examining people's responses to the content of particular TV programmes, as his earlier *Nationwide* study (1980) had done,

Morley turned his attention to the *activity* of viewing, for whole families. In doing so he emphasised, implicitly and explicitly, the need to understand individuals in the social context of their everyday domestic lives.

Morley criticises his own study of responses to *Nationwide*, a relatively lightweight TV current affairs show, for having assumed that 'deep structures' such as class positions would have direct 'effects' upon individuals' responses to the material. He subsequently acknowledges that whilst factors such as class, ethnicity and gender will have some impact upon which 'cultural codes' a person has access to, we also have to consider that individual's own responses to their social situation. 'To paraphrase Sartre,' Morley says, 'it is a question of what we make of what history has made of us' (1992: 136). On a more practical level, though just as importantly, he notes that the method of his *Nationwide* study, in which groups were shown recordings of the show, effectively caused his participants to 'produce' responses to a programme which they, in many cases, would not have had on, or would have ignored. This latter point indicates one of the key differences between Morley's *Family Television* and a whole mass of other studies (of which his own *Nationwide* research was but one example): it recognised that in the domestic context, the TV set being *on* was not synonymous with its output being *watched*. (Morley was partly influenced by the work of James Lull (1982), who had studied the ways in which programmes were selected for viewing in the home environment; Lull's work is discussed further below.)

Acting upon his arguments as outlined above, Morley sought to reject the individual-centred approach altogether and decided that 'the basic unit of consumption of television [should] be the family/household rather than the individual viewer' (1992: 138), although Morley himself admits that in the actual study this would often partly slip back, inevitably perhaps, into an analysis of the individuals who made up the unit (1992: 159). Even so, this would nevertheless produce an account of people's attitudes and behaviour seen within the broader family or household context, which would still be a significant improvement over the approach which assumed that the individual viewer would be 'making programme choices as if he or she were a rational consumer in a free and perfect market', described by Morley quite rightly as 'the height of absurdity when we are talking about people living in families' (1992: 139).

The findings of the *Family Television* study, which involved eighteen households in South London, are discussed in chapter eight (on gendered uses of TV), and also show up briefly in chapter six (on uses of video), as Morley's central finding was that gender was the one factor that cut across all of the other differences in the households that he studied: put simply, the men would almost always dominate the TV. It will also be seen that in the present study, we found that this was not usually the case, and we found little evidence of the polarised gender preferences (men liking realism, women loving romance) which Morley also describes. Although Morley goes to some lengths to emphasise that he does not consider his sample representative of the national population, and that his findings are the social product of a particular quarter of culture, there is nevertheless a kind of implicit claim that he is describing a more general phenomenon, and inevitably Morley's findings have appeared in textbooks shorn of the author's cautious qualifications. This means that Morley's work ends up being curiously *unhelpful*, reinforcing rather than breaking down the gender distinctions which Morley himself is critical of. (It should be noted that Morley himself recognises that this is a problem; Morley 1992: 160.)

Nevertheless, Morley's work was important because of its household-centred methodology, an approach reflected (in a somewhat different way) in the Audience Tracking Study presented in this book. And despite what we have said above, Morley did well to bring the important sociological issue of gender into a field which was dominated by awful pseudo-scientific, individualistic, psychological approaches to media audiences. (The shame is that his polarised report of gender differences sat all too easily with the deterministic work on gender in the self-styled psychological 'sciences'.)

Some other studies of media and everyday life

Morley has perhaps received a disproportionate amount of coverage in the literature on this area, given that a number of other researchers were conducting other interesting qualitative studies of people's uses of the media within everyday life at around the same time. Ann Gray (1987, 1992) conducted in-depth interviews in West Yorkshire with thirty mostly working-class women, in 1985–86. Gray explored their everyday lives and their feelings about domestic technology, with a particular focus on the video cassette recorder (VCR). Like Morley, Gray found that 'Gender is the key determinant in the use of and expertise in specific pieces of domestic equipment' (1992: 187), and identifies quite different gendered attitudes to the VCR, with men considering the watching of an action movie on video a welcome leisure event, whilst women are less interested in the VCR generally, and since the home is not a site of leisure for them, would rather go out. At the same time, again like Morley, Gray finds that some of these women like to steal moments of guilty pleasure from romantic love stories on video (see chapter eight). The detailed and rich interviews which Gray draws upon make this study an important contribution to our more detailed understanding of television and video in the home, and by focusing on women, the research was also valuable for bringing these often marginalised voices to light.

In fact, Gray was not the first to put women at the centre of her ethnographic audience research: Dorothy Hobson had also conducted two ethnographic research projects that are relevant to this study. In the late 1970s, Hobson (1980) undertook a study of the relationship between housewives and the mass media. She found that radio broadcasts provided a series of marker points in the day; housewives used the radio to alleviate stress and feelings of loneliness, and would often have it on in the background whilst they completed household chores. Hobson also discovered that women clearly saw a difference between the type of programmes they liked to watch on television (comedy series, or soap operas) and the programmes their husbands watched (news and current affairs programmes). In her subsequent research on viewers of *Crossroads*, an early-evening soap opera about life in a motel, Hobson (1982) made an important contribution to ethnographic audience research. She interviewed women in their homes and observed the domestic environment, often noting that women were engaged in a complex series of activities, such as cooking the evening meal, whilst at the same time attempting to watch their favourite soap on the television. Hobson found that: 'watching television is part of the everyday life of viewers' and many of the programmes that her respondents enjoyed were transmitted in 'a period of frantic activity in their daily lives' (1982: 110). She also found that in response to this, many women developed interesting ways of half-watching or listening to the programme while they were organising the evening meal. She described the difference between watching *Crossroads* with an elderly woman, who served tea, and put her knitting aside to watch the programme uninterrupted, and watching it with a woman who was 'serving the evening meal, feeding her five- and three-year-old daughters and attempting to watch the programme on a black and white television situated on top of the freezer opposite the kitchen table' (1982: 112). Hobson's research clearly showed that television programmes were incorporated into the framework of everyday life and that people watched television in a variety of different ways.

James Lull has conducted several important ethnographic studies in television viewing, focusing on families in America and China (1980, 1982, 1990). Lull was one of the first American sociologists to apply ethnography to family viewing practices, and he used anthropology and ethnomethodology (observation of routine behaviours) to consider the social uses of television in the home. In the 1970s, over a three-year period, Lull conducted a research project that focused on 200 families living in California and Wisconsin. The researchers lived with the families for two to seven days, making sure that they took part in the day-to-day routine of the household, and these periods of observation in the field meant that Lull had a well-grounded account of television and everyday life. From this research, he concluded that 'the social uses of television are of two primary types: structural and relational' (1990: 35). Television can act as an 'environmental source', or background noise; and it can act as a 'regulative source', a punctuation of time and activity: these are the *structural* uses of television. The *relational* uses are more complex: television can act to facilitate communication, or as a means to open up conversation; it can act as an 'affiliation or avoidance', a means to bring the family together and also to create conflict; it can encourage 'social learning', such as providing information or problem-solving skills; and it can be a focus for 'competence/dominance', for example as a means to exert authority, or facilitate an argument (1990: 36). Lull therefore established some important conceptual reference points for studies of television in the home.

As we are surveying previous notable ethnographic studies of media use from the 1980s, we should also mention Patricia Palmer's study of children and TV, *The Lively Audience* (1986). The study's three-stage methodology involved interviews with sixty-four children (aged 8–12), observation of twenty-three children's viewing in the home environment for a total of nine hours each, and a questionnaire survey of 486 other youngsters. As the book's title suggests, the findings were a refutation of the idea that children's TV viewing is 'passive' and not mentally engaging. Television viewing was found to be associated with 'fun, excitement and finding out about the world' (1986: 132), although the youngsters were selective and critical about the programmes which they watched. Children interacted with the TV set in a variety of ways, although not always with rapt attention: sometimes TV programmes were 'monitored' whilst the child focused on some other activity, and at other times television simply became a 'background' to family life, which carried on around the set (1986: 133–4). Talk about TV with friends was found to be a part of everyday routine, and provided 'an important basis of shared experience for children'. Palmer's study therefore captured a number of ways in which television was a meaningful, but not overpowering, part of children's everyday lives.

Further qualitative research on the family, media and everyday life appeared in two research projects by Rogge and Jensen (1988), conducted in West Germany in 1981 and 1986. The researchers were aware that 'each family undergoes different cycles of development. Such cycles are characterised by continuity and change in communication and media habits' (Rogge 1991: 172). They interviewed 420 families in total and used multiple-level analysis (taking into account other social factors) in order to situate media-related activities within the larger picture of the world of work, or other social activities. Rogge and Jensen talk about family experience and 'media worlds'. Family experience is not static:

> It encompasses the past, present and the future, as becomes apparent from the two concepts, family biography and family cycle. Everyday life is lived out in a field of tension formed by individual and family biographies, socio-cultural and social structures, and socio-historical processes of development.
>
> (Rogge 1991: 173)

This dynamic account of family experience is linked to the concept of everyday media knowledge, a 'media world', where each family constructs an understanding of television programmes which is based on their own interpretation of what these programmes mean to the family. Media worlds, the study therefore suggested, 'are the product of meaning-making within the family' (Rogge 1991: 173). Later studies, such as Joke Hermes's *Reading Women's Magazines*

(1995), based on eighty in-depth interviews, and Marie Gillespie's *Television, Ethnicity, and Cultural Change* (1995), based on more traditional ethnographic fieldwork – two years spent with the South Asian communities in an area of West London – are discussed later in this book.

The qualitative media research of the 1980s, such as those studies mentioned above – and Ien Ang's *Watching Dallas* (1985), which is discussed below – led to a general enthusiasm within media and cultural studies for what have come to be known, as we have already mentioned in passing, as 'ethnographic' studies. This term is not wholly inappropriate, as it reflects an engagement with everyday life and qualitative research; however, its meaning here is rather different from the way in which sociologists have traditionally understood 'ethnography', as research based on truly *lived-in* experience, where the researcher would spend several months or even years with their subjects. Critics might say that it is evidence of the short attention spans allegedly produced by TV, that media scholars have been satisfied with their 'ethnographies' based on a handful of afternoon chats. Shaun Moores, in his book on media ethnography, has to admit that on the whole the set of studies which he discusses 'have relied mainly on audio-taped conversations with viewers, listeners and readers which may not last much more than an hour each' (1993: 4).

Nevertheless, the rise of these qualitative studies, which we can call 'ethnographic' since that has now become an accepted (mis)use of the term, has been an extremely important development in media audience studies. By introducing the everyday context in which elements of the mass media are used, and by allowing media consumers to express or demonstrate what they make of these media in their own ways, such research has provided a much-needed antidote to the tradition of research based in the tradition of 'psychology', where a determination to appear 'scientific' has meant that people's own everyday interpretations have been deliberately excluded from the studies. Ien Ang (1991, 1996), David Morley (1992) and Roger Silverstone (1994), in particular, have all spent a lot of time writing about how valuable this kind of research is, and how important it is that we do more of it.

Silverstone and the paralysis of research

Roger Silverstone's *Television and Everyday Life* (1994) is a theoretical study of the relationship between television and domestic space. Silverstone asks about television, 'How is it that such a technology and medium has found its way so profoundly and intimately into the fabric of our daily lives?' (1994: 2). His book is an attempt to answer this question through consideration of ethnographic audience research and more theoretical approaches to the public and the private, the spatial and temporal in relation to television.

Silverstone is critical of empirical research that does not take into account the social environment, or what he calls 'the experience of television' (1994: 2). Silverstone identifies two general approaches that fail in this regard. First there is the kind of work that emphasises qualities of the *text* (the content of the TV programme) in relation to audiences, such as Livingstone's research on soap operas (1990), and Brunsdon and Morley's work on *Nationwide*'s content (1978, prior to Morley's 1980 study of peoples' actual responses to the show). This kind of research is praised for the way it provides a link between the social and 'text-centred explanations of audience activity' (1994: 148), but is still seen to be lacking in its account of the social environment, television and everyday life.

Second there are the studies that focus on *effects* and the audience, such as cultivation analysis (Gerbner *et al.* 1980, 1986; Morgan and Signorielli: 1990). Cultivation analysis hypothesises that people who watch larger amounts of TV will be more likely to think that the real world is like the world shown on TV. Unfortunately the approach sheds only limited light upon this interesting idea owing to its (American) scientistic, quantitative methodology, which uses surveys in a bid to find statistical correlations which, paradoxically, are often themselves meaningless because of the oversimplistic questionnaire-based data.[1] Whilst Silverstone maintains that 'Cultivation analysis provides a powerful and relevant framework from which to approach television's place in contemporary society' (1994: 140), he nevertheless rejects it for failing to consider the social dynamics of television within the household.

Silverstone argues that in the above types of study, 'the television audience still seems to emerge…rather like plankton floating on the surface of the Gulf Stream and the North Atlantic drift' (1994: 140). What is lacking from this research is proper consideration of the audience's *engagement* with television. As Silverstone explains it:

> We engage with television through the same practices that define our involvement with the rest of everyday life, practices that are themselves contained by, but also constitutive of, the basic symbolic, material, and political structures which make any and every social action possible.
>
> (1994: 170)

Silverstone goes on to define a theory of television, technology and everyday life that is based around the concepts of ontological security (a sense of security in oneself in relation to the patterns of everyday life), questions of agency, and the relationship between domesticity and consumption. However, Silverstone's theoretical account of television and everyday life could be regarded as premature. Before we can begin to understand the symbolic, material and political structures in everyday life, it is important to consider what people have to say about their own experience of television and everyday life, and the practicalities of television in the domestic space. Indeed, Silverstone has been criticised for publishing a book entitled *Television and Everyday Life* which proposes a number of densely worded theoretical hypotheses, but contains very little grounded analysis of either television or everyday life as they are actually experienced in the world.

In partial explanation of this, perhaps, Ien Ang (1996) has argued that the recognition of the need to include the context of everyday life in media audience research has led to a kind of paralysis amongst researchers. She quotes Morley and Silverstone's observation (in 1990) that 'the use of television cannot be separated from everything else that is going on around it' (Ang 1996: 68), but suggests that they have taken this rather too literally and required that research must record absolutely *everything* – not only the domestic context, but the context of that context (the neighbourhood?), the context of *that* context (the nation?), and so on. Obviously here both the baby and the bathwater have been launched into orbit.

Ang suggests that this 'radical contextualism' has produced a feeling – unsurprisingly, perhaps – that, since this approach suggests that all aspects of everyday life have to be studied in order to understand the place of the media, the project is simply too big to do. Only crazy researchers would attempt such a task. This is an interesting point for us, since the Audience Tracking Study, which this book is about, *is* just such a project, with almost every bit of domestic context, radical or not, documented somewhere in the three and a half million words which the respondents produced.

Research where audiences produce texts

The present study is not the first, of course, to get people to produce considered texts about their media consumption. Ien Ang's study *Watching Dallas* (1985, first published in Dutch in 1982) has become one of the most famous projects in the field of qualitative audience research, perhaps because it was one of the first studies to treat audiences of popular media seriously, and did so by sympathetically analysing their own responses to the subject. As Ang notes, at the start of the 1980s, the American soap saga *Dallas* (1978–91) was hugely popular in Holland, and much of the rest of the world ('in over ninety countries...from Turkey to Australia, from Hong Kong to Great Britain' (1985: 1)). Ang was unconvinced by those commentators who saw this success as the height of American cultural imperialism – after all, no-one was *forcing* over half of her country's population to watch the show each week – but also noted the ambivalent, love–hate relationship which she and others had with the series. Ang placed an advertisement in a Dutch women's magazine which invited people to write to her with their accounts of why they liked or disliked the show. The forty-two letters which she received in reply formed the basis of her study. Ang's analysis of these viewers' texts suggested that people enjoyed and related to *Dallas* because they found it *emotionally realistic* – not, of course, because they were oil millionaires themselves, but because the characters' series of domestic problems, rows, moments of happiness, and relationship disap-pointments, were readily identified with. For some of these viewers *Dallas* also presented a fantasy of happiness and fulfilment in its presentation of one happier relationship, between the characters Pamela and Bobby, which apparently gave them some hope for their own lives. Other people claimed to watch *Dallas* ironically, without taking it seriously, whilst even some who purported to hate the show clearly didn't feel that this should stop them watching it.

Inevitably, perhaps, Ang has to observe that there is no singular explanation for the popularity of *Dallas*. Each viewer 'has his or her own more or less unique relationship to the programme' (1985: 26). It is to Ang's credit that she was able to identify common themes and threads from her respondents' divergent comments. Without wanting to sound too self-pitying, we can note that the more data a researcher has, the more difficult it becomes to come up with distinctive generalisations – because the general conclusion that 'everyone is a bit different, everything is very complex' becomes more and more powerful. (In the study reported in this book, we have more than 200 times the amount of data that Ang had.[2])

Ang's *Dallas* study, then, pioneered the detailed study of 'trivial' (but culturally significant) tastes through the analysis of the audience's own responses. It is of particular significance here as the respondents were producing written texts at home, to a particular question about television, because they were willing to participate in that type of research – which has obvious similarities with our present study.

In a group of research projects which took a different angle, seeking to identify media *influences* rather than views and responses, several researchers connected to the Glasgow Media Group have asked participants to write their own news headlines or reports to accompany actual news photographs or headlines which they are given, or sometimes asked to write scripts to accompany other material (see for example Kitzinger, 1990, 1993; Philo, 1990, 1996; Miller, 1994). These studies generally show that the respondents often reproduce the language and ideological approach of the original news reports – although in several of the studies there is the serious problem that the participants may be consciously mimicking or parodying the original material, and the researchers often fail to address this adequately, instead tending to see the reproduced discourses as an 'effect'.

One such study is Greg Philo's work (1996) on the media's representation of mental illness, and the possible influence of this upon viewers. Participants were given the *Daily Mirror*'s 1993 headline 'Set on fire by a maniac', accompanied by a photograph of a young boy, and asked to write the story. The texts produced reflected the tone and assumptions of tabloid coverage of the story. Taking a different approach in the same study, Philo also asked participants to write a script to accompany photographs of scenes from a 1993 storyline in the soap opera *Coronation Street* which involved a young woman who was 'obsessed', *Fatal Attraction* style, with one of the male characters. Only those who had watched the show were asked to participate in this part of the study, and they remembered the language and attitudes of the characters well, and generally found this female character frightening. The report and script-writing elements of this study seem to confirm, then, that the mentally ill are often demonised in the media, and that these features stick in the minds of the audience. They do not really tell us about the extent to which this may have affected the participants' view of the mentally ill in real life, although in discussions some individuals revealed that they had known or spent time with mentally ill people and had not found them to be violent, and yet they still associated mental illness with the kind of violent 'psycho' seen in many movies. Used in conjunction with other interview-style methods, then, this method is an innovative and revealing use of texts produced by audience members themselves.

Also relevant in this context is the qualitative, broadly ethnographic study by David Gauntlett, published as *Video Critical: Children, the Environment and Media Power* (1997). In this research project, the author worked with groups of around eight children at each of seven primary schools, as they made videos on the subject of 'the environment'. The broader aim of the study was to explore the impact of the coverage of environmental issues on television, which had been quite considerable since the late 1980s, on children's awareness and concern about the environment.

The study found that when making their *own* videos about environmental matters, children would tend to reproduce the emphasis found in most children's TV programmes on the subject, which focused on small-scale local solutions – such as recycling and conservation of resources at home – and ignored the macro, industrial and governmental causes of large-scale pollution and environmental damage. When understood as another way of studying children's responses to the media – through their own media productions – this new research method could be seen as a progression from the studies discussed above, with the participants producing video 'texts', rather than written ones (or the spoken 'texts' produced in focus-group or interview settings), which would be taken by the researcher to reflect their responses to the mass media. The method also allowed the children involved to demonstrate their impressive media literacy, and to generate their own repudiation of the other kind of research, particularly from the discipline of psychology, which has traditionally disenfranchised young people and not recognised their capacities in relation to the mass media. In a similar way, the Audience Tracking Study gave a voice to everyday viewers, inviting them to bring their own concerns to the fore in the research process – although then, of course, researchers such as ourselves have to pick up on these themes, rather than ignore them; which brings us to our methodology.

THE AUDIENCE TRACKING STUDY
METHODOLOGY

The 1988 *One Day in the Life of Television* project marked the beginning of the present study. This 'mass observation' project involved 22,000 people from around the United Kingdom who wrote a diary about their television viewing for 1 November 1988. These respondents had been recruited via an extremely visible advertising campaign – in the press, on posters and leaflets, and in particular on television itself, with announcements placed in peak slots next to mainstream programmes. This study's participants included both media practitioners and viewers, and a book (edited by Sean Day-Lewis, 1989) and documentary were produced after the event as a record of what the nation had to say about the role of television in 1988. This project showed that people had a great deal to say about television, and Day-Lewis used extracts from diarists to indicate that the British public is discerning in its television viewing and has 'a firm idea of what constitutes acceptable, and trashy, television' (1989: xiv). In many ways the *One Day in the Life of Television* project marks a period in British television that could be considered as the old order of broadcasting, before the 1990 Broadcasting Act changed the nature of the industry, then dominated by the BBC–ITV duopoly, to incorporate a more competitive, multi-channel approach.

The BFI Audience Tracking Study respondents were picked from this large, self-selected sample, and invited to participate. Janet Willis, Richard Paterson and Duncan Petrie had constructed a sample that was generally representative of the population as a whole. Variables such as sex, age, marital status, region, occupation, and household size and composition were taken into account. The longitudinal study was designed to run from 1991 to 1996, and consisted of fifteen questionnaire diaries completed by an initial 509 respondents, which had dropped to 427 respondents at the end of the project. The problem of attrition – respondents dropping out – is widely recognised as a serious problem for longitudinal studies (Dex 1991: 5), and the fact that 84 per cent of diarists stayed with the study is a remarkable testament to the commitment of the BFI research team, who sent them birthday and Christmas cards every year, and wrote personally in response to major developments which appeared in the diaries (such as serious illness, or the death of a partner), as well as in reply to diarists' other notes and queries.

Table 1.1 shows the breakdown by age group at the start of the study.

Table 1.1 Breakdown of respondents by age group, compared with the general UK population, 1991

Age	Tracking Study	UK population[a]
Under 16	9%	29%
16–39	33%	35%
40–64	29%	29%
65+	29%	16%

Note
[a] *Social trends 1991*

We can see, then, that the sample is under-representative of the under-16 age group and over-representative of the 65 and over age group, compared to the UK population figures for 1991. Women are also very slightly over-represented, with 53 per cent of the sample female, and 47 per cent male. The respondents were fairly well educated; in 1995, 24 per cent had or were about to have a higher education degree, and a further 16 per cent had been in further education. Twenty-one per cent of the sample were in full-time education at the start of the study, and 35 per cent were retired, which shows a bias towards students and retired people in the study overall. The income for the majority of diarists was £10,000–20,000 (25 per cent), with just over 17 per cent receiving between £5,000 and £10,000, and with as many as 27 per cent of respondents earning less than £5,000 in a year, again reflecting the number of low-income students and retired people in the sample.

In terms of geographical location, the sample was spread across a range of areas of the United Kingdom, with people living in the south, central and northern parts of England, Scotland and Wales, with a small percentage of respondents living in the Channel Islands and in Northern Ireland. Similarly, respondents lived in rural areas, villages, small and large towns, and cities. (See Appendix for full details.)

The BFI did not record the ethnicity of diarists, and no questions were asked about ethnicity or racial issues. This has meant that, unfortunately, we were unable to address in this book questions of ethnicity in relation to either broadcasting content or reception. It seems likely that ethnic minorities were under-represented in this study, and this – along with the lack of data on these related issues – has been disappointing.

Because of the nature of this study, which takes into consideration the significance of change over a five-year period within family and household life, our sense of what 'the family' means must take into account the notion that 'the family' is not a fixed entity, but something that is in constant state of flux. Silverstone has noted that 'researchers need to recognise…that families are problematic entities, not only in terms of their composition, but also in terms of their changing character in modern society' (1994: 33). He refers to Pitkin (1985) and Wilson and Pahl (1988), who have claimed that 'the study of the family should be the study of process…the family should be understood in the terms in which family members themselves define it' (Silverstone 1994: 32). This is basically the approach taken in the present study, where the study of process is from the perspective of household members themselves. We have given particular attention to different household compositions, such as single-parent families, student accommodation, and households with only one adult, as well as the more traditional composition of the nuclear family, reflecting the changing nature of household composition in the 1990s. Table 1.2 shows how the households were composed.

Table 1.2 Composition of respondents' households, compared with the general UK population, 1991

Type of household	Tracking Study	UK population[a]
Single person	22%	26%
Two adults	29%	28%
Two adults and two children	24%	24%
Single parents	2%	10%
Others	23%	12%

Notes
[a]*Social Trends* 1991
[b]More than two adults, including families with non-dependent children, student households, halls of residence, etc.

In terms of technology, the respondents in this study had access to a range of equipment. In 1991, 31 per cent of respondents had one television in their household; 38 per cent had two TVs; 18 per cent had three TVs; 7 per cent had four; and 4 per cent had five TVs. In 1996, the figures remained similar. In 1991, 59 per cent of the sample had one video cassette recorder in their household; 11 per cent had two; 3 per cent had more than two; and 27 per cent did not have one at all. In 1996, only 13 per cent said that they did not have a video, and 21 per cent of the sample had two videos in the household, showing an overall rise in the number of videos from 1991 to 1996. The majority of respondents (90 per cent) had a television with a remote control, and 68 per cent had teletext. In 1991 around 7 per cent had satellite and cable services (6.8 per cent satellite, 1.3 per cent cable) and this had gone up to around 26 per cent in 1996 (20.4 per cent satellite, 5.3 per cent cable). Nearly everyone in the sample had at least one radio in the household (98.8 per cent), and around 17 per cent had video cameras by 1996. Those who had telephone answering machines numbered 38 per cent, and nearly half of the sample had a personal computer in 1996 (48.7 per cent), but only 8 per cent had an internet connection.

Janet Willis and Duncan Petrie, the primary coordinators of the study as it ran, explain how the data was collected three times a year throughout the five-year period:

> The first *One Day* project required respondents to complete an unstructured diary about their viewing...For the Tracking Study the diary format was extended to include structured questions relating to television viewing, household compositions, and daily routines, alongside more open evaluative sections soliciting opinions about specific programmes, or TV genres, and topical issues concerning television in general. In addition, a viewing chart was constructed on which respondents could note the programmes

they watched on the day in question, with whom they watched them, the amount of attention given to these and whether they had planned to watch them.

(Petrie and Willis 1995: 4)

Various different approaches were taken, as we began to consider the collected data, to manage and collate the amount of information that had developed over this five-year period. As we have already mentioned, the diarists had managed to write a collective three and a half million words. The question was: how were we to become familiar with this data, and how would we best navigate our way through the diaries? Should we consider each individual diarist on their own, or look at subsets of people, or group responses to themes, such as daytime TV, or media violence?

Ethnographic research, according to Baszanger and Dodier, has three requirements: '1, the need for an empirical approach; 2, the need to remain open to elements that cannot be codified at the time of the study; 3, a concern for grounding the phenomena observed in the field' (1997: 8). We have already discussed the need for an empirical approach to television audiences. The 'need to remain open' is very important to qualitative research. In this study, the data collection was rigorous, with the diaries being sent out three times each year,[3] and including some standardised questions in order to ensure that there was a guide for both the researcher and the people in the study. However, at the same time it was important to remain open to new data and be able to respond to the longitudinal nature of the study, focusing on change over the five years. As Petrie and Willis note above, the respondents were asked a combination of standardised and one-off open-ended questions in each diary, enabling them to give on-going accounts and reflections on their lives in general, and media use in particular, as well as enabling the researchers to collect their thoughts on a range of different issues in different diaries. Some questions about uses of and interaction around the TV were posed in varied ways on separate occasions. In studies involving grounded *observation*, the researcher must ensure that they relate what they have observed to the wider context in which this has taken place (Glaser and Strauss 1967; Strauss 1987). In the case of this study, which of course did not involve physical observation of the respondents at home, we had nevertheless to ensure that any findings were grounded in a specific context, and therefore the diarists' own descriptions of their home life, despite their subjectivity, were vital here. After some exploratory work, we arrived at a way of storing and examining the data which would allow us to access various themes, incidents and opinions whilst keeping the data within its all-important context (see Appendix for details).

How we approached the data

As we began work on this project, some people asked us, 'What theory are you using?' We found this difficult to answer, and slightly bewildering. We were not intent on clamping *any* preconceived theory onto our data. It is not that we have anything against theory: on the contrary, our interests are almost entirely theoretical; we engage with empirical research only because we recognise that theory which has no connection with the world and how people perceive it is, to put it politely, lacking something. But in any case, the way that researchers use the term 'theory' in this context is slightly fanciful. What they basically mean is, 'What are the interests and concerns which you are going to pursue?', which is much easier to answer.

First of all, we wanted to be led by the respondents, as it were, rather than approach the data with a set of questions, concerns and assumptions which the diaries would simply confirm or deny. Naturally, we had a range of interests and issues which we imagined the diaries would illuminate, but we have tried to follow up new leads presented by the data itself, and sought to pay closer attention to the issues and material which the data itself made more pressing. To illustrate this point, for example, when we were securing a contract for this book's publication, we were unable to tell our publishers, Routledge, exactly what would be in it. We indicated a range of areas which we thought would be likely to be fruitful – under advice from those at the BFI who, at that time, knew more about the respondents and their diaries than we did – and some topics which we thought were important enough for us to pursue them anyway, such as gender issues, and views about screen violence (which steadfastly refuses to stop being a controversial area in media audience research). It can be noted that in some ways the latter areas – violence in particular – which we worked on early in the analysis period, are concerned with people's views about TV *content*, and therefore differ from the rest of the book. The way in which our approach steadily changed to be increasingly aligned with the 'grounded' theme of 'television as part of everyday life' can be seen in the way the rest of the book developed. A chapter that we had offered to do on 'technology', for example, which had not at first sounded like a very engaging theme, turned out be full of good stuff as we found that people had absorbed TV-related technologies, such as video, into their everyday lives in a number of creative ways. A chapter on news, which we had originally imagined might involve people's opinions of news programmes, turned out necessarily to be about how people arrange their time and punctuate their days in relation to news broadcasts.

The theme of *change* over the five years of the study also turned out to be enormously important. Our initial focus on some stock 'media studies'-type questions meant that we failed to recognise the real importance of this theme at first: after all, we thought, people's views on TV violence, say, would probably be similar in 1996 to what they were in 1991. This remained true, on the whole, but is something of a red herring, since the important and interesting changes (which we forgot at first) are the *changes in people's lives*. These changes cannot be missed in the diaries: people grow older, get married, get divorced, get a job, become unemployed, fall ill, move house, have children or see them leave home, retire, lose loved ones, fall in love, and experience a massive range of other unpredictable developments, shifts and transitions. We therefore have sought to integrate the theme of change through all of the chapters.

In doing this, we have been informed by the 'life analysis' approach which has been developed in social anthropology and the social sciences. This seeks to create accounts based on the context of people's developing lives, entwined with the individual, structural and institutional factors which affect these on-going narratives. Outlining the area, Shirley Dex has noted that:

> Life and work history data...are a recognition of the importance of the overlap in the chronology between individuals' lives and social and institutional structures as well as between related individuals. Both sets of these relationships are important in trying to unravel social life and gain a better understanding of it.
>
> (Dex 1991: 1–2)

On the understanding that 'individuals' lives are the stage on which societal changes are played out' (1991: 2), this approach assumes that through close study of people's everyday lives over time, we will acquire a picture of broader changes in society which are having an impact at the individual level. Life-history analysis postulates that sociological investigations should not simply describe life histories for their own sake; rather, as Paul Bellaby argues,

> Cases must be treated as samples of the social: if not probability samples of a defined population drawn to test propositions, then what Glaser and Strauss (1967) call 'theoretical samples', selected to explore the various dimensions of social structure, and to enable theory to be built on evidence.
>
> (1991: 20)

Although we have been cautious about drawing deterministic conclusions based upon our sample who are, by definition, people willing to complete quite lengthy diary-booklets for the BFI three times a year, and who unknowingly presented themselves into the sampling process when they completed a *One Day in the Life of Television* diary back in 1988, we have sought to take on board this general approach of life-history analysis: sociological and conscious of wider contexts, but at the same time fundamentally led by the (changeable) subjectivities of respondents.

We should also mention how we considered people's diaries in relation to the demographic facts which we knew about them. We saw above that Morley had come to recognise the flaws in his assumption, in the *Nationwide* study, that individuals' responses to the material would be a product of their class and background. Sharing Morley's subsequent reservations, we have rather gone the other way, and to an extent have consciously *avoided*. generating supposed 'explanations' of things which people have said by referring to their demographic characteristics or background. This is certainly the case with regard to their occupation and geographical location; we realised at an early stage that talking about extracts of respondent's diaries in terms of their being a 'Somerset farmer', 'London-based journalist' or 'Glasgow factory worker' tended to produce mental stereotypes which any other details about a diarist were just 'pasted' on to, creating a veneer of understanding which is often actually illusory. As a kind of compromise to avoid this, we have generally left out geographical information. Having said that, the age and sex of respondents is made relevant at various points in this book. Geography may well be relevant in some ways too, and the data remains at the BFI for those who want to explore this.

For respondents' occupations, we have generally used the terms which the people themselves provided. This sometimes leads to inconsistent terminology; for example, where the woman in a heterosexual couple did not have paid employment outside the home, she would most often describe herself, in this study, as a 'housewife', whilst a man in the same position would most commonly see himself as 'unemployed'. Rather than imposing our own terms in order to avoid problems such as this, we decided to retain the respondents' own authentic descriptions of their status. Therefore the three women who described their occupation as 'farmer's wife', for example, have not been redesignated as 'female farmer' even though this might seem to be more appropriate, given their own detailed descriptions of the work that they did.

The arrangement of this book

In the following chapter we will begin to discuss the place of television in everyday life: how it is fitted into people's internal schedules, the meaning of different times of the day and week, the planning of viewing, interaction around the television, as well as everyday activities not related to television. Chapter three serves as an illustration of some of these themes, as it focuses on the way in which the watching of news programmes is fitted into people's daily business and affects the shape and character of their everyday lives. In chapter four we consider transitions and change in life before the age of 50, and how these affect television use. As people grow up, change schools, do exams, enter the worlds of work or university or unemployment, and perhaps get married, have children, change jobs, get divorced, and so on, we will see that television viewing varies greatly, both in the amount of time spent and in the meaning and purpose of that viewing. In chapter five we turn to the meanings which television has for individuals, bringing companionship, but also guilt; and giving people a common culture on which to base some social interaction, and identification. In chapter six we discuss how people have fitted TV-related technologies, such as video and satellite TV, into their lives, including how they feel about these facilities, and the creative uses they make of them.

We have devoted all of chapter seven to the retired and elderly audience, since there has been little written about this sector of the population in relation to media consumption, and because the Audience Tracking Study provided a rich seam of information on this group. Again, we explore their tastes and uses of television, and what the medium means to them. In chapter eight, we consider television viewing and preferences in relation to gender, including what women and men feel about gendered representations on TV, as well as the ways in which they watch it. In chapter nine, we examine what the diarists had to say about television violence, which continued to be a reasonably 'hot' topic in public discourse during the 1990s, as well as their views on other controversial material, and whether these perceptions changed over time. And finally, chapter ten, the conclusion, pulls together some of the themes which have emerged: time and change, the changing landscape of gender, identity, 'seduction' by TV, and reflections on the research process.

Notes

1   Other criticisms of cultivation analysis include its inability to take into account questions of genre and media content, and its assumption that the audience pays full attention to television, which, as we know from this and other studies, is not necessarily the case. For some further criticisms of the way in which cultivation analysis is conducted, see Gauntlett (1995).

2   This figure is based on the guess that the letters Ang received may have been on average 400 words long. The BFI Audience Tracking Study, it will be recalled, gathered around three and a half million words from its respondents.

3   The BFI sent out diaries in different months, in order to increase the variety in the times at which diaries had been completed and to detect seasonal shifts; similarly, diaries were set for different days of the week.

Chapter 2

Television and everyday life

In this chapter we will consider the ways in which television fits in and around the activities of everyday life. The relationship between television and daily living is a complex one, and it is important to remember that although TV has a significant role to play in the household, it is not necessarily the determining factor in the planning of day-to-day activities. When we look at television in the household, we have to consider a variety of different types of household forms and arrangements. The household is not synonymous with the nuclear family, and in this study households consisted of students, single-parent families, the elderly and people living alone, as well as married couples with children. It follows that if British households take a variety of forms, then these people must also conduct their lives in a range of different ways. Television can be part of domestic routine, but what constitutes routine for an elderly couple living in a rural cottage will be quite different from that of a single working woman living in a city bedsit. In this chapter we will focus on how television is part of the domestic space, but we should emphasise that TV fits into and around everyday life, and other factors such as children, work, friends and leisure activities can be as important as, if not more important than, television.

In the many different kinds of household covered by this study, there were a wide range of ways in which TV viewing would be incorporated into the other activities and routines of daily living. In her work on time and family structure, Jennifer Bryce (1987) focused on the way in which the family's organisation of time has a significant effect on the role of television in the home. Her work drew upon Edward Hall's distinction between monochromatic time and polychromatic time (1973), which sees a difference between the structure of schedules and portions of time, and a temporality that is concerned with more than one thing happening at the same time. Bryce writes: 'The sequencing of viewing, its place in the mesh of family activities, reflects a choice, an organisa-tion, a negotiation process which very little is known about' (1987: 123). Paddy Scannell similarly discusses the relationship between what he calls 'clock time' and 'life time', which are the 'continuous flow of day-to-day life' and the 'temporality of the life cycle of living organisms' (1988: 15). For Scannell, each of these events is part of the daily experience of broadcasting, which he sees as a 'slow, glacial movement of institutional time' (ibid.) that long outlasts our own lifetime. In this chapter we shall see how everyday life is structured by a clearly organised schedule, a schedule for domestic activities and for entertainment activities, which combines what Scannell calls 'clock time' and 'institutional' or 'calendrical time'. However, this schedule is not fixed, and we can see how different types of households, such as single parents, students living in shared accommodation, retired people, and parents with children, negotiate changes to this schedule, changes that can be seen to be part of what Scannell calls 'life time'.

The BBC conducted a survey in 1979 that looked at the way in which people organise their daily routines in the household. Nearly 1,400 people kept diaries which recorded the primary and secondary activities for everyone in the household, for every half-hour from five in the morning to two o'clock the next day. Thus, the research showed what people were doing at all times of the day, and whether they categorised listening to the radio and watching television as primary activities. Scannell discusses the implications of this project:

> The overall implication to be drawn…is that the axes of difference both for daily activities and the proportion of time spent on them are determined primarily by age and gender, with occupation and marital status as major determining differences between adults before the age of retirement…what emerges from the study is the interlocking of lifetime with the time structures of the day.
>
> (1988: 26)

Thus this BBC study of daily life found that how old you are and what sex you are can be quite significant to the way in which everyday activities are organised in relation to the time of day.

Rogge and Jensen (1988) and Rogge (1991), in their research on West German families and media use, found that everyday family life is built upon a daily and weekly schedule that incorporates routine and change. Rogge identifies two levels of reality, an 'objective media reality, i.e. the significance the media have in everyday family life', and on a different level, 'subjective media reality, i.e. the fact that families structure their everyday lives on the basis of greatly varying ideas' (1991: 178). This research shows that media activities are part of a family routine, and that this can help us to understand people's lifestyle choices, even though different family members perceive the routine differently. According to Rogge, the way that the media can be part of family routine 'defines interpersonal relationships and the emotional and communicative climate in a family' (1991: 179). Certainly, we shall see in this chapter that routine and the management of time can illuminate sites of interaction and family conflict in the household.

An American study of television and everyday life by Kubey and Csikszentmihalyi (1990) used quantitative research methods to ascertain whether television viewing was an active or passive activity in the home. They considered when people watch television, who they watch television with, and what they choose to do whilst watching television. They found that '63.5 per cent of the time television was being viewed, people reported doing something else as well' (1990: 75), showing that television is part of the domestic space and is often incorporated into other household activities. However, despite this claim, the authors conclude that television viewing is a passive activity and that many people are affected by television in similar ways (1990: 174). They also claim that television viewing is unchallenging and does not involve a great deal of concentration.

It is certainly the case that in this chapter people talk about relaxing in front of the television, particularly at mealtimes, or late evening. However, this study, and other research on television and everyday life, quite clearly show that the way in which television viewing is part of everyday life varies from household to household. Single parents, students living in rented accommodation, people living alone, all report highly individual accounts of how television is part of their daily routine. Therefore, in this chapter we shall show that television viewing patterns are not standardised, and that watching television is not a passive activity.

TELEVISION AND THE ORGANISATION OF TIME

In this study, every diary contained a question asking respondents to write about their typical day. Answers to these questions invariably led to discussion about breakfast, lunch and evening meal times in the household, and to the way in which the family organised their time in relation to work, school, hobbies and television viewing. In this section we will look at how television is fitted around other routine activities, with certain programmes becoming marker points in the day.

It comes as no surprise to find that television is heavily integrated into people's lives and routines. And because broadcast TV has set timetables, and so is the inflexible party in the TV–viewer relationship – leaving video time-shifting aside for the moment – people's everyday activities are shifted, elongated or cut short to accommodate the programmes that they want to watch. This young woman is typical:

> Television is an important part of my life. I rarely have it on if there is nothing I want to watch, but if there is a good programme on I love sitting down to watch it with a cup of coffee and a bar of chocolate. Often I time my meals to coincide with something good. I like eating and watching television. I also often iron whilst watching. When I clean I prefer listening to music.
>
> (24-year-old female electronic engineer)

The same diarist would switch on her bedroom TV in the morning for the weather forecast, 'to help me decide what to wear'; this would also, of course, mean that she saw an amount of breakfast TV before and after the nugget of information which she sought.

In some households, some people actually woke up to the sound of the TV: 'On a typical day my brother is woken up by an ITV morning programme which is connected by a time switch. The lodger also watches breakfast TV too' (10-year-old schoolboy). One student described her typical morning as follows:

> My mum is normally the first one up as she has to get my sister out of bed. Then the rest of the family appear one by one. We never eat breakfast together as we go off at different times. I like to read the newspaper while I'm eating my breakfast and also watch the television. My mum is around at this time and my Dad is normally doing the breakfast things. My sister has gone off to work and my brother off to school. Television is not so important in the mornings as we never have the time we would like to watch and enjoy it.
>
> (21-year-old female learning support assistant)

Breakfast time is usually very busy for most diarists, and if they do watch TV, it is only for brief periods, or used as background noise whilst other chores are done. In general, 61 per cent of respondents claimed that they did not organise their household chores to fit in with television programmes, compared to 25 per cent who said that they occasionally did this, and only just over 10 per cent who said that they often did this. Afternoons appear to offer slightly more time for relaxation, although this is of course dependent on work, family needs and hobbies. This mother, for example, described the afternoon and early evening as a time when the television would be on, but not necessarily being watched by the family:

> I like quiz programmes so I watch *Turnabout* whilst tidying the house. After the children come home from school they sometimes watch TV. If the weather is good they will play in the garden until tea time. They know the characters in *Neighbours* and *Home and Away* but don't really follow the plot. After tea we watch *Emmerdale* or *Coronation Street* depending on the day of the week. We don't watch *EastEnders* as it is so depressing. The children play together running in and out of the front room. If there is a sitcom on before their bedtime they will sit still and watch it. The TV is on early evening, but often just as 'background' when no-one is really watching it.
>
> (30-year-old housewife)

We can see a very similar account being given for early evening schedules from this young woman, who uses TV as a means to relax after she comes in from work:

> The first thing I usually do when I get in from work is switch on the TV, this means I catch some of the *6 O'clock News*. Tonight I was home in time to catch all of it. One of the presenters was Anna Ford, my brother and I have got this on-going argument about her – I think her hair is a right state and is getting worse, while he thinks she looks quite good! During *Jonathan Ross* I was cooking my dinner, when I came back into the room my brother had now come in and had switched over to ITV to watch the local news. *Cluedo* was just coming on as I sat down, I'd never seen this programme before. I found it compelling viewing, it was cheap and nasty but I couldn't stop watching it. My brother was complaining all the way through it, but I didn't see him turning over either! At 7.30 it's *Coronation Street* time, it always has been and always will be. I've watched this programme since as long as I can remember. My whole family does. If I know I'm going to be out I ring up my mum and dad to tape it.
>
> (20-year-old female secretary)

Although the television is on for the early evening news and the programmes that follow, this diarist is not really giving the TV her full attention until the essential dose of *Coronation Street*.

Many diarists record eating an evening meal whilst having the TV on. This is an important function of early evening television; it provides a focus point, a marker, for the family evening meal, which often coincides with watching the news, or soaps. Fifteen per cent of diarists claimed that they often made sure their meal time was the same time as a favourite programme, and as many as a further 31 per cent said that that they occasionally did this. In terms of watching television (but not a favourite programme) whilst eating a meal, 15 per cent said that they often did this, 17 per cent claimed they did this fairly often, and 28 per cent said they occasionally did this.

This mother uses evening television as a means to relax after a hard day at work:

> At 7.30pm the children go to bed and my husband reads them some bedtime stories. At about 8.00pm we sit down, in front of the box and eat our evening meal. This is the first time I relax all day. I really just collapse at this point. During the week we do just tend to watch television in the evenings.
>
> (34-year-old female secretary)

What we can see from these accounts is how families have very busy, structured days, and television has a part to play in this structure. In many ways, the family schedule is a record of the routine of everyday life, and respondents are quite clear about how regimented this schedule can be. Many diarists chose to write about their schedule in the form of bullet points, giving precise and detailed accounts of what happens where at what time of the day. This schoolboy wrote about his family schedule as follows:

A typical day would be:

6.30 am Mum and Dad get up, and get ready for work. Mum makes everyone's lunches.

7.00 am Dad goes to work and my sister gets up.

8.15 am Mum goes to work.

8.30 am My sister goes to school and I get up.

8.55 am I go to school.

12.05 pm My sister and I arrive home from lunch, with friends.

12.55 pm We go back to school.

3.45 pm I get home, get changed and go out and do my paper-round.

3.50 pm My sister arrives home.

4.30 pm I finish my papers and come back home.

5.10 pm We watch *Home and Away*.

5.30 pm Mum comes home and prepares tea.

6.00 pm We eat our tea.

6.30 pm My sister and I go off into our bedrooms.

7.00 pm Dad arrives home and eats his tea.

9.00 pm We watch the news.

9.30 pm My sister, and usually Mum and Dad go to bed.

10.30 pm I go to bed.

(14-year-old schoolboy)

In this schedule, which is so familiar to the respondent that he finds it the most convenient way to describe his day, particular TV programmes such as the news and *Home and Away* provide fixed marker points in the day, reliable parts of the routine which will be watched, of course, for their own value, but which also mark transitions from one stage of the day to the next – the Australian soap, for example, confirming that the long, busy phase of school and a newspaper delivery round have come to a close, and the more relaxing early evening period had begun. A similar theme is illustrated in the following extract by a working man who records the family's daily schedule from breakfast to bedtime:

> I work. I leave home at 7.30am, return at 4.15pm. My two sons go to school at 10 to 9 and return at 3.30pm. Their mother takes them to and from school. She and the boys have *TV AM* on while getting ready for school and having breakfast, it goes on at about 7am. *This Morning* is usually on while housework and other things are done; and attention is paid to interesting items. *Neighbours* and *Home and Away* are watched by her on their first showing of the day [lunchtime]. *Country Practice* is videoed for her and I to watch in the evening. If she goes shopping in the morning then *This Morning* will be videoed and scanned for interesting items later. Washing and ironing may be done in the evenings, especially if my wife has been shopping, visiting or gardening. So although *Emmerdale* and *Coronation Street* will be on, no great attention need be paid to them. I am an Open University student so I study from 6.30pm to 9pm virtually every evening. Most of my viewing is programmes recorded earlier or from previous days. *Brookside* is about the only 'live' transmission I watch during the evening. I watch my recordings from 9pm. I do watch *Neighbours* and *Home and Away*, though at their second showings during the evening meal with the rest of the family. Any videoed programmes will be seen between 9pm and 10.30pm when we go to bed.
>
> (34-year-old male bank clerk)

Although this diarist was at work and therefore would not witness his wife's activities at first hand, he still felt able to give a detailed breakdown of her daily routine. In many ways, certain television programmes helped him to do this. *This Morning* is a case in point: this diarist could tell whether his wife had stayed at home, or gone out by her *This Morning* consumption pattern. The way in which soaps feature as part of a family routine is something that is discussed later on in this chapter. What is interesting here is that families are engaged in a pattern of work and leisure time that is very regimented – albeit in an unwritten and unenforced way – and it is news and soaps, in particular, that punctuate that day.

This woman, aged 69, provides a typical example of the way an elderly single person's day can also be punctuated and in some ways shaped by media 'events':

I am a pensioner and I live alone so I find my TV set is a vital piece of household equipment, although my radio is a close second. Wednesday (today) has been a typical day in my life. In the morning I went out and purchased my morning newspaper (*Daily Mirror*), read it over breakfast and did both crosswords. Then switched on TV, watched *Gloria Live* then switched over to ITV for *The Time and the Place*. Then switched off and did housework until lunchtime. Over lunch I listened to Radio City for phone in programme. Went out shopping in the afternoon, came back late afternoon and watched Parliament and then *Fifteen to One* whilst having a cup of tea. Then I prepared evening meal which I had whilst I read local evening newspaper. After washing up I settled down to evening viewing and knitting. Made a few phone calls in mid evening and read a few chapters of library book during slack period on TV.

(69-year-old retired female football pools clerk)

The way in which other activities – reading and phone calls, here – are brought into play *only because* TV output has fallen below a certain appeal threshold reflects the power of TV schedules to alter the character of an evening – when fed, of course, through the audience member's own perceptions and choices as to what they think will be worth watching. Whilst good TV cannot *really* hold viewers hostage, there is a balancing act that takes place between domestic activities and watching television, with different viewers being more or less likely to let the balance swing in favour of TV.

Individual and family schedules are not fixed, and vary according to the time of day, week and season. This mother summed it up when she wrote:

I'm a single parent so I spend most evenings watching television. We always watch *TV AM* in the morning, then the boys go off to school and the childminder whilst I go to college. I don't usually watch TV during the day except weekends and holidays. We all watch TV more in the winter than the light summer nights because we would all rather do other things like gardening, visiting, playing and socialising.

(32-year-old mother)

At the weekend, television can be used as a babysitter and as an excuse for staying in bed a little longer:

Saturday and Sunday morning children's TV keeps daughter happy while I stay in bed an hour or so longer than weekdays, though she usually draws or paints while it's on. Husband sleeps all morning (lucky sod) while I do housework.

(36-year-old female archaeozoologist)

As we will see in chapter eight, employed men do generally get away with avoiding housework even when their female partners are employed too – this woman's husband clearly manages to have more relaxing weekends than she does. Weekends generally are seen as a less pressured time, when the respondents felt able to watch programmes which they would not watch on their more time-conscious weekdays:

> During the week, the television is only put on when someone is definitely going to sit and watch a programme. Whilst this is also true at weekends, the set is more likely to be left on for longer and [the family] all watch programmes which we would probably not watch if they were shown in the week.
>
> (18-year-old female student)

Some of our diarists might argue that broadcasters have taken advantage of this weekend audience leniency, as they considered Saturday TV schedules to be less than classy: 'Faced with the dreaded prospect of being in on a Saturday night I usually get in a video, a bottle of wine and a friend!' (18-year-old female administrative assistant). Some people took the precaution of ensuring they would be too busy to have to face this torment: 'Most weekends we are all out, so Saturday TV is not usually watched – probably not a bad thing, since it always seems to be inconsequential drivel' (19-year-old male personnel assistant).

Without wanting to contribute to stereotypes of 'British' concerns, it is worth remembering that a whole range of everyday factors – such as the activity of partners and friends, and time needed for voluntary work or hobbies – are linked in with the *weather*, which is an important factor in deciding how to spend leisure time. These diarists explain:

> Generally, we do not watch television during the day, except on really miserable winter afternoons, when we might run one of the stored videos.
>
> (70-year-old retired male company director)

> You chose a bad day for TV watching. At 8 am the sun was warm, the sky blue and the sea turquoise, the most summery morning of the year, and not one to keep us glued to the box.
>
> (68-year-old retired man)

> Summer evenings are spent gardening mainly as we have a very large garden growing all our vegetables. With the excess veg and fruit make jams, chutneys, sauces and of course freeze lots for the winter. Winter evenings we spend watching TV – we watch a great deal then. I love having the TV in the kitchen, as I can watch and listen while preparing meals etc. and I never listen to the radio now.
>
> (38-year-old housewife)

Whilst some diarists across the whole age spectrum indicated that they might do other things at the same time as watching TV, it was working-age adults in particular who would find other things to do whilst the television was on, particularly in the winter months. As the previous diarist indicates, for some homemakers, the set was switched on as an accompaniment to household chores, such as cooking, which were the main priority. Other working people, such as this teacher, also seemed to feel that they should simultaneously do something more like work whilst also enjoying TV for leisure: 'All of us are likely to do something else while watching, e.g. read, do homework, mark books, sleep, eat, etc' (42-year-old male teacher).

We have seen in this section that people organise their time according to a variety of different factors. However, the way in which diarists describe their day-to-day activities suggests that some points in the day, such as breakfast, or evening meals, are closely bound up with certain television programmes. The repetition of phrases such as 'I eat my tea whilst watching *Neighbours*', or 'we watch the news before going to bed', suggests that family schedules are often organised around television schedules. Indeed, in the following section, we see how *Neighbours* has often installed itself as a regular feature of the day for the whole family.

Everyday routines and *Neighbours* 'addiction'

For many diarists – and a great proportion of those who were at home at the right time(s) of day – the Australian daily soap *Neighbours* was a fixed marker-point in their daily routine. It could be an inescapable accompaniment to lunch, or the juncture at which afternoon slipped into early evening. Partly as a consequence of canny scheduling by the broadcaster (BBC1), *Neighbours* had become an integral part of the day. *Home and Away*, ITV's matching (but mildly more 'realistic') serial, was watched just as avidly by some, but was ignored by others.

A very noticeable aspect of diarists' writings about *Neighbours* was that, wholly unprompted, many would say that they were 'addicted' to it. This was taken seriously by some, and mentioned quite casually by others. It stands out in particular because, across the whole study, respondents did not say they were 'addicted' to anything else, and the language of 'addiction' was quite absent elsewhere (leaving aside a sparse handful of references showing no pattern).[1]

This respondent, whilst self-consciously using a clutch of addiction terms and metaphors, makes clear the concern:

> When I did get home I walked straight into the living room, collapsed into the nearest chair and watched the last few minutes of *Neighbours*. This was as badly acted, stereotyped and predictable as ever, but unfortunately still as addictive. I have to admit, I'm hooked! It's a serious habit but not as bad as it could be: I'm only on one a day at the moment! I stopped once, I got

really annoyed with Beverley and went cold turkey, but I couldn't keep it up and I'm hooked again now as I ever was. Maybe one day they'll start up rehabilitation centres to get people off soap operas!!!

(17-year-old female student)

Another young woman had similar symptoms:

It would be boring and repetitive to explain why I watch *Neighbours* except to say it is an infectious disease that has affected a large proportion of the population.

(18-year-old female administrative assistant)

Even those who had managed to shake off their compulsion could become trapped again by just a sniff of the stuff:

You could say I was addicted to [*Neighbours*], but I can't explain why! I did stop watching it for a while when I came down to London, but I saw a clip of one programme one night and I became hooked again!

(20-year-old female secretary)

Another student described teatime *Neighbours* as 'an unfortunate habit'. One 29-year-old office clerk had become 'addicted' during maternity leave and was missing the show now that her son was older and she was back at work. A 16-year-old school pupil tried to excuse her compulsion by emphasising the ironic distance between herself and the text: 'It is a little escape from reality and I find *Neighbours* funny in a kind of stupid way, i.e. I laugh at it'. A 12-year-old girl also explained that the show 'seems familiar to me, and I want to know what happens next'. Although she felt that the predictability of the plot could be both laughable and annoying, 'the good thing about *Neighbours* is that it's not depressing and I hate depressing programmes'.

But the serial's appeal was not limited to young people. Perhaps surprisingly, older viewers did not worry about its 'addictive' qualities and would list it as one of their favourite programmes, whereas younger viewers, whilst lapping it up, would not actually count it as a favourite show. Some diarists, such as this retired school head, would nevertheless feel compelled to indicate that they were well aware of the drama's failings:

Neighbours: Ramsey Street where people do not die, they go to Adelaide or Perth or Brisbane, New Zealand even. Family members are disappeared, but diverse orphans and drop-outs arrive to fill the gaps. The only 'plot' line is trust, or lack of it, between couples, and farewells to the folk opting out and welcomes to the adopted…Dross – but addictive.

(58-year-old retired female headteacher)

This man, however, was appalled by his teenage offsprings' interest in the soap, again equating it with a drug:

> *They* insist on watching *Neighbours*. I *ignore* it. I could not tell you the name of one character. I think viewers absorb it like valium. A sort of tranquiliser.
>
> (53-year-old male single parent)

So why was *Neighbours* singled out as an addictive product – something so alluring that having a negative view of the show didn't seem to stop people watching it? Its *regularity* was certainly important – addicts could get a 'hit' (or two) every day; coupled with the *timing* and the *cliffhanger*, which meant that if you'd watched one episode with a meal or having just come back from school or work, you would be likely to watch it the next day just to 'see what happened' (...and the next day, and so on). The 12-year-old diarist quoted above identifies two other important elements. First is the *familiarity* and *security* of the world which the characters inhabit – a generally moral universe where no good comes of bad deeds, and threats to happy living are normally minor and quickly resolved. Second is the simply-put view that the show is 'not depressing'; rather, it offers *attractive* characters in a setting where the sun always shines, where everyone is (suspiciously) white and middle class, and there is no crime except for speedily sorted plot-related incidents. (The London-based *EastEnders*, in contrast, was the soap most often seen as 'depressing'.) The regular weekday delivery of the happy *Neighbours* package in 22-minute chunks kept the attention of many diarists throughout the five years of this study.

Planning viewing

The extent to which people's TV viewing is planned, rather than random or based on spontaneous channel-hopping, has traditionally been somewhat difficult for research to pick up correctly – because a lot of people know what is going to be on, *without* having to carefully scan through listings magazines with a highlighter pen, which is the kind of more obvious behaviour that research is able to pick up. In this study, respondents reported that around half of the time, the television would be on because they had read or heard about a programme in advance (58 per cent of respondents said that this was often or fairly often the case, with only 2 per cent saying that they never had a show on because they had read or heard about it). Two-thirds of the time the TV would be on for an already-familiar programme. Word of mouth, trailers, mentions of TV highlights in magazines and newspapers, and in particular what they had seen on the same day of the previous week, all helped people to have quite firm ideas of what they wanted to watch, even where their more obvious behaviour might have led researchers to assume that they hadn't got a clue.

Some people, of course, *don't* have a clue, as this diarist living in a student household was happy to admit:

> As we often do not buy a newspaper we don't know what will be on TV in the evening. We never plan our evening around TV, most of us try and watch *Neighbours* either at lunch or tea-time. One girl watches *Twin Peaks* and makes a conscious attempt to. Otherwise the TV is only turned on when we have nothing better to do. It is not such a focal point in the house as the fridge!
>
> (21-year-old female student)

Clearly, the lack of knowledge as to what would be on television here is linked to a lack of interest in TV-viewing as a leisure activity anyway. Other people could be much more conscientious, such as this man who, having lost his job as a college computer technician, had come to rely on television for daily diversion:

> In the last 2 years I've bought a listing magazine religiously every week and use it, normally the night before, to plan a day's viewing. The programmes I circle, in black ink, I usually watch. This guide lives next to my bed and is an aide-memoire but sometimes gets forgotten – and so I might miss an item. The video recorder sometimes helps but I'll go out and forget. Also, I still have the occasional lapse with 24 hour clock and mess up a recording.
>
> (34-year-old unemployed man)

The TV listings, kept by the bed, are clearly important in this man's everyday life, although the fact that he uses them to watch or set the video for *specific* programmes – and the fact that he sometimes forgets – shows that he doesn't have a wholly TV-dominated life. Quite a number of others 'scoured' the listings just as carefully, and were often also the unemployed diarists.

> None of all this [becoming a grandfather, losing a step-son] has had any effect upon the manner in which I watch television. I preplan for the week using the *Radio Times*, ringing in pen each days' programmes that might interest me when the time comes.
>
> (59-year-old retired male firefighter)

Some had particular psychological reasons for being fastidious about their TV planning. The following respondent, for example, managed to ward off feelings of guilt for watching quite an amount of TV, as he was able to reassure himself that he was only watching shows which he had carefully marked in the listings in advance. As his viewing decisions were therefore documented as the products of prior research and planning, he would not feel that he was watching too much, or too casually:

> By careful programme planning marking paper (*S[unday] Times* weekly TV prog guide) as a 'must' or 'want to see' I avoid guilt. For example we have much enjoyed the repeat screening of *The Village* (Tuesdays at 5.30 on BBC2) having completely missed it on the first showing – although unless it's a particular old film we avoid TV till 6pm.
>
> (68-year-old semi-retired male social work adviser)

(The latter part of this quote, of course, also reflects this man's anxiety about not being seen to have allowed television to 'take over'.) In a similar vein, this woman used the 'family viewing' orientation of the programme descriptions in *Radio Times* to weed out programmes which she feared might potentially offend her, as she mentioned when asked about 'bad language' on TV:

> I don't seem to hear bad language in the programmes I see, but I am very choosy in what I watch. I go through the *Radio Times* with a 'fine tooth comb' as soon as I buy it. I mark everything I want and read the resume of the programmes very carefully, and then decide if I shall be watching them.
>
> (66-year-old retired female nurse)

Others, unsurprisingly, used newspaper TV pages to make their choices, and for some the very act of *reading the listings* in the morning was itself part of their daily routine. Here, for example, the morning newspaper would provide the basis of preliminary discussions which would subsequently be acted upon or rejected at the critical points much later in the day.

> When my husband and I get the newspaper each morning we decide what we really want to watch, what we will video and programmes that we might like if we have time. I am 67 and my husband is 73. Sometimes we are prejudiced and miss a good programme which others tell us about. Therefore one of the many things I like about the BBC is they do repeat programmes – even ad infinitum.
>
> (67-year-old retired female deputy manager)

Others took things a bit more casually – although reading in the *morning* what would be on in the *evening* was usual.

> Second mug of tea [in the morning] is time to sit down and look at *Daily Mail* TV programme page for quick glance to see what's on today – I don't get weekly magazine and don't look ahead – and do the crossword.
>
> (65-year-old retired male GP)

As may be apparent from these examples, those who planned their viewing most carefully were the retired. Those who were working, or young, had a necessarily more hurried approach to culling as much information as they needed from TV listings, combined with the acquired knowledge referred to at the beginning of this section: people would 'just know' that their favourite soap was in its regular slot, that *NYPD Blue* was Mondays at 10.00, or that the decent comedy was on a particular channel on Friday evening. Some were prompted to grab the listings page, supplement or magazine only when an anticipated show failed to appear.

HOUSEHOLD LIFE AND TELEVISION

As well as being built into the lives of individuals, television is integrated into the households in which they live – physically, as a point of focus in the arrangement of one or more rooms, but more importantly, *socially*, as a locus of attention and social interaction. Ninety per cent of respondents had a TV in the living area, 8 per cent had a TV in the dining room, and 19 per cent had a TV in the kitchen. In bedrooms, 36 per cent of adult respondents (aged 18-plus) had one bedroom TV, and in a further 10 per cent of households two adult bedrooms included a TV (mainly students, and people with a lot of TVs). Seven per cent of homes had one TV set in a child or teenager's bedroom, and a further 4 per cent of households had two TVs in such bedrooms. Overall, then, the majority of respondents in this study watched TV in the main living area, whilst the number of TVs in children and teenager's bedrooms was relatively small.[2]

Television is often assigned a kind of everyday priority which means that other interactions take place around and through the watching of it. This idea is illustrated very succinctly here:

> I quite enjoyed the film *Dragonslayer*, despite its predictability. It's the sort of film you can argue with your father through and still keep up with the storyline.

> (18-year-old female clerical assistant)

The centrality of television to her family's social life is considered in a little more depth by this young woman studying for A-Levels:

> Recently *Family Matters* spent their programme discussing the influence of TV on family life. They took a TV away from a family who generally watched it all the time, and gave it to a family without a TV. This was interesting in that the family who had never had a TV found that it disrupted the activities they used to do together, and there was a loss of communication between family members. The family who were addicted to

TV had problems adjusting, but eventually found they became closer and spent more time together.

This programme…made me consider the effect no TV would have in my family. At the moment we generally get on well together, probably due to the fact that we spend a lot of time watching TV and not talking. Although the TV isn't on all day I think that it is a distraction that stops people from making an effort to find things to amuse themselves with.

(17-year-old female sixth-form student)

Whilst the collective focus on TV is seen as a problem here, others, such as this middle-aged parent, would see their family's joint viewing as an impressive show of unity:

The two boys go out more often than we do as parents but we all enjoy to sit down and watch some television together in the evenings especially after our meals.

(49-year-old male management lecturer)

In other households, less happy domestic relationships were intertwined with media use in more complex ways.

My husband is manic depressive and has been for 30 years. However he hit a period of very severe stress last year and his mania shot off the 'Richter' scale. So much so that I moved out for 3 months. He is now at the bottom end and suicidal. These events inevitably affect TV viewing. The grandchildren have introduced me to videos I would not have otherwise found such as *Pingu* (delightful!). The period away from home caused me to rely heavily on TV as a companion and shock absorber. Periods of mania usually mean I am running around picking up the pieces with no time for TV. Periods of depression mean he sits at home slumped in front of hours of TV – mainly sport. However, we have managed to watch several drama series together and become involved with the story lines, e.g. *Band of Gold*, *She's Out*, *Peak Practice*, *Casualty* etc.

(58-year-old female administrator)

In this situation, both adults at certain times sought refuge and comfort in TV-viewing, whilst at others their domestic chaos meant that television was cut out entirely. Naturally, the households in this study do not divide simply into the conventional and the troubled; this diarist, for example, had also written elsewhere, 'I try to take in the news headlines and weather forecast to know if I need to bring in my plants against a frost', which is remarkable only because it sounds so everyday, routine and 'settled'.

As well as negotiations with partners – of which more later – other relatives could have an impact on the household and its viewing choices.

Over the past nine months I have had my sister and brother-in-law living with me. This has altered the programmes I've watched as my sister does not like sitcoms as I do; she likes chat shows which I don't and she doesn't like sports programmes which her husband and I do. There has obviously been compromise all round. As a result of 9 months conditioning I have become interested in *EastEnders* and *Coronation Street*. I still avoid the *Oprah Winfrey Show* etc and still watch any sport apart from wrestling.

(69-year-old retired female headteacher)

It is also worth mentioning that it was not only youngsters who had their viewing sometimes limited by parental censure:

No line drawn for our viewing [sex or violence or swearing], excepting the visits of my elderly mother-in-law (religious and moralistic) – so we have no problems about this most times.

(63-year-old retired male university teacher)

It should be remembered that households today take a variety of forms. As well as 'conventional' families there are heterosexual and homosexual couples, single parents, people living alone, and groups of friends living together. The latter form is becoming increasingly common as, with the expansion of further and higher education in Britain, there are more student households. (In 1982, there were 555,000 full-time students in UK higher education; by 1991 this figure was 747,000, and by 1996 it had risen to 1,182,000 (*Social Trends* 1998).) Unsurprisingly, the students in this study generally had a quite different relationship with television from those with more 'settled' lives at school, work or in retirement. Students' TV-watching could often be less directed, as they did not always have newspapers or TV guides, and viewing had to be taken less seriously since it would often be cast aside in favour of a trip to the pub or, to be fair, study. At the same time, *particular* programmes (such as soaps, or *The Simpsons* or, in the early 1990s, *Twin Peaks*) or groups of shows (such as the channel-hop between Channel Four and BBC2 on Friday evening for comedies) could become the focus of communal viewing events, coordinated with meals, drinks or snacks. This student, for example, in her third year of study at Manchester University in 1995, here recalls her first year:

There were eight of us altogether in the house, and we had one TV in the lounge, and so this involved some degree of compromise in who watched what and when, but in general we had similar taste and especially for *Coronation Street* and *Brookside*, and we made sure our dinner was ready at about 7.25pm so we were all watching together. Thursday nights were also a big house TV night as we watched *Absolutely Fabulous* and Ben Elton with a few bottles of wine and crisps/choc etc. During this year, I would say that TV became a 'social event'!

(22-year-old female student)

Another example of a mixed household, where the student diarist is a lodger, provides some insight into other ways in which television gets used in and around everyday living:

> I share a house with a landlady, who is a teacher and watches very little television herself. She will pop her head round the door and see it if I am watching anything literary or interesting and to keep up generally at school. Thus her tutor group was amazed when she knew all about *Twin Peaks* although she won't watch it with me. My claims to the telly are recognised as sacrosanct on Tuesday evenings for *Twin Peaks* plus *Jeeves and Wooster* on Sunday nights, both of which S. will watch with me if she is in. S. is a Spanish assistant and the third member of the household....The television is important to unwind with, but all of us use books, tapes, radio and going out to stave off the onset of couch potato type malaises. [...The landlady] never checks the television listings thus the news is the only programme she can be sure of seeing.
>
> (19-year-old female student)

Here we see TV being used to make links between people – the teacher gaining credibility with her pupils, and giving her an excuse to 'check in' with her lodger, and the diarist getting to spend time with her Spanish housemate – and imposing demands on the household, with the lounge becoming protected space on Sundays and Tuesdays. At the same time, like many across the age spectrum, these people make some effort to keep TV and its associated 'couch potato type malaises' at bay – although this may often be half-hearted.

Household TV arrangements and arguments

As we have established that television is, at the very least, a *catalyst* for forms of domestic organisation of time and space – or, to be more emphatic, often a *primary determining factor* in how households organise their internal geography and everyday timetables – it is no surprise to find cases where conflict occurs between the participants in these delicately organised social worlds. Disagreements may concern choices of broadcast *content*, or just sheer *quantity* of viewing and differences of opinion as to whether the set should be on or not in shared living spaces.

The Audience Tracking Study very clearly suggests, depressingly perhaps, that once couples have got through an all-forgiving 'honeymoon' period, they cannot help but get annoyed with their partner's mystifying or ill-timed TV choices. For some, these discrepancies did not develop into confrontation, but were forcefully breezed through with the attitude that others could 'like it or lump it':

As to TV I don't really watch as much as I used to do. When daytime TV started I used to watch a lot more but now I don't bother to find out if it is any good. I do still watch a lot of news and current affairs programmes, this annoys my husband unfortunately, but he doesn't have to stay in the same room.

(61-year-old farmer's wife)

Television content, perhaps by virtue of being temporary, fleeting, up to date and glamorously packaged, can seem to take priority, for some, over other more dependably unchanging aspects of a household – like a spouse. In another relatively mild, everyday example, the suppressed conflict has little to do with what is *on* television, but is about end-of-the-day chores versus the luxury of television:

Late Show BBC2: watched this with only half attention, as I was writing this diary. Found the main interview…a bit long winded/boring. (Husband dozed off.) Something on psychotherapy…would have interested me – but husband was 'going on' about clearing up and going to bed. Something about Wren's churches, with some pleasant choral music was interrupted by husband, wanting me to call cat in (we have to do this or they get into fights). Felt pressurised – didn't watch anymore, switched off at close-down.

(47-year-old female part-time lecturer)

In other households, the arguments about TV could be more fraught. This retired couple had to purchase a second set to avoid regular quarrels – although the female diarist feels some (more subdued) resentment about being the one who has to leave the comfortable lounge to watch the small monochrome set, a tension which runs through her diaries.

During the winter we sometimes watch TV in the afternoons, he watches sport, I occasionally watch an old film. We used to argue about which programmes we wanted, especially since we both retired but now that we have two sets we agree to differ, although one is only a small black and white.

(62-year-old retired female teacher)

For the same couple, their different views of TV could produce other irritations too – for example, 'If we have visitors I prefer to switch it off, but am overruled'. Here, the diarist's feeling that TV could detract from a social situation was rejected by her husband – it is not that this woman did not like television. Indeed, two years later, in 1993, she admitted, 'I don't let it rule my life, but I do miss it on holiday'. In 1995, she wrote, 'There is much to be said for TV…but I think it has ruined my social life'.

Other couples in the study would argue about television, particularly those at home a lot, for whom television had become more important – such as the 72-year-old retired woman whose husband 'hates snooker, racing [and] tennis', which caused disputes, although she had limited scope for revenge, as 'I like most of his tastes'. But in one household, one woman's substantial diet of TV shows had led to more serious consequences – her love of television had had a substantial impact upon her marriage, apparently, with the TV set being named as a third party in their divorce proceedings:

> Apart from my college course, I watch less TV (particularly soaps) due to the collapse of my marriage in '94. I lost interest in TV, in general, and spent most of my time visiting friends or talking to them on the 'phone. One of the reasons for the collapse was cited as my TV addiction, so once we decided to 'have another go', this was one area I had to make a positive effort in.
>
> (37-year-old female school catering assistant)

A case of formally identified 'TV addiction' is worthy of closer inspection, and the Audience Tracking Study diaries, which start in 1991, provide relevant 'evidence' on this case. There are, certainly, some elements which could cheekily be used here – this woman would run home from work in order to catch all of *Knots Landing*, for example, and was concerned about her kids watching all of *Children's BBC* every day only because that meant they were neglecting the delights of the commercial channel, ITV. However, this busy part-time working mother of two near-teenage children did not truly have *time* to be a proper TV 'addict'. Housework or shopping would precede the two-and-a-half hours of non-stop 'hard manual work' in a school kitchen; then there would not be much afternoon left – for chores or TV – before the children came home from school, on some days needing travel and support to go swimming, horse-riding or to Brownies. After early evening, 'taken-up with preparing tea, cooking it, eating it and then clearing up', there would not be that much time left for TV. Because of shift-work, her husband certainly watched *less* television, although the diarist would 'sometimes have to tape episodes of a series or a film he particularly wants to see, or a boxing match'. The family did not have much disposable income and this meant that the woman of the household, in particular, was left at home for many long evenings.

> I would say that the television is very important in our family for entertainment and relaxation, even if there is nothing on the 4 channels we wanted to see we would probably watch a video – either rented or bought. I go out very rarely and when I do it is usually to see a film either with my husband or a friend. My husband goes out to the pub at least once a week, but it's very difficult to get a baby-sitter, so we tend to go out together only on special occasions e.g. birthdays, anniversaries, etc.
>
> (as above, aged 33 in 1991)

Given this context, the accusation of TV addiction seems rather an extreme interpretation. In any case, over the five years of the study, major changes would occur. After the marriage came to an end, as mentioned above, the diarist became a full-time student:

> I now watch far less TV due to college assignments. I have also taken on voluntary work, which has reduced the amount of TV I can see. I still watch TV at the same time, from early evening onwards, but I am more discerning in my viewing habits. Due to the course I am undertaking and my volunteer work, I now watch different programmes, usually to do with sociological programmes.
>
> (as above, aged 37 in 1995)

She still found all types of television valuable, however – not least as a babysitter for the children, as she struggled to complete her studies.

> TV is less important to me, but it brings in cheap entertainment...I quite often gain information from it and I am also grateful because it occupies my children.
>
> (as above, aged 38 in 1996)

This diarist *was* careful about what she let her children see on TV, but did not generally find this to be a problem. Other respondents, as we will see below, had less happy experiences of television in the family household.

You just don't understand: parents versus children, mum versus dad

Television could be the source of conflicts between children and their parents, and between one parent and the other as they disagreed over what their offspring could watch. Whilst we might expect the basis of both types of conflict to be 'moral' issues of what the kids might be 'allowed' to watch, they were just as frequently timetabling issues or questions of whether the children 'deserved' to watch a certain amount of TV, depending on whether homework and/or chores had been completed.

In this example, there was little problem getting the children to do their homework, but this seemed to strengthen their hand as they demanded particular programmes:

> My two children go to school. They go out occasionally with friends but are not great mixers. Our lack of social life probably affects them and, arguably, there is a genetic factor involved also. They like working on homework and listening to 'pop' in their own rooms. They get home about 4pm. Programmes they do like they 'must' watch and arguments

occur which aren't always resolved by having a spare TV. Sometimes bargains have to be struck beforehand in order to avoid arguments which, sometimes, are very heated.

(57-year-old retired man)

This diarist, permanently disabled, resented having bad TV imposed on him by his children – although he was, to an extent, resigned to it. Being 'not able to get around much', escape was a little more difficult. For example, in the same diary he wrote: 'The rest of the family watch *Home and Away* at 6.15pm. It's on at the moment. I hate it but find myself involved in spite of myself sometimes.' Once his son had left home for university in 1992, the diarist found himself the only man in the household – leading to another potential problem in the family home:

> I feel I should not watch programmes containing nude or semi-nude young females. I'm too old for a start. My wife and daughter don't like me watching, so I don't or rarely do, eg *Baywatch*, *The Clothes Show*, films containing sexuality and nudity.
>
> (as above, aged 62, 1996)

In any case, this man preferred serious, factual programmes and current affairs shows (although he was suspicious of them). He writes: 'Paradoxically, TV both helps me to take my mind off depressing issues of the day both in my private life and generally; and provides much of the information which depresses me.'

Conflict would develop *between* parents where one of them was more concerned than the other about the effects of television on their children, or their exposure to certain kinds of programme.

> Their father is far more relaxed than me about what they [children aged 13 and 10] watch and how much (causing friction between us, I have to admit!) so they're often in front of the box once homework and music practice is done – or before they start, depending on negotiations.
>
> (45-year-old female teacher)

A bedroom TV for the offspring would naturally ease these tensions, as long as parents were willing to surrender their direct control over what would be seen. It was certainly a happy solution for this teenager:

> Having my own TV means that I generally don't watch with the rest of my family, especially since my parents have a totally opposite opinion of what 'good' TV is.
>
> (17-year-old female sixth-form student)

The much-aired public concern about young people having television sets in their own rooms is, of course, that they may see unsavoury 'late-night' material without parental supervision. This fear was reflected quite strongly in this study, but amongst the over-60s only – it would seem that the generation of grandparents are more troubled by this (somewhat mythic) prospect than are the parents of today's teenagers. 'Teenagers have television sets in their bedrooms now – so who knows what they are watching', a 75-year-old retired supermarket manager complained, typically, whilst an ex-nurse aged 66 noted that 'Parents don't seem aware of when [their children] are watching regrettably' – although it is unclear how she 'knew' this. In fact, those diarists' children who had bedroom TVs were of the kind of mid-teen age where their parents had become more relaxed about viewing restrictions anyway, and some, furthermore, were not allowed to have their sets on beyond their official 'bed-time'.

Whilst the older respondents seemed to believe that *most* children have a TV in their bedroom – 'How many kids don't have TV in their bedroom these days?', a 72-year-old man asked rhetorically – in fact, as we have already seen in this study, it was a minority who did. More importantly, perhaps, the whole idea that TV programmes shown after 11pm are the particularly violent or pornographic ones is, of course, mistaken. The small audiences at these times are usually treated to the more 'serious' programming which populist broadcasters have shunted back in the schedules to make way for something more 'sexy' in the 9–11pm slot, or, later still, to cheap airwave-fillers of limited appeal. As the 17 year old quoted above notes:

> Apart from *Neighbours* and *Home and Away* I generally watch a lot of TV late evenings, and being a near-insomniac I do see a lot of the late pro-grammes, which I'm generally not too impressed with. Apart from the music programmes there isn't really any compelling viewing post 1a.m.
>
> (17-year-old female sixth-form student, as above)

Finally, it is worth mentioning that there were some situations where parents would quite deliberately seek harmony with their children by using communal TV viewing as a 'bonding' exercise. This separated academic father, for example, has his own viewing patterns determined by whether his children are visiting or not.

> Actually, I read a lot! And, to be fair, I watch more TV than before – mainly to be sociable with my daughter. I watch a lot less when the children are with their mother.
>
> (45-year-old male lecturer)

Some families, indeed, were drawn together by their collective enjoyment of an evening's viewing, as this young man, who lived with his parents, notes:

> I think we watch TV in quite a 'healthy' way – often talking about it and discussing after watching it. We bounce ideas off each other. It's a nice way to watch TV…We're a close family and we tend to muck in together – that includes watching TV.
>
> (18-year-old male sixth-form student)

Although this diarist later admits 'I sometimes prefer to watch the box in solitude and silence…without any distractions', most of the evidence about the role of TV in parent–child interactions, to be fair, involved more pleasure than pain. Indeed, parents whose children left home during the course of this study noted that, although they had 'regained' control over what was watched, they missed watching programmes aimed at a younger generation in the company of their children.

Other everyday activities

In a study which focuses on the role of television in everyday life, it is important not to forget that people have a range of other ways of spending time. Our diarists spent a lot of time with friends, and talking with their partners and families – not the kind of activity which is necessarily defined as 'doing' anything in particular, but which is an extremely important part of everyday life nonetheless. To give a flavour of the wide variety of activities which people engaged in rather than watching TV, we compiled some quotes about our diarists' hobbies – although this can actually be seen as a mistake, since the notion of having a 'hobby' is rather dated, and tends to exclude popular contemporary leisure activities such as going to pubs and clubs. As one respondent in his twenties commented,

> I don't have 'hobbies' as such. I think of them as something a bit boring that you do on your own. At school you had to make up that you had a hobby, like stamp collecting, because teachers would always ask about it. I just work, sleep, eat, see my friends, talk…and, yes, watch TV.

Despite this, our sample were not short of hobbies, and these are worth detailing since they show the variety of how people choose to spend their time in and around the household. Indoor hobbyists included the unemployed 19-year-old woman who spent hours on entering competitions ('a lot of spare time is spent researching and inventing slogans'); two different retired people who had taken up painting as a consequence of 'learn to paint' shows on daytime TV (one woman clearly delighted that she'd bought the 'artist's kit' and the book related to The Learning Channel's *Joy of Painting*); a 66-year-old woman who had become fascinated by rubber stamping ('It is gaining interest…You can make lovely personalised cards'); and a man in his early sixties who had read 340 books on 'the lives and histories of American presidents'.

Some retired people were happy to take up quite unstereotypical hobbies – such as this retired man:

> Yes, looking round a supermarket book and paper shop picked up a freebie cross stitch rabbit bookmark to do. Since doing it I have got into it in a big way. I have done some big cross stitch pictures. As one just 9′ × 6′ can take up to 3 months to do.
>
> (61-year-old retired male repair mason)

Rather more active hobbyists included the woman in her mid-thirties who took her mind off her fish filleting job by swimming with a disabled child as his helper ('I enjoy that very much'), and the 71-year-old retired man whose hobbies included 'dinghy fishing, mountain walking, golf, gardening, photography and the wretched *Telegraph* crossword'. Another older man, who had been forced into a more active lifestyle by his doctor, had found a way to make it more interesting:

> Three years ago I contracted circulation problems which necessitated my having to walk a great deal. Since then I have walked more than 300 miles around [a large local] park. To give myself something to think about I bought myself a camera and spent a deal of money and effort learning how not to waste film. I now watch camera programmes and have made some happy snaps looking for subjects which before I never saw as subjects for photography such as the November sun through fog, spiders' webs in the weather, and raindrops hanging on bare branches.
>
> (78-year-old retired male engineer)

Other diverse hobbies included editing the quarterly church magazine (76-year-old retired male chemist), recording books and articles 'onto tape for blind friends overseas' (76-year-old retired male airline official), and making camcorder videos (three retired men – see chapter six). Many diarists enjoyed gardening, and some others who couldn't – or could no longer – do gardening enjoyed seeing gardens on TV:

> Exactly 12 months ago I took an allotment and the extra digging and cultivating has radically changed my TV viewing.
>
> (59-year-old retired male industrial chemist)

> I like to watch the gardening programmes, especially when they are about a specific garden. As I am unable to walk far or in fact go out alone I am not able to visit any of these lovely gardens nor can I drive. But there's a lot of pleasure to be had from looking at gardens on TV.
>
> (65-year-old housewife)

Equally, the loss of gardening opportunities could lead to a greater interest in TV.

> When I wrote my first diary in May 1991 [four years ago], we had just moved to our flat from a large house. TV has become more important to me because we no longer have a garden so now the time I spent in the garden is used watching TV. In the winter I do not find any difference but in the Spring and Summer I do.
>
> (52-year-old female finance collector)

Three or four per cent of the diarists were trying to write other texts; indeed, taking part in this study may have created or reinforced writing ambitions. These ranged from a 71-year-old retired engineer, and two other retired people of a similar age, writing their autobiographies ('mainly for the benefit of my family', as the former says), to a man in his late forties, disabled with severe arthritis and so unable to work, who hoped for wider recognition ('I am yet unpublished, but I live in hope. I took up writing when forced to leave work, and feel I have a good chance of earning something at it'). A retired accountant, aged 70, was trying to improve his poetry-writing ('I sometimes enter poetry competitions but as you will guess have never won anything').

One retired businessman, when aged 70 in 1991, started a short story correspondence course, and between 1993 and 1995 produced two novels and his autobiography.

> This has meant getting up at 6.30am most mornings and getting down to two hours work of 600 words a day before breakfast (ie composing on my electric typewriter editing and printing two pages of typescript). This is enough work at my age plus of course thinking time, research time...
>
> I have entered one of my books into [an] awards competition in America over a year ago, if I am a successful entrant, I should hear something this month, fame and fortune is assured to the winner of 500,000 dollars, with four 50,000 dollar awards for works of literary merit. My book is the special theme of the survival of the planet in the future, was already written before the competition was even announced and is a work of fiction.
>
> If I should have any work published in the future or get any literary success, I could 'go like a train', otherwise I might put everything on the shelf because 'hitting one's head against a brick wall' is pointless, tiring and very painful.
>
> (74-year-old retired male small business owner, 1995)

Two respondents had seen their work in print. The first, a retired civil servant, spent much of his time on a book detailing a complete history of the engines of the London & Birmingham Railway; in 1993, aged 59, he had a reply from a publisher – to his considerable delight: 'I've been tinkering with it for 30 years, but it really is going to be published!' The second, also a retired civil servant, had self-published his own work, the sales and marketing of which then took over his life:

[Spring 1991] I have just finished writing and publishing a book, 'Tower Above All' about my holidays at Blackpool since 1946, and much time is spent replying to enquiries about it and trying to sell copies, going out to people and bookshops where copies may be offered, so in any case I have very little spare time for things like watching TV.

[Spring 1995] After nearly four years since 'Tower Above All' was published, and a 24 page supplement booklet, 'What's Different About Tower Above All?' which I wrote and the first 1,000 copies ordered were obtained from a printer at Blackpool last May. I have enjoyed selling copies whenever possible, which has taken up a good deal of my spare time, and left little to spare for actually watching television, which has always been a low priority anyway.

[Autumn 1995] There is one film from Blackpool which I would like to see, called *Funny Bones*...but it has not yet been shown in Cinemas in the Chester and North Wales area. I would like to get in touch with Mr Peter Chelsom, Producer/Director of this film, as I am wondering whether my book could be adapted for a film about Blackpool (see 'The Tower That Turned To Gold' enclosed).

(retired male civil servant, aged 64 in 1991)

Many of the 'hobbies' reported above, it could be noted, are the activities of respondents who have a lot of 'spare' time and are eager to do things other than watching TV – and to be *seen* to be doing things other than watching TV. Their hobbies are genuine spare-time interests, of course, but also help the diarists to feel that they are 'doing something'.

We should also point out that pets played an important part in the life of many households. Dogs, for example, were dearly loved, and brought structure to their owners' days, with 'walking the dog' being a key part of everyday routine, and the dog's demands affecting the shape and nature of other activities.

Being mostly alone, after breakfast and taking my dog out, washing up, making my bed and always on Wednesdays mornings I attend Holy Eucharist (with my dog – who is wonderful).

(70-year-old housewife)

Cats, like dogs, were seen as good company, particularly for people living on their own.

> I like living alone, although I hate housework. I'm a very independent person, and I have my beloved cat, Patch, for company. Mind you, she's almost sixteen, so perhaps won't be with me much longer. I suppose it's selfish, but I enjoy pleasing myself – no arguments about what to watch on television, what to eat, who does what. I'm middle aged, do a boring job that's not very well paid (but I like most of my colleagues), don't go out much – but I'm not a boring or bored person, I appreciate the beauties of life, and a lot goes on in my head. That's the important thing, after all.
>
> (49-year-old female local government clerk)

Many pet-owning respondents commented on the pleasure they got from the BBC's *Animal Hospital* presented by Rolf Harris, and other natural history programmes. Indeed, these were not, apparently, always selected by the human members of the household:

> I switch on 'Nature' programmes as one of our Siamese cats thoroughly enjoys them. We don't like the killing which always seems emphasised.
>
> (66-year-old retired male schoolteacher)

For some, the needs of their pets were enough to affect major household decisions, such as whether to move house.

> Recently a year old black and white girl-puss [was] dumped on us – now totally adored, [she] rules us and our three elderly rescued puss-cats. So much for 'Never, no more, not never'. Because of increasing severe nerve and joint pains we applied for old folks bungalow in a local complex. We are eligible, but will put 'on hold' because little Tiger Lily puss enjoys the garden here (only one cat permitted in OAPs complex). We decided to stay put!
>
> (67-year-old retired housewife)

It is correspondingly unsurprising to find that the deaths of beloved pets were not only very upsetting, but also changed daily routines. For example, a retired male police chief aged 69 said: 'The terrible death of our 14 year old family dog on Christmas Eve has altered our daily way of life – no 'walkies', etc. Very depressing.' Another retired man, whose wife had taken in an injured stray cat, had to admit that 'his demise, eight years later, distressed me more than I'd expected'. A nurse, whose severely ill cat Zoe 'had to be put to sleep with me holding her', had to endure several months where she 'missed her terribly'. Cats and dogs were not the only important pet members of households, either; the diaries record the sad deaths of goldfish and hamsters, too.

TELEVISION, THE HOUSEHOLD AND EVERYDAY LIFE

In *Television and Everyday Life*, Silverstone (1994) discusses the concept of 'clocking'. Clocking is the organisation of activities in terms of structure, frequency and pace (Kantor and Lehr 1975). This means 'family or household members come together or pass each other, according to a pattern which is set and engrained in their daily routines' (Silverstone 1994: 36). This organisation of activities is not without tension or conflict, but nevertheless, according to Kantor and Lehr, it can suggest 'what the family considers most important' (1975: 86). If we look at what respondents had to say about the organisation of time and daily routine, we can see that the evening schedule is the most significant space in relation to television and leisure time. Certainly breakfast time is important in terms of the family coming together and then dispersing at different times to work or school, but it is the weekday early evening schedule, when the family regularly settles down to watch the news and *Neighbours*, before or with their evening meal, that proves to be the most reliable marker point in their discussion of daily routine. The later programmes are also often the pivot around which other family interactions and activities turn. After the working day, this time is when families engage in discussion, and some conflict, about family viewing, and when household members have often finished the majority of chores and are able to relax in front of the television. If the television schedules are unable to offer satisfaction, then pre-recorded programmes are often chosen (see chapter six for further discussion of everyday video habits).

Whilst the television is clearly an important part of the household, we have also seen in this chapter that the daily life of a household often has an implicit time-schedule, and that TV usually only gets attention during the more relaxed parts of the day (or when viewing can be combined with another activity) – although some items, like the news and soaps, are part of the fixed routine anyway, and take precedence over other tasks. We have also seen how TV schedulers have a certain power over people's behaviour – because when the programmes are all unappealing, viewers are prompted to do something else; this obviously contrasts with the kind of 'media effects' that are usually speculated about.

The television is often the centre of collective attention in the living room of a household, although individuals might be conducting their own activities, focused elsewhere, at the same time. Families and households are therefore drawn together, and sometimes divided in argument, by this shared experience. But finally it is worth remembering that most people have a range of interests separate from television, social relationships more satisfying than television, and other things to do.

SUMMARY OF KEY FINDINGS

- Most respondents' everyday lives were structured by a clearly organised schedule.
- Television programmes, particularly the news and soap operas, provide fixed marker points within the day's timetable. Some people use these points to sit down and focus on the television; others would engage in unrelated activities, and watch less closely.
- This schedule is not fixed, and would change with the differing relationships between members of a household (which could take many forms – single-parent families, students living in shared houses, and retired couples, as well as nuclear or extended families). Individual and family schedules would also vary according to the day, week, and season.
- Some people would watch evening TV until its appeal fell below a certain personal threshold, prompting them to do other activities instead.
- Weekends were often a more relaxed time, meaning that people would view programmes which they would not have watched on weekdays, when time was at more of a premium.
- Some respondents planned their viewing very carefully, marking the listings magazine or newspaper with their choices. At the other end of the spectrum, a few people didn't look at schedules at all. Nevertheless, almost all of the diarists had an idea of what would be on TV on a given night.
- Television can be a focal point around which households bond – particularly families who get on well, and households of students or friends.
- Being a focal point of household attention, however, particularly in the evening, television could also be the nub of some disputes and cause of irritation.
- Away from the television set, hobbies are important to the retired and other people with 'spare time' – who partly use these hobbies to show how busy they are. And pets, too, appeared in the study as important elements of the household.

Notes

1   However, this seems a good opportunity to mention another facet of the everyday experience of television-viewing which received acknowledgement – that of watching programmes which are strangely compelling, even though they're not seen as being good. For example, an 18-year-old female clerical assistant wrote:

> Enjoyed *The Equalizer* too. So what if I've seen it before and I'm dog tired? It's compulsive viewing...You feel like a hare caught in a lorry's headlights; you know what's coming isn't good for you, but you keep watching.

Other unwilling followers of the fascinatingly sadistic Edward Woodward vehicle will recognise this feeling.

2   An Independent Television Commission survey conducted in 1996 gives more general national statistics, showing that our figures are rather low: it found that 24 per cent of households had a television set in a child's bedroom. Two out of every five homes with children had assigned a set to the child's room (ITC 1997: 5).

Chapter 3

News consumption and everyday life

This chapter provides a case study of how news programmes function as a structuring device in family and household routines. Whilst the *content* of news programmes is obviously important to viewers, we will emphasise the often overlooked *context* of watching television news, which is important to our understanding of television consumption patterns. People watch the news for a variety of different reasons, for example to keep in touch with world events, or local news items, but the fact that the news is scheduled to coincide with busy periods in the household ensures that watching the news is also part of the dynamic of everyday life. Thus, news bulletins or current affairs programmes are often watched whilst people are simultaneously engaged in other household activities. The majority of media studies research in television news has focused on such issues as news bias, or what people felt about coverage of specific events, such the death of Diana, Princess of Wales (the subject of a forthcoming BFI study). However, such factors must be seen in relation to patterns of everyday life, and so this chapter looks at what people value about television news, and the way in which the news punctuates the day, in many ways becoming part of daily routine in the household.

PREVIOUS STUDIES OF NEWS CONSUMPTION

There has been a great deal of research on television news consumption, which has primarily focused on audience ratings, the construction of the news, the reception of news programmes, and the relationship between text and audience. This type of research is important in our understanding of news programmes, especially in terms of the construction of the news, and in relation to audience views of local and global events.

The most dominant type of research on news consumption is audience ratings conducted by broadcasters. However, as Ang (1991) has noted, this type of research is not particularly helpful in constructing a picture of what audiences actually do whilst watching television news.[1] What audience ratings do tell us is that television is the main source of news information for the British public. According to the Independent Television Commission in their 1997 audience survey, respondents listed three main sources for information about world news: television, radio and newspapers; and out of these three sources, 'TV was mentioned by almost everybody (94 per cent), followed by newspapers (69 per cent) and radio (37 per cent)' (ITC 1997: 35). However, in terms of local news, respondents relied equally on newspapers and local TV news to gain information about their local area (40 per cent for newspapers, 37 per cent for television).

If we compare this data with MORI opinion polls, we can see that the general public are increasingly dissatisfied with newspapers as a main source of world news. In 1990, a MORI poll showed that '36 per cent of the British public said that they were dissatisfied with the way the national newspapers handled the Gulf War' (Worcester 1998: 44). An NOP poll (for Ayer Advertising) also found that as few as 13 per cent of respondents believed the British press were free of bias (ibid.). This points towards a trend in the British population suggesting that television coverage of world news is increasingly popular with the British public, compared with other sources.[2] Certainly, the fact that in a MORI poll 79 per cent of respondents claimed that they trusted TV newsreaders to tell the truth, and that this figure had increased from 63 per cent in 1983 to 79 per cent in 1993 (Worcester 1998: 47), would indicate that there is something about watching TV news that people find more satisfying than other forms of news coverage.

Research on television coverage of news events has shown that news coverage can have an international impact, and different ways of presenting news events can have different effects on viewers. The Glasgow University Media Group, for example, showed how news bulletins contained a hierarchy of information, with certain types of news items, such as royal stories, being given more importance than others, such as foreign news (1976, 1980). The Glasgow University Media Group also looked at the construction of news events, and Philip Schlesinger (1978) conducted a detailed study of BBC news which focused on the construction of 'reality', a 'reality' which was not free from bias. Recent research into news values and the reporting of 'truth' shows that the question of impartiality is something that will continue to dominate the evaluation of factual information (Gunter 1997).

The issue of 'tabloidisation' is also something that dominates discussion of news programmes in media studies. The study of 'other news' or human interest stories has shown that news coverage can be categorised as 'serious' and 'non-serious' (Hartley 1982; Fiske 1992, amongst others). The way in which the news is fragmented into different types of stories has given rise to concern that the news has become packaged as entertainment, and that non-serious news items are becoming increasingly dominant (Postman 1987). Langer (1998: 9) notes that the 'non-serious' news stories tend to focus on 'the domain of common sense and lived experience' which is popular with television audiences. For Langer, 'rather than distracting audiences away from "more important" issues...the "other news" paves the way into news discourse...functioning not to trivialize the serious news, but instead to act as an identificatory wedge into it' (1998: 30).

This focus on the 'lived experience' is certainly helpful in our understanding of the construction of television in relation to everyday life, but such research primarily focuses on the text, rather than the audience. When it comes to ethnographic research on the 'lived experience' of watching television news in the home, little research has been conducted. The University of Birmingham Centre for Contemporary Cultural Studies (CCCS) conducted research on the encoding and decoding of TV discourse, and the relationship between text and reader. As mentioned in chapter one, Brunsdon and Morley (1978) focused on the way in which *Nationwide*, an early evening current affairs magazine programme, addressed its viewers. Morley (1980) went on to conduct further research on viewers' responses to *Nationwide*, which showed a range of viewer interpretations of news reporting. Similar research has also been conducted by Dahlgren (1988) and Corner *et al.* (1990). Corner *et al.* examined the way in which people talk about the news, and found 'frameworks of understanding', such as the expectation that news should be fair in its treatment of issues (1990: 107).

The problem with such research, as Moores (1993: 31) notes, is that it fails to consider the 'politics of the sitting room'. Within the tradition of ethnographic practice, there has been little research that tells us much about how news consumption practices fit into everyday life. James Lull, in his research on the social uses of television, showed that television could act as a 'behavioural regulator', providing clear marker points in the day. He also found that 'audience members use television to create practical social arrangements' (Lull 1980: 202). This gives us an indication of the way in which television news bulletins can feature as part of everyday life, providing a scheduled framework for the whole family. Similarly, Dorothy Hobson's research on housewives and the media (1980) showed that women regularly tuned in to the radio whilst they did household chores, and radio broadcasts provided punctuation marks for the day. Hobson (1980: 109–10) also found that women tended to view factual programmes and news bulletins as a masculine domain, and some women actively sought to avoid such programmes because they found them boring and depressing.

NEWS AND CURRENT AFFAIRS

Diarists were asked a series of questions about their news viewing habits throughout the study period. In Diary 4, June 1992, a special question was asked about news and current affairs, with a particular focus on news bulletins, asking diarists to write about which news bulletins they watched, at what time, and whether there were any main reasons for watching these particular bulletins. In Diary 13, July 1995, respondents were asked to write about their news consumption practices, and to discuss whether their pattern of reading, listening to and viewing news had changed over the previous three years of the study. Answers to these special questions feature in some of the responses quoted in this chapter, but discussion of news and current affairs also featured in other parts of the diaries, such as in discussion of daily routine, and in sections where diarists were asked to write about something that interested them in that day's viewing. Respondents also wrote about the news in questions concerning their favourite programmes, and in a special question on 'what TV means to you', which is discussed further in chapter five. Thus, the responses in this chapter on news and everyday life are taken from a range of different questions throughout the diary period in order to present a detailed analysis of the role news and current affairs has in the household.

In the BFI Audience Tracking Study, our respondents – in common with the general population – were more likely to watch the news on television than to read about it in newspapers or hear it on the radio. Forty-four per cent of respondents said that they watched BBC TV news more than twice a day, and just over 30 per cent of respondents said that they watched ITV news more than once a day.[3] When it comes to the longer news programmes, *Channel Four News* and *Newsnight*, 17 per cent of respondents said that they watched one of these programmes every day.[4] Only 26 per cent of respondents said that they listened to radio news (of up to ten minutes in frequency) more than once a day.[5] A newspaper was read daily by just over 27 per cent of diarists; around half of these were local newspapers. Thus, we can see that BBC TV news is the most popular news bulletin, with ITV coming second, and radio and newspapers providing an alternative news source. In the following section, we discuss why respondents favour television news bulletins above other sources.

Staying in touch

Diarists noted that although they could access information about world events from newspapers and the radio, they felt they would miss television coverage of news events precisely because of its 'up to the minute' character and because TV is able to actually show these events taking place. John Corner noted in *Television Form and Public Address* that the public trust images of television news, and the impact and memorability of these images is important to viewers, giving them a seemingly direct connection with current events, and a kind of trusting identification with their news-gathering representatives (1995: 59–61). This point was discussed by our respondents. Often diarists wrote about how keeping in touch with world events was an important feature of what TV meant to them on a daily basis. To see the faces of politicians as they discuss topical issues, to watch favourite newsreaders reporting events, and witness events such as the war in Bosnia by watching the daily reports on television: these are all important aspects of why people choose to watch news bulletins and current affairs programmes.

For many respondents, being able to keep in touch with news and current affairs is an important part of the function of television. For example, these two respondents wrote:

> The regular timing of news and programmes is of interest to me, providing a framework for the day. Keeping in touch with world news as well as British and Irish News.
>
> (75-year-old female widow)

> I would miss the current affairs programmes and news features. These are both interesting and informative.
>
> (22-year-old female student)

For both these diarists, television news and current affairs is something they value and would miss if it were no longer part of the 'framework' of daily life. Respondents also valued the way in which news bulletins were part of the daily TV schedule, providing up-to-the-minute information. For example, this respondent discussed how she (and her husband) value the quality of *Channel Four News*, and yet if it clashes with another programme, they do not record it to watch later. This is because this programme is concerned with daily news events: to watch it from video would be to miss the 'up to the minute' feel of the programme:

> Nowadays, there is some competition for our viewing around 7pm – certainly when *This Is Your Life* clashes with *Wogan*. In a perfect world we would like to watch the *Channel Four News* – one of the best news offerings (Jon Snow has proved more than adequate substitute for Peter Sissons). Incidentally, we find it quite unrewarding to record news or current affairs programmes for viewing even only a few hours later. It is amazing how quickly 'topicality' gets outdated.
>
> (66-year-old housewife)

For this couple, early evening schedules compete to gain their attention, and they are aware that if they choose to watch something other than the news at this time, they must forfeit the pleasure of watching what they perceive to be the best news programme of the day. Their observation that they do not enjoy watching a recorded version of the news highlights something that is noticeable in the majority of diaries – people do not write about time-shifting in relation to news bulletins. This is an issue that will be discussed later, but here it serves to show that what respondents value about the news is its ability to keep them in touch with current events, events which are watched by other people in Britain (and to a certain extent around the world) at approximately the same time on the same day.

The following male diarist used the metaphor of drug addiction to discuss how he would feel if he could no longer watch TV news every day:

> I would have withdrawal symptoms for a start. I'm a news addict, especially for instantaneous news coverage. I would feel cut off from the world. (In fact, I had a break from writing this in order to listen to the news....) I feel part of humanity by sharing a television experience with people all over the world. I remember watching the first moon landing and reflecting on the fact that people all over the world were sharing that moment with me. I feel a tingle of excitement that I was at one with humanity at a momentous event in human history. Similar events since then include Live Aid and the Royal Wedding (!). If I could not share these pivotal events with the rest of humanity, I feel that my humanity would be diminished. The ultimate mega-television event will probably be the dawn of the new millennium.
>
> (46-year-old unemployed man)

Here, this diarist accesses other sources of news, but it is television which allows him to feel part of world events. This is one of the ways in which the social activity of watching TV can be linked to news coverage: watching world news events is both exciting and a means to share experiences with the rest of the world. His use of the word 'humanity' suggests that he perceives this aspect of TV as one of its positive benefits to individuals and to society as a whole.

Television news bulletins can therefore be a means of bridging the gap between the public and the private spheres. Here, specific 'media events' bring the public together. As Dayan and Katz (1992) note, events such as the Olympic Games, the World Cup, royal weddings, or the death of a public figure, are live events that unite audience members with a national or global experience. These 'media events', as McQuail (1997: 91) points out, become almost ritualistic in nature, and people interrupt their normal routine in order to take part in this experience. (Typically, in Hollywood movies which reflect anxiety about the new millennium such as *Armageddon* (Michael Bay, 1997), the public are able to take part in the ultimate news event, the end of the world, by gathering around the TV set to witness this global experience.) Audience members in this study praised TV for its ability to bring together public and private experience. McQuail comments that the public experience of 'media events' can involve 'some degree of identification with a wider social grouping – whether defined as fans, or citizens, or a local population or a taste culture' (1997: 91). Certainly, here, we can see that for certain respondents, the need to feel involved with national or global events ensures that they regularly tune in to the TV set to watch the news.

News bulletins

Television coverage of news events is important to respondents. Diarists discussed the construction of news bulletins and current affairs programmes. This young adult developed a keen interest in the news and how different channels construct news bulletins:

> Television news is something that has always fascinated me. The use of music, the importance given to news items, the differences in the different news companies (e.g. BBC News contains a lot of politics whereas GMTV news or *The Big Breakfast* news contains much more showbiz news), the different tones of voice the newsreaders use for sensitive, serious and light hearted issues, coping with breaking news stories and technical faults and the ways in which newsreaders read without appearing to read. I find it all amazing.
>
> (16-year-old male school pupil)

The smooth production values and the techniques used to present the news are certainly apparent to this schoolboy, who takes great interest in observing the constructedness of the news.

In general, diarists praised BBC and Channel Four news coverage. Although not many diarists actually watched *Newsnight* (7 per cent) or *Channel Four News* (9 per cent) every day, those that did were full of praise for these news programmes. This respondent wrote about how he appreciated *Newsnight*'s in-depth and critical approach to national and world news:

> For comprehensive information on current or daily events *Newsnight* is a valuable programme, not simply for its summing up of the daily news, but for its discursive, analytical and critical qualities, perhaps no current affairs interviewer displays quite the authority and tenacity of Jeremy Paxman when he is on top form.
>
> (32-year-old unemployed man)

Another diarist said that '*Channel Four News* is the most "in depth", the other channels mostly give snippets, leaving one feeling cheated' (59-year-old retired woman). However, the majority of people regularly watched BBC news (six o'clock and nine o'clock) and ITV news (5.45 and ten o'clock), with BBC news bulletins receiving slightly more praise for their coverage than ITV. The same male diarist who said he liked *Newsnight* also thought 'in general, the BBC's reporting appears to be of a high standard' (32-year-old unemployed man), and a 64-year-old retired nurse echoed several respondents when she summed up the difference between BBC and ITN as follows: 'On the whole, I feel the BBC takes the establishment line, and shows the news in a more formal way than ITN, which seems to show more human interest stories. I am not accusing either of political bias.' This was a woman who watched the news from the moment she woke up (5.30am news on ITV), through lunchtime (ITV), to bedtime (*Nine O'Clock News* and *News at Ten*) as well as a healthy number of documentary programmes (*Panorama*, *World In Action*, to name two). Her main reasons for watching were to 'keep up to date with what is going on in the world' and 'to keep up to date with disability issues'. One of the ways she could tell if she had kept up to date with what she considered to be the essential news items was by watching *Have I Got News for You*, which confirmed that she was 'as aware as most people of the world and national issues'.

For some people, specific news events remained ingrained in their minds. This diarist, for example, remembered the last few days of Mrs Thatcher's period as Prime Minister as one of the highlights of the 1990s. She explained:

> My favourite clip is Thatcher's appearance before the BBC mike outside our Paris Embassy, to announce, in her ridiculous gown (she never realised that she had no dress sense), that she would stand in the second round, publicly unaware that she'd been ditched – and all this to the music of Nessun Dorma [on *Thatcher: The Downing Street Years*, BBC1].
>
> (72-year-old retired woman)

This male diarist wrote about the impact of television coverage of the war in Bosnia:

> ITN's discovery of the prison camps was a powerful and moving piece of footage – something that genuinely made a difference to Western policy. It's virtually impossible not to associate the image of the storming Croatians with archive material of the holocaust. The bombing of Sarajevo market was another memorable and tragic incident. The blood of the civilian once again staining the pavement.
>
> (35-year-old unemployed man)

Seeing these events take place has had a significant impact on this respondent. The image of war in Bosnia, as seen on the news, is symbolic of another war, and it is news footage of the atrocities of the holocaust which allow this respondent to make the connection. Here, John Corner's comment about 'picture power' is particularly apposite (1995: 59). Corner notes that 'when sufficiently strong in revelatory/dramatic character such picturing may serve to crystallise the whole report and to enter public circulation with a force no other form of contemporary journalism could possess' (1995: 61). Events such as the Ethiopian famine of the 1970s, and the bombing of Sarajevo market in 1993 remain in people's minds, and it is the impact of the pictures on the news which make this memorable. For example, this 44-year-old woman singled out the bombing of Sarajevo market to discuss in Diary 13, July 1995:

Very recently, when Sarajevo's fragile peace was broken – wasn't it a bomb in the marketplace one Sunday morning – I was really upset – I remember seeing the reporter standing in the rubble describing how different the scene had been in the morning. It was a really moving piece of film.

(44-year-old female teacher)

Actually *seeing* the destruction that has taken place is important for this diarist. She did not often watch television news, and the shock of viewing this news report reminds her of the horror of this war:

I remember feeling very angry and upset after a brilliant piece of news coverage uncovering the Serbian government's role in the developing war. I also remember the shock of seeing footage of Sarajevo months into the conflict – up till then, I'd only listened to radio reports and I'd forgotten how beautiful Sarajevo's setting was – made me want to weep. I think I've generally been cushioned from most of the horror because I get most of my news from the radio and the press rather than TV.

(as above)

Although radio and newspapers are this respondent's main source of news, it is television news reports which make an impact. The fact that this woman is aware that by *not* watching the news she is protecting herself from the full impact of the events in Bosnia only serves to reflect the dramatic nature of certain TV news bulletins.

News presenters add to the appeal of TV news bulletins. Respondents discussed how presenters could be perceived as 'friends', friends they can trust.

I would miss nearly all of the BBC announcers – nearly – likewise all of the ITV announcers/newscasters. I would miss Jon Snow. They seem like good-class, dignified, honourable friends.

(63-year-old clergyman)

I enjoyed the authoritative *Breakfast News*. Personalities are pleasing. I like Fiona Foster who combines good looks with competence.

(65-year-old retired male schoolteacher)

The news read by Michael Buerk, is about as trustworthy as broadcast news gets.

(35-year-old male factory operative)

The fact that respondents can actually see presenters discussing world events allows these viewers to feel that they can judge for themselves the authenticity or truthfulness of the accounts given. Once again, John Corner's point about the act of seeing is significant to viewers' appreciation of news bulletins (Corner

1995: 58–61). This diarist, for example, liked watching the news because she felt she could tell whether people were trustworthy or not by the expression on their faces:

> [Without television] I should miss the shiftiness of so many public faces (e.g. the Chief Medical Officer quizzed about BSE); shiftiness one cannot pick up from a newspaper report.
>
> (72-year-old retired woman)

This trust in television news is something that has been noted by other surveys on what the public has to say about television news. At the beginning of this chapter, we looked at MORI and NOP polls which suggested that the public trusted newsreaders to tell the truth far more than they trusted other sources of news, such as newspapers or radio bulletins. This was certainly the case in this study, where the relationship between news presenters and the viewing public is seen to be an important one by respondents and illustrates the power of television news over other media.

News content

Michael Bromley (1998: 25) notes that 'the 1990s have been characterised by a growing obsession with what has been seen as a decline in standards' in British newspapers, in particular the 'quality' or broadsheet press. Bromley sees the spread of tabloid news values as something which television initiated, because of its reliance on 'soundbites' and pictures, and the need to entertain the viewing public. Following the lead of American news (Postman 1987), British television news programmes can also be accused of a decline in standards. In the mid-1990s, ITN, for example, chose to spend less time on foreign and political stories and more time on human interest stories in order to maintain its ratings and challenge potential competition (Bromley 1998: 28–9). However, the fact that the majority of respondents in this study chose to watch TV news bulletins (BBC in particular) should give us some indication that it is newspapers which are thought to contain examples of 'tabloid' journalism, and it is for this reason that many diarists chose to watch the news on TV, rather than read about it in newspapers. As this retired farmer said: '[I watch TV news] to keep up with world affairs and hope to see independent views rather than newspapers' biased ones' (67-year-old woman).

In this section we shall briefly discuss what respondents had to say about news bias and the issue of 'tabloidisation'. There is not space in this chapter to undertake a detailed analysis of news content, although there is certainly material in the diaries to support such an investigation. (As we noted at the start of this chapter, the focus for our discussion of the news is to look at news consumption patterns and everyday life, an area that has not received a great deal of attention in the discipline of media studies.) In general, diarists praised television news bulletins and current affairs programmes, and we saw some of these comments in the previous sections of this chapter. However, some respondents did have criticisms to make about types of coverage used by the different TV channels. Several diarists criticised the way in which victims of a violent crime, or people suffering from illness or grief, were treated by journalists:

> The most tasteless examples [on TV] are often in the news (Dunblane) when reporters kept asking 'How do you feel?' Parents/relatives of missing or murder victims choked with tears on police press conferences are upsetting.
>
> (77-year-old retired woman)

> I have just watched an interview with a couple who have a seriously ill baby needing a heart transplant, and the interviewer asked this couple how they would feel about putting the baby through a transplant ordeal. What a stupid question to put to this worried couple. But interviewers do ask people the most stupid questions sometimes.
>
> (63-year-old retired female cashier)

> I do not like the Americanisation of TV, especially our news services – where the news presenters try to be casual and chatty – 'Good evening Sue, and how's your cancer?!'
>
> (33-year-old female marketing manager)

Diarists were concerned about the lack of 'serious' news programmes available, and ITV was considered by some to be more 'tabloid' than other news programmes. This 30-year-old unemployed man noted that news bulletins were getting more 'nosey', an attribute which he associated with tabloid newspapers: 'Anyone crying, upset, or bereaved is likely to have a camera lens thrust in their face and asked the stupid question "How do you feel?" ITN is more guilty of this than the BBC.' However, on the whole most diarists seemed to feel that this was not widespread, and they could still access 'quality' news programmes. This respondent commented:

> When I started the diaries, I did fear that documentary coverage and coverage of global issues would be greatly reduced. I don't think my fears have been realised, though I have noticed that 'serious' programmes are pretty much all scheduled for late evening.
>
> (45-year-old female teacher)

Some diarists wrote about political bias and different news programmes. This man, for example, watched ITV news coverage, even though he did not like its more familiar style, because he felt BBC news was biased:

I always watch the news on ITV. Whilst I do not enjoy the 'chatty' style with which it is presented, I object most strongly to the left bias of the BBC in all its current affairs programmes. It was Alf Garnett, back in the 1960s who first alerted me to what was happening at Auntie. Remember 'Yer bloody BBC!'

(47-year-old unemployed/disabled man)

Another diarist, a housewife and mother of three children, aged 31, thought the BBC was guilty of political bias, but in the opposite way: 'I find the BBC (including *Panorama*) biased towards the Conservatives. I find the bias offensive.' However, such comments were not widespread. If diarists were critical of the way national news bulletins covered events it was more likely that they would discuss the 'tabloidisation' of news programmes, or journalists' insensitivity to victims or the bereaved. Indeed, these two seem to go hand in hand, and respondents appear to be concerned about an overall lack of ethical standards in journalism, in particular newspapers, and the way in which certain tabloid techniques (aggressive interviewing, for example) are becoming a feature in television news bulletins. This would seem to suggest that respondents' concerns about the spread of tabloid news values in television news programmes are as much to do with codes of conduct and issues of taste and decency, as they are about the feared 'dumbing down' of issues and presentation. Respondents may express concern about 'soundbite' journalism, and the trivialisation of news, but they seem to be more *upset* by what is perceived to be a lack of ethical standards in television news coverage of tragic events, such as the Dunblane massacre (see chapter nine).

In the next section we shall look in more detail at how diarists formed patterns of news consumption. Such patterns were often based around scheduling and how this fitted into daily routine, rather than whether respondents found one channel more biased or intelligent than another. In this respect, the fact that BBC news follows *Neighbours* and coincides with family mealtimes has a great deal to do with how the six o'clock news bulletin became part of daily routine.

PATTERNS OF NEWS CONSUMPTION

There has been very little research on the context of news consumption. Jensen (1986) interviewed twenty-four men in America about their news consumption practices. Although this was a small-scale study, the researcher was able to make the interesting point that the context of viewing the news was as important as the reception of the actual news content. His male respondents talked about how watching the news was part of daily routine:

These news viewers tend to describe television news as a fixed point in their everyday lives, which may even influence the planning of the day...even if television news is not defined as a basic source of information, it may be perceived as a natural and integrated element of daily life, and of other simultaneous activities.

(1986: 178)

Jensen also found that men were more likely to be able to watch the news uninterrupted than their wives or partners, who would be busy with household chores, particularly in the early evening, and unable to give the television their undivided attention. Indeed, Jensen found that watching the news could be used 'as an excuse for evading certain household chores' (1986: 183). What we shall see in the following sections is that news consumption is intricately bound up with daily routine, and that women and men, to varying degrees, watch the news whilst simultaneously doing other activities.

For many people, watching, listening to or reading national and local news bulletins was a daily practice that often coincided with mealtimes or other daily activities, such as housework, cooking or even waking up in the morning. This woman, for example, was critical of the fact that the news was a regular feature of daily TV schedules. She wrote: 'I would not miss the news mainly because it's repeated too often during the day and clashes with meal times' (79-year-old retired female civil servant). Her criticism of the everyday aspect of news bulletins was not shared by the majority of respondents in this study. For these people, news bulletins were a welcome part of their daily routine.

Some examples will illustrate this point. This young woman commented on how important the news was to her daily routine:

> I would miss the news because I am an avid news watcher. It is always the first thing I do when I awake in the morning. Switch on the TV so I can see what is happening in the world. I've got to know what is going on, and at times I think it is the only thing that keeps me sane.
>
> (24-year-old unemployed woman)

The remark that TV news bulletins keep her 'sane' during her unemployment is an indication that the establishment of a regular pattern of news consumption helps some people to feel less isolated, and more in touch with current events.

Another woman, aged 63, also found the news a welcome start to the day. She was disabled, and liked to watch the news to make sure that she did not miss out on anything, especially as she was often confined to her home, and therefore felt isolated from the outside world. She described a typical morning routine as follows:

> Watched the 5.30 early morning news, whilst having a cup of tea, and transferring from bed to my wheelchair. Most of the topics were those that I had seen last night and I still miss the short period of *Cable News* from

the USA as used to be included. After putting the washing in the machine, to catch the 'Night Rate Electricity', I had my breakfast, and watched *Breakfast News*, on BBC1 until 7.45am, after which, I heard, rather than saw the remainder of the programme. I was preparing for my Care Attendant's arrival at 9am.

(63-year-old retired nurse)

These two retired men were often busy in the summer months and watched very little TV, but made an exception for the news:

There are times most days when apart from 7am or 8am news and weather programmes [the TV] is not on again until evening, especially if the weather is good and I can get out.

(75-year-old retired male supermarket manager)

I usually watch news at 1 o'clock and again late in the evening, and I should certainly miss those, because I like to get the weather forecasts and often plan outings on them.

(73-year-old retired male sub-postmaster)

These examples show that the news is an important part of daily routines. Many diarists watched the news because they wished to stay in touch with world events and because the timing of national and local news bulletins coincided with breakfast, lunch and teatime. For example:

Lunch in the kitchen, with the TV on, we watch BBC1 news, then turn over to ITV or CH4 for a film or whatever. 6.00pm a little aperitif whilst the BBC1 news is on, I hate the adverts on ITV, then supper and I watch whatever is on, in the kitchen while cooking.

(66-year-old female housewife)

Television news bulletins can provide marker points in the day. This male diarist, for example, was 29 years old at the start of the study, lived at home with his family, worked as a technician at his local college, and did not watch a great deal of TV (on average less than 17 hours a week). His favourite pastime was going out to the local pub with friends. The news, however, was a regular feature of his day. He got up in the morning and watched *TV-AM*, before leaving for work. Then 'I get home about 3.30 and watch (normally) the 3.50 news on BBC2 while eating my afternoon meal'. He usually watched 'either the Beeb or ITV news around 6pm weekdays, 1pm news BBC Sunday' and occasionally watched *Central News South*, although he believed it did not really cover his local area. Television was one source of news; he also liked teletext, which he accessed over three times a day. He explains:

> My main source of news is teletext – partly as a follow up to the lunchtime news and partly to keep me in touch in the evenings. It's also a good way of avoiding adverts.
>
> (30-year-old male college technician)

He describes no change to his viewing habits in relation to the news over the period of the study, despite the fact that he was made unemployed in 1994. This suggests that news viewing habits can remain constant even though there may be changes to viewers' daily routines. Other references to change in patterns of news consumption will be discussed later.

News consumption can be part of the general routine of television viewing. For example, this housewife and mother lived on the Isle of Wight with her husband and two young children. She was 25 years old at the start of this study. A typical day for her was as follows:

> 1.10pm. I always watch the TVS news and weather. National news is too depressing at the moment.

> 1.20pm *Home and Away*. A lot better than *Neighbours* at the moment, but now both are on at the same time mid-day you can't watch both. Silly! I'll see *Neighbours* tonight.

> 3.10pm *Win, Lose or Draw* (last 10 mins.).

> 3.20pm ITV and TVS news and weather.

> 3.50pm CBBC: Love *Ed the Duck*. My son will watch all the programmes between now and 5.35pm.

> 5.40pm ITV news in lounge. *Neighbours* on b/w in kitchen.

> 6.00pm *Coast to Coast*. A lot better than *South Today* (on b/w in kitchen).

> 8.00pm *Dragonslayer* (film).

> 10.00pm ITV news and weather.
>
> (housewife/mother, aged 25, 1991)

We can see that news bulletins either precede or follow regular TV programmes such as *Neighbours*, or *Children's BBC*, and that this family watches ITV news and local news more than BBC or Channel Four. This respondent does watch BBC *Nine O'Clock News* occasionally but this depends on what has been scheduled for that evening on ITV. She listens to the radio regularly, several times a day, but not for more than ten minutes at a time. The family buy the

Sun and the local paper, but only once or twice a week. She does not watch current affairs programmes. This is what this diarist had to say about the regional news: 'We always have *Coast to Coast* on to see the local news. It is well put together, with a mixture of serious news items and light hearted stories.'

This diarist stopped watching daytime news in 1991 because she did not want to hear constant coverage of the Gulf war. She explained:

> I don't watch TV in the mornings now. I used to have it on all the time but I got so fed up with the Gulf War reports – all day – every day – same thing – that I now either have the radio on or my son has his pre-recorded videos on.
>
> (as above, aged 26, 1992)

In addition, she had noticed that her young son was affected by national news bulletins:

> Something I have noticed lately is that the bombing on the news (IRA etc.) has not as much upset my son but he talks about it. And if he hears an unusual bang (car backfiring etc.) he asks if it was a bomb. We try not to let him see long news bulletins but with all the news headlines throughout the day it can't always be helped.
>
> (as above)

When TV news bulletins are seen to consistently cover events that may be disturbing to young viewers, this places some parents in a difficult situation. As the news is a regular feature of this family's daily routine, we can see why it would be difficult to shield the oldest son from such coverage, and this may be one reason why local news coverage is singled out and praised by this respondent above national news bulletins. In the next section we shall see what young adults have to say about how news bulletins can become a regular feature of daily life. From their point of view, this can be both a positive and a negative experience.

NEWS CONSUMPTION: YOUNG ADULTS

Research has shown that children approaching teenage years gradually watch the news more, and have an increased interest in their political environment. Gunter and McAleer note that 'political knowledge...has been found to be related to children's and adolescents' use of the mass media and in particular to their interest in news and current affairs' (1990: 51). An American study by Atkin and Gantz (1978) focused on changes in television news consumption in children aged 5–10 years. Questionnaires were given to the children on two separate occasions over the space of one year, and the children were asked about their interest in news, and whether they discussed news events with other children or adults. The researchers found that over a period of time children developed an increased awareness of politics, and television news consumption was a key factor in why this was the case. Similarly, a study in Northern Ireland in the early 1980s involved 500 children (aged 11 years), who were asked about the frequency of their news viewing, and their knowledge of the problems in Northern Ireland (Cairns 1984). The study found that those children who claimed to watch the news on a regular basis knew more about the political situation in Northern Ireland.

In the present study we shall see that young diarists develop patterns of news consumption over a period of time. Young adults moving from school to college or university recorded a change in viewing tastes, and this change was often signified by a new-found interest in news and current affairs programmes. The change was often perceived as a sign of maturity. Certain factors may help to influence such patterns of consumption, such as education, and family viewing practices. Gunter and McAleer point out the subtle influence of family viewing practices on adolescents: 'Influence from parents may be less direct and without specific intent, whereby parents provide models of viewing which are matched by their offspring' (1990: 136). This certainly seems to be the case in relation to the development of news consumption practices for young adults.

Young adults were quite emphatic about the perceived changes in their attitude to news programmes, and wrote in no uncertain terms about the new, mature and informed self that they felt they had become. This schoolboy, for example, discussed the changes which he noted over a period of time:

> As I have grown up over the last four years I've learnt a lot of things, formed and changed opinions regarding certain matters and I have even changed some of my likes and dislikes. I have therefore started to watch certain types of programme less while I have also started to watch more of other types. For example, nowadays I think I do not watch as many cartoons or children's programmes as I used to, as I now tend to find such programmes rather childish. I now like to watch news programmes to find out what is happening around the world. As school began to take up a more important part of my life, especially within the last year and a half I have found that if I do work with the television on I pay very little attention to what is happening, and if I have a lot of important work to do in an evening I do not put the television on in my room at all. I now go to bed later than I used to which means I usually have a programme on in the background, usually *News at Ten* while I'm getting ready for bed.
>
> (15-year-old schoolboy)

News programmes feature strongly in this account of the changes that have taken place in relation to television viewing. This respondent watches less children's TV, and more factual programmes so that he can keep in touch with world events, something we saw other diarists discuss at the start of this chapter as an important feature of the role of TV in their lives. By the age of 15 this diarist feels he is too busy to watch a great deal of television, but manages to ensure that he tunes in to ITV's *News at Ten* when he is getting ready for bed, a sign of the way in which news bulletins are beginning to feature as part of his daily routine.

Another student also noticed that she watched less television, and was now more interested in factual programmes. Her reasons why this is the case are very similar to the previous respondent's:

> I watch less television. But when I think about the television I have cut out, it was only the tea-time soaps. I would like to watch more news as I think it's important to know what's happening in the world around us (as I don't always have time to read newspapers either).
>
> (19-year-old female student)

This is a point that is echoed throughout younger diarists' responses to their patterns of television viewing; teenagers have an increased awareness of national and global issues and use this knowledge to situate themselves as part of an 'adult' social group. This is an important point as viewing figures for news programmes in the mid-1990s do not suggest any change in news consumption practices for children and teenagers. For example, in 1994, children aged 4–15 years claimed to watch the news 6 per cent of the time they spent watching TV, and this figure is exactly the same for 16–24-year-olds (*Social Trends* 1996). These figures suggest that there is no change in general quantity of news consumption for children or young adults under 25 years of age within these broad bands, although viewing practices may vary within these parameters. In this study, young adults clearly perceive a difference in their news consumption practices, and the majority record an increase in news viewing as they reach mid-teen years.

Family influence

The previous section showed that young adults experience changes to their taste in TV programmes, and this change is often signified by an increased interest in factual programmes and world news bulletins. However, such developments in taste are also part of the way in which news viewing helps to punctuate the day, providing a reference point, in particular at teatime, for family members. Thus, the family, and the everyday nature of news consumption practices, can influence developments in young adults' viewing patterns in relation to news and current affairs. For example, this respondent discussed how her interest in TV news bulletins had increased, in part, because she was in a household where the news was always on at certain times of the day:

> The TV in my boyfriend's parents' house is on almost constantly and even though I'm in the room I'm usually doing something else e.g. reading and scanning newspapers, but if a news bulletin is on I usually stop what I'm doing and take in what's been happening in the world. When I first started this study, at 6.00pm the TV would be tuned to BBC2 or Ch4, anything but the news (I was at my dad's then), but since moving in with my boyfriend I watch more news (5.40 on ITV, 6.00 BBC1).
>
> (22-year-old female engineer)

In the past, this respondent would deliberately tune in to another channel to avoid the news at teatime, but when she was older and lived in a different household she was more likely to show an interest in news and current affairs issues. Of course, this diarist was not able to have so much control of what she watched on TV, which also contributed to changes in her news consumption practices.

We can see how family members influence young adults' news consumption practices more clearly in relation to two young diarists who noted a new interest in news and factual programmes. This new interest in the news can be linked to family interest in news bulletins at key times in the day, especially at teatime. For this schoolboy, aged 12 at the start of this study, the news was a regular part of the family routine; indeed, it was the one type of programme that was important to the household. In 1991, he wrote:

> Television is not that important in our house except when the news is on. And most times we argue who's going to watch which programme and when. But in the end we all have a vote and then decide.
>
> (12-year-old schoolboy)

If we look at the daily routine of TV viewing in several diaries across a period of time we can see that various different news bulletins were watched by the family, but with different degrees of attention. In 1991, this diarist is not so interested in the news, particularly adult news bulletins. He watched *Newsround* on BBC1 by himself; the whole family watched *Neighbours* and *Home and Away*; and whilst he ate his tea, this diarist watched *Channel Four News* with his father and brother. However, he only watched *Channel Four News* for ten minutes, and he didn't really give the programme much attention. In 1992, there was a very gradual shift in attention towards more adult news programmes. This diarist no longer watched *Newsround*; he watched *Neighbours*, followed by *Midlands Today*. The whole family watched *Home and Away*, and then watched *Channel Four News*. This time, this diarist watched the whole programme, but it was only on in the background. However, he also watched *BBC Nine O'Clock News* with the family, although he again only gave it partial attention. When asked about his news viewing habits in 1992, this diarist wrote:

I sometimes watch *Midlands Today* or *Nine O'Clock News* to see what's happening around midlands or anything that could affect us, e.g. education, money, new inventions.

(as above, aged 13)

We can already see that he chooses adult news programmes, rather than *Newsround*, to mention in this dairy. When asked, in 1995, if he had noticed any changes to his pattern of news consumption over a three-year period, he wrote:

Yes, of course, as I am growing and I intend to read more intellectual stuff and stop watching cartoons because they do not appeal to me as they did when I was younger.

(as above, aged 16)

The changes that he notes are changes that will occur in the future. He wants to read more 'intellectual' material because he sees this as a sign of maturity. His news consumption patterns in 1995 help to confirm this more mature approach. In November 1995, this diarist watched *Neighbours* and *Home and Away* with the whole family, and then he watched all of *Midlands Today* and *Channel Four News* with his parents and gave these programmes most of his attention. Thus, for this schoolboy, a partial interest in the news enables him to regularly watch news bulletins which the rest of the family watch every evening. The news is part of the teatime routine for the whole family, just as watching teatime Australian soaps is also part of their daily routine. Over a period of time, we can see his partial interest in the news gradually develop into a more conscious awareness of the importance of the news in relation to adult viewing tastes.

For another diarist, a schoolgirl aged 12 at the start of this study, her initial dislike of the news was transformed over a three-year period into a more active interest in world events. In 1991, for example, she wrote that she hated BBC *Nine O'Clock News*: 'All those straight-faced newsreaders really annoy me – and they all smile and shuffle their papers at the end!' In 1992, she wrote that her main reason for watching BBC *Nine O'Clock News* was 'because my parents watch it and I can't be bothered to sit on my own and watch something else'. However, by 1995, she said that she now watched BBC and ITV news bulletins about once a day, read the paper (the *Times*) about once a day, and listened to short radio bulletins several times a day. She explained:

Three years ago I would not read the news by choice. I now want to know what is going on, especially with all the political upheaval, the former Yugoslavia etc. As I have grown up I have become further aware of the conflict in Bosnia. It makes me consider how easily that could be us. I am

disturbed how the conflict has gone on as long and how the UN intervention has been so ineffective. I have to wonder whether the Prime Minister
and his freshly reshuffled cabinet actually watch the news. Nobody wants to
make a decisive move to intervene or assist in a permanent peace. The
agenda seems to have been put to the back of many people's minds. TV
reports (the pictures and the words) are used to raise emotions and hardly
ever give a balanced view.

(16-year-old female school student)

At the age of 16, this diarist has developed a sophisticated understanding of
world news events. The way in which she discusses news reports of the war in
Bosnia shows that she has come a long way from criticising the appearance of
newsreaders. Her grasp of the complexity of this war, and her awareness of the
role that TV news bulletins can have in shaping public awareness of world
events, is an indication that this diarist is regularly reading and watching and
listening to the news and forming opinions of her own about TV news
bulletins. Parental influence and changing tastes in TV programmes are just two
of the factors which have contributed to this respondent's increased awareness
of her political environment.

NEWS CONSUMPTION: ADULTS

We can see that patterns of news consumption are influenced by subtle
changes over a period of time. For both of the young adults quoted above,
changing tastes in TV programmes, coupled with family interest in news
bulletins, ensured that they paid more attention to local and world news. But
changes of this kind are not dramatic, and are part of the localised changes
that take place in the family household. This is also the case in relation to
older adults who record changes in their news consumption practices. These
changes take place over a period of time and are often linked to changes to
daily routine.

For example, this woman, who was aged 30 at the start of this study,
was an insurance clerk, and lived alone. She did not watch a great deal
of TV:

I do not normally make a point of watching any news programme but if
there's nothing else I want to see I will watch either *Nine O'Clock News* or
News at Ten. If I have not seen the news for a few days or hear something
of interest either on the morning news or Radio One, or if someone at
work tells me that something of interest has happened I will make a point
of watching the news. I read Sunday newspapers which I usually find can
keep me up to date with any major news stories.

(31-year-old female insurance clerk)

Thus, for this respondent, news bulletins did not feature as part of her daily routine. Living in Scotland, she was critical of national news coverage, which she felt showed a 'bias towards England', meaning that 'major events that have happened in Scotland are never reported on national news'. This comment indicates that this respondent may be more interested in local news bulletins rather than national bulletins, but she works long hours, and does not have time to see regional news programmes as these are mainly transmitted in the early evening when she is still at work. During the diary period she joined a health club, and this meant that she took more interest in exercise, and regularly cycled at weekends. This had an effect on her news consumption. In 1995, she reflected:

> I think nowadays I have less time to watch TV, therefore when I am watching it tends to be a programme I have recorded from earlier on. As a result, I therefore tend to miss news bulletins. I am busier on Sundays nowadays and tend to scan the Sunday newspapers more quickly than I used to.
>
> (as above, aged 34)

Her busy weekly schedule ensured that when she did watch TV it was usually pre-recorded material that she watched, rather than whatever may be on in a given evening. This suggests that regularly having the TV on at particular times of the day may be significant to news consumption practices: she does not mention recording news bulletins to watch at a later date, a comment that was discussed earlier by another diarist, who felt that to record TV news bulletins was to miss the point of the 'up to the minute' nature of such programmes.

Time to watch the news

The fact that many viewers do not record news programmes to watch later is in many ways linked to the amount of leisure time available to members of the household. Some respondents, in particular women, are too busy to watch TV in the daytime or evening. For example, this female teacher, aged 40 at the start of this study, liked to watch current affairs programmes. However, as the study progressed she watched fewer and fewer news and current affairs programmes, and yet did not choose to record them to watch at a later date. She explained in 1992:

> I seldom have the peace now to watch TV for myself until 9.30pm, and since I'm usually pretty shattered in the evenings, I've switched off by 11.15pm – not a big window of opportunity for 'viewing for pleasure'! Still, I manage to catch good drama series and documentaries and the occasional *News at Ten*, *Newsnight*, my preferred type of viewing anyway.
>
> (41-year-old female teacher)

By 1995, she was even more busy with work and family commitments:

> I've hardly watched news programmes at all in the last year, relying almost
> completely on radio news, which I listen to at various points of the day and
> evening. We always read the *Observer* but think I've been reading few other
> newspapers too. Never seem to have the time, so it's not worth buying
> them.
>
> (as above, aged 44)

She chooses radio bulletins as her preferred form of news information, but these
are short bulletins of just a few minutes, so this diarist is opting for news that
she can listen to while she is busy preparing family meals – there is no TV in the
kitchen.

Another example will illustrate the changes that take place to news
consumption practices when respondents find they are too busy to watch
the news. This diarist, aged 58–63 years during the period of this study,
was a housewife, with two grown-up children, and one granddaughter,
born in 1991. She lived with her husband in the south of England. There
were three TVs and three videos in the household. This woman and her
husband watched over four hours of TV per day, with particular emphasis
on the news. In 1992 they both had time to watch the news throughout
the day:

> Television is important to us, we only read a national newspaper
> on Sundays [the *Sunday Times*], we rely on TV and Radio for day
> to day news, information, education, and entertainment. We usually
> watch:
>
> **BBC1**
>
> 6.00pm *News* and *Southern News Weather*
>
> 9.30pm *Panorama*
>
> 10.30pm *Question Time*
>
> **BBC2**
>
> 9.30pm *40 Minutes*
>
> 10.30pm *Newsnight*

ITV

8.30pm *World In Action, This Week*

10.40pm *First Tuesday*

10.40pm *Facing South*

Channel 4

7.00pm *News*

9.00pm *Critical Eye*

9.00pm *Dispatches*

Television current affairs programmes appear mostly well researched. *Question Time* is too party political, but it is nice to see a few more female faces on the panel though. *BBC South* does not cover our area but it is more south coast orientated than *BBC South East*.

(housewife, aged 59)

We can see from the way she itemises the news programmes, and lists them in order of channel and time of day, that this woman is an avid watcher of the news. She has her favourite news bulletins (*Channel Four News*) and current affairs programmes, and offers opinions about which ones give the most satisfaction. Clearly television news is the main source of information for this household, although they appear to watch the news only in the evening, eschewing daytime news bulletins.

All this was to change later in the same year, when this woman began to look after her grandchild. In 1995, she wrote:

Since February 1992 my granddaughter has been in my care all day every weekday whilst my daughter works full-time. From quite early on she has taken an interest in television. I monitor what she views and often watch her particular programmes with her, fortunately our tastes are similar. Her daily presence has certainly changed my viewing habits during and since that time. I used to listen to the news on Radio 4 quite a bit, also watched the news on TV for much longer periods and it is difficult now to find time to read through all *The Sunday Times* but I do make an effort to read the local paper.

(as above, aged 62)

By 1995, this diarist watched BBC news about once a day; ITV news and *Channel Four News* a couple of times a month and BBC *Newsnight* less than once a month. Thus, although she is able to keep in touch with world events (via BBC news) and local events (from the local newspaper) there has been a dramatic decrease in the amount of TV news programmes that are watched. Despite the fact that this diarist is technically still able to watch evening news programmes – she looks after her grandchild during the day – she does not do so to the same extent as she did in the past, and this reflects how being in charge of a busy household means that this woman is unable to find the time or energy to watch the news, even though it is something she had got a great deal of satisfaction from in the past.

The examples used in this section have come from female diarists, and this reflects the fact that many women note that their pattern of news consumption fluctuates depending on how busy they are in the household. This may suggest that news consumption is a luxury for some people, in particular women, who more often find themselves with less leisure time to spend watching television.

TELEVISION NEWS AND EVERYDAY LIFE

In this chapter we have looked at the way in which patterns of news consumption can increase and decrease because of personal and family commitments. The focus has been on how watching, reading or listening to the news can be part of daily routine, a routine that the whole family participate in, even if some members of the family show more interest than others. The way in which respondents in this study situate watching the news as part of the framework of everyday activities is something that corresponds with the findings of Lull (1980), Hobson (1980) and Jensen (1986). Lull's account of the practical social arrangements of television in the home is particularly related to the findings in this study, as is Jensen's finding that watching the news is part of daily routine. However, Hobson's account in the 1970s of the way in which the news is perceived to be part of a masculine domain is not something that we have found with our respondents, who appear to develop news consumption practices that are based (in part) on age, family influence and leisure time as much as on gender distinction and taste in television programmes. Certainly, women showed just as much interest in the news, as long as they could find the time to watch it. This also confirms the finding of Jensen (1986), which indicated that men are more likely to be able to watch the news uninterrupted than women, who were busy with household chores, and therefore less likely to be able to give their undivided attention to the news.

Respondents had different reasons why they liked to watch television, and this may in part correspond with findings by Morley (1980), Dahlgren (1988) and Corner *et al.* (1990) about the range of responses which viewers produced in relation to news programmes, responses that cannot be easily categorised according to socioeconomic status. Our findings indicate that watching the news can be a social activity, one that can be shared with friends or family, and one that allows people to feel part of a larger experience. This is particularly the case with television coverage of world events, where being able to see newsreaders and political figures, and witness visual accounts of world events, is an important part of the function of television. This links with John Corner's comment that 'the offer of "seeing" is absolutely central to the project of television journalism' (1995: 59). As one diarist commented in this chapter, watching news bulletins can make people feel in touch with humanity. Of course, this also means that people are in touch with both the positive and the negative aspects of human behaviour, and so uplifting events such as Live Aid are remembered alongside the atrocity of the war in Bosnia. Although respondents are critical of news coverage, in particular the insensitivity or bad taste that can be seen in relation to victims of tragic events, in general people seemed to feel that British television news bulletins are of high quality and should be praised. This was especially the case in relation to the BBC and Channel Four coverage of world news. Thus, audience fears about 'tabloidisation', or lack of fairness in news reportage, are grounded in an understanding that certain television news bulletins maintain 'serious' news coverage of local and global events.

Everyday life is important to patterns of news consumption, and news bulletins feature as part of people's daily TV timetables and their daily life schedules. Thus, the fact that news bulletins coincide with meal times ensures that many people watch the news because it is a focal point that helps to punctuate the day. News bulletins can provide a means for family members to interact, especially at meal times, and the regular pattern of watching teatime Australian soaps which are flanked by news bulletins on ITV and BBC1 shows that many families do use this time as a reference point, a time to relax and interact. This helps to substantiate the point that patterns of news consumption can be linked to how much leisure time is available to an individual on a daily basis. People change their patterns of news consumption over a period of time, and for a variety of different reasons; for example, in the case of young adults, an increase in news consumption is linked to the subtle changes that take place in overall patterns of taste in TV programmes at this developmental period in their lives. However, such changes are part of the dynamic of everyday life, and we can see that finding the time to watch, read or listen to news and current affairs is not easy in the busy lives of viewers.

SUMMARY OF KEY FINDINGS

- Watching television news bulletins is often a social activity.
- Young adults develop an interest in the news, which is in part influenced by family viewing patterns.

- Patterns of news consumption develop in relation to previously existing or emerging routines within everyday life.
- News bulletins feature as part of daily routine, often coinciding with family and household meal times.
- Patterns of news consumption are influenced by subtle changes over a period of time, such as fluctuations in work or family commitments.
- News consumption practices are dependent upon available leisure time.
- Men and women like to watch television news and current affairs programmes, although women are less likely to find the time to watch the news.

Notes

1   Schlesinger (1978: 112) recorded that there had, at that time, been three major surveys about television and radio audiences and news bulletins, which showed a decline in the dominance of BBC news bulletins since the postwar period. However, as Schlesinger notes, such audience research is concerned with how the different news bulletins are perceived by the British public. Such research projects may tell us about rivalry between BBC and ITN news, but they do little to explain or help us understand how news bulletins fit into everyday life.

2   Indeed, Mullan (1997: 80) suggests that this trend in the popularity of television news consumption originated from the 1950s.

3   Only 13 per cent of respondents said that they watched ITV news two or three times a day.

4   *Channel Four News* is around 50 minutes of news and analysis, and BBC2's *Newsnight* is similar at 45 minutes. Thirty-two per cent of respondents said that they never watched these programmes.

5   Only 11 per cent of respondents said that they listened to radio news bulletins of ten minutes or more, two to three times a day, although 24 per cent said that they listened to radio news about once a day overall.

Chapter 4

Transitions and change

This chapter focuses on changes and transitions in family life, the domestic space and patterns of television consumption. We will be applying the concept of life-course analysis, which is concerned with change over time and change over the life cycle, to the subject of television and everyday life. Our interest is in how children and adults perceive past change, and whether television has a role to play in the transitional periods in people's lives. Chapter seven will consider change in relation to the elderly audience. We shall look at what young adults have to say about studying for exams, going to college or university, or being unemployed. What we shall see is that the role of television alters dramatically in relation to these life changes. Women and men who experience changes to their employment or personal or family relationships are also of interest. The way in which these changes affect television usage can be seen to be more subtle and part of a gradual shift in patterns of television viewing. This chapter includes discussion of normative changes in the family, such as adolescent transition, and less predictable changes, such as divorce. We shall also look at an accumulation of life changes, as well as isolated events, because individuals and families are likely to experience a combination of changes which result in a variety of coping strategies.

PREVIOUS STUDIES OF TELEVISION AND LIFE CHANGES

In chapter one we discussed the significance of life-course analysis in relation to the research methodology used in this study. Shirley Dex, in *Life and Work History Analyses* (1991), comments on the growth of qualitative and quantitative research in life and work histories over the past twenty years. The significance of life-course analysis is to focus on transitions over time. Research topics such as education, unemployment and marriage lend themselves to life and work history analysis, and there have been a number of longitudinal studies in these areas (see Dex 1991). For example, Harris *et al.* (1987) conducted a study in redundancy, and Rosenthal (1991) looked at the dynamic nature of post-redundancy work-history experiences. Similarly, Baker and Elias (1991:

242), in their survey of youth unemployment and work histories, found that longitudinal studies could show the long-term impact of unemployment on the employability and earnings of young adults.

Dex (1991: 13) comments that more topics could benefit from life-course analysis, such as household relationships, or the consequences of motherhood, although she does not mention media consumption patterns. The lack of life-course analysis, or any other qualitative longitudinal research, on media audiences means that we know very little about how children and adults change their media consumption patterns over a period of time.

Nevertheless, there has been a growth in qualitative research on children's responses to television over the past twenty years, and this type of research has been extremely helpful in illuminating how and why children and teenagers watch television in the home. Many of these studies have focused on the positive and negative aspects of watching television, and books such as *The Disappearance of Childhood* (Postman 1982) highlight the negative effects of television for children, whilst others, such as *Television is Good For Your Kids* (Davies 1989), focus on the medium's positive attributes to watching television. The first type of research is by far the most common, and much of this research has concentrated on assessing the impact of violence, sexuality and bad language on children and teenagers (see Belson 1978; Van Evra 1990, amongst others).[1] This shows that there is a widespread assumption that television is bad for young people: it can cause bad eyesight; corrupt innocent minds; encourage anti-social behaviour; and have many other negative effects which parents express concern about. Research by Palmer (1986, 1988), Buckingham (1987, 1993a, 1993b, 1996) and Hodge and Tripp (1986) has attempted to find out what children have to say about watching television. Hodge and Tripp, and Buckingham, focused on how children are media literate, and capable of distinguishing between fiction and reality. Palmer's research suggested that the way adults perceive children's television is quite different from the way children perceive their own experience of watching TV, an experience that they take a great deal of pleasure from. Palmer also noted that children negotiate their relationship with television and everyday life, and often perform other activities, such as eating, reading or playing, whilst in front of the TV. In this chapter we shall see that children do not perceive television as being 'bad' for them, although they are concerned to explore leisure activities other than television.

What is missing from such research is the way in which children change their perception of television over a period of time. In Buckingham's study of children's responses to horror films, it is possible to see that young children distance themselves from children's cartoons, in order to associate themselves with more adult films. As Buckingham notes, the children are very aware of British video ratings such as 'PG', '15' or '18', and 'frequently use them as a means of calibrating their maturity as viewers' (1996: 82). Regulatory bodies such as the Independent Television Commission classify 'children' as aged 4–15 years of age, and for research purposes this suggests that there is a wide range of needs, interests and experiences of this group which obviously change over a period of time. This is something that concerns us in this chapter, and the longitudinal nature of the Audience Tracking Study means that we are able to see how perceptions of film and television change as children become older. Rosengren and Windahl (1989) in their overview of the Swedish Media Panel, a longitudinal study in child development, found that the relationship between children and the activity of watching television altered in teenage years. The researchers suggested that the media can be a substitute for real-life social interaction, particularly in teenage boys, and this led them to consider the 'interaction potential' of the media, which can be used to reduce anxiety or loneliness.

McKenry and Price (1994) note that there has been an increased interest in how families cope with problems such as unemployment, or marital stress. They suggest that the family should be viewed as active rather than passive, and that researchers should be aware of 'the pluralistic and changing nature of the family' (1994: 308). We have already discussed ethnographic research about family audiences in chapters one and two, and research by Lull (1980), Morley (1986), Gray (1992) and others has shown that the domestic space is subject to change, and that audiences negotiate television viewing in complex and diverse ways. This research does not specifically address the issue of life-course analysis, but certain findings about the social uses of television, and the dynamic interplay between household members, will be applicable to this chapter. For example, both Morley and Gray found that the domestic space was not static, and the way in which men and women responded to television in the home was open to change. Similarly, Lull described the relational use of TV ('affiliation/avoidance') as something that is important to family relationships, and his account of how men and women can use television to facilitate communication in their relationship, and also use television to act as a *barrier* to open discussion, is something we shall also see in our discussion of marital relationships in this chapter.

Rogge and Jensen (1988) and Rogge (1991) found in their study of West German families that everyday life and family relationships are in a constant state of flux. Their research showed that changes such as unemployment affect patterns of media use for the whole family. When a member of the household is unemployed, in particular the father, television can become far more central to the family dynamic than in the past, in many ways being used as the sole means of entertainment. Like Lull, Rogge and Jensen reported that television can also act as a barrier to communication within the family, and can encourage members to feel isolated and uncertain about the future.

The BFI Audience Tracking Study contains data that can help us to further understand life changes and television usage. Four years into this study, respondents were asked to write about whether they had experienced changes in their lives over the study, and whether these changes had an impact on the way they use television. This question occurred in Diary 12, April 1995, one year before the study finished, and it gave diarists an opportunity to reflect on television and everyday life over a period of time. It is also the case that throughout the diaries respondents frequently wrote about changes to their personal circumstances (they also filled in yearly updates, charting changes in their lives), and therefore we have used extracts from other diary entries to supplement our discussion.

YOUNG ADULTS: TRANSITION AND CHANGE

The transition from adolescence to adulthood is a time when everyday structures and television consumption patterns alter considerably. There has been some research in young adults which shows that adolescents begin to anticipate belonging to a new group, or status, often adopting new values, or consumption patterns (Rosengren and Windahl 1989; Roe 1994). Peer pressure is a significant factor in this transitional period. As Roe points out: 'With the onset of puberty, and for some years thereafter, peer group membership becomes an increasingly salient reference point for the vast majority of adolescents and is associated with a shift in media use patterns' (1994: 186).

Television plays a significant role in the day-to-day activities of young people: it is watched in the morning, before school/college; it is watched after school/college as a means to unwind; it can be on in the background, or as the focus of collective attention, whilst the family have their evening meal; and it can be a welcome distraction whilst having to complete homework. Television is clearly important to young adults, both as a source of entertainment and information and as a site for social interaction and engagement. However, the structure of the school day, and after-school activities, ensure that young people do not have as much free leisure time as they would like. In 1996, young adults (16–24 year olds) spent 14 hours per week watching television, but they also spent 16 hours per week talking, visiting and socialising with friends, and eating and drinking out (*Social Trends* 1996). As this group of young adults have a total of 40 hours of free time per week, this would suggest that after socialising and watching TV, there is very little time left for other leisure activities.

When major changes occur, such as studying for exams, this places more pressure on young adults to work rather than to socialise with friends, or watch television. These disruptions to patterns of television viewing can also be seen when young people leave school and enter college or university. Television becomes less important the more young adults are away from the household in which they grew up. Whilst at university, young adults tend to develop a range of outside interests and are less dependent on television as a main source of entertainment. Overall, what we shall see in this section is that young adults perceive a shift in both the *amount* of television watched on a day-to-day basis, and the *type* of television programmes that they choose to watch.

It is worth noting here that discussion of parental involvement, or tension between family members, is significantly absent from young diarists' responses to the question of change in their lives. This may seem strange given the fact that many young adults are members of busy households and do not have sole choice of viewing content. It is possible to suggest that there could be parental intervention in levels of television viewing in teenage years, particularly at exam time, when teenagers are under pressure to revise at home. However, according to teenagers themselves, this is not the case. Moores is critical of Palmer (1986) for neglecting to incorporate 'intergenerational ties and tension over TV use in the home' in her study of children's responses to television (1993: 58). As research by Morley (1986) and Lull (1982) has already shown that 'television is an object around which patterns of domestic authority and resistance are regularly played out', Moores finds Palmer's work weakened by this resistance to consider the domestic space and the interaction between family members (1993: 59). We looked at household TV arrangements and family arguments in chapter two, and found that there was tension over TV use in the home, particularly between parents and young adults. And yet, when asked to discuss changes to their life and television viewing over a period of time, young adults chose not to talk about such negotiations in the household. This would suggest that when young adults define changes to their television viewing patterns they see themselves as the primary agent in this transitional period. We shall see, of course, that peer pressure and family influence are significant factors in why children and teenagers change their patterns of television consumption over a period of time, but by allowing the respondents to speak for themselves, we shall also see that the degree of influence from parents and friends is less direct than we might assume. As Gunter and McAleer point out, parental intervention in what is watched on TV on a daily basis is not strong for the teenage group (1990: 137). This is born out in this study, where young adults in a multi-set household are, on the whole, able to make their own decisions about the type of TV they want to watch.

Signs of maturity

Starting secondary school was a major source of disruption to a young adult's pattern of television viewing. The young respondents looked back to the start of the study when they had still been in primary school, and they noticed a clear and dramatic difference in the amount of time they watched television. The following two extracts are typical:

> Since starting secondary school I have watched less and less TV. Recently I have started watching practically no television except decent films and sporting events. I have abandoned early evening TV, like *Neighbours* and *Home and Away* (except for *EastEnders* of course).
>
> (14-year-old schoolboy)

I haven't had any changes in my life, except moving to my secondary school. As my friends changed my tastes in music and programmes changed. I watch different types of programme since I left my junior school. This also could be because I am maturing. Because I have a lot of homework I don't watch as much TV as before in the 4.00–5.00 time period. I also get into my house later and then I always wash my hair. I don't watch as many programmes before *Neighbours* as I did. Because I go out most Saturdays with my friends I also don't watch sport on Saturdays.

(13-year-old schoolgirl)

Both respondents notice a shift in taste, and a reduction in the number of programmes they watch. Early evening television is eschewed in favour of what are perceived to be 'decent' types of programmes, perhaps in this instance more 'adult' programmes. Here television, and in particular the category of children's television, is something to leave behind, to discard along with toys and going to bed early. This is not to say that these young adults do not value television, but to suggest that their perception of the role television has to play in their lives has altered. Children's television is something *they used to watch*, and by saying this these diarists signal a growing sense of maturity. This finding is also reflected in viewing figures for young adults in the mid-1990s. In 1994, children aged 4–15 years of age claimed to watch children's programmes 25 per cent of the time they spent watching TV, whereas young adults aged 16–24 years of age claimed to watch children's programmes only 6 per cent of the time (*Social Trends* 1996).

Peer pressure is certainly important in relation to changes in television viewing, especially when respondents begin secondary school. One respondent, for example, began writing her diary at the age of 9. She came from a middle-class household, which had three TVs, two video recorders, and satellite television. Despite this access to television, she wrote in her first diary: 'Although we have three TVs, TV is not very important in our household.' This is because she was engaged in a variety of after-school activities, 'with Ballet lessons on Thursdays and Fridays, tap on Monday, Chinese on Tuesdays, swimming on Wednesdays, Badgers on Tuesdays, modern dancing on Mondays and piano and elocution on Saturdays'.

She had little time for television, both because she was busy and because she didn't think highly of most television programmes. For seven diary entries in a row she recorded little or no television viewing for the day of the diary, and she was emphatic about how there had been 'NO PROGRAMMES WATCHED' throughout the majority of this period. She also didn't record any programmes, watch any pre-recorded programmes, or rent or buy any videos on these diary entry days. However, by 1994, when she was in secondary school, she watched more television programmes, such as *The New Adventures of Superman*, *Baywatch* and *Don't Forget Your Toothbrush*. By 1995, she talked to her friends about *Casualty* and *The X-Files*. She still didn't watch as much TV as her friends: 'I will say that I don't watch much TV and that most of the people in my class watch almost quadruple the amount that I do', but she was most certainly influenced to watch more TV because of peer pressure at school. She explained in 1995:

> I have had to watch a bit more TV nowadays because my friends talk about TV a lot and so I have to understand what they are talking about but apart from that I still don't attach a lot of importance to TV – I prefer a good book – sometimes I feel guilty about NOT watching TV because I'm seen as a bit weird 'cos I don't watch as much as my friends and sometimes I think that my sister would prefer me to watch a bit more TV and therefore be more normal.
>
> (14-year-old schoolgirl)

Despite this perception that it is 'normal' to watch television regularly, a perception which led the above diarist to watch a little more TV for social reasons, the majority of young adults, both girls and boys, recorded a change in their viewing patterns that indicated they watched less television than they used to. This change took place in periods of adolescence, teenage years and in young adults over the age of 16. If we look at schoolchildren who were completing their final year, we can see that they too noticed a marked change in their viewing habits, which they explained as a sign of becoming more mature. Two diarists wrote:

> My viewing habits have changed over the years because simply, I've got older and more mature. I am doing my GCSE exams this year, so I don't want as much TV as I used to. I'm a quiet person and don't go out much, so TV becomes a companion at times for me. But at the end of the day TV isn't the most important thing in my life. I have noticed that I don't watch weekday children's programming anymore. This is mainly because this is when I'm doing my homework and revision and is also a sign of becoming more mature.
>
> (16-year-old schoolboy)

> My work level has steadily increased over the past 2 years on the run up to the GCSEs, meaning that I usually have a break from working from 5.30–7pm and then work on until I've had enough. I have abandoned kiddies programmes. During the period of the mock exams I was glad to watch some TV as it numbed my brain and gave me a release from the intensive study – I enjoy watching rugby etc. more and midmorning television makes me depressed. I like dramas, like the Ruth Rendell mysteries, I like *Cracker*, I like *Absolutely Fabulous*.
>
> (15-year-old schoolgirl)

Once again, this perception of changes in television viewing is linked to age and the concept of maturity.

If we look at the type of favourite programmes that teenagers in this study watch we can see that peer pressure is probably part of the reason why many young adults say that they now watch different, more 'adult' programmes. The favourite programmes for teenage boys and girls include *Casualty, Neighbours, The X-Files, Friends* and *Have I Got News for You*, amongst others. The first two programmes are aimed at a family audience, whilst the last three are aimed at a more adult audience. It is also the case that many young adults start to look to television for information as well as entertainment, and they are increasingly aware of a desire to watch the news and keep in touch with news events (see chapter three). We can see this in relation to the popularity of a programme such as *Have I Got News for You*, which offers a combination of current affairs (albeit in satirical form) and more straightforward entertainment. The point here is that young adults in this study notice gradual changes in viewing tastes and schedules over a period of time. The very fact that these diarists do not mention parental intervention in relation to revision and levels of TV watching is an indication that these young adults want to be seen to be mature enough to regulate their own viewing, in the same way that they wish to appear capable of regulating other leisure activities.

Television did play a role in providing a break from the routine of study, and those diarists who were studying at school and at college also discussed how they regulated their television viewing. Some young people were particularly adept at weaving their way through the daytime schedules:

> I am studying for my 'A'-levels and spend much of my time at home. Therefore during my breaks I often go and watch television. Often I time my breaks to coincide with something on television – perhaps the start of *This Morning* or *Scene Today* or the quiz show on ITV at 2.50pm – all programmes which entertain rather than educate, a good alternative to revising!
>
> (18-year-old male student)

Another 17-year-old student wrote a highly detailed account of his navigation through the channels, interspersed with short breaks for revision. The programmes, from *Good Morning Britain* and *Crosswits* to *Children's BBC* links and *Neighbours*, were devoured with considerable pleasure, attenuated – or perhaps enhanced – by detailed observations of everything from a newsreader's nerves (improving), and Tom O'Connor's apparent state of health (worrying), to ITV's weather graphics (inferior) and Alan Titchmarsh's mood (wearying). The attention to changing details, and the points of comparison – as seen in his ability to judge whether the newsreader was more or less nervous than last week, or whether Tom O'Connor was more or less red-faced, as well as the detailed ITV versus BBC comparisons of weather symbols, Australian soaps, and news styles – suggests that this student's revision may not have been getting much attention.

These pre-exam students were enjoying an usual opportunity to consume television at a time of day when they otherwise wouldn't be doing anything else socially – even if there was school work to be done – and so felt quite 'free' to do so. Indeed, watching daytime TV to these students is commendably, if very mildly, rebellious. Of course, these heady days of daytime soap, cartoons and anodyne chat do not last for ever:

> I watch a lot less TV because I am hardly at home and if I am I'm trying to get work done. Although I do listen to more music now. I still watch *Neighbours* and *Home and Away*. When I was at high school TV used to be an important talking point, but now I'm at college and older we have much better things to do and say. I do like a nice relaxing night though every now and again when I can just sit in and watch a load of TV and eat loads.
>
> (17-year-old female student)

Although this student makes the point that she has more important things in her life than watching TV, we can still detect a hint of regret for those bygone days when she had more time to spend in front of the set.

University life

Going to university is a key life transition for some young adults. This life transition signifies a marked change in daily routine and in how young people spend their free time. Several respondents did not possess a television for the first year of their study. Going home for holidays afforded some relief from this disruption in television viewing patterns, but in general most students noticed that once this pattern had been broken, they were not so concerned about following programmes that they enjoyed whilst still living at home. This meant that other social activities, and other media (magazines, radio and newspapers) became as, if not more, important as a daily source of information and entertainment. The following respondent describes the key changes that occurred since he started university:

> Over the past four years I have finished my GCSE's off, done 'A' levels and finally last October left home to go to University. Over this time my view-ing habits have changed greatly. I no longer watch anywhere near the volume of programming that I used to. At university this fact is more or less enforced anyway, as I don't have a TV of my own, but even when I get back home (as I am at the present, on holiday) I still don't watch that much. I've found that I have become much more selective in what I do watch. Some programmes that I watched constantly at school – such as soap operas are strictly no go as I got pretty sick of them all, as they

became increasingly predictable and unbearable to watch as I grew older. There are some programmes that I won't miss now, but only a select few. This applies when I am at home. One or two extra special programmes I get my parents to record for me while I'm away during term time, but apart from these I don't watch TV at all. I've found that I can, for the most part, live without TV. The only major thing that I do miss is being kept informed on the latest news, but fortunately I've a radio.

(18-year-old male student)

We can see here that once this respondent moved away from home, he developed a different attitude to television. There were certain programmes he did not want to miss – for example, his favourite programmes were *Vic Reeves' Big Night Out* and the *White Room* – but by getting his parents to record these he could still maintain contact with such programmes. When this diarist first started writing for the study he was studying for his GCSE exams, and watched on average seven programmes a day. However, when he went to university in 1995 he didn't watch any programmes at all. The day he wrote the above passage, he was at home and watched eleven programmes. Once he was back at university the number dropped to zero once more. This take-it-or-leave-it approach to television is perceived by this respondent as a positive attitude. Once again, reduced viewing of soap operas – 'I haven't watched *Neighbours* or *Home and Away* for about 2 years now, and am proud of this fact' – is perceived as sign of increased maturity for this student.

There is a sense in these diary entries that once at university, young adults have better things to do than watch television, a feeling reflected by other teenagers and college students. This is not to say that students do not value television. Certainly many young adults discussed how television became an important method of relaxing with friends, and alone. However, having friends, and socialising on a regular basis, were perceived to be more important than staying in and watching TV. The following extract explains this:

Moving to university has radically changed the way I use television. Previously I used to watch general light entertainment programmes of a varied nature. Now the television I watch has become more specific i.e. relating to my course, only certain programmes that I watch with friends such as sport and videos etc. TV has become less important to me now as my main social and relaxation activities occur with my friends in bars, at their houses and elsewhere. The only usual times when it does become a social activity are when there is a big sport event on or a film. It seems my life has become too full of other activities to have time for television.

(20-year-old male student)

This student wants television to inform as well as entertain. He is too busy to waste time watching 'endless crap gameshows'. However, despite such claims about TV's lack of importance in his life, he does still watch a regular amount of television. His favourite programmes include *The Fast Show* and *Vic Reeves' Big Night Out*. In 1996 he confessed: 'I have started watching more "decent" films and have moved away from the older style of programmes although I do admit to still watching some kids programmes.' This shows us that the changes this student perceives have taken place are more gradual than it at first appears. Life is not so full that he cannot fit in the occasional afternoon programme, although he is cautious to play down this activity in favour of a more 'cultured' taste in films.

Youth and unemployment

For some young adults, leaving school or college does not result in paid employment, but instead in periods of unemployment. Research on youth unemployment suggests that this disruption to 'life-course expectations when young people [are] denied the economic and social resources provided by paid employment' can mean that young adults can experience 'stress and tension and bewilderment' (Allat and Yeandle 1992: 112). Part of the reason that this is the case is that 'adulthood' is equated with a secure wage, and this conceptualisation of adulthood does not take into account the fact that many young people cannot really expect a secure wage once they have left full-time education (Urwin 1990: 62). Allat and Yeandle (1992) conducted a study of the lives of forty young working-class families in the North East of England, and found that a young person's struggle for independence within the family involved a complex negotiation of power. These young adults lacked an externally imposed structure to the day, and parents would often attempt to impose a structure, encouraging their children to adopt a 'work ethic' that would ensure they did not spend all day in the home. Allat and Yeandle did not look at young people's use of the media in relation to these periods of unemployment, but it is possible to see that for young adults in this study, the media, and television in particular, can provide an external structure to the day.

The following respondent was a female student, who finished her college exams, and then faced a period of unemployment. She was aged 15–20 through the period of writing the diaries, and lived in the North East, with her parents. There was one television and video recorder in the household. For this diarist, television was not the central focus of her life:

> I have taken up keep fit, as a pastime/hobby, this takes place at my local community centre, where I have made some new friends. Also, since I finished my college course and have been unemployed, I have been involved in charity work.
>
> (19-year-old unemployed woman)

Here, we can see that keeping fit and charity work take her outside the home environment, and provide an important social element to her daily routine:

> I find TV programmes which are screened through the day are not really aimed at my age group, and therefore do not really watch TV much through the day, and generally watch TV in the evenings. I have become more interested in detective stories such as *Cracker* and *Touch of Frost*, but I still enjoy the programmes I always used to watch, mainly medical programmes like *Peak Practice*, *999*, *Casualty*, etc. I do not watch children's TV anymore, as when I started the study I was 15 and did watch some children's TV programmes. Also I do not watch as many soaps as I used to. I stopped watching *Home and Away* because of the boring storylines, and I sometimes watch *Neighbours*, but not as much as I used to, the storylines are quite unbelievable. I am grateful for TV if I am in by myself as it is a bit of company – and it is good to watch your favourite programmes in peace! I do not really plan my life around TV but I just look in the paper, and see if there is anything I want to watch, and then I watch it. If there is nothing on that everyone wants to watch we either watch a pre-recorded video or rented video, or listen to the radio.
>
> (as above)

In many ways, this diarist presents a picture of herself as quite business-like in her approach to the media. She is unemployed, but seems determined to watch television when she wants to, rather than when she has nothing else to occupy her time. There is the familiar reference to 'children's programmes', and her reflection on the fact that daytime TV doesn't cater for her age group is a sure sign that she aligns herself with more adult-orientated programming, although she is certainly not interested in the programmes aimed at daytime viewers. Her approach to television is to be in control of what she watches, and not to use TV as 'background company', an approach that is less to do with her unemployed status, and more to do with her family's attitude to television viewing in the home.

This 'sensible' attitude to television consumption and unemployment runs counter to the usual image of unemployed youth. However, this 17-year-old seems to rather enjoy his life of 'not doing much', working two days a week, watching TV and skateboarding. Living with his parents and not having a family of his own obviously makes such a life much more viable:

> Usually in the mornings, if I'm not at school, which I am not anymore, I stay in my bed till round midday. I get up and go down stairs to the kitchen, turn the TV on and have my breakfast, usually a bowl of Frosties, yum, yum! After my breakfast I go and sit in the lounge and watch some television and play some card games or read the paper....At around 6 o'clock I have my dinner, then I go out skateboarding with my friends, I've

been doing it for about three and a half years, so I'm not too bad at it. We usually go home at about 10pm on weekdays and whenever we want at weekends, as we usually get drunk or something like that, its fun....On Sundays and Mondays I go to work at Tesco's, where I collect the trolleys and help out in the warehouse, it's okay, but I'd rather be doing something more interesting, something to do with design. In my household I don't feel television is that important, it's just a thing that's there really, I feel that I am the only one that watches the TV a lot, as there is nothing else to do...

(17-year-old man)

In this case, television's ability to 'be there', to entertain when there is nothing better to do, is obviously something this respondent welcomes. His day doesn't come to life until the evening, when skateboarding with friends provides a welcome alternative activity to watching telly and playing cards. However, this life of leisure does not last for ever. Three years later, his lifestyle had changed considerably; this respondent was spending all his spare time with his girlfriend, and he was also doing an apprenticeship in aircraft fitting, which was completed the following year. He then started an evening class in graphic design – the occupation dreamed of four years earlier in Tesco's car park.

For some young adults, long periods of unemployment can lead to depression and family problems, and can cause stress and tension in the domestic space. Here an accumulation of life changes – leaving school, or college, becoming unemployed, parental problems, periods of ill health – can all combine to create a bleak picture of the future for some young people. One young diarist who was aged 19–24 throughout this study was unemployed throughout that time and did not feel positive about her chances of re-employment. She lived in the North East of England, where unemployment levels were high, especially for people leaving college (Allat and Yeandle 1992). Her father was also unemployed, her mother did not have paid employment, and her younger sister was at college. At first, this respondent kept herself busy, and in 1991 she described her busy daily routine, which involved seeing friends, attending an employment training course, and taking an A level in sociology at the local college. However, after several years of unemployment, this respondent began to experience long periods of depression. Television became her main source of entertainment and companionship, but it only served to increase her sense of loneliness. She described one dark period in her life as follows: 'I kept on suffering from bouts of depression, in which I did nothing but cry, and the world around me looked completely black.' Her depression coincided with the divorce of her parents, who had been married for twenty-four years. Here, an accumulation of life changes had a dramatic impact on this young adult. As a result of her parent's divorce, her sister also began to suffer from depression, and the home environment became a negative place for the whole family:

[My sister] makes my father's and my life a misery at times, because she constantly moans. She's like a broken record, and occasionally I feel like hitting her, but I've resisted the temptation up until now, because I understand why she is ill. She misses my mother, but there is very little chance of her ever living with her again, because she thinks as highly of my mother's boyfriend as I do. So my father, grandfather and myself have to put up with her for the time being, and I can't wait for the day I leave home. I may finally gain a little peace then.

(23-year-old unemployed woman)

The fact that this diarist is unemployed is only one problem that she has to face. She not only has to cope with long-term unemployment, but also has to adjust to her parent's divorce, and counsel her sister, and father, whilst at the same time feeling ill and depressed about her future life. It is no wonder that her favourite television programmes are comedies. At times her outlook was not entirely bleak:

I completed a confidence course for women, and I'm going to do a First Aid and a Computing after Easter. I also began to do work at a local Barnardo's Shop every Wednesday from yesterday. I am doing these in that hope that such experience, and such knowledge when gained will help me find that elusive job. Two and a half million unemployed, what poppycock. More like five.

(as above, aged 23)

Although this diarist was acquiring skills that could aid her return to work, we can see that her impression of unemployment figures was quite different from that conveyed by the Conservative government in 1995. This feeling that there are many other young people in a position of long-term unemployment only serves to highlight how finding employment can be an elusive goal.

What we have seen so far is that young adults experience a great deal of change in their lives. Many of these changes are concerned with the transition from adolescence to adult status, and are reflected in a new approach to life, one which ensures that young people are apparently too busy socialising and studying for exams to watch a great deal of television. This shows that young people in this study associate adult status with work, and with an expanding network of friends. However, as we have seen, for those young adults who do not make the transition from education to employment, but instead face indefinite periods of unemployment, life is not so structured, and other pressures, such as family change, or illness, can increase stress levels, and lead to an increase in television consumption. We shall see in the next section how other respondents turn to television in times of turbulence in their lives.

ADULTS: TRANSITION AND CHANGE

Respondents discussed a variety of changes in their lives, but the main life changes that adults experienced were concerned with employment and family and personal relationships. Work and personal commitments ensured that diarists had less time to spend on leisure activities than did young adults. In 1995, 25–44-year-olds had 35 hours of free time a week, five hours less than those under 25 (*Social Trends* 1997). However, when time was available to spend on leisure activities, adult diarists were more likely to use TV as a means to relax on a regular basis than were the young adults we looked at in the previous section. In this study, the majority of diarists under retirement age watched less than 17 hours a week of TV, which is significantly less than the figures for the general population for this period, with 25–44-year-olds spending an average of 23 hours a week watching TV (*Social Trends* 1997). Chapter two on television and everyday life showed how TV plays an important part in breaking up the day, as well as providing opportunities to relax. In this chapter we shall also see that patterns of television viewing are often established on the basis of work schedules and other commitments, to family members, or to personal relationships.

When changes do occur, such as changes in employment, or the break–up of a relationship, these changes are set against the backdrop of an established pattern of work and leisure activities. For some diarists, such life changes mean that their television viewing alters dramatically; for others, the changes are more subtle. When life changes occur, television can be used as an emotional crutch, particularly in times of stress, such as unemployment, or the break-up of a relationship. However, this role of television as a 'visual anti-depressant' is itself subject to change over a period of time. Television can either provide a welcome distraction from the upheaval of change in a person's life, or it can be eschewed in favour of other activities, such as a new social life, or new hobby. Tastes may change, but for adult diarists this is less important than changes in time, time spent relaxing, or socialising, or caring for children.

Employment

In this study we have shown that the concept of the traditional nuclear family does not take into account the changing nature of the family and domestic space in contemporary society. Our respondents come from different family structures, and we have students and single parents, as well as married men and women who discuss their work/family environment. The 'dual-worker' family is one of the subjects of this section, and, as Nickols (1994: 66) points out, this type of family set-up has emerged as a dominant form in recent years. In 62 per cent of married couples with dependent children, both husband and wife were working, either full time or part time (Office for National Statistics 1997a).

Men and women in this study talk about the pressures of employment, whether this be a new job, changing from part-time to full-time employment or vice versa, working overtime, or being promoted. Dual-career couples do not necessarily allocate household tasks equally, and 'women's participation in paid employment is often stressful because they continue to have primary responsibility for unpaid household work' (Nickols 1994: 72). In 1995, working women spent eight hours more than their male counterparts on housework, cooking and shopping each week (*Social Trends* 1996). When it comes to the division of household tasks by parents, mothers spend almost twenty-seven hours a week on cooking and cleaning, whilst fathers spend less than five hours on these household chores (*Social Trends* 1997). This uneven distribution of labour is reflected in female respondents' discussion of work and leisure time in this study, in particular working mothers who are not able to relax as much as they would like.

It is clear that to varying degrees, most adult respondents find it difficult to balance family life and employment, and we shall see in this section how respondents learn to cope with multiple roles. When respondents experience changes to their employment status, these changes influence available leisure time, and in turn influence patterns of television viewing. In general, such changes take place over a gradual period of time, and produce subtle alterations in the amount and type of television that is watched on a daily basis.

Graduates starting work for the first time after university noticed quite a difference in the amount of television they watched. Some diarists watched more because they were no longer near friends or family, and some watched less because they were not able to watch at the same times of the day as they used to as a student. One diarist explained:

> 1994 I finished University. I had my final exams and then was unemployed for three months. It was a very difficult time. I argued a lot with my parents about money and the way I treated their home. TV became a major part of my life – in fact my days revolved around it. I started my new job and career in October. I spend most evenings now with the TV on and watch a lot more than I did when I was at Uni. Most of my friends and my boyfriends all live miles away and I only see them at the weekends so my evenings are my own to veg out, eat and watch TV. My life has changed a lot in the last 4 years. I'm much happier now having my own space and I'm really grateful for my wee black and white TV.
>
> (21-year-old female local newspaper reporter)

For this respondent, television provides a stability to many changes in her life. Living alone, and not having friends nearby, TV is a 'voice' to listen to in the evening. One year later she wrote:

When the study began I lived with my parents and although we did watch some TV together I spent a lot more time in my room listening to music. TV is more important to me now, in that I need it to relax when I come home from work. As I live in a horrible bedsit on my own, I switch on the TV the minute I get in the door. The voices, music or whatever warms the room up and helps me to relax. I have to have it on as background noise.

(as above, aged 22)

Before starting work, television played only a small part in this woman's life, but now it is a regular feature, and helps to bridge the gap between when she is at work and when she is able to socialise with friends at the weekend.

For other diarists, work becomes a dominant feature in their lives. This male diarist was at college when he first began writing these diaries, but a change in career plans caused him to leave university. He was unemployed for a time, and then began a demanding job, and a new relationship. This extract shows how his life has changed:

Where do I start? This has been the most complicated four years of my life. Last Summer I started work. Work meant that I did odd hours and TV viewing waned or became mostly watching stuff on video that had been recorded whilst I was out. My main priority is my private life, so I rarely get the chance to watch TV. It's not worth me watching serials unless I'm really interested, because my working hours are flexible/variable. I don't watch soaps at all now – except maybe a bit of *Coronation Street* as light relief, occasionally. The only thing I've really been hooked on recently has been the *X-Files* – brilliant stuff!

(22-year-old male publicist)

We can see that these changes in his personal and work life ensure that he cannot find the time to watch television on a regular basis, and he prioritises his favourite programmes, dropping most soaps in favour of drama series that are screened only once a week.

When respondents recorded a change in the amount of hours they worked, this had a direct impact on the amount of television they watched. For example, this woman was made redundant from her job as a factory worker, worked part time as a carer, and then returned to full-time employment at the same factory she had been made redundant from. Needless to say these changes had an effect on her television viewing:

I now watch less TV than I did over the last 2 years because I am in full-time work. For the last 2 years I have been able to watch daytime TV and some late night programmes. I cannot do this now as I am at work in the day and have to go to bed early as I start work at 7am and have a half hour journey to work.

(46-year-old female factory worker)

Her way of describing her day in 1991: 'During the day I work in a factory, in the evenings I do my housework' – shows how regimented her day is, and how little time she has to watch television while she is in full-time employment.

For many women, balancing work and home life can be difficult, and when they do find an opportunity to relax in the evening, after a hard day at work, TV can be a welcome source of entertainment. This mother and teacher had this to say about the changing character of educational work in the 1990s:

> The whole tenor of my job has changed under drastic new 'management'. We have endless pointless stupid meetings which get us nowhere and every time anyone objects, 'they' wave the OFSTED stick at us. (Inspection by a load of semi-retired nit-pickers requiring about 3 tons of useless paperwork to read.) So television has become comfort viewing. I watch short programmes because then I can watch a whole one before going off to work – marking, writing stupid policy statements etc. By 9.30 or 10.00, I'm totally exhausted, and fall asleep, even if I am watching something on the television. Then I go to bed, fall heavily asleep and wake up, full of anxiety, at about 4.00am.
>
> (43-year-old female schoolteacher)

We can see from her account of her day that even though she likes to relax by watching TV (in short chunks), she has little time to indulge in this activity as her packed schedule has sent her to sleep before ten o'clock.

Changes in the following diarist's work had an impact upon the type and number of programmes he watched; during this period he also experienced other changes in his life: for example there was a death in the family and he moved house. He reflected on these changes as follows:

> In the past six years since I first completed a diary in 1988 as part of the *One Day in the Life of Television* project, I have changed jobs from being a poorly paid hospital chef to a slightly better paid self employed caterer running a staff restaurant with my wife. As far as TV goes it probably means I watch considerably less than pre 1988. In those days I did shift work and had days off in midweek and once finished at work, because of less money, spent more time at home. Since then apart from the odd very rare holiday I never set eyes on TV during the day and with all the extra work and visits to the cash and carry etc, it's usually 7.30 or later before I sit down to watch anything. I suppose as a result of that I may have become more selective in the programmes I watch.
>
> (40-year-old self employed caterer)

This diarist watched the same amount of programmes over the five year period (less than 17 hours a week), but the type of programmes he watched changed. For example, Friday night comedy programmes on BBC2 and Channel 4 replaced *Kilroy* and *The Time the Place*. He enjoyed this new regime of evening television: 'when I'm shattered from a really hard day, there is nothing better than sitting down, especially on a Friday night and crashing out and relaxing, watching the box in the corner'. He also had childcare responsibilities and admitted to watching *Neighbours* (a programme he watched through both employment periods) because: 'This appeals to children and harassed parents who just want to sit down and watch anything as long as its not too taxing.' Here the multiple roles of worker and father take their toll on this respondent's leisure time.

Unemployment

As Nickols notes, 'there is relatively little research on how families cope with unemployment and other economic hardships' (1994: 66). At the start of this chapter, we cited several studies that concentrated on post-redundancy careers and young people's unemployment (Baker and Elias 1991; Rosenthal 1991). Baker and Elias point out that young people are more likely to experience a high turnover in jobs, and early unemployment can lead to long-term consequences for lifetime earnings. Research shows that individuals and families who experience unemployment tend to turn to informal support networks to alleviate stress (Nickols 1994: 66). Support from friends and relatives can be positive and helpful during unemployment, but it can also cause tension in the household.

For the unemployed, television often had a special importance as a relatively cheap source of entertainment, as well as being valued for news and information, and – for some – a sense of connection to the outside world. Some were more dependent on it than others, of course. One female homemaker wrote: 'My day would be very quiet and boring without TV…As I don't have a job, I feel it keeps me informed and stimulates discussion.' This man, asked to imagine life without television in 1996, had good reason for finding that a disturbing prospect:

> Yes I most certainly would miss TV. It is my means for entertainment and also for information and education. Although I also enjoy reading books and magazines, I do not always have the patience to just sit quietly and read. I find visual entertainment more stimulating, and interesting. The loss of TV would devastate me!!
>
> (45-year-old unemployed steelworker)

This diarist's mother had been living with him at the start of the study in 1991, but she died one year later. He had taken up some new activities – such as writing to a prisoner on 'death row' in California – but television had become particularly important, for company and because he could not afford to go out often. Over time he had 'left behind several programmes…which were among my mother's favourites', and felt that by 1996, he was 'at last beginning to find a new direction in life for myself'. Nevertheless, employment was still elusive, and television still remained 'important and interesting' for him – a central part of his life. Whilst he described himself as 'a fully paid up member of the couch potato club', he felt some guilt at times that he should be doing 'other things', or household chores. (Guilt about TV viewing is explored more in the next chapter.) But television remained indispensable.

Another unemployed man, aged 25 in 1991, said 'I'm in most days and watch TV most of the time', although he later asserted that he would only 'watch TV selectively', or view previously videoed programmes, 'assuming I've no reason to go out'. The following year, he began to learn about video production, 'independently and by using my own enterprise', at a local community resource centre. But he also learned that he had a Repetitive Strain Injury affecting both hands ('That'll teach me to try to learn to type'). By 1996 he had started to overcome some of his anxieties, and had made a few friends as well as taking up tai chi and line dancing. He remained unemployed, and television was still very important to him. Listing his favourite programmes for a 1995 diary, he wrote:

> You may have noticed; most of my favourite programmes [including *The Fall and Rise of Reginald Perrin*, *Have I Got News for You*, *Yes Minister*, *Red Dwarf*, *Friends* and *Hong Kong Phooey*] are comedies. I think it's because I find them filled with fun to lighten a pretty dull life – it's good to escape without having to think about it, and these excellent programmes give the ideal escape.
>
> (29-year-old unemployed man)

There is clearly a feeling of sadness and disappointment about his own life in evidence here, even if TV does offer some respite in its escapist comic fantasies. In particular, this diarist's eclectic unemployed viewing habits lead him to feel somewhat embarrassed about admitting what he watches to others:

> When I talk to people with a fuller life than I, I feel a bit of a failure for watching so much TV instead of getting out and socialising...Some of the childish programmes I watch – *Grange Hill*, *Live and Kicking*, *Top of the Pops*, etc – and others – *Home Improvement*, *Beavis and Butthead*, etc don't fit in with a 30-year-old man. So when I admit I watch them, I expect others to laugh me down for still watching them at my age.
>
> (as above, aged 30, 1996)

The anticipated reaction of others to this man's close relationship with TV only reinforces the feelings of failure often associated with unemployment, so that more TV viewing may lead only to greater feelings of regret. The immediate, escapist pleasure offered by these shows, however – whatever others might say – is enough for him to keep watching them.

For other unemployed respondents, television was not quite as central to their lives. This younger man, for example, seemed surprised himself by his shifting uses of different media at different times of day, and his new-found willingness to switch TV off altogether and do something else.

> Losing my job obviously means that I have much more time to watch TV. However this has not proved to be the case in practice. Before I would use a day off school or work as an opportunity to watch as much television as possible. But as my period of unemployment has lengthened I have found that I watch at differing times. I may watch a lot between 9am and 5pm with the TV switched off in the evening or vice versa. I am using the off switch more and more. It is not unusual for me to listen to either Radio 1 or Radio 4 all day This is certainly different from 4 years ago.
>
> (24-year-old unemployed man)

Over the course of this study, we saw one young diarist's husband lose his job after one year, in 1992, and unable to find work for a further three years, after which the family returned to a state of somewhat happier finances. This respondent had given birth to her second child one month after the start of the study, in June 1991, at the age of 25. Living in a flat on the Isle of Wight, the family in spring 1991 had a well-established routine: the husband would leave for work at 7.30am, with our diarist making the meals, doing housework and looking after their 4-year-old son:

> Afternoons I might go out, but now usually put my feet up and watch TV, or my son will have a video on (favourites of the moment *Pinnoccio* and *Batteries Not Included* films), as with another baby due next month I need all the rest I can get. *Children's BBC* for my son. [Husband] home 4.45pm-ish. I'll cook tea and watch *Neighbours* on b/w TV in the kitchen...*EastEnders* and *Coronation Street* are always watched. [My son] goes to bed around 8 ish, then we watch whatever is worth watching. I will have washed up and made the sandwiches for [husband]'s lunch next day. The TV is always on, whether it be the actual programmes or my son's tapes (*Thomas* [*the Tank Engine*], *Fireman Sam*, *Tom and Jerry* etc). It has certainly kept him amused – he loves his TV. And we don't go out a lot so the TV plays an important part in our evenings.
>
> (25-year-old housewife/mother)

During the years of unemployment, the family struggled, but managed, to cope with pressures which also included some chronically noisy neighbours who were eventually evicted in 1996, the year in which their daughter, born at the start of this study (and a *Mr Bean* addict by the age of 4) started school.

Television had been important throughout, and is even credited with giving the family some psychological stability during difficult times:

> When [my husband] was out of work I think due to a lack of money we never went out, so the TV played a big part in our entertainment and keeping us sane.
>
> (as above, aged 30, 1996)

Ironically, once her husband had started working again, this diarist felt more guilty about daytime TV viewing, and, if she did switch it on, would feel compelled to 'dust or tidy up' at the same time.

Some cases of unemployment were less in the 'conventional' mould. This woman had given up work, aged 28, in order to fulfil her ambition to be a writer:

> Almost a year ago, I gave up my job in the Civil Service where I had worked since 1987 as I became embroiled in conflict with my superiors and decided that the lowly position I held wasn't worth the hassle. I want to write and have been trying to pursue this so mornings and afternoons are supposed to be devoted to a half finished comic-novel. However, when I began, I reckoned without the lazy streak I subsequently uncovered which extends almost exclusively to the area of writing. So, in fact, I spend a lot of time dusting, preparing food, occasionally dropping in on my mother and being angst ridden about the writing I ought to be doing instead. As it's not an idle ambition, I hope that my limited will power will soon force me to alter my daytime activities but for the moment, the basic 'maintenance' tasks I usually carry out are conducted against a background of Radio 4.
>
> (29-year-old unemployed woman)

This situation did not, in fact, last long. Divorcing from her husband the following year, this diarist had to get a job again in order to gain a regular income and, in turn, a mortgage. Although she no longer saw any daytime TV, a further three years on she noted that she was more 'aware' of television and its place in her life; having less opportunity to watch it, she had become more deliberate and focused in her viewing:

> Generally, as the study has continued, although I now watch TV less, its profile has increased. I am likely to think more about what I watch and why, and be more aware of the medium of television.
>
> (as above, aged 34, working in social security benefits, 1996)

In the next section we shall see how several respondents wrote about the break–up of a relationship, and how this life change was accompanied by other stresses, such as illness, or economic hardship, all of which served to influence changing attitudes towards television.

COUPLES, LIFE CHANGES AND TELEVISION

Wright *et al.* note that 'effective marital interaction is commonly considered to be one of the most critical factors contributing to marital quality' (1994: 50). One of the important factors in maintaining a healthy relationship is the amount of shared leisure time that couples have to spend together. Hill (1988) suggests that there are short-term and long-term benefits from shared leisure activities. In this study, we can see that television can be used to facilitate positive marital interaction, such as watching each other's favourite programmes, but it can also act as a means of avoidance, and as a site of open conflict. Couples argue about the number and type of programmes their spouses watch, and when one person is unhappy they may turn to television to avoid discussion and interaction with their partner.

Divorce is an increasingly common experience for British families, and the number of divorces has doubled in Britain since the late 1960s (*Social Trends* 1997). Social theorists such as Demo and Ganong (1994) have argued that changing perceptions of the family and an emphasis on individualism have contributed to an increase in the divorce rate since the 1950s: 'For many adults, concerns with self-development, self-fulfilment, and careers have fostered a declining commitment to others, including spouses and children, rendering marriage and other intimate relationships fragile and vulnerable' (1994: 199). Demo and Ganong note that this is particularly the case in relation to women, who are more likely to recognise that their marriage does not meet their personal needs. Indeed, we found that women in this study were far more likely than men to talk openly about their dissatisfaction with their marriage or relationship. The way that respondents talk about marital problems or the break-up of a relationship can reveal gender differentiation and power imbalances in the domestic setting. After divorce, women are more likely to experience economic hardship, and loneliness, and the consequences of divorce are clear to see in the accounts in this section. However, as Demo and Ganong point out, divorce, or the break–up of a relationship, can be a relatively short-term crisis, and individuals develop new routines and lifestyles over a period of time (1994: 205). In terms of television consumption, TV can act as a bridge between established routine and new lifestyles. Thus, television may provide comfort or a welcome distraction from these changes – it has a role to play in the ups and downs of family and personal relationships – but at the same time, once a new routine and lifestyle has been established, television can assume a more minor role in an individual's life.

First we shall take a look at the positive aspects of shared leisure time and television in the home. For some diarists, starting a relationship can mean an introduction to new programmes, and negotiation about old favourites. Here, two recently married women discuss the change in status from being single to being married:

> Getting married – well, when I lived at home, I had my own TV and video in my bedroom, but when I got married, I had to start fighting for control of the remote (control!). At least I always knew where it was! (his hand). Actually, we usually agree over what to watch, we have more or less the same taste in programmes, and if we want, there's a TV in the bedroom anyway, but I find that it's when there's nothing on that we want to watch that the trouble starts, because the one who has the remote control starts channel hopping, annoying the hell out of the other one.
>
> (26-year-old female accounts clerk)

> The way I watch television has changed because there is another person to consider and not just me. I have to get used to most sport programmes and my husband has to grin and bear the dreaded soaps. We have a television upstairs but we are both reluctant to get up off the settee and go upstairs to watch telly so we stay down and watch each other's programmes.
>
> (25-year-old female learning support assistant)

Both extracts are concerned with the negotiation that takes place when couples are in the early stages of living together. Clearly, the remote control becomes an important source of discussion for the first diarist, who is very aware that whoever has the remote control has ultimate control over the evening's viewing. This gender division is also noted by the second diarist, who watches different types of programmes than she used to (sport), and in return, her husband watches the types of programmes she enjoys (soaps).

This young married woman quickly came to learn the compromised nature of joint viewing.

> In August 94 I got married and this means lots of compromise! – i.e. I have to watch *Top Gear*, *Tomorrow's World*, but mostly when I am at home I get my own way. In November 94 we got cable and though strange at first I'm now hooked on Sky One, Discovery, NBC and UK Gold!!
>
> (22-year-old female housing association support worker)

Interestingly, this woman happens to explain this situation by saying that she 'has' to watch the programmes she's not interested in but which, it is implied, her husband will not go without. It is clearly tacitly assumed and accepted by this couple that they *will both watch* the same material, generally regardless of who has chosen it or their personal feelings about it. This kind of couple-behaviour is not unique to television, of course – couples spend time doing all kinds of activities which are more important to one than the other – but it is perhaps a little more curious when applied to TV, where the viewer can have a similar experience whether they have company or not. (This is particularly the case with programmes – such as *Top Gear* and *Tomorrow's World* – where the viewer had a straightforward, interested relationship with the content; whereas the enjoyment of shows which are watched, perhaps, to be laughed *at* rather than *with*, might be substantially improved by being in company.)

Sometimes, the pressures of a new relationship can lead to feelings of resentment. This man radically altered his leisure activities in order to spend more time with his new partner:

> At the start of '94 I was single living at home with spare time and money. I signed up for an Open University course to start in Feb 1995. I met my girlfriend, we became a couple, a threesome, she has a little girl. More and more of my time became time with her. In '94 she became pregnant. It was a difficult time – she needed more and more of my attention – we started to look for a house together. This difficult pregnancy ended in miscarriage – we need each other even more now. My studies were totally neglected – one month into the course I withdrew. I now live with my girlfriend and we are saving for a house. I watch very little telly now – usually Channel 4 – *Dispatches* or BBC2 documentaries and soap operas – *Brookside* and *EastEnders* only. Occasionally the news. I read less, I barely see the computer I bought, my life has changed inconceivably since Jan '94. TV is useful to relax in front of occasionally but not important in my, our lives. I don't watch the films or film programmes I used to – which I miss. I rarely go out, either to the pub or the cinema.
>
> (29-year-old unemployed man)

When this diarist began writing the diaries in 1991, he regularly watched *Star Trek* and most sport programmes. On the day he wrote the above extract in 1995, he watched no programmes at all. The fact that he ends this discussion of the changes in his life over the past four years with a list of things he has given up suggests that he is not altogether happy with this reduction in his leisure time.

We can see that some of the most notable changes in people's TV use occur when they have major upheavals in their relationships. For some respondents, television is a distraction, or an opportunity to avoid confrontation. For others, television is a means to build up strength, in a similar way that one might build up one's energy after an illness. This is admitted, in general terms, by this respondent:

> During major emotional crisis (i.e. bereavement, separation) I find I watch a lot more TV, for hours at a time. When you have no emotional energy left it's very easy to watch anything. As my energy returns I become more selective with my viewing again.
>
> (33-year-old female office manager)

The diaries cover quite a number of specific cases of relationships coming to an end or breaking down. The younger adults did not generally link together their relationship troubles with TV experience in their diaries for this study. It was the over-35s and over-40s who seemed to find a greater amount of comfort in television during such trying times. For example:

> I moved back to Scotland in Sept 93 [to start a new job] as my contract in work was ending. Was supposed to be a short term move as partner still in England. All decided and arranged. 3 months after I moved, 'dumped' by partner. Had therefore lost partner, friends, sold house and now in new job. Major losses have major effects...
>
> Am starting to find/make new friends...so life is improving. But being alone again has meant I necessarily watch TV more as I'm not 'out' as much yet. Recovering! It is a life saver in these circumstances. I do not feel I am overstating facts here. It's accessible and if selective can be funny, informative, educative, stimulating etc. It is a great relaxant and takes your mind off stresses and strains.
>
> (39-year-old female lecturer, 1995)

Splitting up with her partner brought additional TV-related traumas – since he had possession of a number of her videos recorded from TV (including, singled out for special mention, her *Twin Peaks* collection). A solution to this problem was helping her to see where her new allegiances should lie: 'New friends are taping from cable etc to help me get my collection back! This sorts out who really is a good friend.'

Another example of the way in which television can be used in times of emotional crisis will help illustrate this point. One woman wrote frankly about the role television had to play in the break-up of her marriage. She used television as a means to avoid confrontation in her relationship, but at the same time the very act of her watching television caused tension in the home. For example, in 1991 she described her daily routine as follows:

> We rarely go out in the evenings and spend a lot of time in front of the TV set. We probably spend as much time talking about the nature of television, how it relates to other media and its function in people's lives as about the programmes we watch. I tend to be the one putting the case for television in the face of my husband's hostility. He is apt to be rather snobbish about television and claims he cannot do anything else whilst watching it as I can – because it is too distracting. He often leaves the room to potter elsewhere away from the TV set and is strongly anti the notion of acquiring more than one television.
>
> (29-year-old unemployed woman)

The fact that this couple talk about TV could be interpreted as a positive effect of television in the home, but we can see from this extract that the conversation about TV is dominated, not by discussion about the content of programmes, but by the social use of television itself. This respondent is sensitive to her husband's criticism of TV – the fact that he is hostile towards television during this difficult time in their relationship may tell us something about the way in which TV is being used by this woman as a means of avoidance. It is also possible that this respondent gained insight about her relationship through watching certain types of TV programmes. For example, when discussing talk shows, this woman wrote: 'They can be used to assist in discovery about relationship/gender issues and can be helpful if seen in conjunction with talking to real people in everyday life.' One year later, this woman divorced her husband, and began a new life for herself. In her diary for 1995, she looked back on this time in her life, and talked openly about how TV was an 'escape route' from a stressful relationship:

> At times in the past, I have been grateful for television and appreciate its importance as an albeit third hand means of staying in contact with the wider world. It was important to me as a way of filling the time when I was unemployed and as an escape route from a marriage which had a lot of longstanding inherent problems. Over the four year period with all its changes, the main difference in my television viewing has been that I now watch very much less than I used to. I am happy about this. I think television can be a useful distraction but I would far prefer to be experiencing life at first hand. I have become much happier as an individual over the four year period and increasingly gained in self confidence; a by product of living a happier and more fulfilling existence has been that I watch far less television. This probably speaks volumes about the role of television in late twentieth century life.
>
> (as above, aged 33)

We can see here the way in which her television viewing decreased over a period of time. In 1991, this diarist watched an average of nine to ten programmes on diary days; in 1995, she watched half this amount. As she pointed out, this reduction was due to the fact that she was more self-confident and less in need of television as a source of entertainment. In 1995, this diarist felt stronger and more in control of her own life – she used the word 'happy' three times in the above extract, as well as words such as 'confident' and 'fulfilment'. One of the effects of this increase in self-confidence is that TV does not have the same role to play in this new period in her life, a fact she is well aware of.

Another diarist described how he reduced the amount of TV he watched, after his divorce. This man actually gave up most of his favourite programmes because they reminded him of the previous routine he had shared with his wife:

In the recent past, TV was such a ritual and a crutch to a failing relation-ship. It provided so many ways of evading 'real' conversation – especially from me. It was like a passive third party to the relationship. In this new 'uncoupled' space there's no-one to share it with. I feel for all the world like a recovering addict. The first to go was ritual *Brookside* watching. The second to go was systematic scouring of the TV pages and the circling of programme titles and times. The third to go was automatically putting it on somewhere between 8 and 9pm. The fourth to go was obsessively recording programmes that 'looked as though they might be interesting' just in case. The fifth to go was watching things I had previously recorded. The sixth to go was attending to 'old' favourites, *The Late Show*, *C4 News* etc. The only exceptions being the *Rory Bremner Show* and 'good' films.

(52-year-old retired male lecturer)

The way in which television became a means of avoiding the problems in a relationship are clearly documented here. Each TV-related activity is systemati-cally removed, like building blocks, so that this respondent can start again, as a single person. Parting company with much of his TV viewing, along with his long-term partner, was clearly an important part of this man's reframing of his everyday life. His summary of life changes in 1996, alongside 'mostly stopped watching TV', included 'Spanish in evenings, half dozen new friends, regularly out drinking on a Friday night' and 'got into city regeneration projects'. This represents a considerable change from 1991, where he was watching TV so carefully that his diaries catalogue the *adverts* between a whole evening's programmes.

It is important to point out that for many people in this study, the experi-ence of divorce led to positive life changes, such as a new job, new home, or new relationship, but it could also lead to negative experiences, such as illness, economic hardship and loneliness. This was especially the case with female respondents. The following example documents the changes in one diarist's life over a four-year period. This woman, aged 41–46 during the diary period, was a teacher. She separated from her husband in 1992 and was divorced in 1996. This long period of separation, before the divorce settlement, had dramatic and far-reaching effects on her lifestyle:

The last four years have seen a great many changes in my life. In 1991 and 1992 my marriage broke down completely. As a consequence I almost stopped watching television altogether as my ex-husband controlled what was watched to a large extent and I didn't like to be in the same room as him. At the same time I also had more work than I'd ever had before. I was also becoming increasingly alcohol dependent so in general I stuck to my own room and listened to the radio and played records rather than watched TV except for work related things.

(45-year-old unemployed woman)

Here, we can see that, unlike the previous examples, this woman watched less TV during her relationship because the living room (and TV) was part of her husband's domain, and therefore a place of power and conflict in the home. After she left her husband in 1992, she watched TV occasionally as a source of companionship, but as her economic situation became worse, she became ill, and television became a more regular feature in her life. The more stress that this woman experienced, owing to her separation, poor income and transitional lifestyle, the more she watched TV, during the daytime and in the evening:

> My watching of TV rocketed. I moved into a household where the TV was on much of the time whether it was being watched actively or not. In January 1994 I moved again and shortly afterwards collapsed from physical, emotional and mental exhaustion and was unable to leave the flat very much and so the TV became important as something to do. I began to watch fairly indiscriminately and throughout the day as well as evening – and even night. Up to this time I'd always watched TV on a pre-selected basis and not very much. I saw programmes I would never have watched before – e.g. *Blind Date, Beadle's About.*
>
> (as above, aged 45 in 1995)

Saturday evening light entertainment programmes are seen as characteristic of this low point in her life. This lack of discrimination in her television viewing causes her anxiety, and she measures the changes in her lifestyle by the number and type of programme she watches. Her viewing habits were to change once again, during her separation:

> At the end of 1994 I started on a course which I'm really enjoying. And, of course, my viewing habits have changed yet again. On the days I go to college I come back exhausted (although I'm much better I've still not fully recovered) and it's brilliant having *Babylon 5*, and *Quantum Leap* to flop down in front of and relax after returning home. They suit me well. I do feel TV is rather take it or leave it rather than something I really want to do and if I have the energy to do something else then that's what happens. In many ways TV acts as a baby-sitter or nurse/company rather than a dynamic art form in its own right.
>
> (as above, aged 45 in 1995)

This diarist re-establishes a discrimination in her television viewing. For her, the function of TV is to alleviate loneliness and to provide entertainment and relaxation; however, unlike previously, TV is not a necessary companion in her new lifestyle.

What we have seen in this section is that television can be a 'third party' in a relationship, which means that for some couples, the activity of watching television together can be a positive experience, but for others it can be a source of tension in the domestic space. During times of emotional upheaval, some people turn to TV to avoid confrontation, and to avoid interaction with their spouse. This means that television can come to symbolise the negative feelings in a relationship, and it is no wonder that some people turn away from TV after the break–up of a relationship, as it can serve to remind them of an unhappy period in their lives. Life after divorce or separation is not always easy, and several women in this study experienced ill health, poor income and isolation. During this period TV can became a 'visual anti-depressant', and a primary source of companionship. However, such dependency on television does not last indefinitely, and new routines and lifestyles demand that TV takes more of a back seat in life.

TRANSITIONS AND CHANGE IN LIFE BEFORE 50

Young people in this study were very aware of the transitional stages in their lives, and quite keenly anticipated their future adult status. Indeed, this had an influence on their television viewing patterns, so that young respondents would claim that 'children's programmes' had been eschewed in favour of more adult-orientated programmes. This construction, or anticipation, of a new identity is something Roe (1994) also found in his research on media use and social mobility. When anticipating a more adult status, young people emphasise work schedules and their ability to maintain these schedules. This is particularly so in transitional periods from school to college, and school or college to work, and perhaps suggests that young adults perceive adult status as largely defined in relation to work (Roe 1994). Thus respondents who were studying for GCSE or A-level exams pointed out that they were too busy to watch television and lamented the loss of their leisure time.

   In times of emotional stress, such as unemployment, or marital breakdown, television can be used as a distraction, and it can become a more central feature within the home. This finding corresponds with that of Rogge and Jensen (1988) and Rogge (1991), who found that unemployment changes media routines. However, what we have discovered is that periods of heavy television viewing do not last indefinitely. People who have experienced problems in their relationship, and/or times of unemployment and financial insecurity, do notice a change in their pattern of television viewing, often recording that they watch more television. But this seems to alter again when they actively change their personal circumstances, for example by finding a new partner, or taking up a new leisure activity. Even for people who are long-term unemployed, their pattern of television viewing tends to alter, and in many cases decline, over a period of time. This would suggest that watching television is a coping strategy that people use to help them through stressful situations. However, the fact that watching television can be a source of tension and a means to avoid contact with a partner or spouse is an indication that the role of television in everyday life is not free from conflict. By using life-course analysis we have been able to show how the relationship between television and daily routine alters as individuals experience changes in their lives.

SUMMARY OF KEY FINDINGS

- Young adults are very aware and reflective of the role of television in transitional stages in their lives.
- Young adults clearly perceive a difference between what they used to watch when they were younger and what they watch now.
- This difference manifests itself as changes in taste and changes in the significance of television in their daily routine.
- Major life transitions such as exams, leaving home, and going to university disrupt patterns of television viewing.
- Adults are more likely to have established patterns of television viewing than young adults.
- These patterns are influenced and disrupted by factors such as employment and personal/family relationships.
- Television can be used in times of emotional crisis to alleviate stress.
- After an emotional crisis, viewers appear to eschew television in favour of other social activities.

Note

1   For a comprehensive review of this literature see Buckingham and Allerton (1996) and Gauntlett (1995).

Chapter 5

Television's personal meanings

Companionship, guilt and social interaction

Discussion about the role of television in everyday life has often centred on the dynamic relationship between household or family members and television viewing. However, the relationship between individuals and their TV sets is something that deserves attention, as the way in which people discuss what TV means to them can reveal a great deal about the everyday role of television. Television can mean a variety of things to different people: it can be a source of pleasure, providing companionship, especially for people who are living alone, and it can also be a source of anxiety, or guilt, creating tension in the domestic space. Thus, by looking at how people perceive leisure time, and the value of television, we can understand the range of responses people have to watching television. In this chapter we will also consider the ways in which television is used in social interaction – talking about TV – and consider some issues of television and personal identity.

The research in West Germany by Rogge and Jensen on television and everyday life found that 'media activities can be understood as an attempt to construct a meaningful relationship between the media programme and reality as actually experienced' (1988: 94). This chapter focuses on this notion of a meaningful relationship between individuals and their uses of television. Rogge and Jensen found that television could become part of the family structure, in a sense a member of the family, which household members relied upon to always be there as a means to make them laugh or cry, and to provide a feeling of security in times of change.

There have been studies which have looked at 'over-dependence' on television, and such research has attempted to consider whether watching too much television can be bad for people, causing viewers, in particular children, to have poor social skills, and to find it difficult to adjust to the real world (Himmelweit *et al.* 1958; Halloran *et al.* 1970, amongst others). Some studies have found that 'heavy' viewers of television are more likely to be unemployed, retired, ill, poor, or socially marginalised (Smith 1986). This is hardly surprising, as such people would have more unoccupied time on their hands, but such studies have often implied that these people are elderly or unemployed misfits, 'addicted' to television. As Denis McQuail points out, 'there are reasons for rejecting the term *addiction*, with its associations of drug dependence' (1997: 103), and research by Finn in media use models showed that 'data failed to support any conceptualization of excessive television viewing as a disease' (1992: 422).

As we shall see, audiences are the first to be critical of watching too much television. McQuail (1997) has noted that audiences themselves are concerned about media use, and can feel guilty about watching too much television. A study by Gunter and Winstone (1993) found that 90 per cent of their respondents thought parents should encourage their children not to watch too much television. Other research has linked this concern about 'heavy' television viewing to a Protestant 'work ethic', which encourages individuals to use time in a productive way (Steiner 1963). The assumption here is that watching television is not productive. Barwise and Ehrenberg (1988) and Kubey and Csikszentmihalyi (1991) also reported that audiences can feel guilty about watching too much television, although they did not think that such feelings were especially powerful – after all, the people in their study still chose to watch television. Janice Radway (1984), in her ethnographic study of female readers of romantic fiction, also reported that her respondents felt guilty about the time they spent reading novels, and Radway suggests that this is due to the fact that society places more value on work than on leisure time. Of course, it is also the case that society places greater value on 'culture' than on entertainment, and so spending time reading Dickens or Shakespeare is thought by some to be far more valuable, and educational, than reading romantic novels, or watching television. In the 1990s, popular culture has achieved a more prominent position in society, but it is still often not as valued as other forms of 'high art'.

Morley (1986), Hobson (1982) and Gray (1987) also noted this propensity to feel guilty about watching television, especially during the daytime. Morley noted that women often watched television whilst at the same time engaged in other domestic activities, such as ironing or knitting, because time spent sitting in front of the TV was thought to be unproductive. Occasionally, these women would engage in 'solo' viewing (1986: 160), and would take a guilty pleasure from this form of uninterrupted viewing. Gray also found that respondents in her study organised 'women only' viewing events, where several women clubbed together to watch a video in the afternoon, to save money, enjoy each other's company and avoid feelings of guilt about 'solo' viewing (1987: 48–50).

In this chapter we shall see how respondents in this study perceive the activity of watching television. It is certainly the case that some people feel guilty about watching too much TV, and express concern that they should be doing something more productive than relaxing in front of the telly, but on the other hand it would appear that people do value television as a form of companionship and as an opportunity to relax. This creates an interesting tension between work and leisure time in the home.

WHAT TELEVISION MEANS TO INDIVIDUALS

In Diary 15, March 1996, diarists were asked to write about 'What television means to you'. There were a number of different responses, which ranged from diarists writing about how television can be a valuable source of companionship, to other respondents feeling guilty about the amount of TV they watch, especially during the daytime. It is this focus on TV as a personally meaningful companion within everyday life that provides the background to this section. The way in which respondents discuss how television can be their best friend, and can also be a less than valued accomplice in the wasting of time, is a special feature of the diary entries, where respondents wrote in some detail about the ups and downs of their relationship with television.

It is clear that we can have no singular account of what television means to viewers. TV can mean a number of different things, depending on individual taste, personal circumstances, age or background, and a variety of other factors. For example, for some respondents, television means a great deal to them in the evening, but very little during the day, especially in the summer months. This is because diarists use TV as a means to unwind and to occupy the time when they are not able to work, do the gardening or visit friends. These respondents would often be retired or semi-retired, who may not be able to afford other leisure activities as often as they would like, and find television to be a relatively cheap source of entertainment. However, for other respondents, television meant a great deal to them as a talking point, as a means to socialise with other people at work and at home. This is because watching soaps such as *EastEnders* or *Coronation Street*, or drama series from *The X Files* to *Pride and Prejudice*, is a shared social activity that provides an easy topic of conversation. Such diarists could be of any age or social and economic background: talking about television is a common activity shared by many.

'Electronic wallpaper' or 'a window on the world'

In this section we shall see how diarists search for a means to label what is useful and not so useful about television, compiling lists of what they think are the positive attributes of TV, and often using metaphors or similes to describe what television means to them. For example, this man, who worked in the TV trade, made this observation about the function of television: 'TV for some is nothing more than electronic wallpaper' (51-year-old TV and video engineer). This metaphor, or variations of it (such as 'moving wallpaper'), is a common expression that is used to describe the less positive attributes of television in the home. Here, TV does not serve a useful purpose, but acts as a colourful and noisy background to the comings and goings of the household. Thus, for some diarists, TV is a passive medium, and one that we would do well to be without. This woman explained why she would like to see a world without TV:

Do you know, if there was no more TV, I'd breathe a sigh of relief! I feel as if I've had overload. It's too passive, it's no GOOD for anyone. Everyday the news tells us about awful things and, worse still, shows us these actually happening if it possibly can. I feel I've seen all the beautiful nature films and I'd now do better campaigning to save a few species than sit in front of the TV going 'Ahh' and 'isn't it dreadful'. Instead of staring at victims of torture, why not organise a walk for Amnesty International. I do. As for entertainment, I never did like much of it, and I don't much like the people who sit and watch it. I mean, what are they actually doing? Just sitting there!

(46-year-old housewife)

Her question about what people are 'actually doing' when they watch television is, we hope, something we have started to answer in this book, and we can certainly say that viewers do not 'just sit there', although relaxing in front of the television is part of the enjoyment of TV. As many as 37 per cent of respondents said that they often liked to watch TV because they did not feel like doing anything else, and a further 41 per cent said that this was occasionally the case. In terms of having the TV on as background noise, or for company, 13 per cent of respondents claimed they often did this, 31 per cent of respondents said they occasionally did, and 56 per cent said that they never just left the TV on as background noise. This shows us that people do like to relax in front of the television, but in this study, such relaxation is balanced with a desire to control the frequency and length of these opportunities. The fact that 56 per cent of respondents claimed never to have the television on in the background is an indication that this diarist's fears about the television being used as 'electronic wallpaper' are not substantiated by this study.

People of all ages use television as a means to relax, even if it is just on in the background:

Other than meditation, watching TV is the easiest thing to do in terms of doing stuff. It's a way of doing nothing whatsoever and not getting bored. I would probably find it very hard to find something else to do if there was no TV. Jesus! I might be forced to study.

(16-year-old male student)

The reason I would miss it most is for the escapism factor. It's great to get home from work and completely 'switch off' in front of the TV to give the brain a chance to rest. I do enjoy thought-provoking programmes too, but it's nice to watch without having to think sometimes!

(25-year-old female administration supervisor)

Bringing two girls up as a single parent it became background noise – a friend really – so it is nearly always on whether being watched or not!

(50-year-old retired female art teacher)

When diarists attempt to explain what they would miss about television it leads them to consider the function of television, although there is no consensus about what this is. One man, for example, wrote rather abstractly: 'I think what I'd most miss is having it on in the corner of the room, it would be a bit too quiet without it' (33-year-old store assistant). This general sense of TV as a noise-making piece of furniture echoes the 'electronic wallpaper' metaphor discussed earlier, and yet if we consider the following extract from this retired woman, we can see that TV can be a means to signify the routine of everyday life:

> When on holiday I don't see TV, and strangely enough seldom think about it or miss it, but once home I soon get back into the routine of viewing. After a day out or a day doing things around the house, it's lovely to switch on and settle to view. Some nights I may see only the news and the odd half hour, but I wouldn't like to be without my TV set, it is very, very important to me.
>
> (74-year-old retired female civil servant)

Describing television as a piece of the furniture doesn't really do justice to the function TV has here. To watch television is a daily performance. For this diarist, who watches television on average twenty-five hours a week, particular programmes such as *Coronation Street* or BBC news broadcasts serve as a familiar presence, something she can tune in to on a daily basis.

Other diarists search for ways to describe what television means to them. Here are three different accounts:

> TV is like a husband – you probably wouldn't know what to do without one.
>
> (42-year-old mother and freelance journalist)

> The best TV is like a good novel – totally absorbing and enriching.
>
> (45-year-old female teacher)

> Television is the biggest source of information in my life. I treat television as my window to the world.
>
> (15-year-old schoolboy)

These three different images present different perspectives on the function of television: TV can be a close companion, it can be absorbing, and it can provide new ways of seeing the world. Certainly, the last image, that of TV as 'a window on the world', is the most common expression that occurs in diarists' responses to the question of what television means to them. The fact that television offers information and entertainment from around the world is very important to many diarists in this study. These respondents say they would miss TV for the following reasons:

> The international appeal of TV – being able to turn on and glimpse other cultures and ways of life – it makes the world seem small and accessible.
>
> (21-year-old unemployed female)

> Drama. Contact with the whole world – bringing the rest of the world to us whether it's news, documentaries, travel programmes or nature. Keeping in touch with life, visually.
>
> (55-year-old farmer's wife)

> Travel and nature programmes have added a lot to one's knowledge of the world over the years and could not easily be replaced by any other medium.
>
> (54-year-old male civil engineer)

We can see that people from different ages and social backgrounds agree that making the world accessible, and bringing it into the home, is a significant part of the function of television. But television's role was not seen by viewers in purely utilitarian terms; as the next section shows, some people's relationship with the TV set could be much more emotionally loaded.

A good friend

The Audience Tracking Study very clearly shows that one of the pleasures of watching television is the companionship which the set provides. This is the case for viewers of all ages, but particularly so for the older age group. When respondents wrote about what television meant to them, they often listed the information and entertainment aspects of television, but mentioned as well the company and even 'friendship' that it offers. As this young diarist commented: 'I'd miss the entertainment, the enjoyment, the emotions and the education I get from TV. I'd also miss the company, it's like a good friend' (16-year-old schoolboy).

For some respondents the TV brings 'friends' to their living space, making television presenters familiar companions. This retired woman wrote:

> I would miss most of all the feeling of having company actually with me in the room. I have 'friends' on radio, too, but seeing the people I like is even better. I do not like going out but I like to think I can still keep reasonably up to date with what is going on 'out there'. TV not only provides me with 'company' but it also causes me to react mentally, and, therefore keep emotionally active, without having to face any consequences. I would miss seeing it all.
>
> (78-year-old widow)

Here, television provides company and offers an opportunity to experience emotions that this diarist would perhaps rather not experience in the real world ('without having to face any consequences'). Television allows her to see the world without having to actually travel 'out there', a place outside the home that is not perceived to be as safe or as familiar as the world she sees on her television screen.

Actually seeing presenters, newsreaders or actors on television is an important part of the relationship between the viewer and their TV. This seems to be more immediate and more powerful than radio, which many diarists also listened to on a regular basis. The following diarist wrote about how being able to see the body language of people on television enabled her to make a personal connection with particular actors and presenters:

> As I am very often alone in my flat, I would miss the feeling of personal contact one gets with newsreaders or actors who appear regularly. I never did care for the disembodied voices on radio, and now that I am completely deaf in one ear, it is even more important for me to see who is speaking and to watch their body language. I could live quite contentedly without TV, if necessary, so long as my eyesight allowed me to read, but I do regard being able to watch TV for a change as a great benefit.
>
> (78-year-old retired female teacher)

One of the family

Consideration of the benefits of watching TV also led some diarists to discuss television as if it was a member of the family, not just an occasional friend. For these respondents, television had become an essential member of the household. As this 66-year-old retired man explained: 'I would miss the feeling of comfort in just knowing it's there whenever I want to use it. Quite honestly it has become like a member of the family'. In a similar vein, the following diarist is quite clear about the role TV has to play in her life. She is not married, and her only family members are her sister, who lives nearby, and her son, who lives in the west of England (she lives in Suffolk). Television, therefore, acts as a substitute family:

> I used to do a lot of reading, but, these days (I am 76) I do not strain my eyes more than is necessary – No more TV? I should go *mad*, I think! My sister and I enjoy it so!! I console myself with the fact that when I retired I bought the complete works of Thomas Hardy and Jane Austen, plus the lesser known works of Charles Dickens – and *read the lot*. (Incidentally, I thoroughly enjoyed *Pride and Prejudice* on TV.) TV is our life, our safety valve. It is a husband, a boyfriend, another member of the family! And I quite *love* two of the news announcers! Especially the one who softens his voice when he reads out calamities.
>
> (76-year-old retired woman)

By taking the role of a lover and a friend for this diarist, television – the 'safety valve' (perhaps a means of alleviating stress, or loneliness) – is felt to be absolutely necessary in her life.

The assumption that 'heavy viewers' of television have nothing better to do than sit in front of the 'goggle box' is one that does not take into account the complex reasons why people choose to use television as their main source of entertainment. There are many reasons why television can become a welcome source of companionship. This retired woman, for example, was not shy about declaring her love for her television sets. She lived in the South-East with her husband (her children lived away from home), was aged 66–71 during this study, and proudly owned five TVs and two videos, as well as having access to satellite television. This is what she wrote about the role television had to play in her life:

> The TV goes on at 12 noon for the news on BBC1 and it stays on till 3–4am when I go to bed! Yes, I have always been very grateful for TV. I am a visual person and I like to see what I'm hearing, if you understand me! It is company when I am alone – if my husband is out – and I can't bear a TV that is not on; a picture has to be there even if I don't have the sound on. I could say it is the centre of my life, but that can't be true – my husband and children and their families come 1st and 2nd – if you like, but after them TV is very much part of my life – the family laugh at me, good naturedly, of course!
>
> …I had a nasty accident years ago – I was run over by a mad lorry driver, and it changed my whole personality. Where I was game for anything, and I did everything – skiing etc, I am now too nervous to go out very often and will only go out accompanied by my husband, or someone, so my life revolves around my home, and that is where the TV is on all day from the moment I wake up. I love the old films, and am hooked on QVC the Sky Shopping channel and watch (and buy from) that if there is nothing else that interests me during the day, and night till 3–4am. I am a freak! If there was no more TV God I would die!! I see other countries without travelling. If only they had had TV when I was at school, I would have been a more interested student, instead of listening to old fogies who were our boring teachers. I have learned more of the world and its culture from TV than I ever learned from school or college. I would miss it dreadfully.
>
> (as above, aged 71)

Although this woman is aware that other people may perceive her as a 'freak' for watching so much television every day, we can see that she gets a great deal of pleasure from her five TV sets, and even the shopping channel on satellite TV becomes useful as a means to buy products without having to go outside, a place that this respondent has reason to be afraid of. To categorise this respondent as simply a 'heavy viewer' does not do justice to the complexity of her life, and the social and psychological reasons why she chooses TV as her main source of comfort and security.

So far we have discussed how TV is a welcome companion for many viewers. Diarists have shown that, rather than being just a piece of the furniture, something to have on in the background, television means a great deal to them, offering information, entertainment and engagement with the presenters or actors on television programmes. However, not all diarists are full of praise for the way television can occupy their leisure time. Television and its programmes can fall in and out of favour with viewers in the same way that their friends can. The young adult whom we will discuss below, for example, has a complex relationship with her TV, and if we look at how this relationship developed over the five-year period of this study we can see that, for this respondent and many others, television can be part of both a positive and a negative experience.

This diarist, aged 19–24 during the period of this study, lived in the North East of England and had been unemployed throughout this time. In 1991, at the start of this study, her relationship with her best friend changed and this led to changes in her choice of leisure activity. Reflecting on this in a 1993 diary entry, aged 21, she wrote:

> In years past I used to spend my leisure time around my best friends but that was when we were young…For the past two years the farthest I got on a weekend was doing the weekly shopping in the town centre on a Saturday afternoon, because my best friend spent all her time with her boyfriend. I didn't like it, but I put up with it because we have been friends since we were six years old, so we are pretty much stuck together and would proba-bly miss each other if we didn't meet for weeks on end, so I remained her friend even though at times she didn't deserve my loyalty.
>
> (21-year-old unemployed woman)

With her best friend no longer available, television took the place of her friend's companionship: 'Life was so dull at that time that the highlight of my week was watching *The House of Elliot* and *Birds of a Feather*, which followed each other on a Saturday night, I was that sad.' In the winter at the start of 1993, this diarist went through a long period of illness and depression. In her diary entry for that winter she wrote:

> I've spent the most of this winter watching TV. I'm sick of the sight of it, especially Anne and Nick [on *Good Morning*] but listening to the radio and the trash they play on it only makes me feel worse and I feel giddy when I read, so I've got no other option. Life is so bad at the moment, I'm begin-ning to believe I'm suffering from the disease of the 90s – despair.
>
> (as above)

During this period, this young woman's best friend did not visit her. She perceived TV as the only option as a means of entertainment and regular companionship; but it was not able to make her happy. In fact, television only served to increase her sense of isolation and despair. However, in the spring of 1993 she met a young man who was to become her boyfriend. This had a dramatic effect on her television viewing:

> My life changed overnight as soon as I met him. I began to go out more, we began to visit each other's houses and my viewing of television slumped to an all time low. I'd always been a bit of a square eyes before, but now I only watch programmes I want to watch such as *EastEnders* and *Top of the Pops*, watching TV all the time these days would just send me loopy because it is so bad. TV was so much better when I was a kid.
>
> (as above)

We can see here that when this young woman is happy she watches less television. TV may be a friend in a time of need, but it is not a companion she values or feels obliged towards. Indeed, throughout the diary period she despairs of television, continually writing that TV isn't as good as it used to be, and complaining about the type of programmes that are now available, particularly during the daytime. Her memory of a 'golden age' of TV coincides with her childhood, a period when her best friend could be relied upon as a constant companion, in the same way that TV could be relied upon to entertain. Her favourite programmes, such as *Rising Damp*, *Steptoe and Son* and *Man About the House*, represent a different period of her life – 'All the people who starred in them were my heroes' – and television now cannot match this golden age: 'British comedy is in such a low state now, I could almost cry for it.' The point is that there are two parallel relationships here. There is a relationship with her best friend, someone she feels angry towards and yet nevertheless will remain loyal to, and there is a relationship with television, a substitute friend that cannot live up to her ideal of what television, or 'friendship', should be.

In the next section, this fluctuating relationship with television will be explored further. The pleasure and artificial companionship which people get from watching television has a flip side: feelings of anxiety and guilt.

TELEVISION GUILT

In the final diary of the Audience Tracking Study, in March 1996, the respondents were asked 'Do you ever feel guilty about watching TV?' This – along with other comments they had written during the five years – revealed a rich seam of guilt felt by many diarists, generally based around concerns about wasting time in various ways. This could be guilt about watching television in the daytime, worry that one should be doing something more constructive instead, anxiety about watching purely to satisfy one's own desires, and guilt about imposing one's own favourite programmes on others who were not so keen.[1]

Daytime viewing

In 'time wasting' terms, it was the viewing of daytime TV that prompted the most regret. These are just a few examples from comments made by several respondents:

> Mostly feelings of guilt are confined to morning TV, when there is always some work to be done and I'm quite prepared to ignore it if there is anything remotely interesting on the box.
>
> (77-year-old retired woman)

> The one thing I do feel guilty about is watching TV in the afternoon. Even when I am on holiday. I can offer no real reason for my thoughts behind this.
>
> (30-year-old male office worker)

> I feel guilty when someone puts on TV during the day and I feel as if I am drawn to it even though it is tripe.
>
> (50-year-old retired male fire officer)

> The only times I ever feel guilty is on rare occasions when I watch TV during the day. I feel restless and guilty, feeling I should be doing something more challenging or productive, yet I have friends who are intelligent, bright people who see nothing wrong with dossing about all day watching TV.
>
> (40-year-old male self-employed caterer)

A diarist described in chapter two, the mother of a young son whose husband was unemployed from 1992 to 1995, felt guilty about watching daytime TV once her husband had found work again, in 1996:

> I feel guilty about watching TV in the mornings-weekdays. I feel as if I should be doing housework or something more important. But if you've absolutely nothing to do I think 'What the heck'. Sometimes I'll dust or tidy up whilst Anne and Nick are on so I don't feel so guilty, cos if there is something really interesting on there, I'll tell Steve about it when he comes home from work and he'll say 'Been sat on your backside all morning watching TV eh, whilst I'm working my socks off' meant as a joke of course, then try to find ways of excusing myself!
>
> (30-year-old female homemaker)

Although those who felt guilty about watching television in the daytime included retired people – who might consider that they had 'earned the right' to relax in front of the TV whenever they liked – this respondent did suggest that her age was one factor by which she excused herself:

> I never feel guilty about watching TV as I do not normally watch TV during the day. However, in view of my age, I don't feel guilty about watching if there's anything I want to see – like an important debate in parliament.
>
> (64-year-old retired secretary, homemaker)

We can note that this woman also justifies this kind of viewing – 'an important debate' – on account of its seriousness. Other retired people rejected the idea that they should need to find excuses:

> No, I don't [feel guilty about watching TV]. I have friends who say (rather piously) that they never watch TV in the morning or afternoon. I rarely watch in the morning but if there is something on I want to see and I'm available to watch it, I switch on and sit down whatever time of day it is. What is the use of being retired if you can't do what you want when you want? Why should I feel guilty?
>
> (74-year-old retired female heath planner)

Some were torn between two positions, such as one woman, aged 67, who admitted to feeling guilty if she watched an afternoon film 'when I ought to be doing something useful', although she felt fine about going to theatre matinees, which she considered different from 'solitary TV at home during the day'. However, she then seems to have hesitated, and added: 'though I don't really see why it should be now I come to think of it'.

There is clearly a kind of work ethic at the root of these people's concerns: they have learned the notion that they should be 'doing something' in the daytime hours – the traditional hours of work – whereas in the evening, relaxation is more customary and consequently more guilt-free. As a male teacher, aged 47, reflects: 'I very rarely watch in the daytime and feel guilty if I do. Watching in the evening seems natural and I would only feel guilty if I watched too much and felt I was turning into a zombie.'

Wasting time

Other respondents were worried about wasting time in front of 'the box' more generally. Here, the reasons most likely stemmed partly from the work ethic, and partly from an internalisation of the view that television is an unworthy medium, a banal way to spend time, and the poor relation to reading, listening to music, playing with children, putting up shelves – or any other activity that can be categorised as more mentally or physically challenging, or more sociable:

> I frequently feel guilty about watching television, especially if I watch more than about 3 hours in any one day. This is because one is largely in a passive mode when watching, and there are so many other rewarding things to do (eg reading, writing, walking etc). Feel most guilty about 'soaps' and other superficial series.
>
> (75-year-old retired male school inspector)

> [I feel guilty about watching TV] occasionally, when I have spent all evening slumped in a chair in front of the box and then realise all the things I should have done will have to wait till tomorrow. On the whole I don't think particular programmes make me feel guilty – it's just the amount of time.
>
> (58-year-old female university administrator)

> I don't feel guilty about particular programmes but more generally about the time wasting aspect of it i.e. 'I really should be doing the garden instead of watching this football match'.
>
> (54-year-old male civil engineer)

This mother, a single parent since 1990 with two young boys who spent 'most evenings watching television', was concerned about her own amount of viewing, and more particularly that of her children, whom she describes elsewhere as 'so hooked and glassy eyed':

> Yes I do feel guilty – just in terms of how much it absorbs of my time. My two boys are hooked on TV and I'm already concerned that they spend less time reading books, playing, being imaginative.
>
> (36-year-old female student mother)

For another woman, differing perceptions of the legitimacy of having the television on at all during daylight hours had led to conflict with her farmer husband:

> Yes [I do feel guilty]. Partly because I feel I should work harder and partly because it is a cause of some tension between my husband and I. It is really about the time of the day. I do like to watch the *One O'Clock News* and I usually try to do something while it's on like making a cake or cleaning the table. I would like to watch a bit more Breakfast News but as my husband is around then I have reduced it to the local news, weather and news summary.
>
> (66-year-old farmer's wife)

Here the pressure against watching TV during the farm's long working hours is so great that this woman feels she may only watch if she is simultaneously doing the other work which she is expected to do.

Feeling one should be doing something else

Closely related to the worries about wasting time, as the above example shows, is guilt because the person feels they should be doing something else, instead of watching TV. This retired man, for example, hated the realisation that he could have been doing good work in his garden instead of watching an ultimately uninteresting show:

> If the programme is good, informative and entertaining I feel little guilt. But if I fail to make use of the weather to get jobs done I feel guilty, particularly if I realise that the programme wasn't worth watching anyway.
>
> (63-year-old retired male industrial chemist)

Similarly, a retired woman felt she should be doing needlecraft at the same time as viewing, even though this had become physically difficult for her. Her husband also berated her for watching old films, which he saw as inferior:

> I still feel guilty about watching TV without doing something else at the same time, i.e. sewing or knitting. These two I seldom do now as my wrist is still sore after a bad break two years ago. My husband makes me feel guilty when he puts his head around the door and says 'Oh, a black and white film!' although I know often the standard of many older films were higher.
>
> (67-year-old retired woman)

In a parallel but different case, this woman felt that she should be sewing, knitting or doing something else, but actually had no *inclination* to do so.

> Yes. I feel guilty because I sit watching instead of doing something (what I don't know). I knit only if I need something. I know which end of a needle the eye is. I will sew a button on. But aren't they boring? So why I feel guilty I don't know. I'd like to paint but have no ability. I'd like to write but have little originality. And so I end up watching TV. I will not, however, watch programmes and presenters I do not like. Sometimes the television set is left on but not watched. At times it even has the sound switched off.
>
> (74-year-old retired female lecturer)

Younger people also sometimes felt guilty about watching TV when they felt they ought to be doing something else. For example, this young man, whose GCSE exams were not far away, wrote:

> The only times I feel guilty about watching TV is when I know I'm putting off important schoolwork whilst sitting in front of *Neighbours* and *Home and Away*.
>
> (15-year-old schoolboy)

A perhaps more serious consequence of soap compulsion was this woman's apparent neglect of her 6-year-old son when her favourite serials came on:

> Sometimes I feel guilty at watching *EastEnders* and *Coronation Street* as I tend to 'ignore' my son when these are on. He understands that these are 'my programmes' a bit like his favourites but says I shush when they come on and stop him playing. This does make me feel guilty as really I should play or read to him.
>
> (34-year-old female clerical officer)

One avid viewer, a disabled man, was able to offer an explanation for the roots of the guilt which he had associated, in the past, with TV viewing:

> I never feel guilty watching television now, but I did when I was at school and college in the '70s. Most of the staff were middle class. Not only were you made to feel that reading and studying were more productive occupations than watching those hooligans from Fenn Street, you were also aware of a cultural conflict between the attitude to television at home and that at school.
>
> (36-year-old male senior social services assistant)

The class basis of this account is telling; the middle-class teachers associated with 'reading and studying' are seen as being opposed to the more working-class home life where television is not only a welcome diversion but is also seen as being no less important or useful than those other 'productive occupations'.

My trashy tastes

A few young and not-so-young men admitted to feeling guilty about watching certain shows – often Channel Four's Friday night entertainment – because they were seeking some erotic thrills. A 23-year-old male office worker admitted, 'I feel guilty watching *The Word*, *Eurotrash*, or *The Girlie Show* because I'm only looking out for something titillating or memorable!' An unemployed sculptor pondered:

I do feel a slight sense of guilt viewing programmes like *The Word*, *Eurotrash* and *The Girlie Show*, energetic so-called youth orientated TV which promote tabloid values and titillation. I enjoy reading Austen, Dickens and Dostoyevsky, I like listening to Mozart and The Prodigy, so why I tune into such eroticised extravaganzas must be to satisfy some base bubblings of the id. There is plainly no excuse for such programming, and I don't have any excuse for sometimes watching them.

> (36-year-old unemployed male sculptor)

A man in his fifties was mildly troubled by related concerns:

Sometimes put programme on with 'good looking' women featured – films or plays. Don't feel over guilty about that as a man. My wife is very good looking.

> (54-year-old retired male schoolteacher)

From our sample it would seem that women were less interested in – or less embarrassed by – such voyeuristic opportunities as might be available to them. But then they had other things to worry about:

I realise watching TV prevents giving time to more useful or worthy activities (eg reading novels, and also study time). I do find that I watch some unnecessary programmes at weekends – even bits of *Noel's House Party* as my son (aged 20) has it on, or *Blind Date*. (I enjoy Mr Blobby I am ashamed to say!)

> (52-year-old female part-time lecturer)

'Real-life' crime series seemed to attract a similar mix of compulsion and guilty regret, although the respondents generally took this whole subject more seriously. This young woman, for example, seems genuinely troubled by her interest in relatively 'serious' current affairs programmes about particular British mass murderers of the 1990s:

I feel guilty about watching programmes about real life crimes. The moral part of me says that I shouldn't because it is infringing upon the victims and their families' well being, but the ghoul in me likes watching them. I watched the programmes about the Wests that were shown the day Rosemary West was convicted, and I would of watched the *Panorama* programme about Thomas Hamilton [the Dunblane gunman] if they hadn't postponed it, even though I thought Granada were tactless about showing an edition of *World in Action*, on the very same subject that day. Oh, I'm ashamed to admit that, but it's the truth. The ghoul in me must be larger than what I previously thought.

> (23-year-old unemployed woman)

The self-conscious internal conflict is clear in these deliberations. But even fictional crime dramas could lead to some guilt:

> I feel particularly guilty about enjoying 'crime' like *Silent Witness* [and] *The Bill*...because it preys on people's weaknesses and fears.
>
> (22-year-old female housing association support worker)

Here, we can see that the idea of 'TV as friend' means that TV can bring out the worst in some people, and these respondents feel guilty at the way in which certain types of programmes encourage their fascination with the darker side of life.

Imposing one's programme choices on others

Another type of guilt was that felt by people who had chosen to watch programmes on a shared television which other members of the household did not like, or which were being watched instead of someone else's first choice which was on a different channel. Retired people of both sexes felt this way about watching sport, for example:

> [I feel guilty about watching] sport, when my wife is obviously bored. I always secure agreement first!
>
> (65-year-old male former retailer)

> [I] only [feel guilty] when I insist on watching a sports programme and know my friends are not really interested. Since I have to watch their soaps and the likes of *Panorama* and other discussion programmes I don't feel too bad about it.
>
> (73-year-old retired female headteacher)

A younger woman provided a detailed account of the guilt surrounding her enthusiasm for *The X-Files*, which her boyfriend did not approve of. The show is so engrossing that she even ends up feeling guilty for forgetting to feel guilty:

> Yes I do [feel guilty]. It used to be on Monday at 9pm on BBC2 but then it changed to Tuesday at 9.30pm on BBC1. Every time I watch *The X-Files* I feel guilty. Why? 'Cos my boyfriend thinks it's weird and I think it's great and 'cos any other day around this time is usually our quality and relaxing time together. When the current season ended my boyfriend thought yes, Tuesday night is ours again until the announcer said 'For those *X-Files* addicts who can't wait until the autumn, the first series is being shown again on BBC2 9pm Mondays.' The reason I feel guilty is 'cos whatever we're doing at the time when my boyfriend sees *X-Files* about to start he tells me to bugger off upstairs and watch and he'll finish things off and 9

out of 10 times we've only just started on the sink full of pots and pans. I feel guilty afterwards too 'cos I realise the initial guilt only lasts as long as the opening titles.

(21-year-old female clerk)

Not guilty

We should also mention that a number of people insisted that they did not feel guilty about watching TV, and generally did not see why they should. Some felt that television was light relief, offering a necessary respite from the stresses of everyday life:

I don't feel guilty about watching TV. It never prevents me from attending to matters in real life that require attention. I would never feel guilty about watching daft, light hearted programmes either – I spend a lot of time in real life being serious/having pretty intense conversations with people and sometimes watching something daft can be a relief from that!

(34-year-old unemployed woman)

Some retired people, as we saw above, felt that they had earned the right to relax:

No, I don't feel guilty. Why should I, I have always done my best, brought up my children well, worked until my retirement. If I have time to waste I have earned it.

(71-year-old retired female statistician)

And some people simply saw no need for justifications or excuses:

Never – although some friends think your life is empty if all you can talk about is *ER* and *NYPD* [*Blue*]. Who cares! I love it!

(44-year-old female lecturer)

Others who definitely felt no guilt were often those who lived alone, and for whom television was company. Finally, one woman didn't feel guilty about her own viewing – but found another reason to feel bad:

No [I don't feel guilty watching TV] – I tend to feel guilty that I'm not keeping my partner company when he is watching TV! He likes it much more than I do!

(71-year-old female voluntary charity fundraiser)

Overall, it was interesting to find that so many people attested to feeling guilty about their television viewing. Whilst some rejected the idea, and some others only felt guilty about watching programmes which others in the room didn't really want to see – a feeling stemming from general politeness – there seemed to be a lot of other people worrying about the time they were 'wasting' away in front of the screen, and about all the jobs and chores that consequently weren't getting done. At the same time, it also seemed to be the case that they weren't *so* concerned that they actually took steps to reduce their viewing; or else television was so compelling that they were unable to cut down. Either way, this was guilt which this audience were prepared to live with.

TALKING ABOUT TELEVISION

Ann Gray previously found that 'a very important part of the pleasure of television serials is to gossip about them the following day' (1992: 214), and in the present study we similarly identified the social activity which derives from watching television as an important aspect of TV's place in everyday life. When some respondents consider what they would miss about television, being able to talk to other people about what was watched last night is high on the list. These two examples, from respondents of different ages, reflect the way in which talk about television is implicated in social life more generally – here, in school and family life:

> [If there was no television] I would miss being able to gossip with my friends over the last *ER* or *Neighbours* etc, it has become a social thing.
>
> (16-year-old female school pupil)

> With my husband, we talk about all the programmes we watch – some only by a passing comment, but many more deeply…With our family, when we phone each other – we often mention programmes we have enjoyed to each other. Also if we spot anything forthcoming of interest we point it out.
>
> (58-year-old female school teaching assistant)

Indeed, for some, the pleasure of a TV programme was fully entwined with the anticipation of discussing it with friends later:

> My all time favourite programmes include *Cracker* because it is very exciting and because it's always coming up in conversation the next day.
>
> (14-year-old schoolgirl)

For people who worked in large shared offices, television was frequently a talking point. These conversations seem to be valued for what we might call their textual value – the interest in the subject being talked about – and also for their social value – that they were a way of making connections with people:

I talk reasonably often, usually about the soaps *EastEnders*, *Coronation Street*, *Brookside*, and *Emmerdale*. Almost everyone in my (large) office watches at least one of them, and it's an easy way to get a conversational ball rolling.

(20-year-old female clerical assistant)

Some times in the office we tell each other what's happening in our favourite soaps if, for example one of us has missed an episode. We have also talked about particularly interesting programmes e.g. *Forty Minutes*, *Inside Story* and a few watch *Making Out*.

(44-year-old female medical secretary)

This kind of talk about television helps to create a stronger relationship with television itself – the world of the programmes and, perhaps, their producers – and also serves as a springboard to conversations about contemporary social and moral issues, such as those brought up by soap operas, which also enhance the engagement which an individual has with the social life of their country.[2]

This rich relationship with television, and the way in which it creates shared cultural reference points, is reflected upon by this respondent:

Since I came to university I've realised just what an important part television has played in my development – in conversations and discussions I have frequently referred to TV programmes past and present (as I would refer to books, articles, plays, music or poems) as I often have done in the past, but one of my friends has never watched TV and her ignorance of viewing, from *Mr Benn* [children's animation] to *The Trials of Life* [natural history series] has made me all the more aware of the intrinsic role of TV in the social development of the majority of people of my generation.

(20-year-old female student)

We can note that the six quotes above, selected for being relevant and interesting quotes on talking about television, are from women. Whilst younger men were often happy to admit that they discussed TV with friends and colleagues, it would seem that the cultural codes of masculinity meant that the male respondents in general – who in their diaries showed themselves to be as engaged by, and gossipy about, television as their female counterparts – were less happy to be seen as people who spent their time talking about TV with others. An accountant seemed to want to excuse his TV-related chat by stating flatly:

People will always talk about things which they have in common with one another. Television is one of those things which most of us have in common.

(31-year-old male chartered accountant)

In a similar way, a 70-year-old retired fire service man stated that he would only talk to other people about 'shocking, controversial and important items of general interest', as if to demonstrate the seriousness of such talk; but then he (perhaps reluctantly) added, 'and routine stuff, soaps'. It is hardly surprising that men, like women, seek social engagement through talk about TV. Indeed, for this young male student, conversation in general was not an easy project, and television made life easier, partly because it overcame the need for chat altogether, but also because it provided him with something to talk *about*:

> I think TV can be a really good social activity when you are a student if you do it in group because it gives you something to talk about. I don't like watching it on my own when I feel like doing something else, it can only make you feel more lonely and bored, but if you feel lazy after working for ages it can have a really good effect on you. For example I think that the only time I'm really grateful for it is an excuse to spend time with people in a very 'relaxed' state, without it I would just go up to my room to save the problem of thinking of things to say to people.
>
> (21-year-old male student)

It has to be admitted that some respondents did not like to talk about television and, indeed, seemed to consider that this was rather an *unhealthy* starting-point for a conversation. A 71-year-old housewife, for example, asserted: 'I think its boring and lazy to talk about yesterday's TV programmes when there's so much else of immediacy and positive interest to talk about!' However, this view was not typical; most respondents seemed happy with TV-related conversation, and did not seem to feel the need to qualify this with comments about how television was not dominating their lives, as they did with the issue of the amount of time spent watching TV.

TELEVISION AND EVERYDAY LIFE: MEANING AND IDENTITY

In this section we will take a 'step back' from close examination of the study data and consider the possible meanings which television may have for individuals, in relation to their personal identities in particular. It is obviously the case that television means different things in the lives of different people. It even means different things in the life of *one* person, and, indeed, can mean several things at any given moment. Aside from the more obvious supposed goals of broadcasting – information, education and entertainment – television, as we have seen, can be a distraction, a way of killing time, or avoiding conversation; it can be a source of engaging narratives, which may stimulate new and related ones in the mind of the viewer; or it can be a means by which individuals compare their own identity, or the self which they present to the world, with those on display. The conversations about soap operas which our respondents mentioned above, for example, will have given them an opportunity to compare their own opinion of the performance of particular characters with the views held (or expressed) by others. Marie Gillespie (1995) has identified this more precisely in her discussion of the ways in which the teenagers in her study used the popular soap *Neighbours* when thinking about their own relationships, and discussing them with friends and their more conservative parents.

For some men in the 1990s, television-watching is associated with the search for an acceptable or comfortable masculinity,[3] and women have also been seen to negotiate contemporary femininity with reference to the mass media (see chapter eight, and for a detailed study of how some women come to 'do' types of femininity, see Skeggs 1997). Other viewers may refer to television with an interest – whether explicit and conscious or not – in how the fictional and 'real' people on TV conduct themselves in times of stress, or romantic bliss, or in times of transition.

People may also engage with television because they identify with characters and situations – even where this has to be translated from fantasy worlds, like the 18-year-old woman working in an office who identified with Data, an android man working on a starship, on *Star Trek: The Next Generation* (see chapter six, note 1). We can note that our own attempts to fit into the world of professional academics, which was based on learning acquired from observation of the way in which hot young detectives acted towards their superiors on 1980s American cop shows, demonstrates that this kind of translated identification can lead to problems in later life. However, we do not (of course) want to suggest that television determines or creates people's identities; it is merely a springboard for the imagination. As Kathryn Woodward has put it:

> Representation as a cultural process establishes individual and collective identities, and symbolic systems provide possible answers to the questions: who am I? what could I be? who do I want to be?
>
> (Woodward 1997: 14)

The search for reference points regarding identity issues *within* programmes sits alongside the way in which individuals express their *identity* and *difference* through their programme choices, preferences and pet hates. Of course, few people have a TV programme as their number one identity characteristic, and cultural snootiness means that such people are not highly regarded ('that *Star Trek* nut' and 'that girl who thinks she's *Wonder Woman*', both friends of ours, spring to mind); which may be why such people often form groups and clubs. Frankly, as a society we are not surprised to see people calling themselves 'female Starfleet cadet, 16', 'dedicated Trekker' and 'gay Borg' advertising for pen friends (*SFX* magazine, October 1998). But the fact that such people are nervously seen as having 'gone too far' presumably stems from a general insecurity about the way that almost everyone's lives and personal history are checkered with a tapestry of TV shows which have engaged us and affected our spirits at different times.

As Woodward notes, class has been displaced – to a debatable extent – as a key category of identity (1997: 21). The argument is that until relatively recently, people knew their class and therefore effectively 'knew who they were', whereas today, class has become significantly less relevant than a range of other available categories of identity. Whilst this no doubt represents a heavily simplistic view of the past, and suffers from creating the impression that life in a class-ridden society is easy rather than tough, it remains true to say that identities in contemporary society have become more visible and, perhaps, complex. 'Identity politics' has made familiar a list of categories – gender, ethnicity, sexuality, disability and (to a lesser extent) age – which are now 'up for grabs' in identity terms, although some are easier to visibly challenge in everyday life than others.

What Woodward perhaps fails to make clear is that these factors were of course very relevant to identity in earlier times – *more* relevant, perhaps, because sex, class and ethnicity (for example) were more strongly supposed to determine who you were, how you should behave, and what you might reasonably expect from life. The difference today is that these aspects of identity have, to varying extents, been unleashed from the confines of predictability, and have consequently become more *meaningful* to individuals at an everyday and personal level. And if refusing to conform is less 'risky' than it once was, the less mainstream parts of television and other media content offer a 'selection box' of identities: ways of living and being in the world which challenge the traditional assumptions about the supposed markers of identity, and ally themselves instead with new social movements or new modes of everyday lifestyle politics.

Television, with its nationwide reach, is relatively democratic in this regard: whilst the populations of rural areas have been able to 'protect' themselves from metropolitan liberal attitudes and identities by keeping alternative approaches to lifestyle and sexuality out of their local newspapers and, to some extent, off their magazine stands (Kramer 1995), they have been unable to prevent their more open-minded inhabitants from watching shows on BBC2 and Channel Four, in particular, where challenging views of sexuality, gender and (to a lesser extent) race are not hard to come by. In this way, television may also provide some reassurance to people seeking to come to terms with their identities in any place where they do not have immediate social support.[4]

TELEVISION AND IDENTITY IN THE AUDIENCE TRACKING STUDY DIARIES

Turning to the diaries in the hope of finding some empirical support for the more theoretical discussion above, we are somewhat disappointed. Reading these five-year diaries, we can certainly see that television is important to people, and that viewers become concerned to see what will happen next to their favourite TV characters, for example. We also note the large amount of media consumption overall, and might assume that this is bound to have some influence on how people see the world, themselves, and their relationships with others. However, by the same token, we are assuming that whatever influences there are will be subtle; they will be processed through the filters of an individual's already-established view of the social world, and are not likely to be direct or explicit changes derived from one bit of media consumption. In other words, they are unlikely to be written about by the people themselves. And we can congratulate ourselves on being right about that.

Nevertheless, there are some cases where we can see people making connections between their personal identities and media representations. Several disabled diarists, for example, felt that it was important for their sense of self-identity – as well as for other people's perceptions of the disabled – that television should reflect their lives in a fair and unsensationalised way. A retired transsexual woman (formerly a man) who described herself as '80% disabled' by injuries from two different accidents, wrote:

> I would like to see more documentaries featuring the disabled who seem to be lepers in the television world. Even to bring them in soaps, a few years ago we seen a Down's Syndrome [person] was featured for one or two episodes, *EastEnders* showed a disabled person in a wheelchair. I have set myself a task to help such people gain access which isn't easy. I am well aware that when some people see Cerebral Palsy, they say it disgusts them, but television can help to abolish ignorance.
>
> (68-year-old retired woman)

A disabled man argued that the approach of 'human interest' current affairs programmes, documentaries, and news items on disability served to undermine his own self-esteem, as well as providing an excuse for inadequate government funding:

> The reason why I dislike soft news is that it hides the truth behind the effect of government cuts or social security changes...Instead of focusing on the issues and numbers of people affected, the television news makes a human interest story about the effect of the decision on an individual. As an emotional response, viewers send donations in to help the individuals shown, the TV presenter thanks his generous audience, and everyone thinks that everything is OK – that charity makes government spending cuts OK. I am disabled and resent this approach. Not only does it portray people as passive recipients, the other dangers are that it limits the ability of the disability movement to fight the cuts, and help bolster the wicked Tories who cut, cut, cut.
>
> (31-year-old male senior social services assistant)

The father of a girl with Down's Syndrome felt strongly that soap operas – as on-going narratives which people take into their lives, connecting with the characters – were failing to live up to their potential for changing people's attitudes to disability. In 1991 he made the point like this:

> A major beef of mine is that the soaps do not take on board the issue of physically and mentally handicapped children/adults. There have been the odd one but usually in some dramatic way rather than being used as a means to understand them as individuals. Television is a very important media and rightly or wrongly it does influence people so maybe attitudes could be changed if more programmes had disabled and mentally handi-capped characters in them as the norm rather than being used to dramatise some event or situation. [My daughter] would feel more accepted by society if she could see other children on TV who were like her and her schoolmates.
>
> (36-year-old male carer)

By 1996, five years later, his argument remained the same, as he had seen no improvement, except in the BBC school drama *Grange Hill*: 'People with disabilities deserve to be portrayed as valued members of society and therefore should play a greater role in television. *Grange Hill* is a good example of where a number of the students with disabilities are seen as students first and their disability is not used to get sympathy or for dramatic effect.' Soaps in general were still 'particularly guilty' of using 'people with disabilities...for some dramatic effect or storyline, then abandoned'. (Another minor but interesting change over time is the way that this father's awareness of disability issues has changed over the five-year period, so that he stops using the term 'handicapped' – derived from 'cap in hand' (begging) – and talks about 'people with disabilities' instead.)

In general, disabled people and those close to them felt that disabled identities were not given enough support by television: marginalised into their 'special interest' programmes in daytime scheduling, excluded almost entirely from on-going drama series, and patronised by 'sympathetic' treatment in the occasional chat show appearance and 'pity the weak' coverage in fundraising telethons and the odd regional documentary, disabled people did not do well in this analysis. (See Hevey (1992) and Pointon and Davies (1997) for discussions of representations of disability.) The comments above echo older people's complaints about representations of later life on television (see chapter seven): 'How am I meant to feel good about myself when you represent me like this?', they seem to say.

To consider television and identity in a different way, and to understand the links between individual identities and *particular* TV shows, we can examine the slightly more 'extreme' (compared to the everyday) cases where diarists are openly 'fans' of a specific TV series. Fandom is often associated with science-fiction, although we can note that the internet bristles with personal pages dedicated to everything from the teen soap *Hollyoaks* (and all other soaps) to ancient BBC children's favourites like *Rhoobarb*. In the diaries, a female pools collector in her mid-fifties admitted that she loved David Jason in *Only Fools and Horses*, but the person whom she actually wanted to meet, interestingly, was the *writer* of the series, John Sullivan. Another kind of fan was this railway enthusiast whose nostalgic love of railway films stemmed back to his childhood:

> I studied a catalogue from a mail order company, The Signal Box, who stock a veritable selection of railway videos, ranging from the mainstream to the obscure, from Sentinel steam wagons to the Holborn Tram Station and the Santa Fe Railway…At 8.30, I had enough of general television. I put on a copy of British Transport Film's *Blue Pullman* promotional film of 1960 on my VCR. These films (with a Sir John Betjeman style soundtrack), are as evocative of their age as the Ealing Comedies (I also have *Passport to Pimlico* on tape). I used to love seeing BTF films at the University Railway Society, and now that the real price of railway films has fallen [being on video] owning copies of the films which I loved in my childhood is now possible, and well appreciated. *Blue Pullman* was filmed on the test runs from Manchester Central to St Pancras via Matlock. Much of this route is closed, and Manchester Central is now the G-Mex Conference Centre. BTF films mature with age.
>
> (31-year-old male senior social services assistant)

This interest was a relatively solitary one, although the diarist did have contact with other fans of railways and railway films. In the next example, which does return us to science-fiction, a woman in her fifties had found a way to indulge her fondness for *Star Trek* which was far from solitary:

> Two years ago I joined Manchester Starfleet – the local *Star Trek* club, becoming more involved over the time until I took over as Captain/chairman at the beginning of this year. This has led me to watching more videos as we receive copies of recently run episodes of all *Star Trek* programmes long before they are released over here, we also have to choose a group of different episodes to be shown at our monthly meeting…Through [the club] I have become involved in raising money for charity, and just recently in helping Manchester Museum of Science and Industry in the lead up to the *Star Trek* exhibition.
>
> (53-year-old retired female nurse)

Being a *Star Trek* fan here clearly led to all kinds of social activities and involvements – not only in the club meetings but also in the charity and museum engagements which she describes. In addition, this woman was attending evening classes in GCSE-level music and 'computing for women', leading to a rich social life even though illness made it somewhat difficult for her to get around.

Finally, we will study one fan in a little more detail. This man, aged 18 at the start of the study, had several changes in circumstances over the five-year period; he started university, then dropped out, was unemployed, and then got a job at a cinema. Throughout this time, one thing remains constant: his love of the famous BBC science-fiction series *Doctor Who* (which had its original run of episodes from 1963 to 1989). In 1991, he wrote:

> When I finish my A levels, at the end of June, I hope to spend my summer writing a *Doctor Who* novel and some short stories. Writing fiction relaxes me, sometimes. In October I hope to go to [university] to study Communication and Image Studies or Media Production.
>
> Television is less important than it used to be. As I've had less time to watch it, I've become more selective...I tend to watch videos, frequently – mostly ones I've recorded or bought, rather than hired. With the absence of a new series of *Doctor Who*, for the moment, the video has become a lifeline, in many ways! I like to relax, listening to music, reading, walking, entertaining or visiting friends, drawing, writing or going out to the pub.
>
> (1991, aged 18)

Alongside his obvious interest in this TV serial, we can see that this young man also has a broad range of other interests and social activities to occupy his time. In 1993, after a time of transition and uncertainty, TV in general and *Doctor Who* in particular are again seen as a 'lifeline':

> Leaving University was one of my better decisions, but my life went haywire. I worked for a while; spent a long time unemployed, doing very little except falling in love (lust?) and frittering time away with friends. Maybe TV was a bit of a lifeline, then – I don't really recall, but repeats of *Doctor Who* were nice (if only they'd make a new series...either that or categorically announce that they never will so that all of us Whonatics are out of our misery!)
>
> (1993, aged 20)

Here we see an identification with a virtual community of other fans – 'Whonatics' – who this young man knows share his concerns. By 1995, his social life has become more established again, and takes priority over television-viewing: 'Apart from *The X-Files* and the monthly video releases of *Doctor Who* I watch very little, compared to the old days. I just have to be very selective about what I watch, now. That's probably no bad thing'. When he discusses his all-time favourite programmes in the same year, we start to get some insight into the attachment which he has to the programme:

My all time favourite programme is *Doctor Who*. It always has been and I'm rather afraid it always will be. It has a magical quality that makes it utterly unique and rather beautiful in its own way – the ultimate in escapist fantasy for children of all ages. My other favourites include: *The Avengers*, for its style, charm and eccentricity; *The Prisoner*, for being so odd and the closest TV has come to being art; *A Very Peculiar Practice* for its surreal social comment.

(1995, aged 22)

We can note that all of these programmes are valued for their refusal to fit in with the normal and everyday: the 'magical quality' and 'escapism' of *Doctor Who* is valued alongside three other serials, described positively as 'eccentric', 'odd' and 'surreal' respectively. Attacking the 1990s *Star Trek* spin-off series such as *Deep Space Nine* in the following year, he illuminates this theme further:

I watch it occasionally, trying to find something to enjoy beyond the surface of gloss and competence, but there's nothing but a hollow. Any of the 'characters' wouldn't be out of place in an office! I'm sorry but can you imagine Doctor Who, Captain Kirk, Professor Quatermass, Sapphire and Steel or Steed and Mrs Peel doing that? I don't think so!

(1996, aged 23)

The whole point of good characters in television fantasy serials seems here to be their *difference*: their quirkiness, humour and wit in the face of challenges. Paul Cornell, a writer of *Doctor Who* novels, has argued in a 1998 interview:

I think the core of *Doctor Who* isn't the sort of adventures he has, nor that he is somebody who has adventures. I think it is sort of this ethical thing about a hero who doesn't take up guns or weapons and who defeats the bad guys by being more intelligent and wittier and wilier than they are.

(Cornell 1998: 46)

He argues that this goes to the heart of *Doctor Who* fandom – that *Doctor Who* fans, himself included, are people who as children needed this hero, who was able to overcome those with power by use of his intelligence and wit, and who continue to want this to be true. This commitment to the success of the unusual and different, as opposed to the ordinary and bland – characters who 'wouldn't be out of place in an office' – seems to be perhaps a partial explanation for this man's enduring commitment to *Doctor Who*.

TELEVISION'S PERSONAL MEANINGS

It is clear that television means a variety of different things to different people, and we should be wary of generalising about the function of TV for viewers.

What we have seen in this chapter is that television can offer a front-row view of the world, and in our study respondents praised this aspect of television. We also saw how important television can become as a source of companionship, and this was the most common theme in response to the question of 'what TV means to you'. Television can be a friend, a member of the family, a familiar presence that is an important part of the pattern of daily life. This supports findings by Rogge and Jensen (1988) with regard to the way in which viewers can develop meaningful relationships with television programmes. Rather than getting stuck on shallow questions of whether watching high levels of television is 'bad for' people, we have shown that even for people who do watch television for a lot of the day, every day, there are complex social, psychological and economic reasons why this is the case, and the fact that such people get a great deal of pleasure from this leisure activity would suggest that pejorative terms such as 'addict' or 'heavy viewer' do not do justice to such viewers' range of responses to watching television.

However, it is also the case that TV can be a substitute friend, one that serves to remind the viewer of their own feelings of loneliness or isolation, and this is where the ups and downs of viewers' relationships with television can be seen most clearly. This leads to feelings of anxiety and guilt about levels and types of television watched on a daily basis. It also leads to frustration about the type of television that is available, especially during the daytime. It appears from this study that people feel guilty about watching television primarily because they feel that they could be doing something more useful instead. This work ethic is strong in most viewers in this study, and says something about the common perception of people who sit in front of the 'goggle box' as lazy and unmotivated. As respondents struggle to come to terms with these feelings of guilt, we can see that they would be the first to be critical of 'lazing in front of the TV'. And yet clearly, TV is an important means to relax, and is a leisure activity these viewers enjoy. This supports the findings of Radway (1984) and others who showed that people can feel guilty about reading romantic fiction, or watching television, because they are aware of the value society places on work over leisure time. This perhaps explains why viewers complain about feeling guilty for watching soaps, or old black and white films in the afternoon, and yet are not prepared to give up these pleasures. Overall, the earlier sections of this chapter showed that despite feeling guilty about some of their viewing, television is still a welcome source of companionship for many people.

In trying to consider the ways in which people's identities were formed and changed in relation to television, we found that in most cases any such influence would be so subtle, and spread so thinly across a broad band of time, that we could not comment on it without indulging in an unforgivable amount of speculation. Nevertheless, by focusing on one particular fan of a TV series, we were able to extract some idea of the personal reasons why he valued it so much – why it *meant* something to him, and had done since childhood – which went beyond the predictable kind of answer such as 'a nostalgic hankering for childhood things' or 'a need for escapist fantasy'.

SUMMARY OF KEY FINDINGS

- Television means a variety of different things to different people. Some people saw it as mere 'electronic wallpaper', but more often it was seen as a valuable 'window on the world', absorbing, entertaining and informative.
- Television can be a valuable source of companionship, particularly for those who feel alone, and was even described by some as a good friend, or one of the family.
- People were happy, however, to substitute the 'companionship' of TV for real social interaction when it was available.
- Viewers quite often felt guilty about the amount and type of television they chose to watch. They felt that perhaps they should be doing something more 'useful' instead.
- Guilt was particularly strong in relation to viewing in the daytime, the traditional time of work.
- People also felt guilty about watching or enjoying material which they suspected was indecent or moronic; and for imposing programmes on people who were not keen to watch them, in shared spaces.
- Guilty feelings, however, did not necessarily lead to a reduction in television viewing.
- Talk about, and stemming from issues raised in, television programmes is a part of many people's social lives. For some, an important part of the pleasure of TV viewing was talking about it afterwards. Conversations were able to make use of the shared reference points, in relation to social issues and popular culture, established by television.
- Identities are negotiated in relation to TV and other media material, but in subtle ways which even a qualitative study like this has difficulty picking up.

Notes

1   Other less common reasons for feeling guilty included religious reservations – one unemployed woman aged 22 said that she sometimes felt guilty because 'I am a strong Catholic and I am aware of the sin on television' – and scenes of real poverty in the news – a 46-year-old man, also unemployed, wrote that:

> When I see pictures of starving people in Africa I feel guilty that I'm well fed and living an immeasurably better life than these people. I feel ashamed of being part of a world in which such things are allowed to happen.

2   Of course, viewers in Scotland, for example, may complain that TV presents them with a set of concerns based on English or London-centred interests.

3   The phrase 'the search for an acceptable masculinity' has been borrowed from Lyn Thomas (1997), who uses it to describe a theme which she argues is present in the TV series *Inspector Morse* (1987–); her study is discussed in chapter eight.

4   David notes that growing up in the 1980s, I found some security in my developing sense of identity from the pages of *Smash Hits* magazine and related media, which (as Neil Tennant has noted) reflected the *aspirational* glamour of the time, as various lipstick and eyeliner-wearing male icons radically challenged the stodgy masculine hegemony in general and dodgy 'rock' machismo in particular.

Chapter 6

Video and technology in the home

In this chapter we will consider the ways in which video cassette recorders (VCRs), and other TV-related technologies such as camcorders, satellite and cable TV, and teletext, are fitted into and used within people's everyday lives. A concern with 'technology' may not appear to be the most exciting of topics for those of us who are students of media culture or social life, but in fact the wide range of creative uses which people manage to extract from the technologies which enter their lives makes the subject rather more engaging than one might expect. Electronic goods that are originally sold by companies which, we can assume, will be more concerned about making money than making consumers really happy – though the two are somewhat interlinked – take on new meanings when they become a part of the household. Metaphorically tossing aside their instruction manuals, individuals squeeze the technology for what they want to get out of it – as if saying, 'That's all very well, but what are you going to do for *me*?' As Hugh Mackay has put it,

> When new technologies arrive in households their uses, meanings and forms are not predetermined nor fixed. Encoded in particular ways, with preferred readings or uses, they *may* be used, and carry meanings, as intended by their designers. But they may, alternatively, be rejected or modified through their use in households.
>
> (1997: 278)

We will see that the video does better in this everyday analysis than satellite TV, incidentally: when the latter did not give people what they wanted, they simply had to take it back. Given that video is also the most common of these TV add-on technologies, and was given interesting roles in relation to everyday life, much of this chapter will focus on VCRs and the people who used them.

THE RISE OF VIDEO

Although the domestic video revolution started in the early 1980s, with the number of UK households owning a VCR shooting from zero to 18 per cent between 1981 and 1983, the rise of the video has been relatively gradual and steady after the initial burst of those one-in-five households who had to have a machine as soon as they came on the market. By the time of the 1995–96 General Household Survey, 79 per cent of households had at least one VCR; but at the start of this Audience Tracking Study, in 1991, that figure was only 68 per cent. Perhaps surprisingly, in the mid-1980s, when David Morley and Ann Gray were doing most of the fieldwork for their separate studies which have been the most notable previous accounts of video in the home (Morley 1986, 1992; Gray 1987, 1992), fewer than one in three households actually had a video recorder (Office for National Statistics 1997a).

This means that the overall climate in which video exists and is used today is actually quite different from that found in earlier studies: the video-owning households of the mid-1980s are not like a cross-section or random sample of the larger number of households with a VCR in the 1990s, since the people who bought video machines before the majority had them will be a particular *type*, although not uniform in character. The households with VCRs in the mid-1980s may have been ones where a wage-earner had an interest in films, where the children had successfully demanded one for their entertainment, or where the video was required as a status symbol. These could be factors influencing first-time video buyers in the 1990s, too, of course, but with VCRs now so widespread and everyday, it is less of a distinguishing factor.

The two studies which are cited most often in textbooks and other literature about people's uses of domestic technology in general and video in particular, those mentioned above, by David Morley (covered in two of his books: 1986, 1992) and Ann Gray (also with dual coverage: 1987, 1992), paint a quite polarised picture of gender relations and men's domination of the VCR, particularly the timer, cassettes and remote control. We did not find those patterns in this study. This matter is discussed in a section on video and gender which follows most of the video-related findings below.

Julian Wood (1993) provides us with a glimpse of the 'hidden' world of teenage boys in their own separate sphere within the domestic context. Wood studied young people's uses of video through semi-participant observation, and gives a detailed account of the cheers, jeers and scraps which take place as a group of 14-year-old boys watch Stephen King's *It* – described by the boy who owns it as a 'really bad vid'. They exchange banter, insults and challenges, make knowingly sexist remarks about the female characters (intended to be controversial and humorous, as they have been 'learning about sexism' in school), and fast-forward the 'boring' parts. The boys' vocal support for heroic or diabolical characters is said by Wood to be 'rather like shouting for your 'side'...at a football match' (1993: 190). Keen to assert their masculinity, the boys predictably contest the video's status as 'bad' when it has finished, and marvel at how rich Stephen King must be.

This kind of insight into the everyday lives of teenagers is valuable as it reveals what particular groups or types of people do *whilst* viewing. Surveys may show what people watch, and how much, but tell us nothing about what is going on while they do. Even the diaries which form the basis of the study reported in this book are unlikely to capture this level of detail, particularly in the case of a group such as teenage boys, who would be unlikely to agree to write it all down.

VIDEO AND EVERYDAY LIFE IN THE AUDIENCE TRACKING STUDY

The invention of the video cassette recorder seems to be regarded as a really rather good thing by most of the participants in this study (although it now seems to be taken for granted as a 'necessary' item in most of these households). It might seem cautious and sensible to assume that, as students of the media, we overestimate the general usefulness of the VCR; whilst *we* might find the video machine very useful, it might be wise to guess that most people don't bother using it much, except perhaps for watching rented videos. There is also a popular mythology that lots of people don't really know how to work their video machine. This study suggests that these ideas are quite wrong. Videos were in regular use, often daily, for moving programmes around within people's own daily schedules, entertaining children, for storing and recalling favourite material, and for a number of other applications which people had devised in order to maximise the usefulness of the VCR for their own particular lifestyle and preferences.

Timeshifting

Much the most important, frequent use of the VCR was for 'timeshifting' programmes – recording them upon broadcast for watching at a more convenient time. It is not really an exaggeration to say that this made a significant difference to the way in which these people could live their lives. It was important to them that they should see particular programmes, but being no longer tied to watching them at the broadcast time meant that they were cut 'free' from the fixed schedules by which television previously, presumably, used to tie viewers down. This respondent sets out the positive end of the argument – a little *too* positively, perhaps, for some tastes:

With 2 sets and 2 video recorders we can each watch virtually anything we want to see, whereas, of course, before video, if you did not watch a programme at time of transmission, you missed it. I would say that our ordinary viewing has doubled because of this revolutionary change, and my own special interest, watching feature films, has trebled. Videorecording films has the added advantage over 'live' viewing, that the commercial breaks can be avoided by use of the fast-wind, so a serious mood is not broken by the trivia of advertisements.

(43-year-old male civil servant)

Those who fear that television may be crushing 'ordinary' social interaction might be somewhat alarmed by this vision of a double-video household where there is just so much to view. On the other hand, we can consider that at least what is on will be something specifically chosen, rather than just being what happens to be in the airwaves at the time; and in any case, whilst most households were finding video extremely useful for shifting programmes around within their *own* preferred schedule, they had not taken this to mean that they should necessarily watch any greater amount of TV. A sweeter example is provided by the girl who had to spend each school day waiting for the conclusion of her favourite cartoon, which the education system had unhelpfully contrived to block:

We watch *Teenage Mutant Hero Turtles* every morning and we tape the end because of going to school. Then when we get home we watch it.

(10-year-old schoolgirl)

Video also offered a way of avoiding potential viewing conflicts and rows; in these two examples, the VCR is used to allow the diarists to watch soaps and science fiction (on their own, later), which they would otherwise have difficulty persuading their household to view:

While [the BBC *One O'Clock News*] was on I recorded *Home and Away* on ITV. The rest of my family don't care much for it and prefer *Neighbours* so to save any hassles I record it and watch it on my own later in the day.

(17-year-old male student)

In general, I video record items where there is a conflict of interest between my wife and myself, or because we have visitors or because similar programmes are on at the same time...Because I like science fiction/fantasy I record those items for watching when my wife is out.

(72-year-old retired male analytical chemist)

Of course, not everything would always go according to plan.

On arriving at work I was asked to do overtime that evening. Well that did leave me in a bit of a dilemma. I really needed the money but I hadn't set the video to record *Star Trek – The Next Generation*. It took me a few hours to come to a decision. I eventually risked asking my mother to set the timer. It wouldn't have been so bad if my father would be home in time to read the five easy steps to set the timer from the comfort of your armchair. He was out playing bowls (quel surprise). Anyway I got home several hours later and found it had recorded perfectly...Only to find out a few days later that I had recorded *EastEnders* over it!

(19-year-old male insurance company worker)

The broader range of viewing possibilities offered by a VCR could, as we have seen above, mean that a person's daily schedule and routines would be affected. For example, a woman in her mid-sixties noted that since she had begun to use her video more than previously, her bedtime was getting later in the evening as she 'caught up' with all the taped material. (A lecturer who *failed* to keep on top of similar recordings made the typical academic's analogy, 'it's like xeroxing articles that remain unread'.) Another retired woman noted, with half-hearted regret, that a borrowed VCR was encouraging her to shuttle lots of dross into her TV life, which she would otherwise have survived quite happily without:

I enjoy the use of my youngest son's video, I shall not want to give it back. I watch a great deal of rubbish I think one might say. I like the unreality of such programmes as *Little House on the Prairie*! – Life isn't like that, but it would be nice and right often if it could be. The same with *Flying Doctors* – my husband used to enjoy being entertained by this.

(69-year-old housewife)

Video machines were also deployed in strategic ways. This woman, for example, was able to anticipate that the post-lunchtime quiz *Turnabout* would send her to sleep, and had the video running so that, in spite of her body's own wishes, she would not be able to avoid it:

I turned to BBC1 for *Turnabout*, which has replaced *Going For Gold*, which I always watch and enjoy. However, *Turnabout* is less of a challenge, and I cannot sort out the spheres as the challengers had to do. In fact, I fell asleep during the programme, although I had taken the precaution of recording it, so that I could watch, when I woke.

(63-year-old retired female nurse)

This diligent sixth-former used the VCR to chop up movies into handy chunks, to fit around her lifestyle:

I myself usually work part-time on Sundays, and go out with friends on Saturday nights and so, once again any free time I have is spent on home-work. In these situations, the video is often brought into use and I tend to watch long programmes or films in half hour sections over a period of a few nights.

(18-year-old female student)

These intelligent uses of the VCR, harnessing technology for the ways in which it can be deployed to contribute to one's own life, rather than just using it in the ways proposed in the instruction manual, show that people can be quite creative as they integrate technology developed by others, for the general population, into the unique texture and circumstances of their own life. We are therefore able to lend some degree of empirical support to Sean Cubitt's optimistic view of technology and everyday life presented in *Timeshift: On Video Culture* (1991), a book which paints an attractive but probably over-romantic picture of the liberating, transformative power of video. For Cubitt, video redirects power, quite radically, away from the broadcasting and video production elite and into the hands of anyone with a VCR, who can control, archive, reschedule, compile and cut up TV pictures in a way that was previously unthinkable. Whether this has brought about the 'democratic media culture' which excites Cubitt is, at best, debatable. Most people just shifted programmes around to more convenient times, and some – as we will see below – kept an archive of favourite shows. This can seem very flat and domestic when compared with Cubitt's visions of video breeding a generation of multimedia anarchists who rejig material in self-consciously radical ways. However, just because the latter group of self-styled video artists make up only a tiny minority, we should not lose sight of the broader revolution reflected by the present study – people right across the age spectrum using their VCRs to put TV in its place, by forcing its output into convenient slots.

Particularly interesting, in this regard, is the proficiency which more elderly respondents clearly had with their video machines. Quite contrary to the idea of older people having 'difficulty' with technology, the retired people in this study were very adept at timeshifting shows, and using their video to overcome the problem of interesting programmes being transmitted simultaneously:

Sunday is quite good, as I can tape one of the programmes such as *Band of Gold* or *The Choir*, while watching the other. Tonight though, I am going out and so have arranged with a friend to tape one for me.

(74-year-old retired woman)

Diarists in their sixties and seventies who went out in the evening would often mention that they set the video for programmes that they wanted to see, and, for example, a retired secretary would video the quiz show *Fifteen to One* if she had to go to the shops in the late afternoon, and would watch it upon her return, with a cup of tea – a simple enough act, but an empowering exercise of control over the TV at the same time. (One gets the impression that some respondents saw television rather as a slightly over-enthusiastic dog, always yapping for their attention, and they were pleased to have video because it enabled them to put a leash on it, to regain control over their day's schedule, and only allow the TV to show off its tricks when they invited it to.)

Another respondent used her satellite connection rather in the style of an internet resource, downloading movies onto video for use on subsequent dull days:

> When I'm in the flat all day, I don't necessarily want the television all day, but I want to watch at times convenient to me, and a load of rubbish is usually all that's on offer. This is when I can watch videos, and is the reason why I bought [a satellite receiver], and now pay for the two film channels. There is no cinema in [northern industrial town], so I regularly video films to watch at a later date.
>
> (64-year-old retired woman)

Another group of older diarists had a similar timeshifting technique, using their VCRs to 'replace' the evening's broadcast output with shows which had been transmitted during the daytime, which they actually preferred. In other words, they liked daytime TV best, but didn't like watching TV in the daytime. Resourceful use of their video machines gave them the best of both worlds. These two examples describe reasons for this approach, which was employed by several others:

> With the ever increasing amount of time spent [in mainstream, evening TV] on hospital and medical matters and on sport, I find that I record many morning and afternoon programmes for watching in the evening.
>
> (76-year-old retired man)

> I start with a few minutes of news while I have my breakfast, and then set the video for a discussion programme such as *The Time the Place* and *This Morning*, and I then 'save' these for evening viewing when I am not interested in programmes transmitted in the evening. The gardening programmes I find very useful and was very pleased to be invited to the BBC at Leeds to watch a programme and there meet Geoffrey Smith and Peter Seabrook. These I usually video so I can check on plant names etc.
>
> (70-year-old retired woman)

Again, in the latter part of the second example, an experienced user is seen making sophisticated use of their video facility which parallels advanced internet handling – here, although she may watch gardening programmes 'live' (i.e. at time of broadcast), she has the video recording as a kind of hard-disk 'cache', which she will be able to scan later for details she may have missed whilst 'on-line' (watching the show upon transmission).

Working people with specialist interests would also timeshift relevant material from its daytime slot into the evening, where it could replace the populist output which interested them less.

> *Westminster Live*: I go to work on secondment with the LEA Equal Opportunities Section, and today I worked on the computer-based staff audit database. I leave home at 8.00 and return 17.15. Whilst Breakfast news is on, I set my VCR to save the afternoon's proceedings from Parliament on tape. I replay whilst eating my evening meal – sausages, chips and tinned tomatoes (ie, the Health Education Council will doubtless say I'm on my death bed – but I don't tolerate being lectured to!).
>
> (31-year-old male senior social services assistant)

Again, this video activity fits a model derived from the way in which computers are used to manipulate information – the basic 'cut and paste' function – which is becoming increasingly familiar to people as computer use becomes ever more widespread (the General Household Survey of 1995–96 shows a quarter of all UK households having a home computer, and computer terminals were becoming increasingly ubiquitous in workplaces). In the example above, the social services worker metaphorically 'selects' *Westminster Live* from the daytime schedules, 'copies' it to the (video) clipboard, then 'pastes' it into his own preferred schedule over the top of lightweight early-evening shows. Picturing this rescheduling as a simple electronic mouse movement, of course, obscures the reality of having to fiddle with cassettes, listings publications and the remote control; but we can expect – whether contentedly or cynically – that technology manufacturers will be more than happy to produce clean, all-in-one interfaces of this kind very soon.

Not all timeshifting was as immediate as in these examples. Some people, who had busy lives or lived in households where they could not necessarily dictate what should be watched, had a backlog which they only caught up with at convenient times, often much later:

> If everyone goes out and I'm left in the house alone, I tend to watch a video of something I've recorded a few days (weeks, months) previously. Perhaps I was out when my favourite programme was on, or two things clashed, or it was on while I was asleep. My parents will arrive home around 2200, cunningly timed so my father can see the ITN news.
>
> (20-year-old female sales assistant)

> If [the TV schedule] all looks like crap we may watch something we have previously videoed or a film we have taped (some of which go back to the

Christmas before last). I have a terrible habit of saying 'Oh I really wanted to see that film when it was out' and then leave it on tape for over a year.

(34-year-old female secretary)

Some people were more wary of acquiring too many stored-up programmes, however, with one 69-year-old housewife referring to 'the danger of having recorded videos and no time to see them', which meant that she was careful to tape only shows which she was reasonably sure to watch, and not ones which she thought she 'might', which she would never actually get round to.

Video: the collected works

A number of respondents had created a video 'library' or 'archive' of their own, although not all of them would call it that. As we would expect, these reflected the diarists' own peculiar interests, although it is probably fair to say that the collections were of two basic types:

1   'Cult' programmes, generally collected by some of the younger diarists. Examples include *Doctor Who*, *Star Trek* (in its various versions), Granada's *Sherlock Holmes*, and other TV drama, telefantasy and comedy of the 1970s and 80s.
2   More traditionally 'classic' programmes, the video equivalents of a leather-bound Shakespeare set, stored by some of the older respondents. Examples would include David Attenborough's famous natural history series such as *Life on Earth* and *The Living Planet*, *Pride and Prejudice* and other literary costume dramas, and operas.

Both types of video collection would be upheld, by their respective owners, as preserving a kind of creative brilliance in television programme-making which appears in the airwaves, at best, infrequently. Two examples, from men aged 26 and 71, illustrate the two positions.

Relaxation, on my part, tends to revolve around either the TV or going to the cinema; Streatham, with two picture houses, is ten minutes walking distance up the road. I've built up a substantial TV and film video collection over the last four years, so if there's nothing decent on, which tends to be quite a lot at the moment, me and [my girlfriend] select something pre-recorded to watch. The collection has a definite leaning towards cult programmes, with stuff such as *Dr Who*, *The Prisoner*, *Sherlock Holmes*, and *A Very Peculiar Practice* in it.

(26-year-old male graphic designer)

Our days follow a predictable pattern and we spend most of our time together. We very rarely switch on the television before the news at 5.40

but after that we tend to watch on average for about 3 hours every evening, but quite selectively. If none of the programmes attracts us, then we play something we have previously recorded on video. We have a 'library' of video tapes (including, for example, all Alistair Cooke's *America* series, Shakespeare plays, etc) and we often watch a favourite programme more than once.

(71-year-old retired male school inspector)

The younger man, a joint partner in his own successful graphic design consultancy, working for the music and publishing industries, does not fit easily with the stereotyped image of the cult TV 'anorak' and – simply by being female – nor does his girlfriend, an ideal partner who, working as an illustrator from home, would video the then-new episodes of *Star Trek: The Next Generation* at 6pm for them to watch together over tea, once her boyfriend had got home from work after 7pm. (Indeed, this *Star Trek* series was the subject of enthusiastic remarks from many women and men, young, middle-aged and elderly.[1])

An interest in 'cult TV', then, is not limited to young men with too much time on their hands; nor is it associated purely with space opera. Granada's *Sherlock Holmes*, with the late Jeremy Brett as the eponymous detective, also acquired a 'cult' following (if we take that to mean the kind of following which exchanges videos; discusses the show in fanzines, TV magazines such as *DreamWatch*, or – more often today than in 1991 – on the Internet; and, typically, proposes the show's star as 'the next *Doctor Who*').[2] This middle-aged woman found great pleasure in her complete video collection of the series, which she enjoyed alongside the original books.

Finished off the evening with my passion Sherlock Holmes. I've got them all on tape, all 32 episodes! The last series was variable, I must admit, but I love 'em all really, even when they muck about with the stories. Jeremy Brett is the best ever Holmes, without a doubt, – autocratic, bad tempered, brilliant, and very sexy. And 'The Illustrious Client' is a classic – pure Conan Doyle, even the added mutilation of Kitty was perfectly valid, and the parallel with Don Giovanni was something I'd never noticed, although I must have read the story dozens of times – as a music lover, I should be ashamed. Please Granada, persuade Jeremy and Edward Hardwicke, his adorable Watson, to make another series – there are some good ones left – 'Black Peter', 'The Stockbroker's Clerk', 'Charles Augustus Milverton'...I could go on...

(49-year-old female local government clerk)

One retired man had been one of the first to acquire a VCR, but then had found the blank cassettes to be prohibitively expensive, foiling his plan to tape lots of old films from TV. By the end of this study – some twelve years on – he had worked out a way to collect as many films as he wanted, and improve his health at the same time:

> When I think hard about it, yes there was another big change [since the start of this study]. I, who used to drive the girls [at work] mad by smoking cigars, have given up smoking. It cost me £70 and two visits to my friendly local hypnotist, but I've stopped, and use the money the cigars once cost to buy blank video cassettes (5 × 180 mins at our local [supermarket] for £7.99). £7.99 was the price of *one* cassette in the early 1980s when I started taping, and consequently I could never afford to tape whole films, only extracts. Prices for satellite dishes are also falling (latest £99), so obviously they're spreading. We are getting closer to global TV (we don't think twice now about global radio), and are no longer so dependent on the tin gods of institutions like the BBC.
>
> (73-year-old retired man)

In an essay based on a small-scale qualitative study of people who collect films on videotape, Uma Dinsmore (1998) notes how the collection and their uses of it reflects aspects of the collector's character: some focused on particular stars about whom they knew many anecdotes and pieces of information, and whose appearances in scenes of films might be watched in isolation; others were excited by their 'home cinema' playback hardware and could hardly bear to watch their favourite movies except in surround sound, complete from start to finish and with no adverts, from well-preserved cassettes. The latter are seen as having both a 'material' and a 'textual' interest in their video collections; the interest of the former is more purely textual.

Most of the respondents described above would seem to value both aspects of their collections. The content of the videos – the 'textual' – is obviously important, or they simply wouldn't watch them. But the materiality of the collection also seems to have a resonance – from the young graphic designer who says proudly that he has '*built up* a *substantial*...video collection over the last *four years*' (our emphases here highlight the way he has made it sound like a major construction project), to the retired schools inspector who calls his collection a 'library' and seems proud of the 'high culture' credentials of his tapes (the Shakespeare plays, for example). Similarly, the Sherlock Holmes fan's proud claim that she has 'got them all on tape, all 32 episodes!' reveals her completist pride in the set, which we can readily imagine lined up, neatly labelled, in her bookshelves alongside the Conan Doyle books.

Other video collections were not so much permanent 'libraries' but deliberate stockpiles, which might be erased after they had been watched. Like people filling their cellars with tinned food in case of war, these respondents were saving material that they thought would be well-prepared and long-lasting – often classic films – to help them through the long nights of the barren TV wasteland foisted upon them by the broadcasting companies.

We have had little change in our lives during the last four years, except failing health which, no doubt, will mean more TV viewing...to this end I have been taping war films, classical musicals etc to enjoy when the TV programmes have little to offer.

(72-year-old retired police chief)

We very seldom hire a video film but we do record and keep good films so that when there is nothing on worth watching (like tonight) we can watch a film...I do find that I use my video more now because I find TV at the moment is not very good so I video old films that are on during the day and watch them at night.

(47-year-old female finance collector)

By allowing the respondents to view these comforting classics at any time they chose, video has quite radically altered their relationship with TV. The viewers are happier, now that they feel they have some choice about what they view, and life must be somewhat easier for broadcasters, now that viewers with VCRs do not feel quite so much that they are being held hostage to the TV companies' unfortunate programme schedules.

Parents, children and the VCR

Parents of pre-teenage children found their video cassette recorders to be useful in a variety of ways – giving the kids programmes to watch, allowing parents to vet shows their offspring *might* watch, and timeshifting material the parents want to see so that it did not interfere with their children's activities. This mother, for example, found that a video would at times be useful for keeping her son occupied:

After the rush of getting two children to school I have breakfast with my son aged three and read a newspaper. I then start my housework – washing, emptying the dishwasher and feeding pet animals and fish. My son sometimes watches a video tape, *Thomas the Tank Engine* and *Count Duckula* are his favourites. We often walk to the shops returning for lunch and *Home and Away* and *Neighbours*.

(30-year-old female homemaker)

Grandparents also found that the video was a satisfactory way of occupying children. This woman was particularly active in taping shows, regularly, for their benefit:

Now I have a video I often record programmes of interest for my grandchildren (I also have a daughter who lives in [nearby city] and she comes once a week to see me with her daughters) as well as having films for them to see. Though as the weather gets better we shall be viewing less often as we prefer to be out and about.

(68-year-old retired woman)

Similarly, a 72-year-old retired teacher found that 'looking after grand-children has made a video recorder very important'. However, he did have some qualms about this, finding their cartoons far inferior to the Disney offerings which he 'was brought up on'. 'Why must we feed our youngsters such trash at such an impressionable age?' he demands, although as he is the one with that responsibility, this complaint may seem somewhat misplaced.

All of the parents in this study were careful to express *some* caution about how much TV they would let their children watch. Some were more wary than others, however. This mother, another 30-year-old, used the video for steering TV viewing *away* from the children's time, rather than into it:

> My husband comes in at tea time, but we are both more choosy about what we watch since we obtained a video. If there's something on in the early evening that we want to watch, we video it and watch it when the children are in bed. We spend the early evening playing and talking to our children, they are much more important. In the summer things change a bit if the weather's good, children skip TV and play out, and my husband and I are more inclined to be doing odd jobs round the house.

(30-year-old female domestic worker)

Finally, another diarist had taken this one step further, spiriting programmes *away* on video first, checking them, and then returning them to the children – if appropriate – for viewing:

> I still enjoy much of the same type of programmes but watch more chil-dren's programmes with my daughters. I use these as discussion points, especially in the case of my eldest daughter [aged 5] who has Down's Syndrome. I have become more conscious of the content of programmes as both the eldest daughters will comment on things they hear or see. I cer-tainly record more programmes and check their suitability before allowing them to see them.

(36-year-old male carer)

Again, in all of these cases we have seen that video has proved to be an extremely useful and convenient tool within the household; whilst the spectre of the VCR is sometimes upheld as a damaging presence in the family home – because it is assumed that use of a video leads to increasing amounts of unbridled TV viewing – in fact this data suggests that the technology generally allows parents much greater *control* over the television seen in their household than previously (although the possibility of children sneakily watching 'unsuitable' material whilst their parents are out remains).

Renting movies

Despite the fact that being able to hire and view movies on videotape is one of the most obvious uses of video, and one of its selling points, movie rentals do not feature hugely in this study. The explanation for this is quite simple: the Audience Tracking Study was looking at the lives of a range of individuals spread right across the age range, and sought to take in all of their everyday activity. In this context, the viewing of hired videotapes becomes a minority sport, an activity predominantly engaged in by only a slice of the age spectrum – the 14–35s – and then usually only taking up a couple of hours a week, or none at all. Furthermore, the respondents did not make much of their video rentals in their diaries – the fact that they have rented a video, often at the weekend, features often enough in the diaries of young people (or their parents), but is usually just mentioned in passing. Compared to the detailed video strategies developed in relation to timeshifting, the use of the VCR for watching pre-recorded films was routine and unspectacular, and in any case took up only a small percentage of video time. Whilst there were many people in this study who used their video for recording TV programmes and who did *not* hire (or buy) pre-recorded tapes, there was no-one who used their video exclusively for watching pre-recorded material.

We should mention that by the mid-1990s, it was actually more common for pre-recorded videotapes to be bought than rented (*Social Trends* 1998). The greater number and range of outlets selling videos – including supermarkets and newsagents – will partly account for this. The biggest video sales are in children's videos, whereas video rentals are predominantly of feature films. Pre-recorded retail videos appear at various points in this chapter – for example as some of those used to entertain children, and as part of some people's science fiction collections. We have not organised them together as the fact that they were purchased was usually less important than their various social functions – unlike rented videos, which because of their limited time in the household become social events in themselves.

Reasons for renting videos were straightforward enough. Sometimes it would be a movie that the diarist was particularly keen to see, and had missed at the cinema. More frequently, people were prompted to go to the video shop by the TV schedulers, in a negative sense – for example, a 39-year-old female holistic therapist wrote that 'Friday, Saturday, Sunday evenings are terrible and we always hire videos for entertainment', and similarly, a 67-year-old voluntary charity fundraiser sometimes hired a video (or else watched a film she'd previously taped herself) because she found Saturday nights on TV 'pretty dire'. One parent, a middle-aged civil servant, mentioned that videos were occasionally rented 'for the children [aged 6 and 10] when we go out' – a perplexing finding for readers of the *Daily Mail*, who may understand the 'video nanny' as a purely working-class phenomenon. Finally, for some respondents on a very limited income, watching a rented video was a decent form of (just about) affordable entertainment:

> I usually get up at about 10.30am and have breakfast, get dressed etc. I do housework and read, most days. On a Friday morning my mother and I do a newspaper delivery round. During the day it is usually Mum and I in the house. My dad works and my sister is at college...My boyfriend comes over at the weekend where we watch quite a few rented or pre-recorded films.
>
> (28-year-old unemployed woman)

In a life which this respondent would admit was pretty empty at that stage, the videos – enjoyed in company – added considerable colour to the weekend.

The no-video minority

Not every household owns a video machine, of course; in 1996, 21 per cent of UK households were without one.[3] This was usually due to financial constraints. Although it has been argued that social security benefits should include the cost of a VCR as part of the basic cost of living – because it is such a relatively cheap form of entertainment, and everybody needs some of that – some people simply cannot afford one, and a smaller number of others shun it as an unnecessary luxury. Of the respondents in this study who did not have access to a video, most seemed to wish (to some extent) that they had one. For example:

> My TV watching is [quite] erratic. I wish I had a video to record all those programmes I miss – for example Friday nights is good to go out, but I really love watching Channel 4's tour de force of comedy that night, like *Cheers, Roseanne* and *Who's Line Is It Anyway*.
>
> (19-year-old male student)

> Also if I watch a good long programme, bed time is too late for my condition...For this reason, I wish I could afford a video recorder.
>
> (67-year-old retired woman)

Some felt that broadcasters assumed that their audience was waiting with VCRs at the ready, and so felt correspondingly excluded:

> I have noticed that a fair number of programmes, especially films, are screened in the small hours on the assumption that a video recorder is available. Since I do not have a video recorder I sometimes find this

frustrating. Even if I did have a video recorder, I can visualise a back log of programmes accumulating.

(74-year-old retired male personnel administrator)

And this video-free diarist objected to what she saw as an annoyingly vocal lobby of video owners:

What worries me even more is that those who have videos are now objecting if programmes are overrun. Soon we shan't be allowed to see the end of an opera or watch some important event in case we upset the programming of somebody's machine. *Help!!*

(75-year-old retired female heath planner)

These diarists are clearly annoyed that their relatively mild frustration at not having a VCR is compounded by broadcasters and video owners who assume that everyone has this luxury.

DIY television: the camcorder users

Despite the popularity of the usually serious 'video diary' TV programme format in the first half of the 1990s – in which people would record their local political campaigns, their everyday lives as plumbers or Elvis impersonators, or their untimely deaths, for the benefit of a wider audience – camcorders in everyday life still carry the stigma of unimaginative tourists filming lingering shots of shop fronts and museum displays. The association with Jeremy Beadle's show of 'hilarious' out-takes, *You've Been Framed*, has also enhanced the association between home-made video and general embarrassment. Academic work has focused on video as art (Cubitt 1993), the use of video in TV shows such as those mentioned above (Goodwin 1993; Keighron 1993; Humm 1998), and the role of video in media education (such as Dowmunt 1980; Sarland 1991; Bower 1992; Dewar 1992; Emerson 1993) and environmental campaigns (Gauntlett 1997), whilst *The Video Activist Handbook* (1997) by Thomas Harding, one of the founders of the radical news video *Undercurrents*, has given a more hands-on approach to video campaigning. Little attention has been paid to the everyday videos made by the 'ordinary' people who own (or borrow) camcorders – a group large enough to sustain widely available magazines such as *Camcorder User*, local clubs and evening classes for camcorder owners, and of course the domestic camcorder industry itself.

In our sample, the responses to questions asking what equipment the respondents owned show that 17 per cent had video cameras by 1996. However, the *use* of most of these did not show up in the diaries, perhaps indicating that the camcorders generally sat in cupboards, except on special occasions or for holidays. Nevertheless, three diarists revealed themselves to be camcorder enthusiasts, eagerly making their own programmes or 'short films' in an aspiring-professional style. All were retired men. The youngest, writing in 1996 aged 64, seemed to share Cubitt's vision of video as (media) democracy, allied with an enthusiasm derived, it would seem, from the BBC's *Video Nation* project, which gave short slots to a broad range of people, reflecting their everyday lives and personal views on screen.

> Hoorah for the camcorder! It is democratising the making of television and demystifying it at the same time. *Video Nation* shows that with a little help, people can express themselves in televisual terms as forcefully as the professionals and while doing so they learn to appreciate the professionals' art. 'All professions are a conspiracy against the laity' – B. Shaw. The camcorder is helping the laity rumble the pros! The hour of the Community Programmes Unit has come!
>
> (64-year-old retired male TV executive)

The oldest enthusiast, who died within the first year of this study, adopted a more determined, and less pretentious, approach:

> Both of us, my wife and I are retired. My wife was a school mistress in a combined school. I had a milk business. She is a very keen needlewoman and does some demonstration in embroidery. My hobby is making TV films mostly of our holidays, home and abroad. I possess an 8mm video camera. I do my own editing and dubbing music on to my tapes. Last year I made a 3 hour film about life in our village. This February I made another film of Dick Whittington, the village pantomime. Both films were very warmly received at their showing in the village hall.
>
> (76-year-old retired man)

We can only guess at whether this man's *three hour* film of village life bears out the previous respondent's claim that 'people can express themselves in televisual terms as forcefully as the professionals'. Nevertheless, it is interesting (but not surprising) that, having been a keen television viewer himself – his wife, writing after his death, noted that 'He used to have the TV on all day long' – this man should have gained such pleasure from making his own productions.

The other, a 66-year-old retired teacher, said little about his 'hobby' of 'making short documentary video films of historical subjects'. Like his fellow enthusiasts, however, this man seemed to go about the task seriously and with considerable patience – he mentions that his production process is 'usually [to] spend the summer making the film and then the winter evenings carrying out the editing, putting on the music, etc'.

These men all gained considerable satisfaction from their home-made TV productions. It seems likely that many of the other respondents would have relished the chance to film their own videos, but did not really have the opportunity (or money), and time, to do so.

Video and gender: a brief note

In David Morley's study of eighteen south London households (1986) it was found that the adult women simply didn't use the video machine, and had little say in which videos would be rented or watched. Even where each family member had their 'own' video cassette for recording shows from TV, it would be the woman's which got taped over by others when their own tape was full.

Ann Gray (1987, 1992), researching women's thoughts about domestic video technology in the mid-1980s, imaginatively asked her respondents to think of different pieces of household equipment as either pink (female) or blue (male). Irons were 'uniformly pink'; electric drills, for these women, were all blue. A washing machine was usually said to be pink on the outside – although its motor would be blue. On the video, the basic 'record', 'play' and searching buttons would be lilac (male *and* female), but the timer would generally be blue, and the remote control was resolutely blue, controlled in all cases by the man of the household.

Both Morley and Gray are keen to emphasise that the gender differences that they identified are nothing to do with biological traits, but are the result of cultural norms and expectations. After all, the women were highly competent with a range of other domestic technologies. Indeed, Gray discovered some judiciously 'calculated ignorance', with one woman admitting that she appeared to know little about the VCR because 'If I learnt how to do the video it would become my job just like everything else' (1987: 43).

In the present study, we cannot say that we found the same patterns. There were indeed some women who generally left working the video – particularly setting the timer – to the men of the household, although in a smaller number of cases some men left it to their female partners (or daughters). In general, video use seems to have broadened out, with the technology now so commonplace and everyday – and perhaps somewhat more 'user friendly' than in the past – that we cannot really make broad generalisations about gender in terms of who uses the VCR. (Indeed, Gray admits that the resistance to video technology which she noted in the women she studied might be a 'passing phase' (1992: 188), which would change as VCRs became more accepted and everyday.) If we look back over the accounts which we have quoted in the course of this chapter, there seems to be a pretty even gender balance, and little evidence that women are unable or even mildly reluctant to use the VCR. It was young women, for example, whom we saw chopping up cartoons and movies to fit around their other obligations (school, and going out), and retired women using the video to record the names of plants, and to shift daytime programmes into evening viewing hours. Elderly women were also seen taping simultaneous programmes, and even swapping cassettes with friends when they had been out and therefore unable to watch one of two shows whilst taping the other. Women were also seen storing programmes and movies on tape for watching on later occasions, and both mothers and grandmothers recorded and played videos for the children in their care. Furthermore, whilst we would have been pleased to have been able to give you some quoteworthy examples of men cruelly dominating the choice of video movie rentals, these simply did not appear in the diaries either (perhaps because it was younger people who generally rented out videos, for whom the traditional gender roles for decision-making were, at least, weaker). Video collections, it has to be said, did seem to be more the province of men than of women, but again the Sherlock Holmes fan – to mention just one memorable example – was a middle-aged woman who showed that the careful compilation of a set of cult TV videotapes was not a purely male domain.

We have seen that the camcorder enthusiasts in the sample were all men, and this hobby – along with its associated magazines and clubs – does seem quite 'gendered' at present, although there obviously are female camcorder users in the world. Perhaps if and when camcorders become more popular and commonplace, in the way that VCRs have, this balance will also shift.

Chapter eight of this book provides more information on gendered uses, practices and preferences. As far as video is concerned, this study suggests that by the mid-1990s the use of video technology was not nearly as gendered – or, to be more specific, dominated by men – as studies have suggested it was in the previous decade.

Even more uses of video

We have already seen that VCRs are used for timeshifting programmes, chopping too-long films into convenient chunks, and taping informational programmes so that details can be written down later. We have also found that video equipment is used for entertaining children, *protecting* children, storing shows for a rainy day, collecting a video archive, and making camcorder productions. And the creativity of this sample of everyday owners of household technology does not end there.

One retired man had 'video friends' across Europe, with whom he ex-changed cassettes by post – a hobby which he shared, to an extent, with his wife. The enterprise seemed to be starting to fill up much of his time, although, as in the extract below, he was careful to comment on the unsuitability of the weather, and so on, to 'justify' this activity.

> By 19.50 I was back home, and was able to record *The Golden Girls* myself. All my foreign videofriends are devotees of Blanche, Dorothy, Sophia and Rose. I watched from 9.50 to 1.20am. By chance, a tape had arrived at 9.30am from Bo in Sweden, so [my wife] and I spent the morning watch-ing it – an early Mozart opera, and a Bavarian TV recording ex-satellite of the Kalman/Millocker operetta 'The Dubarray', obviously made 15 years ago as there was the young Julia Migenes in a small part. It keeps us in our armchairs till lunchtime, and as it was a miserable day outside, we didn't

mind. It was also a miserable day on British TV, but that's nothing new either.

My wife and I are retired, and we can do exactly as we please. Yes, we watch a lot of TV. We also watch a lot of foreign videos sent to us by friends across Europe, the best method known to man to improve foreign vocabularies and to acquire esoteric movies like *Martin Roumagnac* (Dietrich/Gabin) the German version of *Anna Christie* with Salka Viertel in the Maric Dressler part, Bette Davis in the Italian *Il Scopone Scientifico* and Maria Felix in *La Escondida*. Our Anglophile correspondents rejoice in anything with Anna Neagle, Jessie Matthews and, stretching a point, Doris Day in exchange. All this activity helps to keep retirement blues firmly at bay, not only for us, but for other elderly foreign videofreaks in Marbella, Vienna, Rome, and Angelholm in Sweden, who pumps Russian movies to us from his satellite dish.

(68-year-old retired man)

Obviously, this is a hobby which could not exist without the technology of portable – or postable – video cassettes, and which involves the sharing of culture across borders. These 'videofriends' – he has even invented his own word for them – would correspond and share their screen enthusiasms and interests, so that although the hobby is somewhat media-centred, it nevertheless involved a measure of social interaction, and a complex web of video-sharing networks.

A middle-aged respondent noted that his 10-year-old daughter was using the VCR to collect television 'cuttings' about her favourite media stars, using the tape like a (rather linear) scrapbook page to gather interviews and performances.

[My daughter] records on the video anything to do with Jason Donovan and some new cartoon/music character, *The Simpsons*.

(49-year-old male civil engineer)

An older diarist was similarly collecting anything she could get on the Royal Family:

I am a strong Royalist so any programme about the Royal Family, on tour, at home, giving interviews I usually record so that I can watch them again.

(65-year-old retired female teacher)

This woman was 'very pleased' to own a VCR because she found there were 'many programmes on TV which do not interest me', and the video meant she could watch some of her royal archive recorded off-air, or 'one of my collection of bought ones – these are musicals, ballets and some about the Royal Family'.

This study suggests, therefore, that domestic VCR technology in the 1990s is something which is most often used for its most straightforward intended purpose – timeshifting TV programmes – and is also used for the other obvious application, viewing pre-recorded tapes. However, we have also seen that people have taken the technology into their homes and worked out a number of ways in which they can effectively 'customise' its functions – not, of course, by taking the hardware to bits, but by devising techniques and approaches to the technology which mean that, by using its built-in functions in inspired and imaginative ways, they can harness its powers to be of optimum convenience and entertainment value in their everyday lives.

SATELLITE AND CABLE

The 1996–97 Family Expenditure Survey indicates that 12.4 per cent of UK households had satellite TV and 5.1 per cent had cable, giving a total of 17.5 per cent with either satellite or cable TV (Office for National Statistics 1997b). This is an increase from just over 6 per cent of households which had either satellite or cable in 1990.[4] In the present study, as noted in chapter one, the proportion of respondents with satellite or cable TV rose from 7 to 26 per cent between 1991 and 1996.

Bob Mullan (1997) provides a useful summary of the development of satellite and cable TV in Britain, although, as he says, it is a simple enough story: Murdoch launches Sky Television in 1982, which gobbles up the one competing broadcaster, British Satellite Broadcasting (BSB) in 1990, to become the rather oddly-named BSkyB, which still dominates (see also Brunsdon 1997; Lax 1997). Even the numerous channels which are not actually owned by BSkyB usually come under their umbrella, being marketed as part of Sky-dominated packages.

One respondent in an ethnographic study of satellite TV viewers by Shaun Moores (1996) enjoyed the feeling of being 'European' that he gained – even when watching Sky, 'because it's from a European satellite'. Hopping around between continental stations gave him the feeling of being liberated from 'the good old British way'. Moores comments: 'Even if his viewing pleasures do take the form of "channel grazing", a kind of armchair "televisual tourism", it remains the case that satellite TV is helping him travel to new places and to reimagine the boundaries of community'. Europe, in this sense, is a wholly 'imaginary' territory until a person becomes part of its community in some more tangible way – here, via television. (Of course, identification is rarely simple or even singular: another British couple interviewed by Moores were eager to keep up to date with news programmes from the United States on satellite TV, and had a strong interest in 'all things American'; but they felt Welsh when it came to rugby matches, were pleased to be mistaken for Germans when on holiday, and also held 'Eurosceptic' political views (1996: 55).) Again we see from these examples that people take different meanings from technologies (and the material that they deliver) than may have been intended by their producers – it is unlikely, for example, that European integration was uppermost in Rupert Murdoch's mind as he launched the Sky satellite channels. We also see that by bringing quite different slices of culture into people's homes and everyday lives, satellite and cable services can bring people to amend their patterns of cultural and geographical identification.

The most obvious and interesting thing about the Audience Tracking Study diarists' comments on these facilities was that, as a group, they were far from impressed. There were some, of course, who found it vital:

> The main difference [in my life over the past four years] is that I have had cable installed at home. One decoder in the main living room and a box in my bedroom. I have been at [my parents'] home for 9 months and am looking to move out – cable accessibility will be a factor in choosing new accommodation.
>
> (23-year-old male television production assistant)

This young man, however, was a *very* big fan of TV, who would say things like 'I can sit in front of a live outside broadcast just for the thrill of watching it', and that without TV 'I would lose the will to live' ('Lame but true', he admits). Indeed, he had found work in the TV industry – working for the Cable News Network (CNN).

But others found things to enjoy on satellite as well, such as this subscriber, the elderly woman featured in the previous chapter, who found it – in ironic contrast to satellite's common image – an oasis of decent programming and traditional values:

> We loved *Are You Being Served* now on UK Gold daily, *Dad's Army*, *Hi-De-Hi* – all good clean funny fun – that's why we have Sky TV – to watch them again – there is nothing much on terrestrial TV to entertain us these days – just smutty, or sexy, or filthy language progs that do not appeal to us.
>
> (70-year-old housewife)

This woman was also loving UK Gold's repeats of the BBC's much-maligned, cancelled 'sex and sangria' soap *Eldorado*: 'In fact I take the phone off the hook whilst it is on 7.00pm Mon–Fri, as we are really hooked on it.' She was also at the cutting edge of interactive media use – if we can call the real-time nightmare of televised mail-order catalogue QVC 'cutting edge' – and gained considerable pleasure, and use value, from this service: 'It is a great boon for me, as I don't go out much, and the local shops are lousy!' Here, the 'virtual mobility' provided by television gets her, mentally if not physically, out of the house – and down to the shops. Her vigorous enthusiasm for this satellite service, however, probably stems more from a general love of TV. Like the young man above, she seemed to have cable because she simply couldn't get enough, asserting that she would 'die' without television, and arguing that she had learned far more about 'the world and its culture' from TV than the 'old fogies' at school had ever taught her.

It is interesting to compare this woman's enthusiasm for UK Gold's 'classic' shows, and the response of this next man, who in some ways was pleased to find that the programmes of the past had not actually been much good, and had only matured in the nostalgic memory:

> Nostalgia programmes on UK Gold and Bravo have actually made us realise how poor some of the old programmes were. Yet some of the old films still have star quality and are worth rewatching.
>
> (76-year-old retired male analytical chemist)

There were some others who, although not wildly excited about their satellite or cable services, did find themselves watching more TV:

> Yes, the arrival of satellite television has changed our viewing a great deal and given television more importance.
>
> (54-year-old male management lecturer)

However, others found that having the choice of so many different channels meant that they began to impose their own, perhaps surprisingly cautious, filters. For example, a 28-year-old female clerk said that she had 'got Sky TV – so I don't have the TV on as often – I'm more selective in my viewing'.

Another diarist explained:

> Probably the most significant event to change the pattern of my TV view-ing [during the course of this study] was the decision to subscribe to Satel-lite TV in May 1994…The satellite has not altered the amount of hours [of] TV we watch in total but has greatly increased our choice and selec-tion, although a lot of satellite output is not to our taste (hence the failure to increase our viewing hours). I think the concept of 'narrow casting' which satellite tends to follow has some benefits though (e.g. VH-1 on satellite is very precisely aimed at my age group/musical tastes), something which the 'broadcasters' cannot do by their very definition.
>
> (41-year-old male company director)

Indeed, some felt that satellite had left them watching less than before:

> I used to watch loads of TV until about one and a half years ago when we got Sky. We got the Sports Channel but not the Movie Channels and, instead of watching more TV I became more selective and watched fewer programmes.
>
> (17-year-old male college student)

A number of other satellite and cable receivers were unimpressed:

> I think one change (a fairly recent one) is that we have recently installed
> SKY TV. I don't really like it much. We cannot get the film channel. We
> have music channel, Eurosport, News and Cartoons. The only thing I
> would watch would be the news and I can get that on the regular television
> channels. I may watch a boxing match of particular interest on Eurosport –
> but little else has interested me. My husband enjoys it, but he enjoys chan-
> nel hopping.
>
> (41-year-old female medical secretary)

Here, even her husband's enjoyment-via-channel-hopping is taken to be a sign
that there isn't actually much gripping content. The following young man was
more vehement in his comments on Sky, feeling that the Murdoch empire had
begun to take liberties:

> We got Sky simply for the football, and are prepared to pay the Sky sports
> subscription to see it. However, I was very angry when despite paying this
> money, for what we believed was all the sport on Sky, the Bruno v Tyson
> fight [1996] was made pay-per-view. This seems to be quite wrong, and
> I would hate to think that any other big events would also be made pay-
> per-view. If football on Sky was ever pay-per-view we might be tempted to
> cancel our subscription, especially if for example you paid the same
> monthly rate to see run-of-the-mill matches, but you had to pay extra for
> big games. The thing that most worries me is that now Sky have done pay-
> per-view once, I'm sure they will do it again, we can only wait and see what
> with and how often.
>
> (18-year-old male college student)

Needless to say, Sky certainly did 'do it again'. Indeed, by September 1998
Murdoch was charging viewers £10 to see the Spice Girls live from Wembley
Stadium, just one of the sport, music and movie 'events' which subscribers
could pay extra to see. This kind of tactic, as well as the general quality of the
regular satellite and cable channels, had led these people to go one step further,
and cancel the service:

> We were without Sky the whole of December [1995], having had it virtu-
> ally since it began. We came to the conclusion that we did not watch it all
> that much, since most is dross, or repeats, or dross repeated. Even new
> films were getting few and far between compared with earlier years. At 38
> pounds per month it was, we realised very poor value. We are solely terres-
> trial these days, and have not missed Sky one little bit.
>
> (75-year-old retired man)

For over one year now we have been cable television free. We do miss the odd film and series but feel better without it. This is the same feeling from friends and neighbours who have also cancelled their subscriptions on cable television.

(43-year-old male police officer)

Both of these men seem quite *relieved* to have shaken off their satellite/cable services, the first stating proudly that he had 'not missed it one bit', and the second, in particular, talking about being 'free' and saying that he does 'feel better without it' – both like ex-addicts who are delighted to have cured themselves.

Several diarists who did not have satellite or cable said that they had quite enough to watch on the terrestrial channels already. There were moral qualms too: both about watching too much television, which as we saw in the previous chapter people quite often see as wrong – they feel they should be doing something more useful or constructive instead – and an ideological opposition to Murdoch-owned media. The latter was expressed most forcefully when the person was also a sports fan – one 34-year-old unemployed man noted that 'The big sporting occasions going on to Sky (spit) annoy me', and a male school pupil aged 17 asserted, after the introduction of pay-per-view events, 'These people are greedy and do not know when to stop. They think of their own pockets and not anyone else's.' Several other respondents also indicated their frustration that satellite TV was running off with the top sporting events.

Overall, satellite and cable TV viewers seemed less thrilled with these services than we might expect. As we have seen, some people gained real satisfaction from the sheer range of channels, or from the greater choice of movies and – funnily enough – TV repeats; but others felt that Sky's provision, in particular, was poor value or, for some, an unnecessary, overpriced bugbear from which they were relieved to have broken 'free'.

OTHER TELEVISION TECHNOLOGIES, AND THE FUTURE

Apart from the TV set itself, video was much the most important TV-related technology for our respondents, as we have seen, whilst a minority made use of the basically 'transparent' technology which brought them extra satellite or cable channels. But the diarists also discussed their use of other technologies during the course of this five-year study, as well as their visions of the future of the media in general, and interactive new technologies in particular.

Despite being gathered under the 'technologies' banner, some of these facilities are quite mundane. Teletext – the blocky text magazine which is encoded in the 'spare' lines at the top of a TV picture, and has been around since as early as 1973 – looks severely dated today. Nevertheless, the service was still experiencing slow growth in the early 1990s, with almost 40 per cent of

UK households having a teletext set, and over seven million people using the service daily (Lax 1997: 100). However, once the sophisticated and increasingly stylishly designed internet has been experienced, it can become difficult to look at teletext's uniform characters and blocky graphics. However, the internet was less well established in the first half of the 1990s, and in any case these aesthetic reservations seem not to have put off those who valued teletext for its content, if not its style. This teenager, in particular, found it compulsive:

> I called up the *TV+* section on [ITV's] Oracle Teletext to read the latest behind the scenes gossip and other viewers letters. I always like to read what other people think about television, especially what they have to say about programmes I like.
>
> Channel 4 was my next destination – for teletext again, though. *Beat Box* and *Buzz* are my daily reads on this channel giving reviews of records, environment news and all the latest pop gossip. Ever since we got a teletext TV we've found it invaluable in giving up to date news, weather, TV listings etc, at any time of the day with Oracle [ITV's service] in particular providing something for everyone.
>
> (17-year-old male student)

Teletext's most valuable contribution to viewing culture, of course, has been subtitles for the hard of hearing (indicated in Britain by the page number, 888, appearing in the corner of the screen at the start of many popular programmes). This affected and improved the TV lives of many elderly respondents. Being able to preserve the subtitles within a video recording made the facility doubly useful to this couple :

> During the last four years, a change in my viewing came about when my husband who is profoundly deaf, purchased a VCR that was able to record teletext programmes which I watch along with him.
>
> (64-year-old retired woman)

An interactive teletext service, being tested by one diarist, had given him a new virtual social life, as he explains:

> The biggest change in my life happened in May 1992 when my mother died. I am still not completely over that...TV has become a more important part of my life, because I now live alone, and cannot afford to go out very often. In 1994 I just happened to see an appeal on [the satellite channel] UK Gold for people to test a new interactive teletext service called Swan. Since then I have made many new friends among the other test users, although my phone bill has more than doubled due to my increased use of Swan, and keeping in personal touch with other Swan users.

Swan is due to open its doors soon to the general public for paying subscribers. We test users are fearful that those among us [who] cannot afford
to subscribe will be forced to leave the service when Swan goes public.

(45-year-old unemployed steelworker)

This technology – or *social use* of technology – had clearly given this respondent
a great deal of interactive pleasure, and at the same time was causing him some
anxiety with his pragmatic recognition that the company would soon start to
exploit the service financially – which he would then not actually be able to
afford. The sense of community which this interactive service has created is
sufficient for this man to write as one of a group – 'we test users' – who
evidently have shared concerns. This teletext-based system has largely failed to
take off, presumably being superseded by the Internet, which hosts similar but
broader-based virtual communities. And indeed, this diarist – if only he had
more disposable income – is just the kind of person that web moguls are hoping
there are a lot of: people who will buy into Internet-by-TV services because, as
this man wrote in 1996 (aged 46), they feel that 'the prospect of more
interactive television is exciting' and 'look forward to [services such as]
shopping from home'.

Technological futures

Several diarists speculated about the *future* of TV-related technology – all of
them quite optimistically. This man's thoughts were informed by looking *back*
at the past:

When I see old TV films or archive material I am always impressed by the
considerable improvement in the quality of TV pictures which has taken
place since we had our first set in 1953 (at the age of 39!). It makes me
wonder what other improvements can possibly be made.

(71-year-old retired male production manager)

Some people wanted more choice and greater control over what they
watched, and when – even imagining the system in some detail:

One thing I'd like is that TV was more like a library and I could call up
what programmes I wanted rather than having to abide by the TV scheduled transmissions i.e. that each week had a menu to choose from, as well
as an archive. I can only video so much and only video one thing at a time
– and it frequently turns out that what I want to see is all scheduled over-
lapping at the same time.

(45-year-old female journalist/teacher)

Another woman had fully envisaged a kind of interactive future in which, somewhat paradoxically, people would enjoy the wonders of the world by staying at home. Her argument that this electronic theatre would have environmental benefits, ironically, is probably also true:

> In the future, the TV room has screens on each wall, and similar seats for movement, smell etc. We go 'on holiday' in there to sample the delights of other countries, cultures, areas without actually going there and tramping all over there causing erosion, letting light in, plundering treasures, risking damage by fire or theft, destroying the countryside by building hotels, cutting down forests, road building etc...Instead those countries can keep their own land for themselves and can sell the videos as a sort of countryright, getting revenue that way. Saves on cost of transport too.
>
> (46-year-old housewife and company secretary/director)

This kind of technology would be likely to have a rather individualising effect, as another middle-aged diarist identified – before outlining his own futuristic lounge fantasy (or fear):

> Since the diaries began, the pace of technological change has accelerated. I would suggest that this is the last time that a survey can be undertaken of common viewing habits. In the near future our experience of television will be totally fragmented. At the beginning of these surveys [1991] technological innovation in TV was mainly concerned with video, satellite and the prospect of cable TV. Now [1996] we have such innovations as virtual reality and computers with TV quality screens. In the future – who knows, perhaps 3D, holograms and screens hung on the wall like pictures.
>
> (46-year-old unemployed male writer)

Concerns about future developments

Most respondents were generally open to ways in which television and home entertainment might develop in the future – although they were not usually as enthusiastic as the companies developing the equipment and services might expect them to be. To an extent, people were wary of businesses which wanted to fill all of their time and take all of their money in the name of some second-rate blockbusters and lots of advertising. Even those who were generally enthusiastic about new technologies were cautious about the three key concerns – *cost*, *aesthetics* and available *time*. In other words, will it rip me off? Will it be ugly? And will I have the opportunity to reap the benefits, or just be overwhelmed by a broad spectrum of dodgy content? All of these worries appear in this example:

I look forward to replacing our present receiver with a NICAM unit, but the whole home cinema scene would be too costly for us and too demanding of space in our tiny bungalow. We enjoy very good quality sound and pictures in our locality, using a roof-top antenna. Cable is not available here and I wouldn't have an unlovely satellite dish outside the house, so we continue to rely on terrestrial TV, which gives more hours of worthwhile viewing than we have time to watch, even when time-shifting with the video recorder. If digital eventually arrives, with its tiny aerial and, we believe, superb quality...we'll see!

(75-year-old retired male company director)

Concerns about the 'unloveliness' of satellite dishes – which seem to worry their owners more than one might assume – are discussed in the studies by Shaun Moores (1996) and Charlotte Brunsdon (1997). Moores found that the modernistic 'innovation' of the dishes clashed with ideas of 'tradition' and 'conservation' in relation to people's houses, so that the neighbours, friends and indeed parents of satellite-dish owners would tell them that the dish was 'vulgar' and would be considerably irritated by it. Local feuds on this subject got so heated in 1989–90 that they attracted national newspaper coverage, the subject of Brunsdon's study. The press lambasted these 'blots on the townscape' (the *Independent*) and 'the blight of the satellite dish' (*Daily Telegraph*) – with the exception of the Murdoch-owned *Times* and *Sun*, which instead chose to cover the soaring popularity of satellite TV in general and 'the fantastic range of programmes being offered by the Sky station' (as the *Sun* predictably reported it) in particular (Brunsdon 1997: 153).

Other diarists identified further, less domestic problems, such as the threat which commercial satellite, cable or digital services could pose to non-mainstream provision.

The development of satellite television and the use of teletext and more interactive communications does interest me but I do fear that more television does not always mean better – and Welsh television may be under threat when the new digital TV arrives in so far as it cannot compete in a commercial market because of the small number of Welsh speakers. The whole field of minority broadcasting does interest me – and the way in which minorities can be catered for in the age of mass communications.

(54-year-old male management lecturer)

Another seemingly well-informed diarist had related concerns about the centralised power of the minority of media producers:

While every receiver is, in principle, a transmitter and cam-corders have become easier to use and more widely distributed, the control of TV output remains rigidly centralised. And the definitions of ways of using the medium remain impoverished. How do you begin to imagine that television can be some other way than the 'active producer/passive viewer' symbiosis. Public access programming, scarce as it is, often displays astonishing technical competence. But that 'competence' is a reproduction of main stream professional routines.

(57-year-old retired man)

Finally, some people simply hoped that the new services wouldn't be rubbish.

The future? Channel 5 seems like a huge waste of money when digital TV is just round the corner. I hope digital TV is handled sensibly. The last thing we need is a proliferation of channels like Mirror Live TV!!

(24-year-old male office worker)

It would seem, then, that our sample are quite interested and curious about developments in media technology, with a few women and men imagining their own futuristic living room in which – most notably – TV takes up much more *space*, and has become more interactive and consumer led. At the same time, many are just not bothered – they feel that they have just the right amount (or, for some, too much) good TV already – and others are apprehensive: they fear that our neatly delivered, relatively cheap, high-quality TV programming will be replaced by unappealingly large screens with all sorts of wires and boxes, with extortionate subscription rates payable for lower-quality services.

ENOUGH TECHNOLOGY?

Video was seen as an extremely useful add-on to the basic television set, revolutionising the relationship between the TV and the viewer, so that the individual was in control, rather than the TV (or, more specifically, the broadcasting schedulers). People of all ages had mastered this technology, and many were using it to exercise power over the way that televisual media fitted into their life – rather than having to fit their life around the TV shows that they wanted to see. Video seemed to have become a widely accepted and used part of the 1990s household, and we did not find the gender divisions identified in some previous studies.

Other technologies, offering greater amounts of TV viewing or other forms of 'information', in the broadest sense, were not half as interesting to most of the group. Most were happy with their terrestrial TV channels, and did not really want to give up more time and money to anything else – unless, perhaps, it was something really special, catering brilliantly for their own specialised interest.

We should also note that whilst video had brought almost 'revolutionary' changes to people's ability to schedule their own preferred material, this was of course not done all of the time: most programmes were watched at the broadcast time, with certain programmes being quite fixed marker points in many people's days, as shown in chapters two and three.

SUMMARY OF KEY FINDINGS

- Video machines were used regularly by people of all ages, often on a daily basis, for moving programmes around within people's own daily schedules, entertaining children, storing and recalling favourite material, watching pre-recorded features, and other applications.
- Being able to record programmes and watch them at a later time – the 'timeshifting' function of video – constituted quite a radical change in how 'free' people were to order their own daily schedules.
- Respondents had devised 'custom' uses of their VCR in order to maximise its functionality for their own particular lifestyle and preferences: for example, by cutting too-long programmes into handy chunks, for 'caching' information which they needed, for storing video 'cuttings' on items of importance to them, for establishing international friendships, and for shifting and checking material to protect children.
- Videotape collections tended to be either archives of 'cult' television classics, owned by younger people, or sets of literary dramatisations, documentaries and classical performing arts, owned by older people.
- Satellite TV enhanced the 'virtual mobility' which TV gave to some elderly respondents.
- Most people were optimistic about the future of TV-related technology, but there were concerns about its ownership and control, and about minority interests being marginalised.
- More common and domestic concerns about new technologies and services were based around three key concerns – *cost*, *aesthetics* and available *time*; and the related feeling that perhaps the existing services were quite expensive, unattractive and plentiful enough already.

Notes

1   Comments on *Star Trek: The Next Generation* are just one of the many subjects about which we grouped quotes – because there happened to be a lot of them – whilst preparing this book, but don't really have space to use. Around 5 per cent of the whole sample offered comments on the series, and these people – almost all enthusiastic about the show – run right across the age spectrum. For example, a 39-year-old female holistic therapist felt that *Star Trek* was 'a must for our family, a time we all sit together', and a 45-year-old female teacher was engaged by the character development and 'the philosophical, ethical and psychological aspects explored in the stories'. Similarly, a 57-year-old retired nurse said that *Star Trek* had been a long-standing favourite because she liked 'the series outlook', and a draftsman aged 34 liked the way the series shed light on the 'very human 20th Century faults'

of civilisations encountered in the series. Amongst those who found it compulsive entertainment were a 63-year-old retired woman and an 18-year-old female clerical assistant who admitted 'I am highly addicted', noting that the cast 'do for tight suits and space travel what Gary Lineker and shorts did for World Cup football'. She identified with the android, Data, whom she felt 'combines ultimate intelligence with a form of consummate naivety'; unlike the 28-year-old unemployed man who wrote crossly that Data 'tries hard to be Mr Spock, but there is only one Spock'. Girls aged 16 and 17 loved the show, the latter happily 'subject[ing] the whole family' to it, and the former arguing that the series 'gives a sense of moral consciousness, promoting the idea that no matter how someone looks, you should treat them as an equal'. This diverse range of *Star Trek* fans, more than half of whom are female, again defy the sci-fi stereotype; it is perhaps significant that absolutely none of them enthused about starships, space battles or learning the 'Klingon' language, instead identifying the heart of *Star Trek* in its well-developed characters and emotional conflicts.

2   Granada's *Sherlock Holmes* series (which began as *The Adventures of Sherlock Holmes*, and became *The Return of Sherlock Holmes*, *The Casebook of Sherlock Holmes* and, finally, *Sherlock Holmes*), was a favourite with 'telefantasy' fans since the first series in 1984, although only the final series in 1993 – the one described by this diarist as 'variable' – included supernatural or vaguely sci-fi elements. Jeremy Brett – who played Holmes as an otherworldly eccentric with an occasional, flickering smile – regularly appeared at or near the top of polls of whom *Doctor Who* fans would like to see as the next Doctor.

3   Source: BARB Establishment Survey of TV homes, June 1996.

4   Based on figures cited in Mullan (1997).

Chapter 7

The retired and elderly audiences

In this chapter we will be considering the retired and older audience, who are here defined broadly as those over 60, although as Eric Midwinter has pointed out, 'the threshold of older age is the completion of work and/or family-rearing, and it could occur at any time from the 50s to the 80s' (1991: 23). Of all the 'minority' groups who have been studied by media audience researchers – or, indeed, sociologists generally – the retired and older are probably the most ignored, given their number. The General Household Survey of 1995–96 shows that 15 per cent of all UK households consisted of one person aged 60 or over, living on their own, and an additional 16 per cent of households consisted of two people, one or both of whom were aged 60 or more (Office for National Statistics 1997a). To put it another way, there were over twelve million people aged over 60 resident in the UK in 1996 – twenty per cent of the population (Office for National Statistics 1998).

Older people do watch the most television of any age group: BARB ratings for 1996 show the over-65s watching 36 hours per week, 40 per cent more than the national average (*Social Trends* 1998). We can also note that they watch significantly more than those younger people who are also unemployed (ibid.). Nevertheless, this rate of viewing – just over five hours per day – clearly leaves room for other activities, and indeed many of the older people in the Audience Tracking Study kept themselves busy, particularly those in the early stages of retirement, and leisure activities such as gardening, travelling and social club events featured strongly in their lives.

Part of the reason why the older television audience has been marginalised in most media research may be because commercial broadcasters themselves are (quietly) not very interested in older people, who are seen as the opposite of the 'sexy' 18–35 'ABC1s' – people with disposable income – who will attract advertisers; and even the BBC, not commercial but increasingly commercially minded, has arguably done little for this group. Businesses and their advertising agencies have recently shown occasional interest in the so-called 'grey pound' (a variation on other terms such as the gay 'pink pound', representing people with disposable income that advertisers might like to get their claws into), but remain, fundamentally, not very bothered about older people.

Eric Midwinter (1991) has catalogued some ways in which older people are marginalised, excluded or negatively portrayed in the media. Taking an approach similar to that of cultivation analysis (Gerbner *et al.* 1986; Morgan and Signorielli 1990), he suggests that the viewing population in general are in danger of developing the impression that the over-60s are uniformly unimportant, ill, stubborn, forgetful, childlike and dependent, or else – most prevailingly – simply non-existent. Myra Macdonald (1995) notes that this invisibility is even greater for older women than for older men in the Western media; she suggests that the close association made in our culture between beauty and identity, for women, makes the physical signs of ageing more difficult for women to deal with. This is compounded by the lack of positive representation in the mass media, the famously short 'shelf-life' of female stars who disappear from the media's gaze when they are no longer so youthfully beautiful, and the proliferation of 'advertising discourses that imply that grey hair and wrinkles are signposts towards the scrap-heap' (1995: 196).

John Tulloch (1989) is one of the few to have paid attention in the past couple of decades to the older *audience*. In a study based on interviews with twenty elderly people, Tulloch found that his subjects were keen to talk about and engage with the world of television, but being often more isolated than young people or larger families, they usually had less of an opportunity to do so. In contrast to younger science-fiction fans (whom Tulloch had studied previously), he found that these retired people – living in Bournemouth, England – related soaps and dramas to their own lives, rather than back to the shows' own on-going narratives and 'back story'. Tulloch also notes that this older audience, being less attractive to advertisers and not being organised into 'fan groups' as some younger viewers are, have to battle valiantly to protect their favourite shows – often by writing letters from their isolated positions which take strength from an assumption that 'many other viewers' share their views.

Tulloch notes that, as in a previous study of older viewers by Nancy Wood Bliese (1986), some of his interviewees were simply too busy to have much time for television, least of all in the daytime, whilst some held 'high culture' values which also put them off watching much TV. However, changing 'needs' at different stages of later life could mean that even these people could get hooked by soap operas, particularly if watching them could be 'excused' because they were on at the same time as a meal, say, so that two activities were performed simultaneously. Soaps were also found to help people focus on their daily affairs; and the themes of organisation and caring in some soaps were seen to reflect the organisation and caring inherent in the viewers' lives in their elderly people's residential home. In addition, some (at least) of the older people interviewed and observed by Tulloch watched TV in an age-conscious way, drawing attention, in their comments about programmes, to the 'older people' and contrasting them with the younger ones – being appalled, for example, when *This is Your Life* featured people of less than senior middle age, who, they contested, had not 'lived a life' at all.

Tulloch argues that elderly viewers, since there are few programmes specifically 'for' them, 'carve out' their own television space, their own '*bricolage* of generic appropriations' (1989: 194), putting together light entertainment shows and the more 'pleasant' dramas and situation comedies to form a television package that is, as some of them put it, 'at our level'. Overall, Tulloch presents a picture of his respondents as full of opinions and engagement with television, using it in a range of ways to satisfy various interests, and as a talking-point.

What do older people actually watch?

In general we would want to say that the elderly and retired audience are a diverse group who watch all kinds of material. But to be rather more specific, the national TV ratings can be broken down into different demographic groupings so that we can see which programmes are actually the most popular amongst different groups of viewers. The 'top 10' of programmes for adults aged over 55, during all of 1996, has the *Antiques Roadshow* at number 1, followed by the sitcom *Only Fools and Horses* at 2; the lightweight nostalgic police drama *Heartbeat* at 3; the least 'gritty' British soap opera, *Coronation Street*, at positions 4, 6 and 8; *Ballykissangel*, a gentle drama about a British priest in an Irish village, at 5; followed by the white-haired Oxford detective *Inspector Morse*; then *Last of the Summer Wine*, the sitcom about three ageing Yorkshire men, and another ageing detective in *A Touch of Frost* at tenth position. Other favourites included *As Time Goes By*, a sitcom about a couple in late middle age, police drama *The Bill*, countryside soap *Emmerdale*, the cosy retrospective show *This is Your Life*, the *Royal Variety Performance*, and a couple of medical dramas, *Peak Practice* and *Casualty*.[1] Whilst a few of these shows (such as *Emmerdale* and *Casualty*) may feature youngish people doing potentially offensive things, in general these programmes have in common a kind of gentleness – they do not tend to feature large amounts of on-screen violence, sex or bad language, they often have light, 'pleasant', nostalgic and middle-class themes (as opposed to reflecting the 'gritty realities' of modern urban life), and they often feature leading characters who are themselves no spring chickens.

At the end of this chapter, we put forward a theory, based on some psychological and gerontological approaches, of why many older people make the television viewing choices that they do. Whilst younger people may see their grandparents' TV selections as conservative and almost idiotically nostalgic, we find that there are sympathetic psychological reasons why people in later life may prefer certain visions of the world to others.

WHAT DOES IT MEAN TO BE OLD?

Being 'elderly' is a highly ambiguous category of identity, varying greatly from person to person, almost to the point where it can seem quite meaningless. The fact of being a certain age does not, obviously, make individuals alike. Whilst at first glance it may seem straightforward to be talking about 'the over 60s' or 'the elderly' as a social group, it soon becomes apparent that generalising about 'older people and the media' can be about as coherent as seeking to generalise about the television use of respondents with blue eyes. That the material should be so resistant to generalisation and categorisation is, of course, a refreshing finding in itself, and accords with recent academic thinking on questions of identity.

The 'identity politics' of the 1970s and 1980s encouraged members of particular identity categories – women, ethnic minorities, the elderly, and so on – to speak out on behalf of others of 'their kind', and to emphasise the universal nature of their experience. Identity theory in the 1990s, however, has blown a hole in the assumptions underpinning such an approach. In her book *Gender Trouble* (1990), Judith Butler pulled the carpet from under these seemingly benign arguments. First she noted that feminist arguments which emphasised the universal experience of women were problematic as they assumed that being female was more important than any other factors such as class, race, sexuality or age. This had been noted previously by some black women, and others, who were unconvinced when white middle-class Western feminists had claimed to be in the same oppressed situation as women in the Third World. Butler took the argument one step further, stating that it philosophically *makes no sense* to base any position on the idea of binary genders, women and men, as these terms have no fixed meaning. There are no essential, universal facts associated with being a woman. Even the basic ones, like 'being able to have children', quickly fall apart, since not all women can have children, and most women spend a great deal of time not having children, one way or another. Age is a similarly fluid category. Whilst old age *can* involve chewing wine gums whilst shouting pointlessly at snooker broadcasts and waiting for *Barrymore*, this is far from being a universal experience. More importantly, there is no philosophical justification for treating a large proportion of the population who are over a certain age – 20 per cent over 60 in 1996 – as being a 'group' at all. On the other hand, it is sociologically useful to consider them as a social group who often face the same obstacles, prejudices and injustices, even if this is not *universally* the case. Nevertheless, we will see that this study shows that the over-60s are – unsurprisingly – diverse in their interests, abilities and concerns. Perhaps their most common characteristic is that they feel, to lesser or greater extents, misunderstood.

The question of 'who are the elderly?' is, therefore, a good place to start, by considering how members of this 'group' see themselves. Since their only collective achievement is, in effect, that they have got through sixty or more years without dying, do they consider their seniority to be an influential part of their lives?

Some of the respondents argued that television programmes had become increasingly youth-oriented, to the expense of older viewers. As previous studies have noted (Coleman 1991), the elderly often feel marginalised by what they see as the youth orientation of society in general, and mass media in particular. Indeed, Rabbitt has said that 'people now aged 80 are time-travellers, exiled to a foreign country which they now share with current twenty year-olds' (1984: 14). Whilst most viewers would find it easy to recognise the youth-friendly TV traits aimed at the latter group – young presenters, dance music, fast pacing, hectic or over-designed graphics, and noise – interesting questions are raised about what the parallel 'elderly-friendly' characteristics would be. The diarists largely sidestepped these issues; elderly self-identity was not pinned down except in terms of what it is not.

> It seems that people in my situation are very neglected. The programme makers cater for the younger people – yet they are the ones who go out.
>
> (74-year-old retired female lecturer)

> [Between 1991 and 1996 I have noticed a] tendency to cater more for younger viewers. It is as if senior citizens no longer count.
>
> (72-year-old retired male BBC engineer)

Perhaps the respondents remain vague about what kinds of programmes they would like to see more of because it would be difficult and counterproductive to characterise 'the interests of the elderly'. Would the style of their shows be the actual *opposite* of the youth-TV characteristics listed above – and therefore involve elderly presenters, classical music, drowsy pacing, large graphics, and a general air of tranquillity?

Some younger respondents found it much easier to identify (with disdain) 'old people's programmes', often shown on Sunday evening, such as the *Antiques Roadshow* and the sitcom *As Time Goes By*. The truth is, of course, that the audience for such shows is not limited to the over-60s, and that those over 60 are not united in their love of these programmes. However, it must be said that many of the senior respondents listed typical sets of 'oldie favourites'.

> I grumble so much, is there nothing that pleases me? Yes. *Inspector Morse*, *Miss Marple*, *Poirot* (not just because I like detective escapism). They are all extremely well done, with typical British attention to period detail and finish. *Antiques Roadshow*. Similarly programmes on collecting and collections. Programmes like *Armada*, *Nicholas Nickleby*. Serialised books and classics. *Songs of Praise*, *Hymns on Sunday*, indoor bowling, *Last of the Summer Wine*.
>
> (72-year-old retired male schoolteacher)

> My favourite is *As Time Goes By* – because the acting is superb – so real life
> and no bad language, no gratuitous sex – a gentle amusing sitcom and of
> course I love the music that introduces and closes it. Judi Dench is a
> favourite of mine but everyone is so well cast in their part – more more
> please – I don't mind how many repeats – I love it!!
>
> (74-year-old housewife)

The reasoning behind these choices – being 'gentle', and part of a perceived
national culture, with attention to nostalgic period detail and the security of
knowing that unwanted language or sex scenes were not going to affront the
unsuspecting viewer – is in keeping with conventional notions of 'older people's
taste'. Indeed, this man in his seventies wraps up what seems like an unselfconscious tirade with his own humorous self-diagnosis:

> I think this survey should have asked for programmes we detest. These are
> 'chat shows', 'game shows', the *National Lottery* and Anthea Turner,
> hospital and most general police, fire, ambulance, and soldier series (except
> for *Morse*), *Coronation Street*, *EastEnders*, *Gladiators*, football, homosexu-
> als and female impersonators like Lily Savage, *The Sunday Show* with Donna
> McPhail and Katie Puckrick,...weather presenters who are too anxious to
> become a 'personality' than to clearly enunciate properly, 'pop groups'
> plonking their guitars to pitiful songs and unable to 'sing' without swal-
> lowing the microphone. I could go on, but I guess you can get the drift
> that I'm just an old codger!
>
> (72-year-old retired male probation officer)

This 'old codger's' taste – which seems to comprehensively rule out much
contemporary programming – again seems to leave room only for serious,
historical and rather sedate shows. This may not be a condition which imposes
itself onto people as they become older, however. This respondent singles out
the same 'elderly' choices but claims that she has brought these interests with
her throughout her life:

> I remember *Civilization* by Sir Kenneth Clarke as being a really marvellous
> series. And the various David Attenborough nature series of course. *An-
> tiques Roadshow* – I really look forward to that. *Chronicle*, *Horizon*, *Time-
> watch*, *One Foot in the Past* – that type of programme, I normally always try
> to watch and always have done. I've been interested in history, literature,
> art since I was at school so I enjoy programmes in these fields and I try to
> keep up with advances in science as best I can.
>
> (59-year-old retired female civil servant)

Elsewhere there is evidence that 'maturer' viewing tastes are grown into over
time: a 34-year-old man – whilst far from being elderly – reported, in 1996,

being 'bloody annoyed' that he had become 'more old fashioned, more fuddy-duddy' than when he began this study, aged 29. Some of the older respondents are willing to accept that their own preferences have fallen behind the times.

> A lot of the 'comedy' they now show on Fridays doesn't do anything for me. I guess I'm just getting old!
>
> (66-year-old farmer's wife)

Others remain unsure whether it is the 'actual' quality of programmes, or their own tastes, which are changing – something which, by the very nature of subjectivity and memory, will always be difficult to distinguish.

> TV isn't what it used to be – we miss Morecambe and Wise, Benny Hill, the *Generation Game*, progs were wonderful years ago, now we never watch the stand up comics, to us they are not funny, unless our tastes have changed – we don't watch *The Bill* or any of the police progs, there again they are nothing like *Z Cars* and *Dixon of Dock Green*, so maybe it is us – maybe our tastes have changed.
>
> (66-year-old housewife)

In particular, a number of the more elderly diarists were very concerned, and indeed upset, about what they perceive as a modern style of programme-making where graphics and visual effects are too fast – to the extent where a handful of the more fretful feel that they will become ill – and, more importantly perhaps, where background music is felt to have drowned out speech in a programme. It is clear that these respondents, rather than objecting to the idea of incidental music *per se*, have developed hearing problems which mean that it is hard to differentiate distinct kinds of sounds. Their objection to music tracks tinkling away behind speech in TV programmes – particularly where it serves a negligible purpose, such as in news and current affairs shows – is therefore a serious concern which has much in common with other disabled access issues (the idea that services should be as accessible to as broad a range of people as possible).

Unfortunately for their own case, these respondents do not set out their argument in such terms. Instead, almost all of those who evidently have failing sight or hearing seem to overlook this and think that programmes are simply being *made differently*, so that none of the audience are able to enjoy these badly mixed shows. Rather than acknowledging their own hearing difficulties, they berate broadcasters for making programmes which they seem to believe are objectively incomprehensible to the entire audience. (This has also been the case with letters on the subject shown on the BBC's feedback show *Points of View*, and enables broadcasters to ignore the complaints, since they are clearly mistaken.) Whilst there would be a strong case for saying that broadcasters should be more sympathetic to those with hearing difficulties in their sound mixing, these complainants undermine their own position by making generalised assertions about incompetent programme-makers who make self-defeating shows with inaudible soundtracks. The point here is not that these are strange individuals; rather, the fact that so many of them make the same mistake suggests that it is a curious facet of human nature, that – whilst we seem well able to admit to most kinds of physical ailment – we are unable or unwilling to accept that our *perceptions* are not what they once were.

In an age of fast-moving, blink-and-you-miss-it mass media, where sharp perceptions are presumed by most media providers, this raises complex questions of access, which – the provision of subtitles on selected programmes aside – have been generally ignored by broadcasters. This contrasts sharply with contemporary concerns in the computer and internet publishing world, where issues of disabled access seem to get more attention.

It must be said, too, that not all of the complaints about 'trendy' new presentation styles were from people with hearing or vision difficulties. Some people simply didn't like these fast-paced and boisterous approaches.

> Some of the advertisements have become much more noisy with flashing lights, and the camera rushing up to the faces and back. I'm sure it can't be good for our eyes. I switch off these adverts. On the other hand some adverts are very clever and more interesting than some programmes! *The Clothes Show* has also changed. A lot of racy bang-bang-bang, so called 'music' and racing images on your brain. I used to watch it. I don't watch it any more.
>
> (67-year-old retired female secretary)

The self-identity of elderly viewers is thrown into the spotlight most conspicuously by programmes which seek to *address* the over-60s audience. By addressing a particular group, such programmes inevitably characterise (or caricature) their presumed audience in everything that they say. In the early 1990s, the BBC's series *Prime Time* – by explicitly seeking to entertain and inform senior citizens – risked annoying its audience at every turn, precisely because that audience is presented with an unusually focused opportunity to say 'What makes you think I'd be interested in *that*?' to the programme-makers. The broadcasters, for their part, have the unenviable task of navigating through a series of pitfalls – being too patronising, too depressing, too cheerful, too serious, too trivial. *Prime Time*, with its tellingly upbeat title, took the cautious route of presenting on screen a kind of Radio Two style cosiness, combined with 'you're having the time of your life!' positivity. This was not universally popular.

> 3.05–3.50, BBC1, *Prime Time*. About wrinklies, by wrinklies, for wrinklies. By the treacly David Jacobs. A gruesome 45 mins. In my throat, a lump of disgust. Expected 'Knees Up Mother Brown', instead got a decrepit

Sir J Mills doing a geriatric tap dance. Plus a heavenly chorus of polyure-
thane sentimentality. Sickening, oleaginous, is this how the BBC think of
me? God save me from David Jacobs.

(74-year-old retired male engineer)

The aghast 'is this how the BBC think of me?' says it all, of course. This
man, trying to retain some dignity in later life, is presented with what he sees
as a hideous, embarrassing programme by the BBC who say – 'This is for
you'.

Of course, different people have different perceptions. A (younger) retired
female nurse said that 'As I am 61 years [*Prime Time*] is just right for me',
and she found satisfaction in its stories about sleeplessness, gardening, 'a vicar
who handles fireworks', and 'some 'gutsy' elderly ladies...abseiling!'. A 74-
year-old woman found it 'a pleasant programme, with good variety'. This
respondent was, nevertheless, wary of being talked down to, concluding that
the show was 'not patronising except perhaps for first item on the difficulty of
getting a night's sleep'. A retired male chemist, aged 59, found it 'sedate' but
entertaining.

The American situation comedy *The Golden Girls* also prompted some
interesting comments about age. The show, about four elderly women, was
produced by NBC from 1985 to 1992. The programme was quickly picked up
in Britain by Channel Four, and as one of their most successful comedy series,
the 179 episodes have been shown and repeated well into the 1990s. *The
Golden Girls* was highly regarded by several respondents for its clever, witty
portrayal of older women which managed to combine its humour with
intelligent consideration of the treatment of older people in society. The show
had great appeal to this diarist, an active woman of nearly 70, who was living
alone in Merseyside, and was retired but engaged in voluntary work several
times a week:

The Golden Girls. Long my favourite American comedy series, I watch the
repeats with even more interest. No other series to me has dealt with the
subject of ageism with such insight, particularly on the issues which have to
be faced when growing older. I never fear old age. What frightens me is the
attitude in general of society to this state.

I have heard the opinions raised against *The Golden Girls* that it is 'over
the top' and unrealistic and maybe it is. But it is not afraid to face issues
which are unpleasant, death, loneliness, illness, fear of rejection, with wit
and charm which have left British series on similar subjects standing. I have
at times been so angry at the way old age has been portrayed here that I
have written in the past to the companies concerned. One comparison on
the same night I found very hard to take was the laughter with the 'Golden
Girls' when they found it increasingly difficult to hold down jobs which
was very, very funny as well as being true, and that of a British series where

the laughter was aimed at showing age through the suspected incontinence of two elderly ladies.

Realistic or not I'm certain that it is only through more images of age on the lines of *The Golden Girls* that is going to give age the attention and the dignity it deserves.

(69-year-old retired female teacher)

Another woman aged 73 felt that the appeal of the show for herself, and for her friends of the same age, was that it was built upon 'a grain of authenticity in the attitudes of the golden girls'. It was 'the best comedy available on TV at present' – despite being American, which they did not usually like – and they 'admired' the central characters. Other retired people made similar remarks. At the same time, a 20-year-old student was just one of the younger respondents who also mentioned that he usually watched *The Golden Girls*: 'It's just it's really original and something about it "clicks"'. This would be good news for the show's older fans, since they particularly liked it for taking positive and well-considered images of old age to a mass audience.

To summarise, we have seen that it is difficult to establish a singular 'identity' for the elderly or retired audience, who are actually a heterogeneous and diverse set of individuals (as we will see further below). Whilst some programming is made in an identifiably 'youthful' style which leaves some older viewers feeling excluded, it is not so easy to define what an 'older' approach would involve. It is certainly more common for the over-60s to praise programmes for being gentle and pleasant, for avoiding 'gratuitous' sex, bad language and violence, and for steering clear of the noise and over-animated presentation associated with younger people's shows. At the same time, when faced with programmes aimed explicitly at the older audience, they resolutely reject both the patronising 'inspirational' approach, and the Radio Two style invitation to 'take things easy' with what they considered to be, frankly, substandard entertainment. Only *The Golden Girls* clearly hit the right mark: neither seeking to hide nor make fun of the age of its stars, the sitcom was rated for its frank, witty, constructive approach to later life. Although the diversity of the over-60 section of the sample meant that they were not going to agree on a single preferred mode of representation, *The Golden Girls* offered an 'identity' and reflection of retirement to older viewers which they found pleasing and, indeed, inspirational, in a subtle, clever way which was much preferred to being given encouragement and advice in annoyingly upbeat shows aimed explicitly at their age group.

LIFE IN RETIREMENT

Writing about older people in relation to television can unfairly reinforce assumptions that people, after a certain age, simply don't go out. Television remains, on the whole, a very stationary technology, and – unlike radios, recorded music, newspapers, magazines and books – usually requires its audience to be sitting in a particular place, such as the living room, facing in a particular direction. Whilst the retired usually have more time to be in this position, it should not be thought that they come to mimic television's inertia, and we should be wary of studies which, by focusing on TV viewing, create the impression that its participants don't do anything else.

For many of the diarists in the Audience Tracking Study, life was far from sedate, as these 'slices of life' demonstrate:

> On Wednesday mornings we usually go to our vintage snooker club in our nearest town. I like snooker but I am no Stuart Hendry. On Friday mornings we go to a vintage sports club at the same venue. I swim, play snooker, archery, keep-fit class, have lunch, go home mid-afternoon.
>
> We try to have a brisk walk each day on either the hill on the North side of the village, or the [moorland hill] on the south side. At weekends we go on longer walks.
>
> (67-year-old female voluntary charity fundraiser)

> I belong to a local history group which usually takes up Wednesday afternoon but [today] we have no class. So if it is warm enough I will be busy in the garden. Mondays are taken up by Townswomen's Guild work as I am publicity secretary for the local guild – and write short notes to the local paper. We have a busy guild with an Arts and Crafts meeting on Thursday afternoons where all sorts of hobbies are followed.
>
> (70-year-old retired woman)

Some diarists had so much to fit into their retired life that the written list itself would take on a frenzied quality.

> I work mornings – out shopping, or housework and gardening. TV on for news at 1pm if in, then turned off until about 4.30. Occasional film watched if weather bad. Out two afternoons with friends, walking sometimes whole day in Dales. To daughter's house once a week, or out in daughter's car. Red Cross meeting with speaker (monthly). Day trips with NALGO, Health Authority (retired member) or Red Cross.
>
> One day a week – lunch at church hall. Evenings – either gardening or watching TV to 9.30. Reading in bed for an hour. Up each day before 8 am. TV not exceptionally important. Verse written and typed for local conservation magazine. Letters typed to family and numerous friends in other towns. Competitions in women's and TV magazines entered. Supermarket either Thursday or Friday afternoon. Phoning kept to a minimum because of low income. Visiting elderly, (sometimes housebound people).

Visiting sick members of the retired Health Authority either in their home or hospital.

(67-year-old retired female secretary)

Of course, these respondents represent the most healthy and active band of this age range. However, the people who are retired cannot easily be grouped into those who are ill and those who are well – rather, the diaries show that health can fluctuate quite considerably (from poor health to good, as well as the other way around) over five years, as well as varying greatly between different respondents of the same age. As diarists got older, issues of health and the death of loved one(s) rose to greater prominence. In the following sections, we will see that income, health and the family are three key factors in the number of changes that occur in the everyday lives of these people. For those diarists who have a more generous income, relatively good health, and regular contact with friends and family, it can be seen that they are more likely to find television of less importance in their lives than other leisure activities, such as gardening, or visiting friends. However, those diarists – the majority in this study – who have an insubstantial or low income, moderate or poor health, and intermittent contact with friends and family are more likely to find television increasingly important in their lives: TV replaces other leisure activities to become a primary source of entertainment and information.

The transition into retirement

The way that respondents discuss the issue of retirement would suggest that this life transition is perceived in a number of different ways. Retirement can be a positive and rewarding experience, but it can also be a difficult and traumatic time. What is more, as Chris Phillipson suggests, 'retirement is shaped at least as much by continuities and discontinuities in life experiences' (1990: 156). Thus, diarists can alter their perception of retirement over a period of time depending on other life factors, such as health, outside interests and family relationships. Often the changes that take place in relation to retirement are subtle ones, such as going to bed earlier, or watching television at lunchtime.

These two women give very different accounts of retirement:

There were no changes to my life until October 1992 when I retired from my job in the Health Service. I was Personal Assistant to the Director of Facilities at my local hospital. It was an interesting and very busy job. After 19 years there retiring was shattering. Working then waking up the next day to nothing…no company and no-one to chat to.

(67-year-old retired female health service PA)

I retired one month ago and just can't believe how wonderful life is. It is like being born again, and freedom to do what I like whenever I like. It is like riding the crest of a wave and always being at the top. I am able to watch TV whenever I want and then stay up till the early hours watching TV. I am able to watch a good British film without worrying about work the next day. My husband (accountant) has also just retired so we do household chores together, and spend a lot of time socialising, meeting friends watching TV and going out to concerts and seeing films. All the family relax in the evenings. In the summer we sit out on the beach garden till late. In winter we all enjoy watching TV around the coal fire and rent videos at weekends.

(59-year-old retired female community nurse)

For the first respondent, retirement is obviously a very negative experience. Her work was very important to her, and offered a social network that she does not have anymore. The concept of 'nothing', nothing to wake up to, no one to talk to, no set tasks to perform, suggests that this respondent has a strong work ethic and found it difficult to make the transition into a leisured lifestyle. With the second diarist, we can see that family and friends play an important part of her retirement. For this respondent, the image of rebirth serves to indicate that retirement is something she has looked forward to; it now offers her freedom and energy, something she felt she did not have to the same extent when she was in employment. Here, retirement involves a number of different leisure activities, with her husband and with her family, in an almost idealised setting.

For people in the early stages of retirement, life was often very busy. Many diarists wrote about the lack of time they had to watch television, and a strong work ethic ensured that a majority of these people said they did not really like to watch television before 5pm in the day – a point which will recur in this chapter. This meant that during the day people in early retirement were engaged in a number of different activities, such as pursuing hobbies like gardening or writing, or taking part in charity work and family responsibilities, such as childcare.

Since the diaries started the only change in my life has been that I have retired (1993). The only difference in my lifestyle is that I don't go to work anymore. My hobbies have expanded to fill the time available. I do more cooking than I used to. My TV watching is exactly the same as before except that as I don't go out to work in the evenings I don't have to record so much! I rarely watch TV during 'working' hours unless it is snowing or something, as I feel slightly guilty that I'm not getting on with some job and with three and a half acres to look after no wonder.

(60-year-old retired male helicopter engineer)

I am retired, and over the past 4 years my involvement in charity work has increased, by holding more fundraising coffee mornings, and writing more

letters and articles on behalf of these charities. I had to cut back on TV –
but I do enjoy what I watch, and would not be without it.

(63-year-old retired female secretary)

For both of these diarists, retirement has not led to increased television viewing.
The first respondent uses 'working hours' to devote time to gardening and
cooking and the second respondent is so busy with charity work that she cannot
watch as much TV as she would like: for example, she has had to abandon
watching the soap *Emmerdale*.

Stability and change in retired life

As respondents became older and more accustomed to retirement, they
generally noticed an increase in the amount of television that they watched. If
we take a closer look at the female diarist who said that retirement was
'shattering' at the start of the previous section, we can see how she altered her
perception of retirement over a period of time. Before her retirement she wrote:
'I am 60ish and a widow. Television is very important to me. As soon as I wake
it is switched on. It is like having others in the room with me.' She watched
three or four hours of television a day, which along with her busy and engaging
full-time work – the centre for her social contacts – seemed to keep her quite
happy. Retirement in 1992 ejected her sharply from the world of her colleagues
and work which had been so important in her life, and everyday life therefore
became very difficult. After the death of her husband, it would seem that this
woman's whole sense of identity had become rather dependent on her working
life; losing that was a fundamental shock. However, she later began a watercol-
our painting course at a local college, and started to go out on day trips with a
friend (although this friend later moved away). In 1995 she wrote:

> As far as TV was concerned I did watch more on retirement – for a start I had
> never watched during the day before, so I tried some – like *Kilroy*, and *This
> Morning*. They vary in interest from day to day. I still occasionally watch
> these. Currently I don't find afternoon programmes very good – a lot of
> repeats. The fact that I am a widow and live alone means I watch TV more.
> Sometimes it is just background, but this occasionally gets me interested in
> various topics. In the earlier days of retirement my best friend and I went out
> quite often, but before Christmas she was unwell and moved to live with her
> daughter – another reason for being at home and watching more TV. TV is
> important to me, especially Monday to Friday. I assess programmes daily and
> if I am going out record anything I wish to see. I see my family more at
> weekends. I don't watch much during the day. I still check though and
> record if necessary. Although I drive, being on my own I seldom go out at
> night in the winter so TV really is important during this season.

(67-year-old retired female health service PA)

Here we can see how television came to play an increasingly important role in this woman's life in the three years following retirement. She would half-heartedly sample daytime TV, although the programmes were not always to her taste. Once her friend had moved away, the diarist found herself alone at home even more, and the daily planning of TV viewing became a more routine operation. The day of the week and the time of year were also an influence on how much television she would watch. Gradually taking a more established role in her life, television seems to have helped this diarist come to terms, at least in part, with the amount of leisure time which retirement brings.

Some of the older diarists liked to go out to the cinema. During the course of this study, the number of multiplex cinemas in Britain continued to rise dramatically. These cinemas, usually away from town centres and with lots of well-lit parking, are able to attract older would-be cinema-goers who had previously given up travelling into city centres, which are perceived as busy and dangerous. This diarist explains:

> When I was young, we had no TV, no videos and no TV games, no drugs. We could go out at night to the theatre or cinema, and walk home late, and never ever think of being 'mugged' or attacked.
>
> (63-year-old retired female nurse)

In 1986 there were just 18 multiplex cinemas in Britain. By 1991 this had shot up to 510, building steadily to 875 in 1996.[2] On the whole, the over-60s, like a majority of the over-35s in fact, do not go to cinemas. However, a handful still made the effort to go, with even the oldest, 88-year-old woman saying, at the end of this study in 1996, 'I have been fortunate to find friends [recently] with whom to enjoy my usual pastimes – bridge, theatre, cinema'. Although multiplexes are generally frequented by young people and fitted out in a garish neon-lit interpretation of youthful style, they still did not deter the more determined older cinema-goer, who found them preferable to other possible kinds of evening out:

> Since the opening of an MGM multiplex cinema in Belfast I do now go to the cinema more often, both with my wife and on my night out with my friend – as neither of us are heavy drinkers – so a night in a pub is not to our taste.
>
> (60-year-old male civil engineer)

Social and economic factors, of course, are influential here. For some, cinema is a welcome escape from the household.

> Weekends I don't watch much [television], except in the evenings if our son is home for the weekend he stays up very late and watches documentaries and political programmes. We don't have a video. I go to the cinema, I prefer it that way as it is a change of scenery.
>
> (62-year-old retired female teacher)

More commonly, trips to the cinema were the stuff only of fond memories. Harsh financial realities ruled them out. This man, for example, said that 'Films are the main interest of my wife and I', but they now were enjoyed only on television and video:

> We no longer have any desire to go out in the evenings. There is no longer a cinema in [town] and as we drink very little there is no desire to go to the pub – particularly of an evening...My parents did not get on well when I was a boy and to get out of the situation my mother used to 'escape' with me to the cinema. I thus saw many classic films during Hollywood's Golden Years. After marriage, my wife and I continued to enjoy the cinema for many years until it declined and the admission prices etc went skywards.
>
> (68-year-old retired male probation officer)

This view of cinema prices shooting through the roof appears again below, and put into the context of the increasingly heavy financial burdens which the elderly must find a way to accommodate.

> [1992] Shorter of money, now that interest rates have dropped steeply and various unavoidable charges (water, Council Tax, electricity – and TV licence) have risen remorselessly. TV has now become our main source of information and entertainment, since newspaper prices and the cost of theatre and cinema seats have rocketed.
>
> [1995] We now tend to spend most of our evenings indoors. We live six miles outside [south-west city], so confine our visits to the city to daytime shopping trips, about once a week. As pensioners we are no longer able to afford cinema and theatre tickets, except for one or two visits a year – we saw *Forrest Gump* at a matinee...long before it won its Oscars.
>
> (retired male photographer, aged 71 and 74)

Indeed, for many retired diarists, the diminished income meant that they were less likely to choose other leisure activities over watching television, which was recognised as relatively cheap in comparison to going to the cinema, or eating out. This diarist puts it quite succinctly when he writes:

> There have been few changes of any real significance [over the past four years] which have seriously altered our lifestyle – except that our own standard of living has deteriorated, very slowly and insidiously. In this respect we actually go out for meals and entertainment a good deal less than we used to. Hardly at all.
>
> (72-year-old retired male schoolteacher)

Some diarists felt that their lack of income was compounded by the fact that others did not seem to appreciate the extent of retired people's poverty. Again, in such a situation we see that television (and radio) become much more important within the limited range of affordable entertainments:

> Money is a bit of a problem but one learns to do without things. I wish the cost of living figures were based on more realistic items. I know that my pension doesn't increase at anything like the rate of the price of gas, electricity, water, food and clothing. The cost of theatres, concerts, cinema etc has increased and consequently TV and radio play a greater part in my life.
>
> (74-year-old retired female heath planner)

Some respondents felt resentful about the decrease in income due to their retirement. This self-employed man wrote at some length about being forced to retire because of an ailing business:

> The main change has been growing economic panic. We had two shops. I (now 65) ran the man's shop which we had to close in Feb '94. I have done nothing financially useful since. My wife (63) still runs the woman's shop and the takings are going down rapidly and we face bankruptcy. (Satellite villages are losing out completely to one-stop shopping-complexes. A retailing colleague said to me recently: 'I wish I could have had this final bit of life with more dignity.') So TV's main purpose is distraction and comforter. I rely on a framework of the popular favourites (*The Bill, University Challenge, Neighbours*, repeats such as *Auf Weidersehen Pet*) to keep me going. Probably watch the same amount, going to bed earlier, recording later films I never see. (In fact, films are the major disappointment: the scale is wrong, the effect lost.) I no longer watch (so much or even at all) the arts or current affairs programmes; they seem trivial or irrelevant. But it would be an empty, anxious house without the evening TV. And I have lost my appetite for reading. I'm whinging.
>
> (65-year-old retired male retail assistant)

The loss of his business has made this respondent feel that he has been forced into early retirement, and forced into a difficult financial situation. The quotation from a colleague is telling. The description of his life now he has retired is quite different from his description of life whilst at work (in the 1991 diaries), when going to the pub for an hour after work was a regular feature of the day. By 1995, evening television had replaced this, becoming important as a distraction from his anxieties, although he shows some signs of irritation at particular programmes which do not seem to give him the same enjoyment as in the past. Other leisure activities have been dropped in favour of television, but television is only able to offer mild consolation, and no real satisfaction.

Of course, we do not want to create the impression that life after 60 is a story of bad times getting worse. The following diarist reminds us that not all positive life changes happen in early or middle age – and that they are often nothing to do with television:

> [This year I] started a new relationship. After many years of indecision I realised I was gay and have formed a strong relationship with [my male partner]. Also: last October I stopped smoking (after 40 years of bondage to the weed!).
>
> (63-year-old retired male Relate coordinator)

Two years later, this man went on to comment:

> I have discovered that even being in the older age group does not mean the end of life. During the period [of this study] I met [my male partner] and have come to think a great deal of him. One day, we might decide to share a home together.
>
> (as above, aged 65, 1996)

Here, happily, we have a man for whom fresh new horizons, new ways of living are appearing, *after* a period in his life where, it would seem, he had perhaps given up hope that life would get better. Even his contributions to this study's five years of diaries reflect this, with the earlier ones spartan and uninterested (or simply not returned), the later ones much more vigorous, lively and opinionated.

As respondents entered into later stages of retirement, however, they were more likely to experience illness, and spells in hospital. This could have an effect on the role television played in their lives. Most diarists were aware that they used television as a means to recuperate from a period of ill health. Here, watching television becomes a useful exercise that involves little physical exertion and can be beneficial because of increased relaxation and long periods of rest. The following diarist describes how her pattern of television viewing altered during and after a period in hospital, which we see moving through three different stages, the last of which is a reduced version of her original habits:

> I broke my wrist in December 1993 and had barely recovered when I broke my left hip and elbow in the autumn of 1994. The latter injuries necessitated a spell in hospital followed by three months in my son's house. In hospital I was exposed to programmes which I found positively repellent. At my son's, my viewing had a different pattern and I was introduced to some sit-coms and saw a lot of very old films (often black and white) mostly videoed from Channel 4. Since I came home my viewing has reverted mostly to my previous pattern. Since I am not yet fully fit, I normally go earlier to bed and sometimes miss late programmes. Also I am not out so often in the afternoons and can watch the programmes from Parliament.
>
> (70-year-old retired female bookkeeper)

Another example illustrates other changes that can take place after someone has had a visit to hospital:

> This past winter I have spent 3 months in and out of hospital and in again twice. I was offered a TV for rental but I didn't bother. I felt no desire for it. I did not even go down to the rest room to watch communal TV. I didn't miss it. I no longer watch question and answer progs. They seem so banal. I don't know if this a consequence of being ill, but now that I am home, I watch more TV than before. I scan the *Radio Times* trying desperately to find something worth the while. I have resumed my walking and photography. I am really grateful for the 'Wild Life' programmes and other natural history progs.
>
> (68-year-old retired male inspection engineer)

Once again, this diarist – seeming somewhat deflated by the whole hospital experience – describes a series of stages in his illness and in his television viewing. Whilst in hospital, he feels no desire to watch television, and upon his return home he notices a change in the type of programmes he wants to watch. Other leisure activities appear to be important to his recovery, and influence the type of TV programme which he chooses. Illness seems to bring a desire to watch more television, then, for comfort and entertainment during recovery, and can also be a time of change in viewing patterns as the individual seeks material which matches their state of mind as they struggle to achieve some stability of health.

Coping with grief

Unsurprisingly, another theme runs through the lives, and therefore contributions, of the older respondents: that of loss. This was particularly common for the female diarists – in Britain, half of the women over 65 are widowed.[3] Whilst the deaths of loved ones would obviously be upsetting to say the least, the diarists tended to write about these losses in a stoical, concise way. We cannot doubt that these deaths were perhaps devastating to those who remained, but the written accounts might suggest that, as people get older, they come to expect – to some extent – that not all of their friends and relatives will be around forever, and that, of course, they themselves are not immortal. (Peter Coleman (1990) notes that whilst the approach of gerontologists to old age has often been focused on crisis, illness, loss and misery, many surveys and studies show that the elderly cope surprisingly well with their circumstances, and, indeed, generally report high levels of life satisfaction. Given that loss is likely to figure often in their lives, he notes, 'the rates of depression observed in later life are not remarkably high but remarkably low' (1990: 90).)

The way in which television fits into the process of grief and the prospect of living alone in older age is complex. Often, television (and radio) becomes a welcome friend, something to listen to whilst alone in the house. However, television can also serve as a reminder of what once was, and a marker of loneliness. Thus television can be a double-edged sword in relation to the grieving process. The following quote, from 1995, sets out movingly a number of themes: the transition into more noticeable 'old age', the on-going pain of grief and loss, and overcoming it through the pleasure of new life.

> In May 1991 I was still only 68, now (quite recently) I do feel 'elderly'. I am by now nine years on from my husband's death in January 1986, and have grown used to living alone. I am neither the J. [maiden name] of my youth nor D.'s wife, but a new character who has developed from both, distilling her experience. In 1991, I had two four-year old grand-daughters and the new baby grand-daughter Natalie; now I have also two grandsons. My relationship with these five young people has helped immeasurably to ease the blow of D.'s loss. Yet I found it very sad – almost unfair – that he had not lived to watch with me the inauguration of Nelson Mandela as president of a Liberated South Africa.
>
> (72-year-old retired woman)

The latter point reflects the power of seeing world events on television, and the importance of sharing these experiences with others – and sadness when one no longer can. In the next example, being unable to share television viewing (or other activities) with her late husband meant that the diarist, in 1991, felt little inclination to do it at all. A pet dog had given her an on-going reason to be active, and afforded some company. By the end of this five-year study, he had also died.

> [1991] My life has completely altered since becoming a widow five years ago...I do find winter evenings long and miss my husband so I tend to go to bed early...I am lucky with my health, just a few odd aches now and then – the worst of course being the ever constant ache at the loss of my husband.
>
> [1995] Lost a small dog which has left me a rather longer day on my own. Trying to do more reading – have dropped some activities as I do not now want too many outside commitments...[Television has increased in importance to me over the past five years] very much – especially this last few months. Having lost my little dog I do not walk out quite so much. Also as I get older I am inclined to watch more than I did.
>
> (retired female telephonist, aged 78 and 82)

This woman managed to cope with some of her on-going grief in the earlier years of this study by spending time participating in activities run by 'Life Long Learning', an organisation for retired people which encouraged learning about 'whatever interests people request' in groups, as well as social occasions, musical performances and outings. However, older age (by her own account) caused interest in this, and other things, to wane.

Another diarist also learned to cope with the death of her daughter by ensuring that her life was extremely busy. Like the diarist above, she also lost a beloved pet dog, and this was the first time in forty years that she did not have a dog to walk every day. She writes:

> Three years ago my only daughter died – now I am quite alone. I coped with grief by keeping myself occupied, and in attempting to answer your question see I have done this rather too thoroughly – I haven't time to sit and watch TV until after 7.30 even if I wanted to now, and am often out in the evenings at meetings. Wildlife programmes and gardening programmes of various types continue to be excellent, and very good viewing – no complaints there. Sit-coms – mostly very poor, and depressingly un-funny, so seldom stay with any for more than the first ten minutes of the first one in any new series. TV features less in my life now than it did 4 years ago because I have taken on too many commitments which leave me very little time to relax. But although I do not watch a great deal, I am very glad it is there.
>
> (67-year-old retired woman)

This respondent is all too aware that she has learned to cope with the death of her daughter, and the fact that she now lives alone, by making her life very active. Television is only a source of occasional comfort. The exact opposite can be seen in relation to another quite typical diarist, whose husband died in 1993. Living alone and having also suffered a period of ill health, she explains what effect these factors have had on her television viewing:

> Being a widow and living alone gives me more time to watch TV during mornings and afternoons when I am not out. After the 9 am news I look to see what *Kilroy* is discussing and occasionally if it is interesting to me I take the time to look at it. Also Anne and Nick and *Pebble Mill* but I have lots of other things to do and would enjoy it better in the evening. If my husband was alive I'm sure we would have a video as he loved gadgets and looked after all electrical matters – I'm no good with new gadgets at all. I watch more TV than I used to and at times I am indeed very grateful for it. I'm reasonably happy and cheerful when I am alone but there are times when I feel lonely and television fills the gap.
>
> (74-year-old housewife)

Here, television acts as a friend, something to 'fill the gap' in her social life. We can see from the way in which this respondent writes about her husband that she still thinks of him in relation to everyday household matters. Another diarist also discusses her late husband, in relation to taste in television programmes.

She notices that she still watches many of the same programmes they used to watch together before he died:

> My life has changed pattern a bit over the four years. I lost my husband in May 1992 and also began a series of periods in hospital as one of my new hips proceeded to dislocate 4 times in 2 years, culminating in another major op 6 months ago. I can drive again and am back in the groove, Church Mother's Union, my garden (limited), painting, and an interest in television – more so of course, now I live alone, and can selfishly please myself entirely as to what I watch. I enjoy the use of my youngest son's video, I shall not want to give it back. I watch a great deal of rubbish I think one might say. I like the unreality of such programmes as *Little House on the Prairie*! – Life isn't like that, but it would be nice and right often if it could be. The same with *Flying Doctors* – my husband used to enjoy being entertained by this – I still watch rugby and cricket, as much as I did with him, enjoying them both. I watch more documentaries, but not so many of the social problems unless they are ones that I actually know something about or have had experience of – my husband did not like to watch these problems, life was hard enough without dwelling on them, he felt. I think men do tend to take a different view to women on this altogether.
>
> (69-year-old housewife)

Illness and the loss of her husband led to this woman watching more television, which was valued for its escapist entertainment. However, watching certain programmes served as a reminder of what her life was like before the death of her husband. Her recounting of conversations which they once had about television is both poignant and also a means to keep her memory of her husband alive.

Ways of adjusting to and living in retirement, then, were quite varied and diverse. Some people were delighted to have the freedom to do what they liked in retirement, whereas others found it to be a traumatic separation from the world of work. Some of the respondents had deliberately filled up their days with responsibilities, voluntary work and hobbies in order, perhaps, to maintain a perception of themselves as active and useful. Others, inevitably, owing to physical and financial restrictions, spent much of their time at home where, as we saw in previous sections, they might allow themselves to watch some television in the daytime as long as they could 'excuse' it in some way (although some felt that excuses were not necessary). At the later stages of life, in illness and particularly if loved ones had passed away, television would be turned to increasingly for comfort and entertainment, even though it was often a cause of sadness for such diarists that these viewing experiences could no longer be shared with their late companions.

ELDERLY PEOPLE'S RELATIONSHIP WITH TELEVISION

Television will have arrived in the lives of most of these people in the early 1950s, or later – around forty years prior to their participation in this study. They will therefore have spent between twenty and forty years of their early lives with no television at all (the oldest diarist was a sparky, bridge-playing woman, aged 88 in 1996, who would be unlikely to have seen a television until she was in her mid-forties). Some diarists discussed these changes, unprompted. This man, born in 1931, wrote in 1996 that television 'opens up new vistas and enhances my life a great deal,' but he nevertheless felt nostalgic about the TV-free days of his childhood:

> I am glad to have lived in a period when there was no TV so that I can think about the difference it has made. As a schoolboy in WW2 I went to the local Cinema in Appleby – paid 4d to sit on a backless form to be fascinated by Will Hay, James Cagney and even Diana Durbin! to name only a few. This year (50 years on) I re-visited my little cinema. Sadly, no films are being shown now even though the projection room and ticket office is still there. Ah well, happy days.
>
> (65-year-old retired male Relate coordinator)

Cinema, of course, was a 'treat' and occupied another place both geographically and metaphorically – not invading the home itself, as other media would. In domestic terms, as Haddon and Silverstone have noted, the over-60s of the 1990s are really the *radio* generation:

> Television was...their children's medium. As such it had to be domesticated into households with different values to those offered by serials, series and advertising...Such domestication did not pass without continuing tension and, for many, increasing bewilderment and dismay with the creeping consumerism of the sixties, a consumerism that fundamentally challenged their own moral economies forged... in periods of austerity and depression.
>
> (1996: 153)

Whilst television was quickly welcomed into the heart of their lives, it was not always there, and the relationship retains areas of ambivalence. For some, television, like an appealing but cheeky guest, has become a little bit *too* settled into their households, and they are starting to regain the will to resist its advances – largely because of an awareness that, as the years creep by, they don't want to waste too much time on trivialities. More precisely, there is the point of view – particular to this age group – that, whilst one may have had time to waste on rubbish programming in years gone by, there is now less excuse for idling away the remainder of one's life in the company of second-rate shows.

> Sometimes my critical judgement is lulled or seduced into watching that which is not worth the time it takes to view. I do not need yet another holiday programme, or another Premier league goalless draw. I'm in my sixth decade and time is not on my side any more.
>
> (64-year-old retired male TV executive)

The idea of 'seduction' by television, used here, is common to many TV viewers across the generations, as seen in chapter five, on the guilt associated with television viewing. However, it is a particularly powerful metaphor for those retired people who, being at home in the daytime, could so easily be 'tempted' into watching the alluring, companionable box all day long. This respondent, for example, was still fighting temptation quite strongly:

> The day-time viewing is contrary to the intention I made when I retired. At the time I didn't watch the early morning news, but after starting to do so the habit grew and now I switch on automatically to view whilst having my breakfast – the excuse I give myself that whilst eating I can't do anything else, like housework etc.
>
> (72-year-old retired female civil servant)

Daytime television viewing is here seen as a developing, regrettable 'habit', and 'excuses' have to be made in order for such respondents to, effectively, 'forgive' themselves for giving in to temptation. These catholic terms are echoed even more strongly in this 1995 quote from a man who had retired in the previous year, aged 62.

> Retirement has given me the opportunity to watch at times when before I was not able to. The only thing is that I don't. I do not watch TV in the daytime – it's probably because I regard it as a cardinal sin!! (However, I have no trouble about going to the cinema in the daytime!!)
>
> (63-year-old retired male statistician)

This man, a film buff and member of a film society, was able to put cinema-going into a separate, 'cultural' category, about which one would not feel guilty. Television, on the other hand, described elsewhere as 'not particularly important to me', was subordinate to the radio and his other interests, which include playing squash, bridge, music and family history.

Others are keen to emphasise that they are keeping TV at arm's length.

> I am a woman of 55 years of age who lives alone. Since October 1990 I have been retired due to severe arthritis. Before that I spent 30+ as a civil

servant with the Inland Revenue, so being at home is a new experience for me. I have not yet become accustomed to watching TV during the day and do not normally do so, except for news programmes at lunch time and occasionally a pleasant old film if there's one on in the afternoon. I do not, ever, watch soap operas of any sort, chat shows, game shows, crime series, American comedy, sport...

(55-year-old retired female civil servant)

Only in circumstances which this diarist feels the need to register as unusual – as in the case of the occasional, irresistible old film – would she allow herself to watch television by day. The news, though, is also exempt from her worries about watching TV by day, as is the case for most of these respondents. Whilst most respondents across the age spectrum watched TV news and felt something of a need to keep reasonably up to date with news developments, some elderly diarists seemed to feel a particular need to be on top of the news, watching several bulletins a day. It seems likely that a (perhaps exaggerated) fear of being 'out of touch' leads to a degree of over-compensation in areas where it is actually interesting to them. The respondent quoted above would go on to explain, four years later, the importance of the link which the media provides between herself and the global community:

I can of course remember life before TV – before the world was brought to you in your home. I think that this is its most important aspect – to make me, alone at home, feel connected to the rest of the world.

(as above, aged 59)

By this stage, five years into her retirement, this diarist had become more accepting of the important role which television plays in her life. Similarly, a 72-year-old retired teacher somewhat reluctantly admitted, four years into the study, that he 'wouldn't want to be without...news and special interest programmes'. (This is a man who would feel obliged to leave the house for a walk each day at 5.35, while his wife watched *Neighbours*. Nevertheless, as a moving testament to their relationship, if she was out he would video the hated soap for her.)

Not all of the elderly diarists were self-conscious about their media use, of course, although most would find some way of demonstrating that they would not sit and watch just *anything*.

The main change [over the course of this study] has been that my husband retired at the end of 1991 and for a while we were out a lot more than usual, but when we were at home the television was switched on earlier and inevitably I found myself watching at different times of the day. However in the last 3 years we have not been able to follow our favourite pastimes quite so energetically as he has been waiting for a hip replacement, and it

meant we were home a lot more. The television thus became more important to us, and indeed there have been many times when we have been
grateful for television. This does not mean that we are addicts, we are quite
selective and turn it off when there is nothing of interest to us, in favour of
listening to a concert on Radio 3 perhaps.

(69-year-old retired female administrative assistant)

If we consider this passage as a piece of spontaneous writing, with each
handwritten sentence following the next for a reason, we can note the defensive
relationship between its parts. Having been able to preface the reason why they
came to be spending more time indoors with the – in these, embarrassed-to-be-
watching-TV terms – more 'impressive' note about how they used to go out
much more, this diarist finds herself paying a heartening tribute to television.
Eager to avoid being seen as TV-dependent, she quickly leaps to regain her
credibility by saying that they are not 'addicts' – a group of implicitly inferior
'others' – and asserts her cultural discrimination by insisting that they might
listen to a classical concert instead. The word 'perhaps', however, sitting
uncomfortably at the end of the sentence, suggests that the writer may have just
realised that this is rarely what she actually does.

Others are happier to pay unselfconscious tribute to the role of television in
their lives.

TV is of enormous importance to me. It is a constant source of entertainments and interest, and keeps me in touch with world events. The nature
programmes are outstanding, and sport is very good.

(85-year-old retired male civil engineer)

I would be lost without TV. I value it a lot. For one thing as you get older
you rely on it for company – you are not alone while you have TV. There is
always something for everybody.

(73-year-old retired woman)

The two themes of being 'kept in touch' with the rest of the world, and
television as company, recurred frequently in the elderly diarists' writings. For
those who could not get about as they used to – for physical and/or financial
reasons – television creates what we might call 'virtual mobility':

We don't read daily newspapers, we need TV for all our local, national and
world news. We are very grateful for being able to travel all over the world
from our armchairs, which replaces the real thing we used to do.

(70-year-old retired male small business owner)

As one who watches TV on most evenings of the week (though very rarely
during the days), I would miss the contact with a far wider world than the

one I inhabit. In old age one's financial and physical ability to travel are limited and through television we can visit the farthest corners of this world and worlds beyond. Through films and drama we are given insights into the lives of people, periods and places which would otherwise remain unknown to us. If there were no TV, we would read a lot more and listen more to recorded music, but TV is, in itself, an exciting medium and, for the reasons given, its disappearance would leave a considerable gap in our lives.

(75-year-old retired male company director)

These people expressed no concerns about bias or having the world presented to them through particular sets of eyes. Rather, they were very happy just to be able to see places around the world which they would – by this stage of life in particular – be unlikely to visit themselves. Some even found television to serve the ancient function of debating contemporary issues in a public forum, with some reservations:

[Television provides] an opportunity, like a citizen of some ancient city state, to go down to the city square and listen to the great and the good debating affairs, and judging their quality in the process. [TV can be] a source of news; a natural theatre in the widest sense. A series of extra mural lectures for working class self improvers like myself, often splendidly illustrated. Guided tours to remarkable places. Entertainment that crowned one couldn't afford.

On the other hand it confronts me with a procession of quacks, con-men, chancers, people trying to talk me into condoning rash, ill advised action; people who are talking what I know to be bullshit. In other words it forces me to keep my wits about me, to consult, as Burke said, the wisdom within me.

(73-year-old retired male university teacher)

This testing of one's critical abilities is perhaps the more-educated version of the trait identified by Willis (1995), where elderly people would watch quiz shows in order to keep 'mentally agile'. This can become almost a *necessary* task; the same diarist had written four years earlier that '*Westminster Live* is rarely wildly exciting, but one feels duty bound to watch it'. The need to keep on top of public affairs, in an informed and critical manner, was paramount here. A 74-year-old woman echoed these thoughts, directly linking them to increasing age: 'I believe [television] has become of more importance as I get older. It stimulates me, because it brings new/modern ideas. I disagree with them frequently but it does mean I think about them.'

Finally in this section, we should note that for many others, television brought much more generalised pleasures – in this case, being seen as a sweet paracetamol:

I have arthritis and rheumatism which rather limits my activities, I have a
home help for 3 hours a week to do my laundry, shopping etc. Television
gives me hours of pleasure and helps me forget the pain!

(65-year-old retired female teacher)

On the whole, the elderly respondents – in common with almost all of the
diarists – were grateful for television and that which it contributed to their lives,
despite the various greater or smaller points of annoyance which they all found
with its output. Having grown up without TV being a taken-for-granted part of
everyday life, some of this group were somewhat wary of its seductive charms,
but were more commonly grateful for its varied entertainments and regular
supply of news, even where they felt the need to spell out that it had not taken
over their lives. Television, they felt, kept them in touch with the world, and
mentally active. The 'virtual mobility' offered by television's ability to take the
viewer to places which they recognise, by this stage, that they may not see with
their own eyes, was particularly welcome.

THE ELDERLY ON WATCHING TELEVISION

As we have established, the elderly respondents in this study were diverse in
their interests, which, we have noted, should be unsurprising since all 'the
elderly' have in common is being above a certain age. Nevertheless, in their
comments on particular programmes, or types of programme, we can find some
common themes and perspectives – such as nostalgia, a (variable) interest in
younger people's programming, a mixed relationship with *Westminster Live*,
and some concerns about sexual content and other material which they felt
would not have a positive effect on their grandchildren. It is these issues which
are discussed in this section.

An air of nostalgia wafted through many – though not all – of these respondents' diaries. This yearning seemed to stretch beyond the actual programmes,
to a time which they represented for the diarists. In other words, the romantic
thought was not simply that 'the television programmes were so much better
then', but that the whole *world* was far nicer previously. Take this example:

My favourites are any of the adaptations in serial form of classic novels
especially Dickens and I particularly enjoyed the Jane Austen [sic]
Middlemarch serialisation. I also used to enjoy *Upstairs Downstairs* and
the *Duchess of Duke Street*. These kind of programmes were enjoyable
chiefly because they portrayed a more leisurely kind of life with no
violence, or drugs etc.

(69-year-old retired male office manager)

Since most programmes in the 1990s do not feature drugs or drug use, in
particular, and it is easy to find shows which contain no violence, this comment

may seem strange. The explanation is, perhaps, that it is the *spectre* of drug-taking and violence which the respondent associates more broadly with modern times and youthful programming, and which fills him with nostalgia for less 'dangerous'-seeming times.

For others, the nostalgia is simply for programmes which they enjoyed in the past.

> I am more nostalgic in old age, enjoying old black and white films I missed in the past. I have loved all the *The Avengers* and *New Avengers* repeats – they are classics I feel.
>
> (69-year-old housewife)

This kind of nostalgia is common to almost all age groups – even teenagers had fond memories of programmes they'd watched when growing up. But some contemporary programmes were enjoyed for their counter-nostalgia value. The ITV quiz *Blockbusters*, where educated teenagers got on so well with the congenial older host Bob Holness, seemed to particularly reassure older viewers that society had not gone completely down the pan after all.

> *Blockbusters* we so enjoy and the background information about contestants – but *Champion Blockbusters* – when it comes around, we enjoy more. So interesting to see maturity of participants 3/4 years after leaving school/university. Very encouraging for our country's future!
>
> (69-year-old housewife)

> ITV 5.10pm *Blockbusters*...Very good. It is always encouraging to watch bright teenagers. Raises hopes for the future. I shall watch this again.
>
> (74-year-old female author)

Other older respondents were keen on a range of programmes aimed at young people – perhaps in part because they would rather identify with children than with, say, the presumed audience for the 'senior citizen's' show *Prime Time*, discussed above. At the same time, they did find them to be genuinely interesting, well-made programmes.

> *Zig Zag* is a fine programme for adults as well as children. Very well presented and bringing back the Greek Myths of which I'm very fond.
>
> (70-year-old housewife)

> *Zig Zag* was an unexpected 'find'; I realise it is intended for children, but it really was very interesting. I'd love to know the extent to which it was based (re household in Ancient Greece) on knowledge rather than imaginative guesswork...I watched the final episode of *Tom's Midnight Garden*

deliberately: it has been an enchanting serial – many of those Wednesday 5.05 serials are more enjoyable than some of the serials intended for adults.

(63-year-old retired female mathematician)

I appreciate the pace and verve of the *Rough Guide* series (now repeats) on BBC2. This may seem an unexpected comment from a 63-year-old, who is housebound and 'stuck' with MS/Arthritis, but this lively, well-informed, off-beat programme fills a gap in my life nowadays admirably. The young presenters speak well and use words skilfully – and I love the fashions!

(63-year-old retired housewife)

In addition, some grandparents enjoyed watching children's programmes with their grandchildren, and participating in related activities – for example, a 66-year-old grandmother had collaborated in an artistic project demonstrated on *Blue Peter*: 'We made a beautiful artificial flower in a pot!' In the previous chapter we also saw that grandparents took an interest in videotaping programmes for their grandchildren to watch.

Of course, we cannot generalise and say that all elderly people find pleasure in children's programmes. One 76-year-old housewife, for example, said 'I dislike intensely the manner and presentation of most children's programmes'. A more 'serious' interest of several older respondents was *Westminster Live*, BBC2's afternoon coverage of proceedings in the Houses of Parliament, broadcast throughout the five years covered by this study.

Westminster Live perhaps appears most in the retired respondents' diaries because they were at home to watch it, and did not (usually) have pressure from young children to switch over to something more invigorating. Indeed, not all of these elderly viewers tuned in because they wanted to see the cut-and-thrust of Parliamentary debate; one 70-year-old enjoyed the fact that he would 'invariably drop off to sleep for 30 minutes or so'. However, some were clearly paying more attention:

[1991:] The televising of Parliament has been a revelation: the failure of the Prime Minister (especially the ex-Prime Minister) to answer questions, the inanity of as many of the younger Tories, the deep sincerity of a very few, the Speaker/Skinner relationship, the speaker always a conjunction of the right man and the right time.

(68-year-old retired woman)

This woman continued to keep a close eye on proceedings through to 1996. Looking back over her memory of the diaries at the end of the five years, she supposed that a key theme would be 'my hatred of Margaret Thatcher'. Others found a (less passionate) interest in the general proceedings:

I regularly watch *Westminster Live* and I find this particularly interesting when it moves away from Prime Minister's question time, and shows the working of various committees.

(68-year-old retired male probation officer, 1991)

However, over the course of the study, disillusionment set in.

I no longer am a regular viewer of *Westminster Live* as I now regard the proceedings as a charade.

(as above, aged 73, 1996)

This diarist was turning instead to Radio Two and 'reading non-fictional books'. He was not alone, either, in finding Parliamentary goings-on a disappointment.

I am interested in the opportunity TV gives to us all to see politicians and hear them expounding their views. I do not watch the House of Commons live because I find the confrontational style, now so common, unpleasant. My friends and I used to go to the public gallery nearly sixty years ago and politicians then seemed more sensible and less keen to score cheap points. Although some TV interviewers may be too aggressive, and certainly interrupt too much, the politicians do give a better account of themselves and their principles when being interviewed on TV than they frequently do in Parliamentary debates.

(77-year-old retired female civil servant)

Westminster Live was an unsurprising choice for the older respondents, who generally liked to 'keep in touch' with current affairs, and preferred less fantastical, straightforwardly presented programmes. A few respondents were seriously concerned about what effect some other kinds of television programmes might be having on their grandchildren.

I feel strongly that although I avoid apparently violent and sex programmes, we are being exposed to these elements in advertisements, early programmes and, please note, too early screening of trailers for possibly offensive programmes to be shown later in the evening. I fear for the future of my grandchildren because of this.

(68-year-old retired woman)

After my husband's death I gained five grandchildren, each seen first as a tiny infant, a few hours old, with a mind unsullied by the world (yes I know they recognise the signature tunes they have heard in the womb!). My husband, a teacher of older pupils for most of his life, would have worried greatly about the diet of programmes these children absorb every day, and

would, I think, not have been too reticent as I have tried to be in convey-
ing his worries to their parents. (I risk breaking off relations with both sets
if I really let go: 'For God's sake can't you see what all that ghastly tripe is
doing to your children? etc, etc').

(73-year-old retired woman)

That the discussion here should be about *their own* grandchildren, rather than
young people in general, makes the argument much more personalised.
Television here is not (only) a vague threat to the future stability of society, but
is a direct threat to the happy continuation of one's own family. At the same
time, in the second quote, it creates another immediate threat to family
harmony, since the grandmother fears that the rest of the family will reject her
'warnings'. Both aspects of this dilemma could be seen as being somewhat
overwrought, given what we know about media effects (see chapter nine), but it
is clear that these concerns are causing this woman considerable amounts of
anxiety and stress.

A number of older women were more happy to discuss sex than younger
generations might expect. Several were keen to make the point that they did
not object to sex *in itself*, separating reality from television representations.

I really don't worry about sex as I'm nearly 87 but the sex I enjoyed with
my dear husband (older than me) made me very happy. I think there is too
much nudity [on TV] and get bored with that.

(86-year-old retired woman)

Widowed for years, I regard sex as something special and sacred between 2
people. I can appreciate a subtle smutty yarn. I am not straight laced but
leaping from bed to bed is dangerous anyway...Full sex acts on TV disgust
me, yet I still think sex is God's gift to mankind properly used.

(82-year-old retired female nurse)

Obviously my views are those of an old lady but when I was young, children were allowed to develop naturally and we were none the worse for it.
It was quite delightful to learn all the mysteries of sex with the partner who
had made a faithful vow to care for us 'till death us do part'.

(75-year-old female home-maker)

Comments such as 'Obviously my views are those of an old lady...' reflect the
somewhat self-conscious, circumspect way in which these respondents put
forward their views about sex. They seemed to feel that they were basically
right, but knew that they were out of step with the younger part of society.
Rather than having an assertive, angry reaction to this, they were apparently
resigned to it, or perhaps were embarrassed and saddened by sex on TV, which
was felt to devalue real-life sex.

One respondent analysed her own, changing reaction to sex on TV rather more closely. Knowing that her growing aversion is not a traditional, 'unthinking' rejection of all things sexual, she ponders other explanations. (At the back of her mind there seems to be the question – 'is this just part of getting old?')

> Rather to my astonishment, I find myself increasingly bored by sex scenes and repelled by the sorts of stories in which boy meets girl, they spend all of three minutes talking to each other and, lo and behold, there they are in a sex scene so steamy that you marvel at the fact that the screen doesn't fog over. The first may just be a sign of my age: boredom is a recent reaction. Or they might both be a feature of upbringing. But neither reaction is due to the sort of unthinking, conventional disapproval I remember fighting against when I was a teenager.
>
> (68-year-old retired female mathematician)

In general, few of the elderly men or women wanted to see *more* sex on television, but many seemed happy enough with the present amount. Some suggested that it should be implied rather than shown, and some others felt that sex scenes were acceptable in moderation, but had become too obligatory. A number of respondents said they did not want to see simulated sex on television as it was 'unnecessary', whilst others admitted that it made them feel uncomfortable. A few asked why bed scenes had to be 'humping and groaning', rather than more tender aspects of lovemaking. (For views from the full range of diarists about sexual matters on TV, see chapter nine.)

A retired teacher seemed to summarise the concerns of many of his generation when he asked, 'Sex is a private matter – I wonder why some people want to make it a public one?' For those who had grown up before they were first introduced to television, perhaps when it reverentially covered the Queen's coronation in 1953, the idea that cameras would enter so far into the most intimate parts of life – intruding into a household's mature secrets – remains largely unthinkable. At the same time, they are often willing to give way to what they feel are the interests of a younger generation. For example, this same retired teacher nevertheless adds, 'As my wife Maria said, in the sex scenes in *Our Friends in the North* – "you can always go out and make a cup of tea".'

TELEVISION VIEWING IN LATER LIFE: SOME THEORY

Overall, as we have already emphasised, the over-60s audience was as diverse as you would expect any 20 per cent slice of the population to be. And yet there are certain themes which do shine through. The psychologist Erik Erikson (1950) has argued that in the later part of life the individual's task is to attain 'ego integrity', an assured sense of meaning and order in one's life and in the world more generally. The individual comes to terms with their own life as they have lived it, and confronts the fact that they lived it in one way and not another. There is something of a struggle, in which it would seem that most people generally succeed, to keep despair and disgust at bay: despair that one has been a failure and can now no longer choose to go along alternative paths to integrity, and disgust in younger people who are doing things differently.

We can see television being used by older people in ways which fit with this model. Entering the later years of their lives and getting many of their images of the world from television, older people seek to preserve a picture of the world as they like to 'remember' it – fundamentally polite, civilised and good-humoured. The lighter sitcoms and dramas help to support this view of the world. (As the television writer Dennis Potter once said, 'Nostalgia is a means of forgetting the past'.)

In addition, costume dramas and programmes like the *Antiques Roadshow* provide reassurance that the past is relevant to the future. The popularity of the situation comedy *Keeping up Appearances* amongst the more senior audience reflects this interest in maintaining an idealistic, traditional view of the world, even though the show affectionately satirises this tendency at the same time. Another Sunday evening sitcom, *Last of the Summer Wine* (where 'Sunday evening sitcom' is a genre popular with the elderly, as much as it is a scheduling description), is also humorously concerned with the displacement of traditional values into a (semi-) modern world.

Whilst younger people may dislike the sentimentalised, exaggeratedly pleasant view of the past presented by shows like *Heartbeat* and costume dramas, and the past-in-the-present of the sitcoms mentioned above and *Coronation Street*, there is evidence that there are good psychological reasons why older people find them fulfilling. Reminiscence about the past 'contributes to the maintenance of self concept and self esteem in old age' (Coleman 1991: 130). Gerontological studies have suggested that the elderly may denigrate the present, indeed, in order to feel better about their past lives. The present may threaten their sense of self, and emphasising the greatness of the past enhances their sense of security (ibid.).

The older audience seem somewhat baffled by the tendency of the younger generation to reflect the contemporary world as a dark and nasty place in the name of stylish entertainment, when they themselves are struggling to retain an integrated picture of the world as not at all bad. The urban realism of *Cracker* and even *The Bill*, as well as most contemporary movies, may be enjoyable for young and some middle-aged people, who can take the dark aspects of their reflections of society as warning signs or as mere entertainment, but they are not welcomed by those in the later years of life because they do not want to think that, within their own frame of reference, this is where we have ended up. Of course there are exceptions, older people who enjoy modern, gritty images of life, but perhaps these are the ones who are best adjusted to the world and their place in it, and so have a lesser 'need' for television to provide traditional-ist reassurances. For most, whilst they may have enjoyed more challenging texts in the past while they had the luxury to do so, they would now prefer more reassuring programmes which might help them to maintain some stability in their perception of the world and their place in it, and ward off the depression which would come from feeling that all the good things which they had enjoyed in the past had been lost.

SUMMARY OF KEY FINDINGS

- The retired and elderly audience are actually a heterogeneous and diverse set of individuals.
- Whilst some people adapted easily to retirement, for others the transition was quite traumatic. In early retirement, people would often occupy them-selves with a range of activities, stemming from a general work ethic and a need to feel active and useful. They would try to resist the 'seduction' of daytime TV, and were well aware of the changing patterns of their viewing between working and retired life.
- The self-consciousness of the retired about watching television stems partly from having grown up in a world where television was not part of everyday life.
- Physical and financial restrictions, and often diminishing numbers of social contacts, meant that as time went by they would generally spend more time at home and 'allow' themselves to watch more television. It was both comfort and company in times of illness and grief, although its reminder of happier times made it a double-edged, bittersweet pleasure.
- Older viewers felt that television kept them in touch with the world, and mentally active. Television gave these viewers a 'virtual mobility'; its ability to show them other parts of the world was frequently acknowledged.
- Whilst programme tastes were varied, as we would expect from such a large group (representing 20 per cent of the national population), the over-60s did generally prefer more 'gentle' and 'pleasant' programmes which avoided 'gratuitous' sex, bad language and violence.
- These preferences may be explained by the individual's process of coming to terms with later life. Programmes are valued which support a view of the world as these viewers would like to remember it, and which suggest that the past is of relevance to the present and future. Bleak views of the present and future may be enjoyed by younger viewers, who have the psychological luxury to do so, but older viewers are usually less able to find them entertaining.

Notes

1   Source: Taylor Nelson AGB/BARB/AGB Television, 1997.
2   Source: CAA/CAVIAR, in *Media Data Summary 1997*, published by the Ogilvy Media Company, London.
3   This fact was noted by Eric Midwinter (1991: 18) and confirmed by *Social Trends* publications from the 1990s.

Chapter 8

Gender and Television

In this chapter we will consider what men and women feel about gender-related issues in TV content, as well as women's and men's uses of television in the household. Is this drawing attention to a contrived issue which is of little relevance in contemporary, 'post-feminist' Britain? We think not. Despite decades of feminist argument, statistics show that things may not have changed as much as we might think. A reliable, large-scale survey by the Office for National Statistics conducted in 1995 showed that women, whether they worked or not, typically spent *three and a half times* as much time doing cooking and routine housework as men did. In an average week, men would spend under five hours doing 'cooking and routine housework'; women would spend almost seventeen hours (*Social Trends* 1998). This fact alone suggests that assumptions about gender roles remain rather traditional in many households.[1] Furthermore, a number of studies involving television have drawn attention to gender-related issues, and the BFI's Audience Tracking Study can shine important new light upon the arguments and assumptions which have been made in the past.

PREVIOUS STUDIES OF GENDER AND TELEVISION

Studies which consider associations between television and gender can, unsurprisingly, take a number of forms. They can be categorised most simply into three types of research, differentiated by quite different research questions, and consequently distinguished by separate approaches and methods. There are studies of *gender representation* – the (different) ways in which women and men are portrayed on television; studies of *gendered behaviour* – the (different) preferences, interests and usage of television which may be held by men and by women; and studies of *gender influences* – the ways in which women and men learn and adopt their (potentially different) gender attitudes and roles from television.

It should be noted straight away that the premises of all such studies are built on shifting sands. All three types of study described above obviously have assumptions of *difference* at their heart – they expect to find that men and women are portrayed in different ways, that women and men will use television in different ways, and that television may produce different attitudes and behaviour in men and women. (This does not mean that the studies are *determined* to find differences: if a researcher went looking for differences, but found that there were none, and said so, that would be fair enough.) But the amounts of difference are changing all the time. A study of gender representations in television published fifteen years ago will be of marginal application to today's broadcasting; and one published twenty-five years ago – apart from its notable historical value in showing us the representations of yesteryear – will be virtually useless. There is an obvious knock-on effect here for the studies of gender influences: the influence of 1970s television on people developing their gender identities then, will be different from the impact of programmes and adverts in the 1990s; and, more than that, the changed expectations of 1990s culture and society will form a wholly different environment in which these 'messages' – if they constitute that – are received. And these changes will mean that people's media usage will be continually changing too. It could be that looking for differences in men's and women's behaviour becomes redundant, a backward-looking question which is seeking to make distinctions which have become meaningless. (In fact, as we will see below, in 1990s Britain there are still some differences in the kinds of programme that women and men like to watch, and, to a lesser extent, who gets to choose. But there is also evidence that these tastes have changed a lot since the 1970s and even the 1980s.) Indeed, even the categories change: the soap operas that were largely shunned by 1970s man were clearly different in content from the soap formulas which have become relatively popular with men today.[2] Therefore the percentage of 'men who watch soap operas' actually has *a different meaning*, regardless of whether the figure has gone up or down or stayed the same, in studies from different decades.

In this brief introduction, therefore, we will only concern ourselves with relatively recent studies. We will outline some studies of gender representations – matters which diarists in the Audience Tracking Study have their own ideas about, as we will see subsequently; and we will describe some studies of gendered uses, preferences and decision-making in relation to TV, which we will also be able to compare with what our own respondents recorded. After the discussion of gender representations, we also briefly cover questions about their possible influence, although the five-year diary project – in common with virtually all other studies, to be frank – is unable to shed useful light on this matter. Gender identities are so entwined with social development that it is practically impossible to measure an 'effect' from the mass media, which is only one of a range of potential influences which people encounter every day. None of the diarists chose to write that their gender identity had been affected by the media, although in some cases, which appear below, there was some concern that certain images were sexist and so could potentially influence or reinforce sexist ideas. Furthermore we obviously cannot make the leap of judgement involved in claiming that any particular respondents have 'turned out the way they have' as a consequence of their media choices. This is not to say that the media plays no part in people's developing gender and sexual identities (indeed, one of us is writing a book on this very subject – Gauntlett, forthcoming). However, these variables are very difficult to distinguish and pin down empirically.

Gender representations

Earlier studies of representations of women in the media tended to focus on the identification of stereotypes (for example Friedan 1963; Tuchman 1978; Gallagher 1980). They found that women were under-represented generally, were often shown in the home, and were often valued (only) for their physical attractiveness – women on TV tending to be young and pretty. They were less often treated as authoritative or as experts, were generally shown taking a more passive role in relationships with men, and were frequently seen as subordinate to men in a variety of other ways.

Over the past ten or fifteen years, both representations and ways of studying them have developed significantly. Television programme-makers and advertisers have taken these criticisms on board, and have altered their modes of representation in relation to each point, to varying degrees; although of course, examples of each of them can still be seen on TV today (see Gunter 1995). At the same time, academic approaches have changed in recognition of a point which has become increasingly obvious, that there can be no direct link between stereotypes and how people will perceive them, let alone how they might affect their attitudes or behaviour. (Ann Brooks (1997) provides an excellent account of some of the recent changes in feminist cultural theory, showing how certain key ideas like *identity, pleasure, masquerade* and *performance* have become increasingly important in the more sophisticated approaches which are replacing the simplistic assumptions that identity would be absorbed from media representations. See also Whelehan (1995) and Skeggs (1997).)

In *Representing Women: Myths of Femininity in the Popular Media* (1995), Myra Macdonald has examined the ways in which images of women, and 'myths of femininity' in particular, have managed to survive various direct attacks (by feminist critics, for example) and more subtle cultural shifts (as some feminist ideas have become accepted into the mainstream). She argues that these often contradictory but surprisingly durable myths depict femininity as enigmatic and threatening, nurturing and caring, and portray women's sexuality and women's bodies in ways which are frequently unrealistic. Rather than arguing that these notions have been imposed upon popular culture by men, Macdonald seeks to account for why women have colluded in, and taken pleasure from, their reproduction.

She understandably criticises 'post-feminism' for giving new life to old ideas of femininity which feminists had aspired to erase. Advertising in the 1990s has been able to show women as sexy vamps, workers in a variety of fields – who are sexy, and even as sexy housewives, with an ironic wink added which legitimises the whole package as clever and contemporary, rather than regressive. Adverts which have shown women as sexual predators, rather than in the former passive role awaiting male attention, are an advance in one sense, but ultimately still show women as flirtatious and feminine and in need of a man. Of course, we also have adverts showing men as flirtatious and masculine and wanting a woman; Macdonald notes that change might come quicker if 'masculinity's stability as a sign' is also unsettled (1995: 101).

Ultimately Macdonald gives us an insightful and engaging discussion of a selection of images of femininity, but does not actually manage to answer her own question about why women as well as men are complicit in the continued survival of these ideas. However, she does note the increased amounts of playfulness in texts (particularly advertising) which address women about their femininity. One interpretation of this, which Macdonald tends towards, is that it is 'a ruse of consumerism anxious to revitalize worn myths without alienating an audience whose social and cultural position is changing' (1995: 221). However, she also notes that there may be something to Angela McRobbie's more optimistic argument (1991, 1994, 1997) that this post-modern playfulness puts an ironic distance between the text and the reader, and so may in turn encourage women to be playful with their own identities, opening up interesting cultural and political possibilities.

Gender representations are about men as well as women, of course. Researchers such as Sean Nixon (1996, 1997), Tim Edwards (1997) and Frank Mort (1996) have explored the way in which men have become increasingly targeted, since the mid-1980s, as consumers of fashion and 'grooming' products, and of related fashion and 'lifestyle' magazines. This work focuses in particular on the 'spectacle' of masculinity displayed in advertising – images of men in general, and of the 'new man' in particular: stylish, strong, sensual, caring and sensitive all at once. In film studies, Steven Cohan and Ina Rae Hark (1993) have compiled studies of the representation of masculinities in Hollywood cinema, and Yvonne Tasker (1993) has explored the presentation of male (and female) bodies in popular action movies.

In-depth analyses of masculinities on television have been somewhat slower to appear, although Lyn Thomas (1997) has produced a valuable study of changing masculinities in everyday texts in her work on the enormously popular detective series *Inspector Morse*. Thomas notes that the TV series – which had its main run of twenty-eight two-hour films from 1987 to 1993 (with subsequent one-off 'specials' later in the 1990s) – replaced the 'sexually predatory' Morse of Colin Dexter's novels with a substantially different, 'romantic' Morse as played by John Thaw. Combining textual analysis with interviews with fans, Thomas charts how the TV *Morse* reflects changing perceptions of gender roles in society. To make their hero attractive in the late 1980s and 1990s, the programme-makers recognised that some break with tradition was in order. As we have noted previously (Gauntlett 1995: 112–114), the contrast between Thaw's *Morse* and his previous noted role as Regan in *The Sweeney* (1975–78) is one of the clearest demonstrations that some interpretations of masculinity were changing, the latter's macho aggression being almost wholly replaced by the gentle melancholy of the sensitive Oxford detective. Thomas's comparison of the book-version Morse and his TV counterpart makes much the same point. Emotional, caring, and not afraid to express his (frequently unrequited) feelings, Morse is often contrasted with the repressed murderers whose secrets and sexual intrigues lead them to their crimes. In this sense Thomas sees in *Inspector Morse* a critique of heterosexuality, and more importantly, an on-going theme of 'the search for an acceptable masculinity'. We can add that the theme of searching for an acceptable and comfortable form of masculinity can be found in a range of 1990s shows, from Homer's often flawed attempts to 'be a better husband' in *The Simpsons* (1991–) and the domestic sexual politics in *King of the Hill* (1996–), to the struggles of both 'harder' and 'softer' male characters to find their places in life in numerous soap operas. In *NYPD Blue* (1993–), two styles of masculinity 'worn' by Sipowicz and Simone are contrasted, and also shift in relation to each other, whilst their colleague Greg Medavoy is seen (in 1996–98 seasons) struggling to 'try for size' a more aggressive kind of masculinity, based on the model of Sipowicz, which doesn't really suit him.

What impact do these representations have?

There is certainly evidence that people do not simply absorb the ideologies which critics say are implicit in texts. Elizabeth Frazer (1987), for example, conducted focus groups (group interviews) with young women in which they discussed the girls' magazine *Jackie*, which featured photo love stories where girls would swoon over boys and shun their female friends in the all-important quest to find true happiness in the arms of a man. Frazer found that the teenagers were well equipped to resist the potential influence of these messages, since they saw the stories as laughable fictional entertainment. Taking the photo strips seriously, as lifestyle advice, would be unthinkable. Therefore the assumption that ideologies are put 'into' texts and then feed straight into their reader's beliefs and behaviour was shown to be, at best, flawed. At the same time, it remains the case that the magazines may have influenced their readers in more subtle ways, giving them certain messages about society and its expectations, even though they outwardly found the photo love stories quite silly.

To take a more recent case, the sexist humour featured in *Loaded* magazine and the sitcom *Men Behaving Badly* is excused as it is supposed to be deliberately ironic – the idea that readers won't take these texts seriously is here an assumption made by the media producers themselves. The same kind of assumption was made by the makers of *Till Death Us Do Part* (later, *In Sickness and in Health*, and in America, *All in the Family*), who believed that the audience would recognise that Alf Garnett's racism was being satirised. They expected that the frequent racist comments made by their star would be seen by the audience as the rantings of a laughable fool. But in an autobiographical article, Jeremy Clarke (1998) has noted that when he was growing up, in 1960s Essex, Alf Garnett was a hero, 'a man who dared to say on TV what everybody we knew said in the privacy of their own homes'. Language and behaviour which we would now regard as appallingly racist was everyday currency, and Alf was loved as the one man who 'spoke for us all'. This disturbing news leaves us with the likelihood that *Loaded* and the magazines, comedies and adverts that it has inspired will also be received by people who short-circuit the 'ironic joke' element – the almost classy notion of 'satire' doesn't even really come into it here – and gain less progressive pleasures from these texts.

In general, as we have noted before (Gauntlett 1995), it is virtually impossible to produce firm empirical evidence that television cultivates sexism, racism or other prejudices, since they are deeply rooted in our culture. We are therefore unable to separate any influence that television may have from the range of other possible influences – although we do know that more direct social contacts, such as family, peers and friends, usually have a much stronger impact on attitudes and beliefs. A review of literature by Kevin Durkin (1985) found that studies had predictably failed to find 'a strong or convincing relationship' between children's television viewing and sex-role stereotypes. Instead, children seemed well able to distinguish between real life and the sex-stereotyped depictions they saw on TV. An overview of research on the effects of gender representations in television shows and advertising on both children and adults, by Barrie Gunter (1995), also reflects the difficulties with these 'effects' studies – oversimplistic methodologies, which fail to examine the question from more than one angle, and are often badly devised and inaccurately written-up, characterise much of this unsatisfactory research (1995: 137). This body of studies certainly holds out the *possibility* that television feeds into people's perceptions of gender roles, norms and expectations, but the methodological flaws (and the complex nature of the research question itself) mean that these studies cannot tell us the extent to which TV is or is not an influence, let alone give us any understanding of the processes that may be involved.

Studies of gendered television uses and preferences

In chapter six we have already seen that David Morley (1986) and Ann Gray (1987, 1992) found that the use of video machines was dominated by the adult male in the households that they studied, although our own more recent evidence does not support this. The two studies identified some other points about gender and media uses which are worth mentioning here.

Morley (1986) interviewed eighteen white families, all living in South London in households of two adults and two or more children. Morley is careful to emphasise his recognition that these households would not be representative of all households. He found that for men, home was the site of leisure where they could give television their full attention, whereas for women, the home was primarily a place of work – whether they were employed outside the home or not – and so television could only be viewed distractedly and guiltily. It was usually the men who chose what to watch, and in houses with a remote control, it would be the man who generally used this device – 'a highly visible symbol of condensed power relations' (1986: 148). Indeed, 'a number of' the women complained that their husbands would obsessively flick around the channels whilst they were trying to watch something. Interestingly, the households which did not fit this pattern and where the husband might give way to his family's preferences were those where he was unemployed and his wife was working. The economic power of the 'breadwinner' role is here revealed to be tied to other forms of domestic power.

In contrast to this rather polarised view of gender relations, we should consider the findings of James Walker and Robert Bellamy (1996), who produced a comprehensive overview of largely quantitative studies conducted by both academic and industry researchers in America and Britain, from the mid-1980s to the mid-1990s. This found that overall both women and men used TV remote controls frequently, although it was more likely to be men that used the device for hopping around several channels and for avoiding adverts. Men seemed to take more *pleasure* from using the remote control, whereas for women it was more purely functional. The studies also showed that in some households it was the woman who dominated use of the remote control. Whilst quantitative studies offer less detail about the intricacies of everyday life, it seems sensible to assume that these results should be more or less representative of what really goes on in people's living rooms, whereas Morley himself warns against generalising to the whole population from his own qualitative findings.

To return to that study, Morley (1986) also found that when they had the rare opportunity to do so, the women would take 'guilty pleasure' from watching 'a nice weepie', a sentimental or romantic film or serial, on their own. This was the kind of material which they were unable to watch in the family context, as the man had defined an implicit hierarchy of material on behalf of the household, and this kind of show came at the bottom. Morley's men preferred factual programmes and 'realistic' fiction, whereas the women favoured fictional shows in general and romance in particular, although the author quickly admits that this may be an exaggeration of the 'real' differences (1986: 166).

Nevertheless, similar patterns were found in Ann Gray's study of women and video recorders (1987, 1992). Here, too, the women find pleasure in watching the romantic fictions derided by their husbands, when they get the guilty opportunity to do so on their own or with female friends. Their male partners prefer physical action to emotional interaction in TV and films (Gray 1992: 160), and the women seem to have taken this value system on board, being embarrassed or apologetic about their own supposedly inferior tastes. Whilst Gray relates these preferences to the cultural worlds which men and women are expected to maintain around themselves, she ultimately ends up with very polarised gender categories, where male texts involve heroic tales of public life and physical action, whilst female texts are romantic stories with an emphasis on the domestic and the emotional. The fact that these women want romantic fantasies as an escape from their everyday reality, and yet do not feel able to defend their preferred genres, can work as a critique of domestic patriarchy; but the study, like Morley's, is also in danger of simply reinforcing gender stereotypes.

Janice Radway (1984) also emphasised the link between romantic fantasy and an implicit critique of patriarchy. She found that a group of women who enjoyed reading formulaic romance novels gained pleasure from them as they were an *escape*, not only psychologically through the enjoyment of the romantic fantasies, but literally and physically an escape from the women's everyday duties, since they made it clear that they were not to be disturbed when reading. The novels were therefore a 'declaration of independence' from the patriarchal assumption that they should be always available as a mother and housewife. We are not being unfair by describing the novels as 'formulaic', incidentally: the women themselves were well able to recite their favourite formula, and some had even written their own stories which stuck closely to this narrative pattern.

Joke Hermes conducted a detailed ethnographic study of how women (and some men) related to women's magazines, published as *Reading Women's Magazines* (1995). Although not about television, this study is still worth considering as it relates to women's use of media. The work was based on in-depth interviews with eighty people, sixty-four women and sixteen men. Hermes found that the magazines were fitted into women's lives when they had spare time, but – disappointingly, perhaps, for those who produce or are fans of magazines – were often not regarded as particularly important and were 'easily put down'. The men who read women's magazines (whom the researcher had some difficulty tracking down) also read them for swift, easy pleasure. Hermes herself seems a bit sad about it: 'I wanted to know how women's magazines became meaningful for readers and readers told me that women's magazines have hardly any meaning at all,' she writes in the conclusion (1995: 143). Nevertheless, the magazines were said to have practical uses (in terms of home-making, lifestyle, craft and fashion tips, for example), and gave the readers a sense of learning about other people's emotions and problems. Furthermore, Hermes says that in the course of her interviews she would catch an 'occasional glimpse' of other aspects of magazine-reading: the pleasure of picking up a magazine within an otherwise busy daily routine, and, most interestingly, the 'fantasies of control and perfect selves that reading women's magazines also occasionally gives rise to' (ibid.). The recipes and everyday tips, for example, became meaningful because they could be stored away and enabled a fantasy of being well organised and on top of household tasks. Other fantasies – of being an ideal partner, of being a well-informed consumer, or of being a wise woman, for example – could also be built upon the everyday experience of reading the magazines.

The way in which some of Hermes's respondents considered their own lives in relation to the emotional learning which they felt they gained from the magazines is partly similar to the way in which young people considered their own lives in relation to the soap opera, *Neighbours*, in a study by Marie Gillespie (1995). Based on two years of ethnographic research within the South Asian diaspora in Southall, West London, Gillespie's study indicated that these young British Asians would 'draw on the soap as a cultural resource in their everyday interactions both in the peer culture and with parents and other adults, as they endeavour to construct new modes of identity for themselves' (1995: 143). Talk stemming from discussion of *Neighbours* gave young people and their families the opportunity to discuss changing gender roles in the family, for example, and the serial fed into the teenagers' emotional learning about relationships. (Although Gillespie devotes one chapter of her book to *Neighbours* and the related issues of gossip, kinship, courtship and community, her study covers a range of other issues, most notably how television and video were used in the recreation of cultural traditions within these households.)

As with gender representations, men and masculinity are as worthy of study as women and femininity, but in the past have been 'problematised', and studied, less. (In the male-dominated research culture, men's media use would traditionally be equated with 'normal' media use.) Just as Macdonald found that ideas of femininity were malleable but fundamentally resilient within culture, so masculinity has also proved to be somewhat flexible (within boundaries) in adulthood, but remains pretty monolithic to children (as we will see below). Whilst it can seem positive that young people were using TV as a 'cultural resource' in Gillespie's study, we might be more troubled to remember that this can also mean that they were learning norms of masculine and feminine behaviour from *Neighbours*.

Discussing cartoons with groups of boys aged between 7 and 12, in English schools, David Buckingham (1993c) observed that masculinity was 'policed' within the group by the boys themselves. Although they were able to have relatively complex discussions about sexism in cartoons, the boys kept each other's masculinity in check, so that any boy who began to step out of line – by expressing an inappropriately 'feminine' view, or even by suggesting that they liked a female character – would quickly be 'corrected' or made fun of, so that they were pulled back into the junior masculine hegemony. Masculinity, then, which is at least partly constructed through discourse in this way, becomes defined, in certain conversations, in *relation* to the media, but only in ways which are constantly interfered with by more powerful social forces – such as the respect of one's peers.

Studies of gendered *preferences* in the media – what men like and why, and what women like and why – have tended to be somewhat unsatisfactory and problematic as they seem to reassert differences between women and men. The findings of Morley, Gray, Radway and Hermes above could all be seen as confirmation of traditional stereotypes of women – as lovers of romance, for example – even though the women's behaviour is generally seen as a kind of *resistance* to the male domination of their everyday social world. And once again, intelligent studies of men's preferences have also been thin on the ground. The most notable association between gender and preference in media research has been the work which has investigated soap operas as a 'women's genre'. Unsurprisingly, we find this problematic too; this is discussed later in this chapter.

WHAT DO MEN AND WOMEN ACTUALLY WATCH?

The statistics gathered continually by the ratings organisation BARB give us the firmest indications of the viewing habits of women and men in Britain. (As anticipated, these figures reflect the behaviour of the diary-writing sample discussed in this book; however, the BARB figures are obviously the most precisely representative.) In the 'top 20' of programmes watched by men in 1996,[3] nine of the shows were sport (all football, in fact), with the *Euro 96* soccer championship dominating positions 2–6, and the *FA Cup Final* in at number 7. These fixtures were beaten only by the David Jason sitcom *Only Fools and Horses* at number 1, hotly pursued by the David Jason detective drama *A Touch of Frost* at number 8. Other non-sporting chart-toppers included the sitcom *One Foot in the Grave* at number 9, the Christmas Day *EastEnders* at 11, dinosaur movie *Jurassic Park* at 12, northern soap *Coronation Street* at 14, 15 *and* 17, comic set-ups by Jeremy Beadle in *You've Been Framed* at 16, heart-warming police drama *Heartbeat* at 18, and Dawn French as the comic female *Vicar of Dibley* at 19.

The women's 'top 20' programmes of 1996, by contrast, featured no sport whatsoever – demonstrating not only that women enjoy televised sport less than men, but also that they will actively leave the room and do something else (or watch other shows on a different TV set) rather than stay with their partner and watch football. The 9.7 million men who sent *Only Fools and Horses* to the top of their chart were joined by 11.7 million women, for whom it again sails into first place. *Coronation Street* then occupies positions 2, 3 and 4 (appearing again at 13 and 17), followed by *EastEnders* at 5, 6 and 10. The emergency services are well represented next in the chart, with *Heartbeat* at 7, hospital drama *Casualty* at 8, *A Touch of Frost* at 9, fire-fighting drama *London's Burning* at 11 and yet more detective work in *The Bill* at 14, *Inspector Morse* at

15, and *Prime Suspect 5* at 20. Providing light relief are *One Foot in the Grave* at 12, and *You've Been Framed* at 16. The rural dramas of *Emmerdale* and *Ballykissangel* fill positions 18 and 19.

We can supplement this picture with data from the Independent Television Commission's 1996 survey *Television: The Public's View*, which invited respondents to express their level of interest in a range of programme types.[4] Many categories were rated 'very interesting' by similar numbers of women and men – for example films (new and old), nature and wildlife, news, crime reconstructions, adventure or police dramas, sitcoms, holiday programmes and music shows. Men, however, showed a distinct preference for sport (58 per cent of men found it 'very interesting', compared to only 15 per cent of women), alternative comedy (20 per cent men, 12 per cent women), science (20 per cent men, 7 per cent women) and adult films (19 per cent men, 9 per cent women). Women were more keen on soaps (45 per cent of women, and 16 per cent of men, called them 'very interesting'), plays and drama series (33 per cent women, 18 per cent men), quiz shows (26 per cent women, 18 per cent men) and chat shows (20 per cent women, 7 per cent men).

In sum, the data in this section show a clear divide on sport, which men rate highly and watch much more than women. The next greatest difference is with women's preference for soap operas, which the chart shows *are* watched, but not so highly rated, by men. The lack of sport in the women's chart leaves room for a broader range of other programming, but the not stereotypically 'feminine' crime and action-packed emergency service dramas figure strongly, and indeed women confess to a greater liking for them. Otherwise women and men seem to watch sitcoms, light entertainment and current affairs with similar levels of attention and enjoyment.

SHOULD WE TALK ABOUT 'WOMEN'S' AND 'MEN'S' INTERESTS?

In a special section on women's and men's television preferences in the Audience Tracking Study diary of February 1993, female respondents were asked, 'How do you think women's interests and concerns are represented by television?' The male diarists faced a matching question about 'men's interests and concerns'. Perhaps the most notable thing about all of the responses to this question is the number of individuals who refused to accept that we could sensibly talk about 'women's' and 'men's' interests and concerns separately in this way. This point was made by numerous respondents, young and old, male and female. Young women commented:

> I don't really agree with dividing men's and women's issues in the media because I feel this leads to segregation in society.
>
> (18-year-old female student)

What are women's interests and concerns? Are they only the stereotypical concerns of make up, men and making homes? There are not my concerns at all. I think my concerns are the same or similar to many men's.

(18-year-old female student)

I don't think you can specifically define what is supposedly 'men's' and 'women's' TV. It's not as black and white as this question suggests...In my view man (or woman!) is too complex an individual and suggestions that he is only interested in certain things and issues has no foundation whatsoever.

(22-year-old unemployed female graduate)

And the point was made by many young men:

Firstly it is difficult to say what is a man's 'interest' (cars, sport, business?). I personally don't find these at all interesting but I do take an odd sort of pleasure from 'spying' in on supposedly women's daytime TV shows...

(18-year-old male school pupil)

What are men's interests? Sport? DIY? I don't know. I'm not particularly interested in either of these. The programmes I enjoy don't cater to a specific sex (unless you want to be really chauvinistic and include soaps as women's TV)...

(18-year-old male school pupil)

It's absurd to suggest that men and women have different interests and concerns. I think that each sex is equally interested in themselves and others, and that you cannot split their differences very much.

(21-year-old male student)

Older women were similarly unhappy with these classifications:

How does one define 'women's interests'? Surely childcare, cooking and craftwork – once mainly women's subjects – are now shared by men. Most women I know do most of the gardening and house decorating, maintenance and repairs.

(69-year-old housewife)

I hope that neither 'men's interests' or 'women's interests' are or will be represented [separately]. I really do not like male/female segregation.

(65-year-old housewife and freelance writer)

Several older men also rejected the premise of the question, contradicting the possible assumption that those who are both male and have had longest to become entrenched in tradition would be the most happy with such distinctions. For example:

> I am puzzled as to the difference between men's and women's interests...I know women who are mad about football, snooker and other sports but I would not cross the road (which I could) to watch a football match or switch on TV for *Match of the Day*, I honestly don't care who wins, what difference does it make, it's only a game.
>
> (71-year-old retired male dental technician)

> I don't really think men and women's interests are all that far apart. I find that many programmes labelled as 'for women' are more interesting than programmes labelled as 'for men'. I am not interested in sport.
>
> (74-year-old retired male analytical chemist)

It could be said that these responses are dealing in stereotypes even as they try to reject them – taking sport as 'male' before negating the idea, for example – but this only shows that the diarists are *aware* of stereotypes which exist; perhaps they have become aware of (but not influenced by) the idea of sport as 'male' because of the predominance of sports with male players, and male commentators and presenters, on TV. Nevertheless, their arguments draw distinctions between the possibly 'gendered' TV presentations, and their own quite different experience.

Curiously, a larger proportion of the middle-aged respondents were able to accept the question at face value. (Their responses consequently appear in other sections below). More specifically, although many respondents across the age range struggled somewhat with the extent to which we could talk about separate 'men's' and 'women's' interests, it was only the younger diarists, and the elderly, who rejected the premise outright. A possible explanation for this could be that the world of work, or the separation of work and home lives, leads women and men to believe that they do indeed have more distinct interests; and that when heterosexual couples come to retire and spend far more time with their partner, they come to feel that the sexes are not so different after all.

IS TELEVISION OUTPUT BIASED TOWARDS WOMEN OR MEN?

Those with strong feelings about television output being 'gendered' – programmes being aimed, in the imaginations of broadcasters at least, at one sex rather than the other – tended to focus upon daytime programming, which was generally seen as being dominated by 'women's interest' programmes. Some women found this to be an excellent service.

> [Women's interests and concerns are represented by television] very well. I especially enjoy the morning programmes e.g. *This Morning* (ITV) or *Good Morning with Anne and Nick* (BBC1). They cover everyday things, family, fashion, health problems etc. – great if you've time to watch during the day! I also love *The Clothes Show* on Sundays! Sometimes there are debates, discussions etc. covering very interesting topics, mainly for women e.g. *Kilroy* can be very good, also *The Time and the Place*.
>
> (40-year-old housewife)

However, several others – particularly young respondents – considered the content of daytime television to be trivial and insulting to women. Some of the language used here reflects the way in which anti-sexist and feminist ideas have become part of everyday discourse.

> I think that women's interests and concerns sometimes get highlighted more during the day because men are meant to be at work. I don't think this is fair and it is very sexist. I was ill a few days ago so I had to stay home from school, I spent most of my time watching daytime television, nearly all the programmes were aimed at women.
>
> (15-year-old schoolgirl)

> I think broadcasters believe they are representing women's interests with the patronising programmes offered on daytime television. In fact, not everyone who stays at home has an IQ under 100. The 'cosiness' of Anne and Nick and items on patchwork are condescending. Women's interests and concerns really aren't that different from men's...
>
> (20-year-old female student)

> Most weekday day-time television programmes seem to be suited for house wives only and are quite boring. I am a female but I feel there should be more programmes to suit the male at home.
>
> (14-year-old schoolgirl)

In the examples above, we can see that young women have taken the idea of sexual equality on board to the extent that they feel *sorry* for male viewers, who are perceived as being poorly served by the range of daytime programming. Of course, this argument also contains the less progressive notion that the cosy, housewifely, patchwork-informed programmes are not for men; but on the other hand, the 'patronising', 'condescending', 'quite boring' shows are not seen as being what modern women want either. Others made similar arguments.

I think television tends to concentrate on the more frivolous aspects of women's lives.

(32-year-old female homemaker)

If I were in to watch daytime TV, I wouldn't watch it. Mindless drivel, useless banter, blatant sexism, and insulting to the intelligence. Blagh.

(30-year-old male student)

The 'magazine' programmes I saw – *This Morning* and *People Today* – seemed to be clearly aimed at young women staying at home with children of whom they did not appear to have a very high opinion judging by the superficiality of their content. The emphasis of such programmes has not changed since I last completed a TV diary; there is still plenty of coverage given to cookery, craftwork and childcare although *This Morning* began a new slot, *Work Wise*, which gave a potted history of feminism and an address to send for a fact sheet for more information.

(29-year-old unemployed woman)

The idea of daytime programmes being actually 'insulting' to their audience – a pretty damning criticism, particularly for public service broadcasting – was recurrent. Even some men seemed embarrassed by the 'daytime ghetto' programming supposedly aimed at their female friends:

[Television caters for men] a lot better than women. Men have a lot of action, police, sport, etc. aimed at them. Women on the other hand seem to have been allocated soaps, daytime TV, cookery and food shows, even gardening programmes – media authorities still seem to think that women are tied to the sink with nothing better to do than learn how to improve their home, themselves or partake in idle useless gossip.

(32-year-old male student)

Mothers at home also found that in some ways the values of daytime television reflected those of women's magazines in their focus upon an 'ideal' of the independent, glamorous woman with no dependants (Anderson and Mosbacher 1997; Gaudoin 1997):

I'm so fed up with seeing the mother's role undermined!!! Being a mother is the hardest job in the world.

(34-year-old single mother, college student)

Some retired men expressed regret that daytime television was dominated by 'women's interests', soaps, and self-congratulatory presenters. Indeed, some men of all ages who spent their daytime at home were unimpressed by the programmes which they felt were not aimed at them.

[Men's interests] are covered fairly well, but since being made unemployed and looking to daytime TV for entertainment I find that TV planners do not cater for men. Most of the people who call in on [the] phone to BBC and ITV are women. This is because I feel that it is aimed at the female population. They should remember that we're not all retired female, housewives or unemployed people sitting aimlessly watching television.

(34-year-old unemployed male technician)

There are not enough programmes aimed at men who for one reason or another play a major role in looking after the household, children etc.

(38-year-old male homemaker)

My youngest daughter with baby enjoys the morning programmes. But knowing there are so many unemployed a lot of men could get bored with viewing just family matters.

(68-year-old retired female farmer)

The reverse side of the argument that programmes aimed at women are too trivial is that particular *serious* issues are generally ignored in the rush to provide a cheerful blanket of woman-friendly programming.

I don't think [women's concerns are covered] really – the Oprah Winfrey show or Sally Jessy Raphael are the nearest you get to discussions on issues which really affect women – abuse, violence, serious issues.

(25-year-old female accounts and payroll clerk)

I find this question incredibly difficult. My first reaction was to think [that programming for women] had improved, as it does not confine women's interests to the 'Watch With Mother' slot. It has broadened the female representation over a number of programmes during the day. However I feel it has lost a specific focus. By trying to provide a mass appeal to women's concern, I feel it doesn't really answer anyone's needs.

(36-year-old female lecturer)

Whilst daytime programming was seen as being biased towards 'women's' interests, television in general was most frequently seen as being of interest to both sexes, reasonably fairly. However, some felt that broadcasting was male dominated:

There are more women than men in the population but the TV is male dominated interest-wise.

(50-year-old female part-time primary school teacher)

The Oprah Winfrey programme sometimes deals with women's problems, as do some of the Channel 4 documentaries and medical discussions but I think that women's interests are under represented, probably because the producers and directors are mainly male. I don't watch TV much during the daytime.

(64-year-old retired female teacher)

I think a woman's – a 'female' perception is almost entirely absent from TV…So many current affairs and news type programmes leave it out entirely, so I watch very few of those, especially when there's an all-male panel, even if there is a woman presenter.

(43-year-old female writer, journalist and teacher)

Satellite and cable television was seen to have the worst service for women, being centred on stereotypically 'male' interests and additionally failing to provide the 'token women's' programmes which other broadcasters were seen to at least put on in the daytime:

There is nothing specific to females on any channel and satellite is even worse – not even anything like *The Clothes Show*, *Good Morning*, or *Food and Drink*…

(63-year-old retired female nurse)

As far as satellite is concerned, it seems to be planned for the younger macho set, if not to say yobs – all football teams, chips and rottweilers. Sky sends out catalogues of goods obtainable from them – all heavy boots, T-shirts, and leather jackets. This would to some degree explain their choice of films, all muscle men and destruction. Yet occasionally they include good old classics and up-to-date French movies.

(70-year-old retired man)

We have seen that some women liked daytime TV, but a significant number of both women and men felt that the programmes were an insult to the women that they were apparently aimed at; and television in general was seen to have a reasonably fair balance of material for both women and men, although some felt that it was biased towards men and overly male-dominated. Obviously, the responses to these kinds of questions vary according to the respondents' perceptions of what kinds of material are of interest to women, and to men – or their rejection of the idea that we can categorise interests by sex in this way. These issues are explored further in the following sections.

SHOULD WE *STILL* CLASSIFY SOAP OPERAS AS 'WOMEN'S PROGRAMMES'?

Academic studies and student textbooks have frequently assumed that soap operas are a 'women's genre', and have sought to investigate the 'special relationship' between female audiences and soap opera texts, or have tried to identify characteristics *of* the texts which might link them with women's psychological or social lives. Surprisingly, perhaps, scholars publishing in the 1990s still feel able to talk about soaps in this way, with books by Christine Geraghty (1991) and Charlotte Brunsdon (1997), for example, seeming quite happy to treat the genre as being essentially for and of interest to women – Brunsdon, admitting that men do watch these dramas, nevertheless asserts that 'the connotational femininity of the genre remains overwhelming' (1997: 38). Even some recent texts which begin by seeming quite cautious about this issue – such as Christine Gledhill's Open University text on gender and soap opera (1997), which notes early on that terms like 'women's culture' are problematic as they suggest a sex-based essentialism – nonetheless often fall back into an infuriating separation between 'women's' and 'men's' genres and preferences. In our experience, students in the 1990s reject these gender-divided approaches completely, finding them bewildering and laughable.[5] The general perception today is that whilst this treatment may have made some sense twenty years ago, soaps have had significant numbers of both male and female followers for some time now; and, indeed, it is felt that identifying women with soaps is a strangely conservative approach which creates parodic images of both 'women' and 'soap operas', trapped in a world of 'emotion' and romanticism, and does no service to our understanding of either. Liesbet Van Zoonen, in her useful guide *Feminist Media Studies*, has sensibly criticised this kind of work for having a fixed view of gender, and for presuming that we can find 'a stable and easily identifiable distinction between women and men' (1994: 40). She suggests (in common with several contemporary feminist thinkers and, indeed, ourselves) that gender should be viewed as a discourse:

> ...a set of overlapping and sometimes contradictory cultural descriptions and prescriptions referring to sexual difference. Such a conceptualisation of gender does not deny the possibility of fragmented and multiple subjectivities in and among women (or men for that matter), and allows for difference and variety.
>
> (ibid.)

It seems obvious that this kind of formulation is the appropriate one: it is true to the real world – we all know that people differ in their levels of what we label 'masculinity' and 'femininity' (even the most traditional bigots recognise this, or they would have no 'effeminate' men or 'masculine' women to abuse, for example) – and it is also politically attractive, allowing for people to be different, and for people to be able to change.

The 1996 figures quoted near the start of this chapter showed that, whilst women were three times more likely than men to rate soap operas as 'very interesting', men nevertheless do watch soaps, and they are the genre which appears most frequently – with four entries – in the men's 'top 20' after sport (although they are beaten in ratings terms by two sitcoms). Indeed, back in 1982 when Ien Ang noted that more than half of Holland's population were hooked on *Dallas* (Ang 1985: 1), it seems unlikely that the male and female populations had precisely split, with every one of the women watching, and every man in the country sloping off to the pub for a pint instead. On the contrary – although the explanation itself deals in gender stereotypes – *Dallas* is famous for having managed to appeal to men with its big-business storylines and macho characters, *as well as* the women who would watch it – quite unlike any men, of course – for its emotional rollercoaster of love-life crises, lust-loaded mishaps and long-lost offspring. Even if men had managed to avoid becoming soap viewers entirely, prior to this – which seems highly unlikely – there must have been a notable change in the way that soap operas, or gendered behaviour in relation to them, are perceived since the 1980s, for there are certainly considerable numbers of men watching British soaps like *EastEnders* (BBC1), *Brookside* (Channel Four) and *Coronation Street* (ITV) today, as well as the Australian imports *Home and Away* (shown on ITV) and *Neighbours* (BBC1), and others.

In the present study, one of the youngest teenage girls, as well as a few of the much older viewers, were able to apply the traditional stereotypes:

> It all depends on the channel, programme and time but [women's interests and concerns are represented by television] quite well I would say. I mean *Home and Away* and *Neighbours* are on every weekday and that is an interest of nearly every female. The concerns are showed through drama where you can see things going on and how most women find a solution.
>
> (14-year-old schoolgirl)

> I simply cannot abide 'soaps', but women lap the stuff up.
>
> (55-year-old unemployed man, single parent)

Generally, however, the present study suggests that soap operas have become well accepted as at least semi-respectable entertainment for both men and women, particularly amongst those who have yet to meet middle age. As this is an important point to make – given the assumptions of many previous studies – and since they provide interesting accounts, we will here quote a larger-than-normal handful of men, who enjoyed soaps for a range of reasons:

My favourite programmes are soap operas – especially *Brookside*, which I have watched ever since it began. I like soaps because I like the idea of becoming involved with other people's lives – their good times and their bad times. But it is great that at the end of a programme you can forget about the characters (until the next time!), unlike friends and family. I prefer *Brookside* because I think it is the most realistic of the soaps and perhaps the fact that I live in a small cul-de-sac means I relate to it more.

(15-year-old schoolboy)

I enjoy soaps as does [my wife]. [My daughter] has been hooked on *Neighbours* since she was a baby and sings the signature tune. She also enjoys *Home and Away*. Australian soaps seem to dominate British TV. When they are good they are very good. At their worst they are atrocious. *Coronation Street* is and always has been my favourite soap. It mirrors life in that it has its high and low moments, but for most of the time nothing too major happens. The small developments maintain interest because of the quality of acting. It doesn't attempt to moralise or ram messages home at you, so it means that it is a lot easier to tune into than *EastEnders* which is becoming more the gloom and doom show.

(36-year-old male carer)

Coronation Street has recently become the backbone of our viewing during the week. On arriving home from work, the thought 'Coronation Street tonight' is a cheering factor. I had not watched the programme regularly since the 60s, and am not normally keen on soaps, but, seeing the 30th anniversary celebrations, and the Roy Hattersley lecture last year, persuaded me to give the programme another look, and I was pleasantly surprised to find a series of little sit-coms, one of which is generally amusing or funny in any particular episode.

(43-year-old male civil servant)

Thankfully my life is very stable and I'm completely in control. I am single and self employed and I keep life as simple as I can. In the last year and a quarter I've discovered *Home and Away*. It's perfect to watch after a hard day's work because it's pure fantasy.

(42-year-old male taxi driver)

Neighbours and *Home and Away* are as nice and easy to chew as my tea which I eat while I watch them. I would no more like to be without either as I would my tea. It's my wind down hour after a day at work. *Coronation Street* is an entirely different thing altogether, still the best drama, comedy, soap or whatever it is, on TV.

(35-year-old male factory operative)

What is striking about these quotes is that the men clearly have strong connections with their soaps – 'my favourite', 'I like the idea of becoming involved', 'quality', 'the backbone of our viewing', 'perfect to watch', as essential as an evening meal, 'the best [thing] on TV' – and they have quite carefully thought-out reasons for liking them: the soaps are variously described as realistic, engaging, reflective of life, well acted, easy to watch, an amusing high-point of the evening, 'pure fantasy', compelling, well made, and relaxing. Another man, with satellite TV, was an even more keen soap-watcher, with his own specific preferences – namely escapism and entertainment, rather than realism:

> I enjoy American programming and follow three 'soap operas' on video daily, *Santa Barbara* (Sky One) and *Edge of Night* and *Search for Tomorrow* on Lifestyle. I know some of the situations are a little far fetched, but it is good escapism. I don't enjoy 'gritty realistic soaps' like some British ones. I want entertainment. The standard of acting on [*Santa Barbara*] has become much better (it has 11 Emmys). I also like them because it shows that people *with* money and other luxuries have problems too.
>
> (32-year-old male magisterial officer)

Another man, 43 and unemployed, enjoyed *Prisoner: Cell Block H* because 'It provides an insight into life in Australia and it tends to show things from a woman's point of view', as well as showing 'how people cope or fail to cope with crises'. A male senior social services assistant, aged 31, said 'I love *Coronation Street*, and have done for many, many years'. He praised the serial for its humour, and described a particular storyline as 'delightful', even though he was concerned that the show reflected 'a world how conservative people wish it was', without black or disabled people settling in the street. All of the men quoted above were unembarrassed by their enthusiasm for soaps, and ignored or were oblivious to the idea that soap operas may be seen as a 'feminine' interest. However, some other men clearly felt more defensive about liking soaps. A teacher aged 46 admitted that he was 'a long standing fan of *Coronation Street*', but added 'God knows why', before providing his own answer: 'familiarity, humour, good characters, etc'. An unemployed steelworker aged 41 said that he enjoyed *EastEnders*, 'much to my amazement'. And of course, there were some men who hated soaps, and perhaps even *enjoyed* expressing their disgust as other family members sat 'glued' to the unfolding stories.

In general, most men were happy to admit to liking soaps, and this was unproblematic for them. The approach of those theoreticians or researchers who support illusory gender boundaries by studying soaps as a 'women's interest' seems perversely backward today.

THE REPRESENTATION OF WOMEN

Whilst the majority of respondents did not volunteer views on the depiction of women or men, interesting points were made by some. It was noted above that younger respondents, including teenagers, employed feminist or anti-sexist discourses when criticising broadcasters' ideas, or lack of them, for daytime television. The use of those discourses was also a notable trend in younger diarists' analysis of gender representations on TV:

> I think women's interests and concerns are represented quite well on the television. Although many programmes show the women in the house, doing the housework, looking after the children.
>
> (13-year-old schoolgirl)

> Women and their views are clearly represented mainly on daytime TV e.g. *This Morning*. I think some of these programmes give a very stereotypical view to women.
>
> (15-year-old schoolgirl)

Young women felt that some television presented stereotypically glamorous, feminine women who addressed their counterparts in the viewing public:

> Women's interests and concerns gets a fair representation, but there are times when I think it's all too much. Daytime television seems to be full of programmes about women's sex lives, women dieting, make-up, exercise etc. TV seems to still think that it is all women think about. Although these programmes may be useful I can't help thinking that perhaps we don't need so many diet programmes.
>
> (19-year-old female bar worker)

Dramas were also seen, by some, to overestimate the distribution of female beauty, and its importance to men:

> ...The only gripe I have is the way women are portrayed, too many are too young and too attractive, though this is improving.
>
> (26-year-old female electronic engineer)

> More large women in romantic roles would be more realistic because thin women don't always attract husbands. Some men like big girls you know.
>
> (38-year-old female voluntary worker)

A number of women felt that their sex was stereotyped, narrowly defined and/or marginalised on mainstream television:

[Women's concerns are represented by television] very inadequately – women's interests are trivialised or reduced to minority channels. Male violence and domination are never challenged. Childcare limited to morning programmes. Parenting never concerned or covered. Women are still stereotyped or ridiculed in the media.

(35-year-old female secretary)

[Women are served] very badly! The stereotype is portrayed constantly. Adverts are, in the main, appalling – very few 'normal' women are portrayed except in the soaps e.g. *Coronation Street* or *Brookside*. The male patriarchal view of woman is dominant. It is a pity there are not more positive images.

(41-year-old female lecturer in women's studies)

At times they make out women to be indecisive, weak and boring.

(41-year-old unemployed woman)

Other women were concerned that the distribution of naked bodies was rather biased:

Nudity is really only shown for the titillation of the viewer – mostly nude women for the men folk viewers. Let's face it, full frontal male nudity is more funny than anything else!

(51-year-old female secretary)

Nudity is OK if it is a genuine reason for being there and if it is equally applied to both sexes. Usually sex is superfluous: if it is made known that a couple are to have sex then why the need to show it, unless it is just an excuse to get an actress to flash her boobs about.

(29-year-old female voluntary worker)

More specifically, some of the comments on stereotyping deployed the concept of television's '*responsibility*' towards the whole viewing population – and indeed responsibility to provide role models for a changing society – as in this example:

I think TV has a big responsibility to represent women's interests and concerns as the way women are represented in the media is in large part responsible for the way we are seen in society. I don't think TV serves women very well. It could take a lead – as a section of the media that's present in most women's lives – broadening the range of women's interests. I enjoy driving; I'd like to see a *Top Gear* type programme aimed at women with information about basic car maintenance. Or a programme about DIY aimed at women, DIY and general property maintenance. I recall a few years ago, there was a half hour show about women's issues – on Channel 4 I think – which unfortunately disappeared after two or three series.

   In general, I believe there are still too many stereotypical images of women on TV and I would like to see a broader spread of women and their lifestyles. Young women need to see more positive images of women on TV. I often still get the impression that the women that many programmes are chiefly addressing are white, middle class and married with 2.4 children. TV could and should be enabling women and broadening our horizons as well as entertaining us. Working class women are not well represented on TV – they are often patronised.

(31-year-old unemployed woman)

In some ways this diarist seems to be calling for the kinds of shows – a car programme *for women*, a DIY programme *for women* – which could easily offend her by replacing the masculine posturing of *Top Gear* with equally stereotyped 'feminine' coverage. This, of course, is not to deny that there remains a lack of programmes about cars and DIY for *any* people who don't know much about them, presented by women (or men). Similar ideas about the *responsibility* of television to counteract sexism and include issues of relevance to women appear in the following example, although the argument is carefully tempered by the feeling that such material should not be presented in a way which might be threatening to male viewers.

Television has in part a responsibility to equally represent the population who watch it. Sitcoms and dramas still tend to reinforce sexist tendencies. Many women's interests are only dealt with in programmes directed at the young such as *Reportage* and the *DEF II* series. Otherwise they might be late at night and probably teach the converted. If they were at a more popular hour and were made in a format accessible to men (not to alienate them), they would be given more credibility. Women's programmes should not be made only for women, otherwise any complaints that there are too many programmes directed only at men falls flat. I don't think there should be too many, as men go on the defensive if they are too much under attack and the whole exercise does not benefit anyone.

(23-year-old female postgraduate student)

   Television's depiction of certain, well-developed female characters was seen to be superior to women's more peripheral and stereotyped image in some films, however:

Women are portrayed better on TV than they are on film. Films these days are terrible, women are either portrayed as victims, bisexual killers, bimbos, or nannies from hell, but at least on television there are a few good strong characters like Bet Gilroy and Bea Smith.

(21-year-old unemployed woman)

There is not a singular ideal of how women should be shown on television, of course. Whilst some respondents wanted to see more successful women being used in factual programmes, for example, others resented the focus on successful working women in magazine programmes, and the promotion of their lifestyle as some kind of ideal for women:

> I find all questions relating to women as such very depressing because of the emphasis on women being out at work, in great careers – I'm an un-employed housewife.
>
> (43-year-old woman)

In general, the women in this study were not radically dissatisfied with television, but many of them expressed a reservation or two from the range detailed above: women poorly represented by the stereotyped approach of daytime TV, and some mainstream programmes; broadcasters showing an overdeveloped preference for young and glamorous women; female nudity used for titillation; and, in general, a lack of intelligent or practical programmes not aimed at a masculine audience. The raw self-reports of these ordinary women and men suggest that women are not (quite) as well served as their male counterparts by TV broadcasters in Britain.

CATERING FOR MEN WITH SPORT AND SEX?

Defining 'men's interests' is not likely to be any simpler than defining 'women's interests', of course. This young teenager, for example, reflects the importance which soap operas have for the younger male generation:

> I think that men are only interested in storyline programmes like *EastEnders*, *Neighbours*, *Home and Away* and *The Bill*, and show a lot of considera-tion to those programmes. And watch a lot of football.
>
> (14-year-old schoolboy)

Soap operas were not described as a 'male' interest by older respondents. The mention of football here, however, accords with many males across the age spectrum. It is perhaps surprising to note that those men who liked to watch sport on television seemed to be nevertheless aware – and almost embarrassed – that there is quite an *amount* of it:

> Men's interests are well represented by TV at least if you like sport (I do).
>
> (48-year-old male, retired from fire service)

> What are men's interests and concerns? I guess most men are interested in sport and there seems to be a lot of sport on TV.
>
> (31-year-old male chartered accountant)

I think the TV people believe men wish to see masses of sport from football to snooker...Whilst I am interested in sport (or some sports – soccer, cricket, tennis) I still think far, far, too much is shown. Men should be out *doing* sport, not sat watching.

(52-year-old male teacher)

[Men's interests are] more than adequately represented. Huge amounts of sport especially football, rugby, snooker, cricket which are predominantly male interests, plus a good deal of 'sex and violence' stuff.

(36-year-old male barrister)

It could be seen as puzzling why these men feel almost apologetic about the amount of sport which they (seem to) enjoy on TV. In the 1990s football had largely overcome its lager-and-violence image of the 1990s, rehabilitated by all-seater stadiums and Nick Hornby's *Fever Pitch* (1992) as a charming middle-class and, to an extent, family interest. Nevertheless, football and other sports never lost their image of general 'blokeishness', and the 'new men' amongst the fans remained, of course, men. However, *Fever Pitch* and the numerous imitators and articles that it spawned may have contributed to men's self-consciousness about their sporting obsessions. In any case it seems likely that a large part of the apologetic stance has developed as a response to partners and friends who have less time for the athletic arts than these men do.

Of course, not everyone welcomed sport on TV:

[Men's interests and concerns are represented] not all that well unless you are a sports freak.

(62-year-old male coordinator for counselling service)

I think too many evenings and weekends are taken up with sport which is mainly for men. I also think we are now getting too many violent American films such as *Rocky* which is on tonight and these films do not interest women but do interest men and children.

(49-year-old female finance collector)

One woman had a suggestion about TV sport:

Most women tend to like soaps and drama so we do well. *But* – there is too much sport on TV. Hours given over to football, snooker and darts could be used for more quality drama. I think Sky has the right idea by having a channel for sport, leaving the other channels free of it.

(23-year-old female graduate trainee)

Other women had identified an obvious but much-overlooked way in which sport need not be implicitly *male*:

Football, racing, men's golf – what about women's hockey, women's football, women's golf – there isn't any! Why not? I want to see more women's sport, especially on Saturdays when all that sport is sooooooo boring.

(13-year-old schoolgirl)

Men's interests are represented far too much, especially at the weekend. Most Saturdays at least two channels have men's sport. Once I remember all 4 channels were covering sport. If television showed women's sports, cricket, hockey etc. they might be taken more seriously.

(23-year-old female postgraduate student)

Returning to the definition of men's interests, another suggestion was:

Most men are interested in violence more than women and there is plenty of violence on TV at the moment.

(14-year-old schoolboy)

Comments such as this invite the question of where perceptions such as the association of violence and masculinity come from, of course, with TV itself as one candidate for blame. Indeed, Gunter (1995) notes that studies have shown that on television, men are more likely than women to be involved in violence, and in particular are most commonly the perpetrators of violence. But others saw men's interests as being somewhat broader:

Men's interest seem to be interpreted as sport and politics. If you like neither well that's just too bad. It would be nice to see more male health shows and fashion for men. Also DIY shows.

(27-year-old male office worker)

Interestingly, a greater number of men than women argued that television is oriented towards men. For some, this point was made from a standpoint of empathy with women, whose interests or voices were excluded; for others, the argument was that the 'men's interests' represented by television were too stereotypical (sport and cars) and so did not cater for the full range of *actual* men. Those who felt that television is too male-dominated said:

There still seems to be a marked bias towards male-oriented programming – i.e. football (in fact, almost any sport), interest shows (*Top Gear*, gardening), and the general tone is towards men. I don't mind (I'm a man) but feel it is unbalanced.

(31-year-old unemployed man)

TV very much represents men's interests too much and is therefore a wrong representation…Why is it for example we have such as BBC's *Question Time* frequently with three men and just one woman?…Until women see themselves in equal numbers in Parliament, they are unlikely to stir from their understandable apathy to take on men in the running of our society.

(57-year-old male, retired from fire service)

There's a plethora of sport, which is predominantly, if not exclusively, a male interest. A number of serials and series made for TV, seem to include almost a formularised quota of bonking scenes. These, I would think are aimed specifically at males. Overall, though many programmes, perhaps, reflect interests of both sexes, specifically female interests seem – from [my] male point of view – to be under represented. Which is another way of saying male interests predominate.

(52-year-old male part-time schoolteacher)

The TV medium is male dominated, but not overly so. As a male, I am well satisfied with business, sports and news coverage.

(49-year-old male company director)

Inevitably perhaps, these engagements with the idea of 'men's' versus 'women's' television could be said to crystallise supposed differences, rather than break them down, and make them material where otherwise they would be undiscussed. Furthermore, we can see that when these middle-aged men begin to make 'feminist' arguments, they not infrequently stumble and reveal some of their own preconceptions – women don't like to see sex on TV, business and sport are for men, women are in a state of 'understandable apathy' about their place in society, and so on. These viewpoints are not transparently 'wrong' – or 'right' – but could be expressed with greater caution. Nevertheless, we can assume that these respondents are trying to be sympathetic to women's views.

The arguments of those who felt that masculine interests were anticipated too *narrowly* ranged from the gentle to the lusty. For example:

It is generally considered that sport, cars and violence are the items most men are interested in and TV caters for this group extremely well. I am not so sure that these men are in the majority as they are of the type to let their views be known more than those with the quieter interests.

(67-year-old retired man)

I don't know what women think about spicy or steamy sex scenes. My wife doesn't like them – but she's 72. I enjoy permissive steamy sex scenes which are now returning to our screens, but not pornography or violence.

(70-year-old retired small businessman)

It is perhaps the case that no-one likes to have their interests defined for them, as it makes them feel like limited, rather predictable characters – which would explain some of the venom directed by women towards daytime programming, and the way in which men become uncomfortable when 'men's interests' are pigeonholed. This self-conscious distaste may be supplemented by an awareness that men and women famously see the stereotypical interests of the opposite sex as 'boring' – which is not a distinction that most people would want to be recognised for.

More on masculinity

Whilst some women (and, indeed, men) felt that television had yet to learn the lessons of feminism, a minority of men argued that women had already fixed too firm a grip over their viewing. For example:

> Men's interests are mainly represented by sports programmes, and pro-grammes to do with motoring, and finance. Personally, I would like to see more uncut action films, erotic films etc., on TV. Feminists are getting too much their own way with television, and on what cannot be shown.
>
> (43-year-old unemployed male steelworker)

In contrast, this woman was relieved about the relative paucity of sexism on television, and was only disappointed that real life did not reflect such a change.

> Things have changed so much over the last few years [on TV], the male chauvinist attitudes come as quite a shock on the rare occasions they do appear. One of the best things about 'alternative' comedians (male) is the trashing of macho attitudes towards women or men – God bless Ben Elton et al! But it has to get even better – you should hear the male conversation at work, to know how deep the old fashioned crap goes!
>
> (51-year-old female local government clerk)

A couple of other men felt that the pressures and strains of masculinity could be treated more sensitively.

> There is a lot said about crime, and such things as wife bashing, but not about the stresses of being the Master of the Home.
>
> (63-year-old retired male weather forecaster)

> There is nothing about men in society in the 'feminist' sense of women in society.
>
> (37-year-old male window cleaner and teacher of Spanish)

However, there was little enthusiasm for introspective men's programmes elsewhere, an explanation for which is offered by this respondent:

> There is no doubt that men's interests are more than adequately served by television, politics, sport, etc. I don't feel that having a magazine type programme aimed at men would be successful as the average British male is a fairly suppressed person emotionally who I cannot believe would respond to a woman's hour type TV programme.
>
> (38-year-old male self-employed caterer)

Emotional analysis seems to still be interpreted by most British men as, if not 'feminine' behaviour exactly, then as unnecessary and somewhat embarrassing. The respondents did not comment upon Channel Four's forays into this area, such as *Sex Talk*, which have staged studio discussions of sexuality and gender, albeit in the style and time-slot of minority programming which would perhaps go unwatched by the respondent quoted above.

THE REPRESENTATION OF HOMOSEXUALITY

A minority of the diarists (around 2.5 per cent) expressed some distaste for homosexuality in their diaries – this ranges from an objection to the representation of gay sex acts, to extended and repeated diatribes opposing any appearance by gay people in the media. (These points were made spontaneously, rather than being prompted by a specific question about homosexuality.) The respondents who made these comments were spread evenly across the age range.

> One thing I must say, if I learn from the media that anyone is a homosexual (as a lot of first class actors are) I never look at them again, or for that matter if they are, or have been, drug addicts, as I feel they are all disgusting and weak willed.
>
> (80-year-old retired female secretary)

Here, typically, the opposition to homosexuality is so strong that other positive factors – being a 'first class actor', for instance – cannot alter it. The dislike of homosexuality was often listed alongside other prejudices:

> I dislike lavatorial 'humour' and programmes about homosexuals (whom I loathe) and [racially] mixed marriages/relationships.
>
> (73-year-old retired male probation officer)

This clustering of discrimination indicates that the positions are not thoroughly thought through, and inevitably undermines the force of any one argument by throwing in other reprehensible views. Other common themes

were that gay lifestyles were being represented as a 'trendy' lifestyle in too
many programmes, and that homosexuality shouldn't be allowed to enter
prime-time soap operas. This view appeared in the findings of Kieran *et al.*
(1997: 33), in a study for the Broadcasting Standards Commission, who found
in discussions with fourteen focus groups that a number of people felt that gay
people themselves should be 'tolerated', but that the presentation of
homosexuality as an everyday lifestyle in soaps like *EastEnders* was offensive
and worrying.

Our respondents often revealed curious contradictions, such as this man who
is wholly in favour of broadcasting freedom – except in certain cases:

> One thing I find very offensive, ITV and BBC are equally guilty. The
> 'cutting out' of bad language or violent scenes in films. After the 9.00pm
> watershed, as long as a spoken warning is given, the full film/programme
> should be screened. I find Mrs Whitehouse and her group an offence to the
> freedom of the individual...I am also appalled that this group have suc-
> cessfully banned videos from private home viewing. This self righteous
> group should live in reality, not pretend that there is no sex, violence, or
> swear words used in today's world. It is a shame sometimes that the BBC
> and ITV have had to bow to government pressure. There is an On/Off
> switch. And a warning. So these people should use it. They should look at
> the POSITIVE role of TV and videos, not the negative...The ONLY
> EXCEPTION to this is UNNATURAL SEX. Whilst this may be okay for
> people on home video (I certainly would never buy it), I do not think it
> necessary to have HOMO-SEXUALS or LESBIANS PROMOTED on TV
> in films and talk shows.
>
> (32-year-old male magisterial officer)

Obviously, the implicit call for representations of homosexual life to be kept
from our screens, and the 'unnatural sex' label, sit uncomfortably alongside the
protests against 'self righteous' censorship, and concerns about 'freedom of the
individual'!

Of course, not all comments on the appearance of gay people on television
were negative.

> Over the last few years there has been a minor increase in the time given to
> lesbian and gay programming in a positive way. Channel 4 and BBC2 have
> adopted these 'minority' programmes in a more advanced and professional
> manner than mainstream channels. I feel that more could be done in this
> area of programming to address the diverse needs of this section of the
> population.
>
> (23-year-old male social services worker)

I find many types of 'gender' specific shows appealing like *The Girlie Show* and the Gay and Lesbian series on C4.

(30-year-old male office worker)

Channel Four is still very good...But what happened to all the 'gay interest' progs? I liked those.

(40-year-old female archaeologist)

Finally, it seems worth quoting the mother of a gay man who is proud of the careful control which she exercised over her children's viewing when they were younger – and proud of her children today. This is a interesting counterpoint to those other elderly viewers who felt that the small amount of supposedly 'depraved' pro-homosexuality broadcasting available today would be the ruin of modern young people.

There is always an OFF switch for us to use. When my children (they are now in their 40s) were young I took great care to monitor what they saw. They have had no problems in their adult life and marriages and careers. Even my son who is homosexual has shaped his life and partnership with dignity and is respected in his work place.

(75-year-old female homemaker)

GENDER ISSUES IN THE HOUSEHOLD

At the start of this chapter, we outlined studies from the mid-1980s by Ann Gray and David Morley which suggested that the television set and video in a household were typically dominated and controlled by the men. It is also worth recalling that national statistics for 1995 showed that women spent three and a half times as much of their waking hours doing cooking and routine housework as men did, whether they were employed outside the home or not. Given that the latter stands as a pretty incontrovertible fact about life in 1990s Britain, it is at least something of a relief that the Audience Tracking Study suggests that – when they did get to sit down – women did have greater TV power than those previous studies have suggested. In chapter six we have already seen that video machines, which are now more common, were also more commonly used by both women and men. Television-wise, Table 8.1 shows who the respondents said 'usually' decided what was watched, in households where there was at least one adult man and woman (based on responses from 244 such households).

Table 8.1 Who usually decided what was watched on television in a mixed household

Joint decision, or household dispersed to multiple TV sets	81%
Man usually decided	11%
Woman usually decided	6%
Children usually decided	2%

The 81 per cent who said that the decision was jointly made includes 2.5 per cent (six people) who expressed this slightly differently – that the man chose some programmes, whilst the woman chose some others; a way of putting it which brings to light their distinct, non-agreed interests. The most interesting aspect of this is that there remained some 78 per cent of couples who felt that they had actually arrived at joint decisions about what to watch.

Table 8.2, based on the responses of the 132 diarists in mixed households who revealed which person usually held the remote control, shows that men certainly do dominate when it comes to actually *using* the channel-changing device itself. But even though the man alone had this control in almost half the mixed households, as opposed to only a fifth where the women held this symbol of power, this role does actually seem to be just that – symbolic, and relatively illusory. We have already seen (in Table 8.1) that only 11 per cent of respondents said that the man was actually *deciding* what to watch. Most households came to joint decisions, or did not face this problem in any case as its members were happy to make use of the multiple TV sets.

Table 8.2 Who usually used the TV remote control in a mixed household

Man usually had remote control	46%
Woman usually had remote control	22%
Either man or woman had remote control – no pattern	20.5%
Children usually had remote control	11.5%

It remains the case that men hold the remote control much more than women, and make unilateral decisions about what to watch on the main TV set more than women. But the detailed evidence in this study clearly shows that previous studies which have noted men 'hogging' the remote, and so have concluded that men are imposing their own programme choices on households who resent those options, are not really painting an accurate picture. It seems more likely, from this evidence, that women 'allow' men the mild feeling of power which may come with physically holding the remote control device, but will not in fact have programme choices made for them.

The following quotes reflect the situation in four out of every five homes in the study, where the decision about what to watch was made jointly, or – most commonly – was not a difficult single decision to be made, as household members simply used different sets.

> Each family member watches TV in a different place. Mum and Dad in the living room, my sister in her bedroom, and I usually watch TV in the kitchen. I prefer watching TV on my own, because my parents talk through everything.
>
> (18-year-old male student)

> We usually watch together, but when there is a difference of choice one watches in the lounge and the other in the dining room.
>
> (64-year-old retired female clerical worker)

> Since we have two main colour TV sets, various recorders, and subsidiary TV sets about, there are no decisions to be made, although my wife and I would normally watch together, by mutual consent.
>
> (69-year-old male lecturer)

> Generally watch the same programmes so there's rarely any problems. Majority decision wins if there is an argument but my brother and I have TV's in our rooms so we can watch anything there.
>
> (18-year-old female student)

Of course, there would be a problem with this data if it were the case that male respondents were imposing their programme choices on a household but wrote this up in their diaries as democracy in action. Cynics might fear that in cases such as the two below, the male respondents are glossing over such a situation:

> If a consensus view does not emerge, dissident members go and view a different programme on a different TV in a different room.
>
> (49-year-old male company director)

> My wife and I have been married for over 50 years. During that time there has developed a complete unspoken agreement about what programmes we would wish to watch, and which not. Only occasionally do we ask each other whether we should watch an individual programme.
>
> (73-year-old retired male schools inspector)

In some households there were self-conscious struggles for possession of the remote control:

My flatmate tries to seize the remote control but since the TV belongs to me it's usually about 50–50. My flatmate is male. When I was married my husband always took charge of it.

(43-year-old female journalist and teacher)

Yes, I control the remote control, and my wife and I have regular quarrels about it.

(61-year-old retired male BBC executive producer)

Some households did seem to have relatively democratic decision-making, which was approached in various ways, but usually involved a small-scale supremacy battle where marginal viewing choices, such as those of younger members of the household, would have to be pitted against the (parental) mainstream default option. In some houses this would be more of a struggle than in others.

A joint decision between myself and my wife, although if one of our two boys really want to see something we would consider their view but normally they will watch on their own televisions in their rooms.

(51-year-old male lecturer)

If there is something worth watching on I suggest it to everyone else. If no one actively doesn't want to see it, we usually watch it.

(16-year-old male student)

It must be said that there are some men who *do* impose their own TV tastes upon their families, even where we would expect this to make them less than popular.

As far as the main TV (in the lounge) is concerned, I (if I am home) seize the remote control – for my own protection. My wife and our daughter invariably know if there is a programme they want. I acquiesce in their choice until it begins to annoy or insult me, and then I begin rapid channel-hopping until I find something less annoying to settle on. When I feel it might be safe, I switch back. If this system fails, I switch the set off. Those who wish can go and watch in another room...I am (when present) the virtual exclusive user [of the remote control]. I'm probably politically and genetically incorrect, but I intend to remain basically un-challenged as a husband and father – at least in my own home.

(40-year-old male office worker)

As the male of the family I believe it is my duty and right to monopolise the remote control.

(38-year-old male self-employed caterer)

> My husband sits with [the remote control] in his hand all evening and flicks from channel to channel – it drives me batty.
>
> (72-year-old housewife)

These men take for granted their 'right' to control the collective viewing (in the primary TV room at least). Readers who do not find this problematic might note that they would probably regard the same behaviour in a woman as positively insane. (There were no women in the study who exercised control in this way.) To focus on one example, the first man in the group of quotes above – the 40-year-old office worker – seems to have a paranoid anxiety about the choices made by the women of the household (who 'invariably know' what they want to watch, as if the TV schedules are fed to them by supernatural forces), and he appears to usually make a unilateral choice to start hopping around other channels instead, which we can expect to be infuriating for others who are watching – 'it drives me batty', as the woman of another household says above. Sometimes he makes the decision to switch the set off altogether. He shows some awareness that not everyone would approve of his style ('I'm probably politically and genetically incorrect...') but asserts that he will nevertheless keep his masculine roles of 'husband and father', which he obviously identifies with his domineering and wilfully obnoxious approach.

Of course, this case is relatively unique. It was more common for men in the study to get their way insofar as their own choices were viewed on the household's main TV set, whilst women's choices were videoed, or were viewed on a secondary set in another room.

> My husband is the TV addict, I fall in with whatever he switches on. On the whole we like similar programmes, but if I'm really keen on something specific I will record it.
>
> (60-year-old housewife)

> My husband has the most choice as he is the bigger viewer but if there was something I especially wanted – it would be videoed.
>
> (64-year-old retired woman)

> When the men folk are watching their sport on Sky, I watch the programmes I wish to see on another TV.
>
> (53-year-old housewife)

In a handful of households it was women who usually held the remote control – one commenting, 'she who holds the control holds the power' (52-year-old housewife). However, they apparently wielded this power less emphatically and selfishly than did their male remote-hog counterparts. For example:

Up until 9pm what we watch depends on what we think is suitable viewing for our seven-year-old daughter and ten-year-old son. After 9pm I usually decide, unless there's football on.

(32-year-old housewife)

Overall, then, we have seen a few men, and fewer women, dominating household viewing decisions, but in general the choices appear to be made quite fairly. Admittedly, the remote control is 'usually' in the possession of the man in twice as many households as where it is 'usually' held by the woman, and this is likely to mean that men more commonly do have the opportunity to sneak their own preferences onto the screen. However, it would seem to be a mistake to conclude that the men holding the remote controls are actually making complete viewing decisions without consultation, since only 11 per cent of people indicated it was a man of the household who usually decided what would be watched, whereas in 81 per cent of the households there was a joint decision, or else it wasn't much of an issue because there were enough TV sets.

A CHANGE OF GENDER

Our findings, summarised below, generally indicate that the sexes are somewhat less divided than they apparently were in previous decades. The diarists largely rejected a question which asked them consider the 'interests and concerns' of women and men separately; women and men felt that daytime TV was aimed at an imaginary housewife whom they had never met; and both men and women enjoyed soap operas. Whilst previous studies have suggested that men have dominated control over the television, our evidence indicates that in the 1990s this is relatively rare (although there are a minority of men who *do* insist on making the channel-changing decisions). In general, the choices were made jointly.

These findings should not be taken as an attack on feminist arguments in general – indeed, the range of findings in this chapter leave a number of areas where changes are still required (the representation of women, and men, for example). However it does seem that people's gendered attitudes and behaviours are changing somewhat – even within the ten years between the mid-1980s and the mid-1990s – and that the general perception of gender is becoming, to some extent, more variable and fluid. In a number of areas, our evidence suggests, broadcasters are actually failing slightly to keep up with these social changes. Whilst the shifts and changes in people's perceptions of gendered identities may not be as great as we might like, this is still quite an encouraging finding for the contemporary form of feminism inspired by Judith Butler's book *Gender Trouble* (1990) – see previous chapter – which seeks to collapse the divided, binary approach to genders.

SUMMARY OF KEY FINDINGS

- Many people rejected the idea that men and women have different interests in TV programmes, especially the younger and older respondents. (Being regularly apart during employed life may have led the middle aged to feel that men and women differ more, whereas being together in retirement led to the belief that they have more in common.)
- Younger women and many men found daytime television 'insulting', trivial and rubbish. Unemployed men, as well as a number of women, did not like being addressed as housewives.
- Academics (and others) should stop talking about soap operas as a 'women's genre'. Many men were keen viewers, engaged with the characters and unfolding storylines, and were not afraid to talk about it.
- Some women felt that the range of women represented on TV, in terms of appearance and skills, could be extended. Several women felt that women's sport should be featured much more, both because they wanted to see it and because it would lead to women's sport being taken more seriously.
- The minority who objected to gay and lesbian lifestyles being featured on TV often combined this with other prejudices such as racism, and made contradictory arguments.
- In households with at least one adult man and woman, decisions about what to watch were usually made jointly (in four out of five households). In 11 per cent of these mixed households, the man made the decision and in some cases felt it was his 'right' to do so.
- In nearly half of the households with at least one adult man and woman, it was the man who usually used the remote control. Despite this being a symbol of power, the power was generally illusory since the men in most cases (see previous point) did not make decisions without consulting the other viewers. Women may often give way to the man's desire to hold the remote control, but will not actually have unwanted programming foisted upon them.

Notes

1   Incidentally, women spent just under four hours per day watching television, on average, in 1996, whilst men watched a little less – just under three and a half hours (*Social Trends* 1998) – although previous studies have shown that women are more likely to be doing a household chore, such as ironing, whilst watching TV.

2   The American soap *Dallas*, as noted later in this chapter, was one of the first shows to find a recipe which successfully appealed to an audience of both women and men. Soaps in the 1990s increasingly used attractive young characters of both sexes, more sexual themes and involvements, a proliferation of contemporary 'issues', and (in some cases) a greater smattering of violent scenarios in order to attract a mixed audience (see *EastEnders, Neighbours, Brookside, Home and Away, Emmerdale*, and most other soap operas on British TV in the 1990s).

3   Source: Taylor Nelson AGB/BARB/AGB Television 1997.

4   Source: Unpublished survey data from *Television: The Public's View* project, courtesy of the Independent Television Commission.

5   In her book *Women and Soap Opera* (1991), Geraghty notes that from the 1980s onwards soaps were changing in order to broaden their appeal to men. But since she has argued that soaps 'address women in a particular way, [and] that women are the skilled readers by whom the programmes are best understood' (1991: 167), she seems to find this development rather disappointing. (The case for why we would want to hold on to this strange kind of essentialism in television studies, however, is unclear.)

Chapter 9

Television violence and other controversies

This penultimate chapter is concerned with the way in which people respond to television violence, bad language, sexuality and issues of taste and decency. The focus of this chapter is on media violence, as we found that the majority of people in this study had a great deal to say about this emotive issue. We look at a range of responses to fictional and factual violence, and consider how people change their perceptions of television violence over a period of time. Case studies of popular family dramas such as *The Bill* and *Casualty* have been used to provide a sense of how viewers are concerned about levels of fictional violence in family entertainment. We also look at diarists' responses to the question of 'effects', paying particular attention to what people have to say about the James Bulger case and the Dunblane massacre, two events that sparked a great deal of controversy in Britain with regard to the issue of media violence.

PREVIOUS STUDIES OF TELEVISION VIOLENCE AND ISSUES OF TASTE

There has been a great deal of interest in audience response to violence, sex, bad language and taste and decency in relation to television. Television is primarily perceived to be a medium for family entertainment, and not only are representations of violence or sexuality seen as unsuitable material for family entertainment, but, for some members of the general public, it is questioned whether this is suitable material for *any* type of television programme. Showing pub brawls, or the consequences of rape, in television drama is a far cry from John Reith's ethos of public service broadcasting which was to 'carry into the greatest number of homes everything that is best in every department of human knowledge, endeavour, or achievement'.[1] It is no wonder then that organisations such as the Independent Television Commission (ITC) or the Broadcasting Standards Commission (BSC) spend a considerable amount of energy and time researching what the public have to say about these issues in order to control and regulate violence, sexuality and bad language on television.

Certainly, the issue of media violence is one that has caused considerable concern in the public domain. Politicians, such as the Liberal Democrat peer David Alton, anti-violence campaign groups, such as the National Viewers and Listeners Association (NVALA), and newspapers, such as the *Daily Mail*, regularly bring to public attention what are commonly perceived to be the 'risks' of watching representations of violence (see Hill, forthcoming).[2] These 'risks' include such alleged negative effects as copycat crimes, where someone is incited to commit a crime after they have watched a media text which contains violence; desensitisation, where someone who watches a great deal of media violence becomes desensitised to real violence; and an increased fear of real violence in our society, where someone who watches a great deal of media violence may develop a distorted picture of real violence as a result of this (see Bandura *et al.* 1963; Belson 1978; Gerbner *et al.* 1980, 1986; Van Evra 1990 amongst others). Although there is no research to prove whether there is a direct causal link between these negative effects and media violence (see Cumberbatch and Howitt 1989; Gauntlett 1995, 1998) there is still great interest in the *possibility* of finding definitive proof that such negative effects do exist. High-profile events such as James Bulger's murder by two schoolchildren in 1993, the Dunblane massacre, where Thomas Hamilton shot and killed sixteen infants in 1996, or the murder of four schoolchildren and their teacher by two young boys in Arkansas in 1998, give rise to heated discussion about this difficult and emotive topic.[3]

Studies which attempt to listen to what people themselves have to say about media violence are few and far between. This type of research does not look for 'negative effects' but rather asks television viewers how they respond to watching scenes of violence, and what they think should be done about showing representations of violence on television. Research by Palmer (1986), Buckingham (1993a, 1993b, 1996) and the BSC (1996) have focused specifically on qualitative, ethnographic approaches to the study of children's responses to television. This research is concerned not with effects, but with children's emotional responses to television. The research shows that children are much more intelligent and media literate than parental figures would have us believe. Certainly, David Buckingham (1996) finds that children understand the difference between reality and fantasy, and are far more upset about depictions of violence on the news than in television fiction. This does not mean to say that children are not concerned about the issue of media violence, but that they are aware of the contexts of violence on television.

It is important to note such a research finding, because as we shall see in this study, children are the primary cause of concern in relation to public anxiety about media violence. Research by the Joint Industry Group suggested that there is an 'extensive tendency to deflect concern about TV violence and its effects onto others, especially children' (1997: ix). Even children are worried about children younger than themselves, and how they may emotionally respond to depictions of violence, whether this is on the news or in a fictional context (see BSC 1996; Buckingham 1996). When it comes to adult responses to media violence, there is even less audience research in this area. Work by Gunter (1987), Gunter and Wober (1988), Schlesinger *et al.* (1992), Hill (1997) and BSC (1997) has focused on using a variety of qualitative and quantitative research methods to attempt to understand adult responses to violence in film and television programmes. Such research is not concerned with effects, but instead focuses on how people respond in a variety of complex and diverse ways to watching media violence. For example, Schlesinger *et al.* found that personal experience, social class and ethnicity help to shape women's responses to representations of violence, and that 'viewers are active interpreters and evaluators' of media violence (1992: 168). In *Shocking Entertainment: Viewer Response to Violent Movies* Hill (1997) found that viewers in this study, who regularly watched films such as *Reservoir Dogs* (Quentin Tarantino, 1992) or *Natural Born Killers* (Oliver Stone, 1994), were sensitised to film violence. Rather than developing an increased desensitisation to fictional and/or real violence, these viewers used a range of physical and emotional responses to understand and interpret violence in a fictional context.

If people talk about what it is acceptable and unacceptable to show on television, such talk generally focuses on media violence first, then moves to discussion of representations of sexuality, and other controversial issues such as bad language, negative stereotyping and bad examples to children. This is certainly born out in the way in which diarists respond to questions of media violence, sexuality, bad language and taste and decency. Media violence is by far the most important topic on the agenda. This finding may appear obvious – after all, media violence is something that is continually under public scrutiny – but such a finding contradicts ITC research which suggests that bad language comes top of the list in terms of what people find offensive on television (ITC 1997: 47), and BSC research that suggests the most common type of complaint about television concerns taste and decency (BSC 1998: 11).[4] Throughout the course of this chapter we shall see why media violence, rather than bad language or taste and decency, is the primary cause for concern in this study.

It is worth bearing in mind that unlike the ITC's research into the public's view of television (1997) or similar BSC research into public perception of regulation (1997), the BFI's Audience Tracking Study can offer a wide-ranging and detailed view of public attitudes to television controversies over a period of five years. This is why this present study has important contributions to make to our understanding of sex, violence, bad language and issues of taste and decency. Unlike other audience research in this area, this study offers a longitudinal, ethnographic account of how children and adults perceive and respond to such representations on television. We come to see over a period of time how people think about this issue, what other factors they regard as relevant to an understanding of it, and, most importantly, how they deal on a day-to-day basis with existing levels of sex, violence and other controversies on television. Consequently, we have a unique opportunity to see what the general public have to say about these issues over a five-year period (1991–96) when the death of James Bulger, the Dunblane massacre and the Bosnian war were part of everyday discourses about television, violence and contemporary society.

MEDIA PORTRAYALS OF VIOLENCE

There are two stages to respondents' comments on media depictions of violence in the BFI Audience Tracking Study. First, diarists were asked to write about the issue of violence in Diary 7, 10 July 1993. In this diary they were asked two questions: 'Have you watched any programmes, today or recently, which contained scenes of violence?' and 'There has always been a great deal of discussion about violence on television and its potential effects but recently those debates have intensified in the media. What do you think to this rather difficult question?' These two questions produced a flood of replies from respondents who had a great deal to say both about the types of programmes that they considered to contain scenes of violence and about the potential negative effects of media violence. It is these responses that will form the first half of this chapter, as we look at the range of discourses used to discuss factual violence, regulation, negative effects, censorship and specific programmes such as *Casualty*, or *The Bill*.

The second stage of responses to the issue of violence is contained in the Diary 15, on 24 March 1996. Here, diarists were asked 'Where do you draw the line, if at all, on the following issues: bad language, sex/nudity, violence, issues of taste?' We shall consider what respondents had to say about bad language, sex/nudity and issues of taste later in this chapter, but what is important here is that diarists were asked to respond a second time to the topic of media violence. This means that the two diaries mark a passage in time, and what we shall see is that diarists' responses were both varied and recorded changes in perceptions of media violence over a three-year period (1993–96).

The question of violence

When asked to write about television violence and the 'effects' debate, many diarists registered their difficulty in forming an opinion, or in coming to a decision about an issue that appears (to them) unresolvable at present. A few diarists chose to answer extremely briefly, offering one-line replies, or odd snippets of information, such as this diarist: 'Snuggles, our son's little Yorkshire terrier, hates violence – he always barks at the TV and tries to protect us from violent scenes or voices!' (77-year-old male chartered accountant). However, the majority of diarists chose to write at length about the problems they encounter when forming an opinion about media violence. Here, three respondents explain:

It is indeed difficult and one reads contradictory opinions. I do not have sufficient reliable data to form a judgement. Instinctively I think that TV violence does have a harmful effect, especially on young viewers.

(65-year-old retired male schoolteacher)

It's difficult to have a sensible, coherent discussion on such an emotive subject...

(37-year-old male writer)

I think that it's a basic instinct for humans (read 'men'...) to be violent so on the one hand you could say that TV violence is just a reflection of society or can serve as an outlet for violent feelings. But on the other hand, I suppose it could influence/desensitize persons of low intelligence. I honestly don't know which side of the argument I side on – a bit of both, I suppose!

(19-year-old female student)

As the first respondent pointed out, the public hear contradictory evidence, they are asked to take on trust evidence which may not be reliable, and one reaction to this is to rely upon 'instinct', a word used by many diarists to suggest a grounded, common-sense approach to this issue.

Factual violence

Although respondents found it difficult to formulate a coherent argument regarding media violence, one point that the majority of diarists seemed quite clear about is that factual violence, especially violence shown on the news, is different from fictional violence. This finding corresponds with BSC research (Hargrave 1993) and the findings of the Joint Working Party (1998) on violence on television, which also suggests that viewers differentiate between fictional and factual violence. There were a few diarists who did not make this distinction. For example, a 61-year-old female school assistant felt that 'the showing of violent scenes on TV, either on the news programmes, or as fiction must have an influence, particularly on those people who have a potential for violent behaviour'. Such comments, however, were not common. Respondents expressed concern about the way in which factual violence is portrayed, especially on the news, but on the whole they did not equate such mediated images of violence with fictional representations of violence on TV. For example, this business student was an avid watcher of the news, and watched BBC news and CNN two to three times per day. He had become concerned about the graphic representations of violence on the news:

With reference to television news programmes – both BBC and ITV, is it my imagination or have we been seeing increasing violent pictures on our screens? Repeatedly, with news reports from the 'former Yugoslavia' we are seeing images of dead people, some burned alive. Although these pictures are not violent in themselves, they are the result of violence. Showing dead people is unnecessary and it is disturbing. There is no need to show these pictures. Why not simply state that people have died without the aid of pictures, or do news editors believe this will not put the message across strongly enough? However, violence on television should not be banned, however much violence in the 'real world' may disgust me. Nevertheless, in TV news, editors should cut down on the number of violent images.

(20-year-old male student)

His criticisms of mediated images of real violence were seen as quite separate from his perception of fictional violence. He commented:

In TV (or film) drama for example – we know that the violent scenes portrayed are 'drama' – are 'pretend' and are not real. Therefore, if viewers dislike programmes which contain or may contain violence, then they can SWITCH OFF!!

Ultimately, this diarist suggests two different approaches to the regulation of media violence. On the one hand, violence on the news should be regulated or censored because it is too graphic, but for fictional violence, people should be allowed to make their own decision about what they can watch or not watch. This is because there is a perceived difference between the context of watching mediated images of real violence, and watching fictional violence.

Another diarist, for example, did not watch violence on TV because he found it offensive; he also believed that 'programmes based on violence must have a disadvantageous effect on viewers' and yet he perceived a difference between violence on the news and in fictional programmes. He was critical of the news: 'The *news* often (to my mind) has too many close ups of violence'; but at the same time pointed out: 'I know that violence occurs on the news but this is in a different context from entertainment' (69-year-old retired male production manager).

Indeed, many respondents noted that they were more upset by what they saw on the news than by representations of fictional violence. This student wrote about her different responses to fictional and factual violence:

I find images of real violence far more disturbing and upsetting than anything fictional. I often cry at TV news programmes, but I think they are still very necessary. I'm not really affected by violence in dramas or films. Sometimes it's just plain pointless. But on the other hand I enjoyed *Reservoir Dogs*. Violence can be funny when it's only actors but is never amusing in real life.

(18-year-old female student)

It is not just women who expressed this concern; many male respondents also made the same point. For example: 'Scenes of violence or its aftermath on news programmes worries me more than fictional violence' (31-year-old male chartered accountant). Hargrave (1993: 26) also found that people were more upset by factual violence than by fictional representations of violence, although violence in factual television was considered more acceptable because it was real, and therefore showed people the consequences of real violence in society.

Although the majority of respondents expressed concern about real violence, or mediated images of real violence, they did not necessarily wish to see such images toned down or censored. This mother of three children was worried about her son watching the news, but she didn't think that violence should be banned: 'The news of late has had a lot of violence, but it's life around the world and something we all need to see' (50-year-old female community care assistant). Another mother, living in Belfast, said that she avoided violence on television at all times because she found it so disturbing, and yet she wrote: 'I still find that children have no difficulty in distinguishing between "real" wars on *Newsround* and fictional violence in other programmes' (40-year-old female journalist).

Some respondents even wanted to see more graphic images of violence on the news so that the real horror of violence and its devastating effects could be shown. This unemployed woman grew up in Northern Ireland, and felt strongly about the need to show people the consequences of violence in society:

> I do think that people should be aware that the images we see on the news are often 'cleaned up' and occasionally a little more indication of the violence which had occurred might be appropriate. For instance, I've grown up with continual news reports of IRA atrocities but I'm afraid it's not very easy to get worked up about endless shots of damaged buildings. The only incidents which have had a real effect on me, made me angry, are those where the cost in lives has been made more apparent, such as the Brighton Bombing where you SAW victims being pulled out of the rubble. For me these are examples of the effective reporting of violence because they show the real suffering involved. And these are the images which stay in your mind.
>
> (30-year-old unemployed woman)

In this study, the majority of diarists perceive a difference between the portrayal of mediated images of real violence and fictional representations of violence. This does not mean that people are not concerned about the alleged negative effects of media violence, but it does suggest that viewers are aware of the context of watching violence, and treat factual violence in a different way from fictional violence.

Popular discourses

Respondents drew upon common discourses regarding the alleged negative 'effects' of media violence. In fact, throughout the sample as a whole, we can see repeated use of phrases, expressions and arguments that owe a great deal to the way in which television, radio and the print media present this issue. For example, this woman wrote at some length about the types of discourses and high-profile figures that are associated with the topic of media violence:

> There probably is a connection between exposure to violence and violent behaviour. Towns all over the country were affected by TV news coverage of window smashing a few years ago: 'Copy Cat Violence' trips easily off people's lips when things go badly wrong. Michael Medved has succeeded in drawing the nation's attention to the problem of violence in the media. Mrs. Whitehouse in the past voiced similar concerns and was harangued. Now we are seeing a generation of 'anti-Whitehouses' producing kids of their own and waking up to the reality of the situation. The moving image is intended to affect people's thinking during advertising, it has done without trying from fashion to fags to furniture in the past. BBC1's *Antiques Roadshow* incites thousands to visit car boot sales. Films (I do not visit the cinema) often glorify dangerous driving scenes which may/may not be personified in 'joy riding' in our towns and cities. Sometimes I think we see the projected images of mad brains. The old films were violent sometimes in act and speech but there was usually an obvious moral ending, perhaps too society on the whole was then more moral. I think it is a question we should consider seriously, especially so for the sake of the young and im- pressionable, even though TV is only one of the many influences that form our psyche.
>
> (58-year-old housewife)

This diarist begins by writing that there is 'probably' a link between television violence and aggressive acts, and then soon moves to mention 'Copy Cat Violence', using quotation marks and capitals to signify her recognition that this is an argument in common currency. However, she is still cautious about whether such effects can be proven to exist, and therefore we can see this diarist place some distance between herself and the 'learned' popular discourses on this topic, despite that fact that she uses such discourses to frame her concerns.

Certainly, if we consider the topic of 'effects' in more detail we can see that in general most diarists know about and are very familiar with the most common arguments regarding negative 'effects' in relation to media violence. Two respondents discuss different types of negative 'effects':

This is the issue I find most worrying and I do think programmes should not be graphically or gratuitously violent. I subscribe to the view that it desensitizes and normalizes violence and TV should not bow to consumer tastes for more violence.

(21-year-old female student)

I believe the amount of violence on TV, videos and films has produced gradually a desensitizing of people so that violence becomes more and more acceptable...Children are brought up on violent cartoons where characters are hit, squashed and promptly spring back unharmed...Before long I believe they will accept violence as a part of life.

(62-year-old male civil servant)

There were some diarists who did not subscribe to this view:

It's all hypothetical. You only have to visit certain areas, pubs, to see real violence is not inspired by TV or film violence.

(25-year-old unemployed man)

I think that violence on television doesn't make people violent. It's daft to say TV makes people violent, if you are violent you are violent but not because of the telly.

(10-year-old schoolboy)

But even if some respondents felt that 'television doesn't make people violent', many were still concerned that children should not be exposed to excessive screen violence. Children are perceived to be vulnerable, and parents express their anxiety at the way in which they believe children are subjected to increasing levels of violence, whether this be in cartoons, or on the news.

In the following extracts it is possible to see diarists responding to the issue of violence through the subject of children, using their concern about children as a yardstick for what they believe to be acceptable and unacceptable levels of violence on television and in society as a whole. It is this link between media violence, society, and the lack of clear family values or moral guidelines for today's children that echoes the kind of anti-violence rhetoric that is popular in tabloid newspapers and daytime talk shows (see Barker and Petley 1997). Two extracts illustrate this point:

I have always hated violence and find it very disturbing. People have often said to me things like 'It's only a film. It's just pretend – they're acting you know!' But to me that's not the point. My daughter was very sensitive too, and I had to be careful about what she saw as a child, and she is now with her own children...I'm sure it can only have bad effects on children to grow up accepting the portrayal of violence as a routine day to day means of entertainment. To me, to consider violence as entertainment is sick.

(55-year-old retired female civil servant)

As a mother of three children (14, 13 and 8) I am constantly on my guard against violent images which tend to pop up unannounced upon the TV screen. It's like teetering on an emotional tightrope – my justification for an almost obsessional fixation of violence on the TV coming simply from those natural maternal instincts of wanting to shield your growing children from the horrors of gratuitous violence. I do think this is something that people without children find difficult to perceive. But when a child arrives as a ready made innocent package it's only natural to want to keep that going as long as possible. I'm not talking about cocooning children in a cotton wool cloud cuckoo land – but being able to explain on my own terms the degradation of violence, instead of having it thrust upon us when there may be neither time nor opportunity to discuss the issues in question and the implications they raise. Carry on like that and I think the definition is that of being desensitised – and that's the last thing I want my children to be...I'm sure if you canvassed the views of most ordinary families, the vast majority of parents would come out in favour of a harder line by the TV companies on the kind of violent subject matter that slips through the net.

(37-year-old mother)

The first diarist clearly abhors violence on television, and perceives the types of people who may watch violence for amusement as 'sick'. Here, we get a definite sense that family discussion and normative family behaviour have had a great impact on perceptions and attitudes towards parental regulation and media violence. In the second extract, although there is no mention of current regulation by the ITC, the BSC, or broadcasters themselves (for example, the 9pm watershed), this mother describes herself as 'obsessional' about her 'fixation' with monitoring media violence, and her desire to protect children – not just her own but *all* children – from media violence.

Many diarists responded in similar fashion to the subject of children, media violence and violence in society. Contrary to the diarist's comment above that people without children cannot be as sensitive to this issue as parents, a significant proportion of single men and women showed a great deal of concern about the potential effects media violence may have on children, and even if they themselves did not condone fictional violence, many respondents felt that television should be regulated in order to protect children. As one diarist explains: 'At the end of the day if I had children I might very well feel more strongly about [media violence], but as there's just me, I simply switch off what I don't like' (25-year-old unemployed woman). And another adds: 'Certainly children should not be confronted with real or fictional images that they cannot intellectually and emotionally handle' (59-year-old retired male TV producer).

There are some respondents who do not feel that children should be 'wrapped in cotton wool'. Two diarists wrote:

> My mother and I usually use the violent scenes to show my younger brother (11) what's 'wrong'. I think it would be harder to explain without some of the scenarios on TV. In every life there is a certain amount of violence, some more than others. If television was to completely hide all violence so as not to influence people, it would not be showing a true resemblance to how our society is today. A certain amount of violence shown on television is fair enough, and maybe if we watch it with open minds we'll realize what a mess we're making of our society and instead of complaining because it's on TV, maybe stop using it in everyday life.
>
> (16-year-old female student)

> Sometimes my teenage sons watch films (usually on satellite) with more violence than I can bear, but it doesn't seem to worry them and it doesn't seem to turn them into violent criminals! I would choose not to watch programmes with a lot of violence in them, as it would disturb me and probably keep me awake at night. We should all be able to choose what we watch, with of course young children being directed by their parents.
>
> (44-year-old housewife)

Both responses can be seen to address the issue of consumer choice, parental guidance and the idea that television drama should deal with a variety of topics, some of which may include violence. However, it should be said that such responses were not common when it came to discussing children and media violence, and this reference to consumer choice was certainly more apparent when diarists discussed adult entertainment and regulation, an issue that will be discussed in a later section.

One of the reasons why there were so many respondents who were sensitive to the need to protect children from media violence is the fact that high-profile events such as the murder of James Bulger and the Dunblane massacre took place during the writing of the diaries. In the next section, these real crimes and their alleged links with media violence will be considered in relation to diarists' perceptions of children, media representations of violence, and real violence in society.

The James Bulger and Dunblane murders

The two diaries in which respondents were asked to write about media violence were sent out in July 1993, five months after the death of James Bulger, and March 1996, ten days after the Dunblane massacre. Two-year-old James Bulger was murdered on a railway line in Bootle by two 10-year-old boys on 12 February 1993. In the ensuing investigation of his death, media discussion of the case centred around 'permissive' parenting, working-class children and media violence. The judge, the Honourable Mr Justice Moreland, 'suggested that "exposure to violent video films" may have been part of the explanation for the killing' (Buckingham 1996: 22), and a specific video, the horror film *Child's Play 3* (Jack Bender, 1992), was linked to the murder of James Bulger, even though there is no evidence to suggest that either child had actually seen this film (see Smith 1994).

On 13 March 1996 Thomas Hamilton shot sixteen schoolchildren dead in the Scottish village of Dunblane. There was no evidence to suggest that Hamilton had been inspired to commit such a crime after watching a violent movie, but in the wake of the massacre politicians, social commentators and the press focused on discussion of the role of media violence in relation to violent crime. In particular, the film *Natural Born Killers* (Oliver Stone, 1994), a movie about a couple who go on a killing spree, had been accused of inciting copycat killings in America and France (French 1996), and this film was also linked to the Dunblane shootings, even though Thomas Hamilton had not actually seen the film.

With this type of 'moral panic' (Cohen 1972) occurring in the media in relation to media violence and real violence, it is not surprising to find that diarists were familiar with the common discourses associated with the media violence debate, and were particularly perceptive regarding media discussion of this issue. One respondent commented:

> I notice that after Dunblane, scenes dealing with gun violence were cut or programmes postponed. After a week or so they will come back. Why? (Before Dunblane the *Daily Mail* carried an article to the effect that if you felt downtrodden, assert yourself – it was accompanied by a picture of a person holding a gun!)
>
> (52-year-old self-employed man)

This is a somewhat unusual response. Those who spoke about the James Bulger case or the Dunblane massacre in association with media violence were in general shocked and appalled by these tragic events. However, what is surprising is that despite the enormous amount of media coverage of both events and the alleged relationship between these crimes and media violence (see Barker and Petley 1997; Buckingham 1996), very few respondents chose to specifically mention these events.

Only two diarists wrote about the James Bulger case in Diary 7 in 1993. One student wrote:

After the recent copycat incidents of murder etc, seen through the media, e.g. Jamie Bulger's murder, I think that strong violence should not be shown until after 9.00pm.

(18-year-old female student)

Six more respondents mentioned James Bulger in Diary 15 in 1996, ten days after the Dunblane massacre. Two women discussed their shocked response:

Well, that is terrible and it shows these stupid brainless types how to exert their violence in the way they see with TV, I think of the Bulger child, tho' that was with a video – and look what we've just had – Dunblane – that had me crying for days, the senselessness of a loony with a gun.

(73-year-old housewife)

A few days before this diary arrived sixteen children died in the village of Dunblane, shot by a mad man with four hand guns...Because of this there has been renewed talk about violence on TV...There is only one answer and that is not to show violence at all and to ban all violent videos. Until we do, children will grow up thinking violence is normal...When small boys go out and murder a three-year-old, Jamie Bulger, after watching a violent video...TV and parents have got to change their ways of life.

(47-year-old female sales collector)

Such responses are to be expected only ten days after the Dunblane massacre had occurred. However, what is not to be expected is that only five diarists chose to write about Dunblane in relation to media violence – two of these responses being those quoted above. What seems significant here is the *lack* of reference to two notorious and well-publicised crimes that were allegedly linked to the negative effects of media violence. Four hundred and twenty-seven diarists wrote about media violence in Diary 15 in March 1996: why did only five people choose to refer to the Dunblane massacre? It is certainly possible that when respondents discussed their concerns about children and media violence they may have been thinking about and responding to the murder of James Bulger and Dunblane. Such diarists may not mention either event, but the type of universal appeal to protect children from media violence that we saw in responses to the question of negative 'effects' could be a direct response to public discussion of how to come to terms with such senseless and shocking acts of violence. Taking this into account, and acknowledging that the vast majority of diarists chose to discuss children in relation to television violence, this still does not explain why more diarists did not refer specifically to either event. In fact, nineteen diarists did refer to the Dunblane massacre in Diary 15, but they did not refer to this event in relation to the issue of media violence. These diarists were concerned about *media coverage* of Dunblane. They were shocked at the way in which reporters were seen to be insensitive to individual feelings;

they criticised invasion of privacy, and saw this type of reportage as an example of bad taste. What people had to say about this event in relation to taste and decency will be discussed later in this chapter.

TELEVISION DRAMA

When diarists wrote about media violence they often referred to specific programmes to illustrate points, and to situate their own thoughts in relation to viewing habits. In this section, we shall first take a look at the way in which respondents used American TV drama as a means of measuring just how violent British TV drama has become. Following on from this, the two most popular British television dramas that diarists referred to in relation to screen violence – *Casualty* and *The Bill* – will be discussed in some detail. It is important to remember that diarists form an opinion about media violence based on what they choose to watch or not watch on a day-to-day basis. In ITC research on children's viewing habits and action cartoons, parents claimed that their children were more upset by scenes of violence in *Casualty* or *The Bill* than by cartoons (Chambers *et al.* 1998: 40). *Casualty* and *The Bill* are the two most common programmes that are referred to in relation to the topic of media violence, primarily because they are popular programmes screened (usually) before the 9pm watershed, and therefore targeted at a family audience.

American imports

American television drama can be perceived as a troublesome genre by some diarists. This does not mean that American TV programmes are not watched by the respondents – on the contrary, programmes such as *The X-Files* or *Friends* are extremely popular. However, American television drama is seen to be far more violent than British television drama, and this violence is seen as a bad influence on the British viewing public as a whole. Respondents referred to these American imports in a very general sense. One woman succinctly summarised the feelings of several diarists in saying that 'Many American productions seem to heave with [violence]' (58-year-old housewife). This man agreed:

> I think, on balance, the worst offenders are the imports from the USA. The numbers of murders, cars exploding and redneck racial attacks are legion. So I rarely watch that type of prog. Praise be, the off switch!
>
> (55-year-old male helicopter engineer)

American shows were generally not popular with older respondents. Many younger diarists, however, did not feel the same need to mention 'American imports'. Indeed, even if such American dramas as *Star Trek: The Next Generation* or *The X-Files* were popular with respondents, they tended not to refer to their American origins, but praised them for aesthetic qualities such as acting, direction or dialogue. However, some younger respondents were aware that American drama can be violent, although they were not necessarily critical of this. As one man explained:

> Yes generally American films contain scenes of explicit violence as part of the contrast between good and bad. I do not find these images disturbing or unnecessary as without them how would a thriller be good entertainment?
>
> (30-year-old male engineer)

Certain older respondents may be critical of American imports and their negative effect on levels of violence in British television, but in terms of British television drama, diarists offered a mixed response. As we shall see, *The Bill* is perceived to be violent, perhaps too violent by some, but is praised by others. Similarly, many diarists referred to *Casualty*, in particular the last episode of the seventh series, as an example of a shocking and disturbing representation of violence, but other respondents felt that this episode was very powerful and realistic.

The Bill: a case study

The Bill is a popular crime drama series on ITV. It originated as a play by Geoff McQueen (written for Thames TV) in 1983, and was then made into a TV series. In 1988, the fourth series of *The Bill* targeted a family audience with a new half-hour format screened three times a week at 8.00pm. The opening credits set the scene: blue flashing lights, short sharp editing, images of conflict, a strong theme tune – this is a serious drama. The closing credits, showing the feet of a policeman and policewoman walking 'the beat', serve to reinforce the subject matter of this TV drama series which focuses on the everyday working lives of a community police force and their battle to keep crime off the streets.

On Saturday 10 July 1993, the day of Diary 7, the episode of *The Bill* 'Dived We Fall' was concerned with outsiders, and how travellers and criminals can be excluded, even in their own community. We see Billy Staggers, a traveller, attempt to get in touch with his mother, but in the process he becomes involved in an altercation with the local police. Staggers is obviously unstable, both mentally and emotionally, and the police officers involved have to find a way to deal with his erratic and sometimes threatening behaviour. In this episode the police are seen to be sympathetic but firm. This leads to this episode's ending, which has Staggers leave, but not before he makes a fool of himself and those around him. In this drama, the violence is understated, and Staggers is symbolic of the threat of outsiders, especially those that can terrorise family members – in this instance Staggers's elderly mother who lives alone and is clearly frightened by what her son now represents. This episode could be seen to be fairly representative of *The Bill*, with its aim to concentrate on 'problem' members of society and topical issues, such as travellers, drugs, or living alone.

Diarists discussed *The Bill* in Diary 7 and Diary 13 in relation to media violence (thirty-seven diarists in total), and rather than detailing specific instances or narrative strands, respondents focused on what *The Bill* represents – a family drama series that deals with the issue of violence. For some, *The Bill* is the kind of programme they wish to avoid, precisely because of its 'violent' subject matter. One diarist explained: 'I tend to shy away from violent programmes. When I receive the *Radio Times* each week, I scan it and mark what appeals to me, and avoid anything like *Crimewatch* and *The Bill*, and anything else that appears creepy' (61-year-old retired female nurse). For others, *The Bill* proves a useful stick to beat programme-makers with: it is too violent, and is on far too early in the evening to be classified as family entertainment. Two diarists wrote:

> Watched *The Bill*, because you can usually guarantee there will be some sort of fracas or fight. But tonight's episode was rather tame by usual standards (Thank goodness)…I am opposed to violence on TV. I do not think that violence in such shows as *Taggart* and *Inspector Morse* is as appalling as that shown in the unruly, yobbish, disgusting behaviour in *The Bill*. Perhaps *The Bill* reflects life in Britain today, but is that a good thing? And as it is on three times a week at 8.00pm (which I think is too early), is it corrupting a young nation of TV viewers?
>
> (25-year-old male office worker)

> *The Bill*, which you see a lot of unnecessary violence, this programme should be given a rest, as it encourages violence when seen by teenagers, such as stealing cars etc., muggings, especially elderly people.
>
> (68-year-old retired male train driver)

These diarists use *The Bill* as an example of what they dislike about television violence. The first respondent actually watched the episode of *The Bill* 'Divided We Fall' so that he could criticise it in the diary that day. As this episode proves to be 'rather tame', this respondent is forced to discuss what he hates about the programme in more abstract terms.

When diarists wished to praise *The Bill* they did so in guarded terms. Two examples will illustrate this:

> Have a slight addiction to 'crime' programmes: that is why I watch *The Bill* frequently. I accept violence as part of a programme unless I suspect that the scenes are gratuitous or unessential to the plot.
>
> (76-year-old retired male director of education)

Watched *The Bill* today and saw a policeman attacking and pinning down a man. It's not the most violent thing I've ever seen. I think it was appropriate to the programme.

(12-year-old schoolgirl)

In both examples, respondents evaluate the acceptability of the violence shown in *The Bill*. In a sense, they use this programme as a way of justifying fictional representations of violence: is it 'appropriate' they ask? Is it 'gratuitous', or 'unessential to the plot'? In this instance the answer is no, but for some diarists, as the previous examples illustrate, *The Bill* is thought to be a prime example of irresponsible scheduling on behalf of TV companies. It is exactly this charge that is also made against *Casualty*.

Casualty: a case study

Casualty is a long-running hospital drama screened on BBC1, scheduled in a prime time 50-minute slot on Saturday evenings, around 8.00pm, where it has been able to attract over 15 million viewers. With a complicated, interwoven narrative, *Casualty* aimed to be gritty and realistic, and was not afraid to deal with difficult and/or taboo issues, such as homosexual gang rape, or incest abuse. Because of its treatment of difficult subject matter before the 9pm watershed, the programme often attracted a degree of negative criticism and the BBC felt compelled to push the scheduled slot for the last episode in series seven, 'Boiling Point' by Peter Bowker (episode 104), back to 9.30pm. This episode attracted a considerable amount of criticism.[5]

'Boiling Point', which was watched by 17 million viewers, depicts an escalating situation on a housing estate, where youths terrorise local inhabitants, breaking into their homes and committing vicious attacks on helpless victims. Community members retaliate and a riot breaks out. Ambulances are called to the estate, but the situation is so out of hand that even the ambulance team are attacked. The injured are taken to the hospital, but friends of one of the injured youths, unhappy with the way the hospital staff are treating him, decide to burn the hospital down. The doctors and nurses are unaware of this arson attack, and whilst they are treating the wounded, the sounds of explosions warn them that they must evacuate the building. As the main exits are blocked, the hospital team have to work fast to ensure everyone has left the building; people panic, falling debris and thick clouds of smoke make the evacuation difficult. At the end of the episode the hospital is in ruins and it appears that one member of staff may have died in the fire.

Viewers who wrote to the BSC complained about the unacceptable level of violence in this episode. 'Many of the complainants expressed anger and deep disappointment about a depiction of violence which they believed had demeaned a well regarded series' (BSC 1993: 2). The BBC defended the episode, claiming that *Casualty* 'had built up considerable expectations of authenticity since its inception' and they had taken particular care 'to ensure that the violence depicted was not glorified, and that the consequences of anti-social behaviour were fully apparent to viewers' (ibid.). The BSC's Complaints Committee upheld the complaints: 'it felt that this episode's exaggerated treatment of contemporary urban violence, and the consequent sanctity viewers normally associate with hospitals, would have betrayed the expectations of many of its audience, despite its later placing' (ibid.).

In this study, thirty-five diarists discussed this episode of *Casualty* in relation to media violence. Like *The Bill*, *Casualty* represented what respondents disliked about current television violence:

> I avoid 'violent' programmes if I can. The only one I can remember is the last episode of the *Casualty* series and that upset me – that was really frightening.
>
> (41-year-old housewife)

> I don't like to see violence on TV and would deliberately avoid programmes which showed it to excess – like the controversial *Casualty* programme recently.
>
> (49-year-old male civil engineer)

> There is so much violence in real life on the news that I do my best not to watch any extra if I can help it, but there often seems to be a violent film on every channel at the same time. One of the most horrific programmes I can remember was the final episode of *Casualty* when vandals ran amok in the hospital, and I can only pray that it was not really typical of hospital life today.
>
> (67-year-old widow)

Each respondent prefaces their discussion of *Casualty* with a general disclaimer that they do not like to watch TV violence. In this respect, *Casualty* symbolises unacceptable violence, and a type of violence that taps into a deep-rooted fear in these viewers. For the third diarist, her fears about TV violence are also linked with a fear that TV violence may reflect real-life violence. These diarists describe their response to this episode of *Casualty* using terms such as 'frightening', 'excess', 'controversial', 'horrific', which leave the reader in no doubt as to their shocked response to this programme. If these viewers deliberately avoid violence, then one could assume that they would choose to not watch this drama series at any time, given its reputation for hard-hitting realism. But, from the responses above, we can see that it is precisely because *Casualty* is scheduled in a prime-time slot, for all the family, that they feel justified in criticising this programme in such a definite manner.

Even those that claimed to enjoy this episode of *Casualty* were critical of its prime-time slot. The series may have a reputation for dealing with violence in a responsible manner, it may be well scripted and acted, *but* the very fact that it is popular with children, and situated in a Saturday evening slot, means that the BBC are criticised for irresponsible scheduling. The following extracts from two diarists explain this further:

> I do not enjoy watching senseless violence but realise that a certain degree is required to make a drama realistic. In adult drama I do not mind it as much but I feel that it should be controlled before the 9pm watershed. An example is *Casualty*, and the episode about the teenage hooligans and the vigilantes. I thoroughly enjoyed this one and was glad to see the hooligans get what they deserved, but it was on too early. I know children like *Casualty* and want to watch it but this is no excuse for showing so much violence so early.
>
> (21-year-old female student)

> The only programme which actually stays in mind (minor miracle) is the *Casualty* episode where youngsters – teenagers go on the rampage. I can't remember all the details now but I was upset over it. Something unusual for me. I think possibly because it reflects our society as it is today, and I find society like this objectionable. But it was so brilliantly acted as to be 'too realistic', just too near the bone and yes it was disturbing, and I don't know if it really was necessary as entertainment? I know I kept flicking channels – as I couldn't hack the mindless vandalism and aggression. But it was a brilliant episode nonetheless.
>
> (46-year-old female art teacher)

Both respondents enjoyed the episode, but at the same time expressed concern about its suitability as prime-time television entertainment.

A few fans of *Casualty* felt that if the programme was to retain its reputation for hard-hitting realism, it needed to portray violence in a realistic manner. This retired teacher wrote:

> I saw the episode of *Casualty* about which there was so much fuss, but it seemed to me that the scenes of the attack on the hospital were totally justified since they portrayed violence as appalling, terrifying and utterly stupid, and were an accurate image of much violence in our world today.
>
> (65-year-old retired male teacher)

Some diarists were also not convinced of the possibility that this episode could have inspired copycat effects, as was suggested in the press.[6] As the following diarist makes quite clear, such alleged links can be seen to be fabricated and alarmist in nature. For this diarist the representations of violence in this episode are unrealistic, and therefore harmless:

I thought all the hoo-ha over *Casualty* was stupid. The episode was totally OTT, I thought. Maybe that kind of thing does happen, I'm sure it does. But I hardly think it was going to encourage the public to go out en masse as vigilante hospital-burners.

(23-year-old female clerk)

For one respondent, reflection on this episode of *Casualty* led him to defend his rights as a viewer to *enjoy* such a programme. He wrote:

The final episode of *Casualty* was slammed because of its violent content. I very much doubt that gangs of youths across the country were suddenly compelled to rush out and set fire to their local hospital after blowing up an ambulance and beating up people with baseball bats, just because *Casualty* showed them it was possible. I certainly didn't see any newspaper reports the next day of any such incident. Violent images could be damaging. Those who have a mental disorder or a past experience of violent crime are more likely test cases for the copy-cat theory. But what can be done to stop them watching such images? Not a lot I think. Warnings were given before *Casualty*...so that those who wanted could switch off and leave the psychopaths and voyeurs to watch in peace.

(17-year-old male student)

For this respondent, the complaints about this episode of *Casualty* bring to light negative perceptions of viewers of this type of programme. This diarist uses humour to get across his impatience at the common view that such a programme could inspire copycat crimes. He is not quite convinced that such crimes do not exist, but he does not feel that other viewers should have to pay the price for the unlikely possibility that this *might* happen. By allowing himself to be classified as one of the 'psychopaths and voyeurs' who watch this type of programme, this diarist pokes fun at the dominant view that those who admit to liking media violence must be unstable and perverted in some way.

What these two case studies reveal is that in this study television viewers use specific examples to illustrate their opinions about the acceptability or unacceptability of media violence. Such programmes can engender contradictory responses, and it is this point that needs examining in further detail in the next section. If there is one issue that invites a wide range of complex and diverse responses within these diaries, it is media violence.

PERCEPTIONS OF VIOLENCE

What is very specific to the BFI Audience Tracking Study is its in-depth, longitudinal approach to television viewers. In relation to the subject of violence, such lengthy written discussions of viewers' perceptions of media violence means that there are illuminating insights into the way in which respondents construct and deconstruct their attitudes towards this difficult issue. In this section we shall see how respondents often hold contradictory and quite complex views in relation to media violence, and this reveals a great deal about how diarists form perceptions of television violence and television viewers. In particular, we shall see that some diarists *change* their perceptions of media violence over a period of time.

It is not uncommon in diarists' written responses to find contradictory arguments. Respondents may dislike media violence, but find that they like to watch crime dramas which include it, or they may call for less violence on television, and then complain about the lack of realism in television drama. Diarists who say that they believe television violence can cause harmful effects may still watch shows which contain violence. As one diarist neatly put it: 'I am sure [TV violence] causes copy-cat behaviour and ideas for crime. Yet I like or appreciate *Crimewatch*' (77-year-old retired female nursing officer). Another example helps to illustrate this paradox:

> I think the potential effects of watching violence will be devastating. Violence on TV should be used with great care. The more we watch violence – the more hardened to it we all become. Also, on TV you never see the true effects of violence – pain, more violence etc. You may see pools of blood, but most people think 'oh just special effects'. Violence should be shocking and will remain so if it is used sparingly and not as if in comics or cartoons, when we all know that no one is really hurt.
>
> (50-year-old female Justice of the Peace)

This diarist begins with a familiar denunciation of television violence but then goes on to say that when fictional violence is depicted on screen it is not shocking enough. We can see that for this respondent the type of fictional violence they do not like is a violence that fails to show the consequences of brutal acts. And yet it is this type of fictional representation of violence, as shown in *Casualty*, which attracts the most amount of criticism from television viewers.

Not all diarists are sure of their responses to media violence, and for some, this involves being aware of changes in their perception of media violence and its alleged effects. One student wrote: 'Having ridiculed Mary Whitehouse in my teenage years, I now admire her for standing the abuse she received' (21-year-old female student). This student doesn't explain why she now admires Mary Whitehouse, but implicit in this acknowledgement is a sense that Mary Whitehouse has something important to say, something that this student did not take seriously when she was younger. Here is another diarist discussing a perceived change in her attitude to media violence:

Previously I've said there was too much violence on TV and thought it a bad example to the immature in that it would seem to sanction brute force as macho and acceptable. However, your question gave me cause for deeper thought...There has always been brutality with or without TV. At my Senior Citizens Lunch Club, Dolly said to Mary: 'You knew Joe Peters, didn't you?' 'Aye, we lived next door to 'em in't Long Rows when I were a girl. When we sat by't fire at night and his father came in, we could hear him kicking Alice an' she cry doan't, doan't. She were a lovely woman, loverly. Aye, but she died young.' Me: 'I should think she did if she was being clogged all round the kitchen!' That comment came as a surprise to the other women, some ten years my senior, who had never thought other than husbands had the right to slap them around. Then they all began to talk at once of being hit by fist, poker, leather belt, showing me the scars where visible. That wasn't caused by watching TV.

(64 year-old retired female clerical officer)

For this respondent, the diary is a means for her to think through her thoughts about media violence. At first, she thought that media violence could be harmful to viewers. However, when she begins to consider what violence means on a day-to-day basis, this causes her to think about domestic violence. The women at the Senior Citizen's Lunch Club have real experience of violence, and this fact alone gives this respondent pause for thought. As she says, domestic violence isn't 'caused by watching TV'; the reasons for this type of violence are complex and take into account factors such as childhood experiences, alcohol, and marital relationships.

The fact that there were two separate questions about media violence, in the space of a three-year period, means that there are some examples amongst the diarists of changes in perceptions of media violence over this period of time. Respondents are not always aware of such changes themselves, but when comparing two sets of written comments, we can see changes taking place. One young respondent wrote at some length about media violence in 1993 and 1996:

[1993, aged 15] I think that there is too much violence on our television screens, even children's programmes nowadays have been said to contain too many violent scenes. I agree with John Major PM when he says that the level of violence in society is linked to violence on TV, many people may try to copy the violent acts and injure or kill people. Most films in my opinion contain needless scenes of violence and swearing which don't contribute to the plots. I have difficulty in understanding why people watch these films and even find them 'entertaining'. I certainly don't find someone being punched, stabbed or shot to death 'entertaining'. I find it brutal and disgusting.

[1996, aged 18] I think that programmes with needless violence shouldn't be shown before 9pm. After that time, when the vast majority of viewers are adults then moderate violence should be OK to be shown...On the whole I get completely outraged when a film gets censored in any way. What is the point in showing them if they don't show them in their entirety? It is the viewer's choice whether to watch a programme or not, they can always switch off. You find it is a small minority that complains about a programme content if it displeases them. I like to think I have an open mind, it isn't often that I'll find a programme in bad taste or is over explicit. I do believe that children shouldn't watch programmes containing bad language, violence or sex, as they can pick up bad 'habits' or even bad practice. Isn't it true that adults should be able to choose what they want to watch, not for the TV companies to censor a programme?

(15–18-year-old female student)

Her first comment about media violence in 1993 shows that she is aware of public debate about this issue, and she agrees emphatically with the view that media violence can have negative effects. However, by 1996, she is somewhat older, and she chooses to watch programmes that contain scenes of violence. Certainly, she is not in favour of showing such programmes before the 9pm watershed, and she still feels that children should not be exposed to fictional violence, but the crucial difference is that she now sees herself as part of the adult world. She even goes as far as to say that she is 'open minded', that she is not part of a 'small minority' who complain about programmes that contain violence or bad language after the watershed.

Another female diarist, who was unemployed, also changed her perception of media violence over a period of time:

[1993, aged 21] Now this is a rather difficult question to answer because it inflames passion in so many people. There's Mary Whitehouse on one side, and Michael Winner and you can't imagine getting any further apart in views than these two...Violence and crime has nothing to do with television. But that's not to say violence on TV doesn't affect some people. You hear of such cases, when someone has watched something sexually violent and goes out and rapes a woman, but these people are usually mentally deranged and can't rationalise between fact and fiction. Most people are not affected by it all and like Arnold Schwarzenegger movies as much as they like the puke inducing saccharine sweet *Little House on the Prairie*, and anyway, TV is not as violent as it used to be, just think of *The Sweeney* and *The Professionals*. They were incredibly more full of violence than the average cop show of today. I personally can't think of any show that regularly shows violence at the moment, so it is not as bad as some people say it is.

[1996, aged 24] Violence: Now this a hard one. I don't know where I stand on violence. Some days I think violence on TV corrupts the minds of the young and shouldn't be allowed on TV whilst other days I think violence on TV doesn't influence people to commit violence on the street, and that it is caused by our present day society's worship of materialism. I personally though don't like seeing people being kicked in the head, or their head being pushed against the wall. That always makes me wince.

(21–24-year-old unemployed woman)

We can see the change that has taken place in this diarist's response to the issue of media violence by her change in tone. In 1993 she was confident in her response to violence on TV, and quite clearly did not see a link between real violence and media violence, but by 1996 she was no longer so confident. Her reference to particular types of violence she personally does not like may suggest that this respondent views the issue of media violence from a more personal perspective that she did previously. Certainly, her views are more extreme, and represent the two different sides of the debate about media violence that she notes in her first diary entry.

One more example will serve to illustrate such changes in perceptions of media violence. This woman, a retired social worker, noticed a change in her attitude towards television violence:

[1993, aged 69] In the past I have watched programmes where I believe some of the violence was gratuitous. At the same time I would not like programmes to become too bland, and unrealistic. I have seen programmes which show violence has occurred but without being so graphic. That suits me. I have listened to some debates, but as usual, the extremists on both sides appear more vocal and I feel will never change their minds or agree a compromise.

[1996, aged 72] I now believe that some of the violence on television is too explicit and detailed, and at times sadistic. I have been against too much censorship, but I am beginning to feel that some of it has a negative effect on some youngsters and adults who may already be emotionally disturbed.

(69–72-year-old retired female social worker)

In 1993, this diarist is unsure about her position on media violence. She is familiar with the common debates that argue for or against increasing regulation and control of television violence, but she doesn't find such debates very useful. However, by 1996, ten days after the Dunblane massacre took place, she has changed her attitude to media violence. Television violence is 'too explicit', it is 'sadistic', and the fact that she is beginning to believe that certain types of people may be negatively affected by watching television violence is enough to suggest that she is rethinking her anti-censorship approach to media violence. She does not mention Dunblane, but it is likely that such an event, and the ensuing discussion of media violence in relation to this crime, may have had some effect on her perception of media violence.

These examples demonstrate that some television viewers in this study did not have rigidly fixed opinions on this difficult subject. Diarists may sound sure of their first opinion, but they also reserve the right to change this view in light of discussion with their peers, in response to news events, or because their tastes have changed in relation to what they choose to watch on TV. In the next section we shall see that for some diarists, the right to choose is important to adult consumers, and even though some may feel uneasy about the alleged negative effects of media violence, they still feel that it is up to individual people and parents to regulate television viewing.

REGULATION AND SELF-REGULATION

Regulation is an important factor in the debate about media violence, and it would appear that most diarists are very familiar with current television regulation. Regulatory bodies such as the Independent Television Commission and the Broadcasting Standards Commission monitor standards of fairness and decency and regulate levels of television violence, so that any type of programme or advert that may cause harmful or widespread offence is carefully monitored – although this is often retrospective. Examples of current regulation are the 9pm watershed, whereby programmes of a more adult nature are shown after 9 o'clock, and pre-transmission warnings, whereby viewers are informed that there may be scenes of violence, bad language or sexuality in a film or TV programme that they could find disturbing.

Research by the Joint Industry Group (1997) points out that most people are aware of the 9pm watershed, and although there may be some concerns about its effectiveness, most people felt that the watershed and the remote control were the best way to regulate viewing. This finding is reflected in the present study, where many diarists pointed out that people can choose whether to watch or not watch scenes of violence. Although a few respondents claimed that they did not want to have to switch off, other diarists felt that even if they themselves did not like to watch scenes of violence, this would not mean that all television violence should be banned. Regulation and self-regulation therefore become important to the way in which respondents think about and come to some understanding about media violence in relation to their everyday viewing practices.

Here are some female diarists describing how they choose what to watch and not watch on TV:

I do not watch programmes (except the news) which I think may contain violence, being naturally squeamish and disliking violence intensely. If I get caught out, I shut my eyes or turn it off.

(74-year-old retired female teacher)

No, I avoid violence in films, and the *Radio Times* warns us if a programme contains it. I am too violent myself to enjoy watching it. It makes me want to smash the set.

(65-year-old retired female librarian)

I try whenever possible not to watch anything that is likely to show violent scenes. If, in the *Radio Times*, something is described as being a 'tense, powerful drama' or something to that effect you can usually bargain on lots of violence.

(38-year-old female laboratory technician)

Increasingly, films seem to be very violent, and I don't watch them. Fortunately, days before it is due, the channel will show clips from it, and that is enough to put me off.

(61-year-old retired female nurse)

Each example serves to show that viewers who do not like to watch depictions of violence respond in a variety of different ways in order to make sure that they do not see such scenes. Each respondent regulates their own viewing by using warnings, information about programmes, and the on/off switch to ensure that they only watch films and television drama that they can expect to be to their liking.

The way in which television programmers provide warnings about potentially upsetting or disturbing images seems to be welcome information to diarists. As one schoolboy (aged 11) put it: 'It's good when we're told roughly what the programme contains before we watch. That way if people are likely to be offended then they can choose not to watch it.' Similarly the 9pm watershed is something most diarists praise. Some felt that the watershed should be moved to 10pm, but overall the majority of diarists seemed to be in favour of the present degree of regulation.

These respondents, indeed, felt that the watershed was a good marker-point, after which they should be able to expect programmes and films to be uncensored:

I think the line currently drawn by the terrestrial channels – the 9 o'clock watershed – is the only one that needs to be drawn. This is an all adult household, and I trust the programme makers to use bad language only when necessary – usually in adult drama. In one sense there is not enough bad language. After 9pm I think feature films should be shown as originally presented in the cinema – even if that means hearing the word 'fuck' in every other sentence. The same point would apply to sex/nudity in feature films – if it is in the original, don't mess with it.

(43-year-old male civil servant)

In my opinion I dislike violence on screen, much of which is unnecessary, more than I object to sex scenes, many of which are also unnecessary. However, sex and violence are the main stays of drama and life and are therefore bound to be of interest to the general public and I do object to certain people setting themselves up as my censor. We all know where the off switch is.

(34-year-old female fish-filleter)

Some viewers feared what might happen to TV if all violence, sex and bad language were removed:

If TV and video had all violence (or sex or swearing) censored by the state, so that all programmes met government approval and were suitable for the easily influenced or readily offended, we'd have no news, no dramas, no films, no plays, no documentaries, no sport, no nothing: just wall to wall soft toys and mind numbing game shows.

(25-year-old unemployed man)

We can see from these responses that even if viewers may be concerned about media violence, they still want adult television drama to feel 'real'. Current levels of regulation seem to be acceptable to most diarists, with the 9pm watershed and pre-transmission warnings providing viewers with the information they need in order to choose whether to watch or not watch TV programmes which contain scenes of violence.

BAD LANGUAGE, SEX AND NUDITY, AND ISSUES OF TASTE

In Diary 15, March 1996, diarists were asked to write about bad language, sex and nudity, violence and issues of taste. As we have already looked in detail at the way in which diarists responded to the issue of media violence, this section will briefly consider the other categories. We should point out that, as mentioned at the start of this chapter, diarists were most inclined to write about media violence at some length, and quite clearly see this as the most important and problematic factor in relation to acceptable and unacceptable entertainment. The majority of diarists seem to be quite clear in their minds about whether bad language, or sex and nudity, should be shown on TV, whereas when it comes to discussing media violence, diarists need space to work through a complex series of arguments. As we saw in the previous sections, even then, respondents find it difficult to do justice to the question of violence. Certainly, if we compare diarists' responses to bad language with some of the previous extracts we shall see here the entries are, in general, short, sharp and to the point.

Bad language

The majority of respondents do not like to hear bad language unless it is after the 9pm watershed and in context. They object to inappropriate use of bad language when children may be expected to be watching television, and when expletives are used merely for effect and not to add to characterisation. Some diarists object to bad language in any context. One man explains:

> I do not like BAD LANGUAGE – even after 43 years in industry – most of the time spent in factories. If a programme contains a lot of bad language – especially words other than damn and bloody I will switch off. I still find swearing by women worse than by men...especially Fucking. Swearing does not occur in our household – hence why should I listen to it on TV?
>
> (67-year-old retired male senior manager)

Some diarists object to misuse of the English language, which they classify as 'bad language'; however, most diarists feel that the context in which bad language is used is most important. As this respondent says: 'if it is in keeping with the character and drama, OK. If it is put in simply to shock, simply because the writer didn't know what else to say – NO' (64-year-old retired female clerical officer).

Similarly, most diarists appear to think that if bad language is used in television programmes after the 9pm watershed then it is broadly acceptable, as long as it is felt to be in a justifiable context.

> Before the watershed bad language should be avoided except where it is absolutely necessary in a serious drama.
>
> (73-year-old retired female teacher)

> I dislike most 'bad language'. However, only if its usage is associated with malice, violence, or bad taste i.e. gratuitously. I can't think of ANY word I'd actually ban i.e. that couldn't be acceptable to me in some context. An informative documentary on behaviour could well include 'Fuck Off' – acceptable because it would, within a context, be describing reality. Similarly, in *Four Weddings* didn't it start with 'fuck, fuck, fuck'? It was OK. Sort of nicely humorous, my children saw the video: I didn't mind at all.
>
> (41-year-old housewife)

9pm watershed broadly reasonable. *TFI Friday* 'fuck' is not acceptable at 6pm, even if it is the language of youth. I am uncomfortable with the slang of *Birds of a Feather* while *Only Fools and Horses* is OK. It is hard to define what these differences are. I don't think a 'bloody', 'bleeding' or 'plonker' count would actually prove anything!

(36-year-old unemployed man)

We can see that for these diarists, context is all important. Bad language can be used in serious drama even before the watershed, *if* it is appropriate to the narrative. Respondents have a reasonably sure sense of what they like and don't like, and this seems to be based on whether they feel the language is used in an appropriate setting. In general respondents do not favour tougher regulation. As the third example argues, content analysis will not help because the idea of counting instances of swearing, as in research which the BSC and ITC sometimes commission, would not provide useful information precisely because it ignores the all-important context. Recent research by the BSC (Hargrave 1998) suggests that people do not like bad language to occur in programmes transmitted before the watershed, especially if these programmes are aimed at children, and yet despite this, people still feel that bad language is a fact of life, and can be acceptable if used in certain circumstances, for example as an expression of shock. In this study, it is also the case that adherence to the watershed and responsible use of such language is considered to be a pragmatic and sensible solution to the problem of bad language on TV.

Sex and nudity

When discussing the subject of sexuality and nudity on television, diarists offer a range of responses. In general diarists did not discuss sex and violence together, and indeed, many respondents felt it necessary to point out that sex should not be conflated with violence. When diarists discuss the subject of sex and nudity they do so in relation to sexuality and gender, and loving or consensual sexual relations, rather than violence. Certainly sex and violence can occur together in the same film or television programme, but when this does take place, the context is very different from when scenes involving sex and/or nudity occur:

People always put sex and violence together when complaining about standards on TV. I do not. Sex on TV (at the right time of day) can be pleasant. And there is nothing wrong with a little titillation. However it is when sex and violence are portrayed together (as in a rape scene) that it becomes offensive.

(46-year-old male TV engineer)

A small minority of respondents wanted more, not less sex and nudity on television. One diarist said this about TV sex: 'FANTASTIC, if you're not watching with your parents. Again should be kept until late (kids know too much too soon these days)' (16-year-old male school pupil). For this diarist, 'kids' must be children younger than himself, for he certainly has a curiosity to know more about sex and does not see any need to chastise himself for growing up too quickly. Another diarist wrote: 'I love sex and nudity, but for the sake of innocent children, it should only be shown after they are safely asleep' (41-year-old unemployed male steelworker). It was not only men or young boys who wrote about the need to see more not less sex on TV. One woman explains her attitude to sex and nudity:

> Have no problem with either at any time. If anything I feel there needs to be more of both on TV to help broaden people's knowledge of what sexual expression is, and to help foster a climate where neither males or females are ashamed of their own and each other's bodies.
>
> (41-year-old female writer)

It must be said that such a response is not typical. Women in particular seemed either unhappy about sex and nudity on television, especially satellite and cable programmes, or dismissive of the type of men who enjoy seeing such images, or both. Three women discuss this:

> All pornographic channels should be banned along with magazines because they exploit women and corrupt the minds of a certain type of male who shouldn't be exposed to a beauty contest never mind filth such as *Playboy*.
>
> (20-year-old unemployed woman)

> I dislike this and avoid it. My husband has the knack of channel hopping and arriving at nude scenes instinctively! If he wants to watch something and I just don't feel like it (the sex scenes) I go to bed...In our house my husband chooses what is watched. So if it says sex/nudity he would choose it.
>
> (41-year-old female)

> If my husband gets gratuitous pleasure in watching tits on TV, then so be it. I usually read the paper! Sex: It can be mildly embarrassing if daughter is watching, but this is usually relieved by joking about it. I only rarely find film sex erotic. (My husband has brought home pornie videos in the past, which I found hilarious.)
>
> (36-year-old female archaeozoologist)

All three women are dismissive of the need for showing sex scenes on television, and regard men's tastes in erotic material with some suspicion.

Some respondents found that although they did not object to sex and/or nudity being shown on the television after the watershed, they were embarrassed about watching such scenes with other people, especially parents or children, in the room. As one diarist explains: 'Sex should definitely only be after 9pm, if only to spare children the cringing embarrassment of watching it with their parents' (21-year-old female student). Many of the older generation objected to sex and/or nudity being shown on television because they found it unappealing, often prefacing their remarks with 'I'm no prude but...':

> I'm no prude but I do think the sex act (and the manoeuvres leading up to it) should take place in privacy, e.g. the bedroom with closed doors to the cameras and their crews. There is nothing edifying about two people gyrating to the accompaniment of moans and groans, and the sight of unclothed posteriors is enough to put one off one's food.
>
> (69-year-old retired female civil servant)

However, it should be noted that not all older respondents are against sex and nudity on television, and older respondents' tastes in different types of TV programmes are discussed in chapter seven.

Issues of taste

There were many different types of responses to the issue of taste. It would be possible to write a whole chapter on what people found distasteful, ranging from such diverse subjects as public lavatories, Channel Four programmes such as *The Girlie Show* (a 'post-feminist' and 'post-pub' Friday-night show), certain types of 'cheap' game shows and, bizarrely, children's presenters. One thing that seemed to be clear is that diarists are well aware that taste is a subjective issue. Certainly, when some diarists list their favourite hates, we can see that it would be very difficult to find a general sense of 'public taste'. Setting aside issues of bad language, sex and nudity, and violence, what is left seems to be a mix of different subjects. One housewife (aged 51) lists a range of subjects that she finds distasteful: 'throwing up', 'scenes in gents', 'under arm sweat', and, curiously at the end of the list, scenes that involve 'carnage and dead bodies'.

Respondents seem very aware themselves that taste is a subjective issue and therefore very difficult to classify or regulate. This schoolboy gets to grips with the issue of taste as follows:

> The fact that I am not entirely sure what 'issues of taste' means probably underlines the fact that taste is very much a matter of personal opinion. So in my view, the best approach is to veer towards a 'no-holds barred' approach after 9 o'clock in any case. The 'off' switch can always be used. Before 9 o'clock when many more (young) children are likely to be watching, care should be exercised (but by whom?) although children are perhaps not so negatively affected by many things as adults assume.
>
> (15-year-old schoolboy)

Another diarist also attempts to list what is and is not distasteful, and she too comes to the conclusion that it is really up to the individual. She writes:

> I'm not sure what you mean by issues of taste. I feel that humans encompass such diversity that it's inevitable that some, or even most things, will not suit people's tastes universally. If you mean 'taste' in people, say, making jokes about serious things, or supposedly dignified people, I feel the more the merrier...For me universally a great deal of TV recently is in bad taste – especially, sadly, a lot of Channel 4's programming – *The Girlie Show*, *TFI Friday* for example, but I just don't bother watching shows like that – *Blind Date* is a show where I feel the whole premise is in bad taste. But others enjoy it and good luck to them.
>
> (41-year-old female writer)

Numerous diarists wrote one-line responses to this question, basically saying that taste is in the eye of the beholder. As a 30-year-old housewife wrote, 'This is subjective and I feel I have wide tastes and anything I don't like I don't watch. You can't legislate for taste.'

However, one issue that many diarists did feel strongly about was the issue of ethics in relation to journalism, especially when the media were seen to invade people's privacy, an issue about which there was an uncommon degree of agreement. Many diarists wrote about the insensitivity of reporters who would do anything to get a story, often at the expense of basic human dignity. As one diarist writes:

> One thing I consider bad taste is the way TV reporters, mainly ITN, are always shoving mikes in the faces of people who have just suffered tragedies or injury. The victims are usually so shocked that they forget to do the obvious – tell the TV man to put his mike where the sun don't shine.
>
> (55-year-old male helicopter engineer)

In particular, nineteen diarists wrote about the Dunblane massacre, which had occurred ten days prior to the writing of Diary 15. These diarists discussed the way in which reporters were seen to be insensitive both to the victims of this violent attack and to the way in which the general public were shocked and upset to learn about this crime. Respondents repeatedly wrote about journalists abusing their profession:

> I hate journalists abusing people who are bereaved or making a meal out of others' grief, i.e. Dunblane.
>
> (18-year-old female student)

The only issue of taste which has struck me recently is the Dunblane tragedy. I did not like to see TV jumping on the media bandwagon in the
aftermath of the killings, e.g. not only a Breakfast TV unit evidently
camped there, but *Songs of Praise* inveigling its way to the local church. On
the day of the tragedy, it is legitimate for TV to report as news, thereafter it
becomes sensationalist exploitation – fortunately after about seven days, the
TV companies did seem to get the message.

(43-year-old male civil servant)

I have been appalled in the last few days in the media coverage of the
events in Dunblane. I would expect that many other participants in this
survey will agree. Initially everyone I came into contact with was shocked
by the event but very soon turned into anger at the media intrusion.

(35-year-old female insurance clerk)

The fact that this is one issue that respondents seem to agree upon would
suggest that media intrusion and ethical behaviour is an important topic that
needs further attention. Certainly, so soon after the Dunblane massacre, it is
not surprising that diarists chose to write about their response to this event;
but, as mentioned previously, diarists chose to write about media intrusion
rather than the relationship between violent crime and violent television in
relation to Dunblane.

STUDYING VIOLENCE AND TASTE

In relation to other studies of media violence, sex, nudity, bad language and
taste and decency, we can see that the findings discussed in this chapter
corroborate certain types of audience research concerned with these issues. We
can see, for example, that people are concerned about the negative effects of
media violence, but they are also concerned about the way in which the news
reports crime events such as Dunblane. This backs up David Buckingham's
point in *Moving Images: Understanding Children's Emotional Responses to
Television* (1996) that children in his study were more upset by media coverage
of the James Bulger case than by the video *Child's Play 3*. We can see too that
the way in which diarists take the issue of privacy very seriously when it comes
to victims of crime also corresponds with the BSC's research (1997) into what
the public have to say about privacy.

What the BFI's Audience Tracking Study data adds to our understanding of
audience concerns and tastes is that when diarists say that they are concerned
about media violence, they still may hold contradictory or even changing views
about this issue. They readily admit that media violence is a difficult and
complex 'problem' and one that is not easy to resolve. Even when events such
as the murder of James Bulger or the Dunblane tragedy take place, diarists are
still aware that there is no easy answer to the problem of media depictions of

violence. This acknowledgement of the complexity of media violence and an unwillingness to find easy solutions to this 'problem', even when diarists themselves believe media violence does have negative effects, is an important finding.

The way in which respondents are more willing to spend time and effort writing at length about media violence than about sex or bad language also suggests that ITC (1997) and BSC (1998) research into what the viewing public find objectionable may need further attention. Diarists were asked to write twice about the issue of media violence, but even taking this factor into account we can still see that diarists perceive the issue as difficult and complex. Viewers find it difficult to define boundaries for acceptable and unacceptable portrayals of violence on television; some diarists are not sure whether media violence can have negative effects; other diarists wish to protect children from violence on TV, and yet at the same time feel that adult drama should be realistic. This reflects the fact that media violence, like issues of taste, is a subjective issue, and this study suggests that further discussion of TV violence is necessary before a coherent picture can emerge as to what the public find acceptable and unacceptable on British television.

SUMMARY OF KEY FINDINGS

- Viewers distinguish between fictional violence and factual violence on television.
- There is more concern about fictional violence than about other forms of controversial televisual material, especially in relation to negative effects.
- Viewers express concern that children should be protected from violence, sex, nudity and bad language on television, especially in family entertainment.
- The nine o'clock watershed is thought to be an acceptable means of regulating controversial material, especially in relation to sex/nudity and bad language.
- Viewers find it difficult to agree on what levels and types of violence are acceptable and unacceptable on screen.
- Viewers can change their perceptions of media violence over a period of time.
- Viewers do not necessarily equate events such as the death of James Bulger or the Dunblane massacre with the alleged negative effects of media violence.
- Indeed, viewers are more likely to criticise coverage of such real-life violent events on the *news* as lacking in ethical standards.

Notes

1   Quoted in Ang (1991: 108).
2   David Alton is a member of the Movement for Christian Democracy, an anti-violence campaign group (see Barratt 1995). For information about the NVALA see Barratt (1995) and Newburn (1992), and for discussion of the *Daily Mail* and its coverage of the issue of media violence see Barker and Petley (1997), and Barker (1984).
3   For detailed discussion of the James Bulger case and the Dunblane massacre see Barker and Petley (1997) and Buckingham (1996), and see the *Independent*, Thursday 26 March 1998, and other daily newspapers, such as the *Times* and the *Guardian*, for reportage of the playground killings in Arkansas.
4   The report on programme complaints for the ITC (1998) suggests that the ITC also receive the greatest number of complaints regarding issues of fairness and taste and decency.
5   See the *Daily Mail*, 25 February 1993, p. 5 and the *Guardian*, 25 May 1993, p.11, for discussion of *Casualty*. For specific reference to the BSC outcome see BSC 1993: 2.
6   See the *Guardian*, 20 April 1993, p. 19, section 2.

Chapter 10

Conclusions

So what have we found? Well, quite a lot of things, so readers who have jumped to this conclusion to get a summary of the whole book should really look at the bullet-point summaries which appear at the end of each main chapter. We mentioned in chapter one that the findings of this kind of study, because it is based on a lot of qualitative data from an unusually large number of people, can tend towards the finding that we can only say that 'everyone is a bit different, everything is very complex'. However, by looking at different groupings within the sample, by looking for patterns, and by focusing on certain issues which the data pushed forward, we have been able to identify a range of more substantial points.

In the BFI Audience Tracking Study, respondents came from a variety of different household forms and arrangements, and the fact that we had students, retired people, single parents, people living alone and married couples with children writing about the relationship between television and everyday life means that we can offer a more comprehensive picture of people's responses to living with television. Unlike previous ethnographic studies of television in the home, we have not privileged one group of people, such as women or married couples, but allowed a range of accounts of television and everyday life to shape our understanding of this issue. Roger Silverstone (1994), it will be recalled, pressed for 'the experience of television' to take centre stage in media audience studies: this would prioritise people's *engagement* with television, and the study of the ways in which people consume and interact with TV would be seen in the context of their broader environment – both immediate and more distant. Silverstone noted that such a study had not yet been achieved. Whilst it is unlikely that the present study has fulfilled all of Silverstone's more ambitious dreams, we do have some solid findings about the experience of television in the households of 1990s Britain.

TIME AND CHANGE

Time emerged as a factor which our diarists were overwhelmingly conscious of. Although their timetables were not in the written-down form which we normally associate with such schedules, most people did have a mentally timetabled routine. Even those whose day did not have to start at a specific time, or who had avoided the rigidity of '5.20: Make cheese on toast, 5.35: Watch *Neighbours*', still had a clear idea of how long particular activities should take, and approximately when they should occur. Television schedules partly contributed to this need to be aware of the time, since programmes such as soap operas and the news were adopted by viewers as marker-points, breaking up and adding interest to the day, as well as being a social opportunity for members of the household to meet and interact around the TV set. This suggests that the significance of TV programmes is not their content but other formal features (such as when they show up) – an idea dating back at least as far as Marshall McLuhan's famous declaration of the early 1960s, that 'the medium is the message' – and is not an argument we fully subscribe to, since the content of programmes *was* clearly of great importance to our respondents. Nevertheless, time and the social meaning of that time were important factors as well, and this is often overlooked in media studies.

Furthermore, as well as being aware of time in terms of their personal schedule, and the broader timetable of their family or household, respondents were conscious of the *amount* of time which they spent watching television. Some regretted the amount of time which they found they spent in front of the screen; others were keen to emphasise that they spent a minimal amount of time viewing and so had little to regret – an emphasis which we shall return to below. Most people, it should be said, were not overly worried or disturbed by the amount of time they spent in front of the screen, but they were certainly aware of it.

Time was also a factor in broader terms, as over the five years in which the participants wrote diaries we were able to observe the significance of transitions, changes and shifts in the character of their lives. Starting or finishing a relationship, periods of depression or grief, or changes in a person's perception of how generally 'busy' they were (for example, if exams were imminent, or had just passed), as well as the changing attention requirements of other members of a household or family, could all have an effect upon how much TV was watched, and the quality of engagement with it.

When this study was established by the BFI, it was thought that the impact of the 1990 Broadcasting Act would be an important factor in the changes which would be observed over the succeeding years. Whilst this matter perhaps needs more consideration than we have been able to give it in this book, it is our general impression that although the changes which this act brought about – deregulation, the 'auctioning' of ITV licences, the scope for more channels – were of tremendous consequence to broadcasters, they made very little conscious impression upon the everyday viewing audience in the first half of the 1990s. Of course, there was the relatively small but growing number of households which took up satellite or cable TV, but even this did not radically affect viewing *practices*. (Channel 5 finally appeared in March 1997, a year after our respondents had written their final diary.) As far as our diarists were concerned, in general, they had enjoyed the output of the four TV channels in the 1980s, and continued to enjoy them in the 1990s. They noted some changes in channel identities – such as Channel Four's increases in both quality and sexual adventurousness (the latter not welcomed by all), and the growing ITV-style populism of BBC1 (not welcomed by anybody) – but as they went about their everyday lives and daily viewing, there was little sign that the Broadcasting Act of 1990 made any difference to them, except insofar as the TV output available to them was affected by it. Even this difference, as far as our viewers were concerned, is slight. For example, when TV-AM lost its franchise in the ITV licence auction process, in 1993 – meaning it had to shut down its whole breakfast TV broadcasting operation – this was quite earth-shaking in the broadcasting industry, and even in Westminster, prompting Margaret Thatcher, extraordinarily, to apologise for one of her flagship policies. But as far as the consumer is concerned, TV-AM and GMTV are like two makes of cola, bubbly but basically indistinguishable, and probably bad for you.

GENDER: CHANGING LANDSCAPES

When looking at issues of gender, we generally found some breakdown of the polarised distinctions between men's and women's tastes and uses of media which some previous studies had emphasised. Soap operas in particular have been studied, in the past and recently, as a 'women's genre', and our diarists rejected this dated notion quite categorically. Many men in our sample enjoyed this genre just as much as many women did. Furthermore, the diarists themselves – particularly younger and older respondents – rejected the idea of there being distinct 'women's' and 'men's' tastes or interests. In terms of the uses of technology, women and men were equally adept at operating videos and other equipment – an unsurprising point, but one which again contrasts with some previous findings. Another finding of that kind is that women were just as interested as men were in the news; current affairs was not seen as a 'masculine' domain.

In all of these ways, gender distinctions were breaking down, and we would suggest that the much more polarised views of gender relations which emerge from those much-written-about studies conducted in the 1980s, such as Morley (1986, 1992) and Gray (1987, 1992), should be regarded more as products of their time – and their small, local samples – than they usually still are. These texts make very valuable theoretical and methodological points, and Ann Gray's *Video Playtime* (1992) in particular is a very good read, but we would warn against taking them as representative of gender relations in Britain today (as textbook writers, at least, seem to), since our own large-scale qualitative data did not support their findings.

Furthermore, there is something curious about overtly polarised gender 'findings', and we are supported in this view by the large number of our respondents who thought it was rather odd that at one point they were asked to comment separately on how TV catered for women's and men's 'interests and concerns'. When David Morley (1986, 1992) ends up presenting his basic argument from the *Family Television* study in a chart which under 'Masculinity' lists 'Activity', 'Factual programmes' and 'Realist fiction', and under 'Feminine' lists 'Watching television', 'Fictional programmes' and 'Romance', it is difficult to see why he thinks this is helpful.[1] The problems that these findings are simplistic, polarised and based on an unrepresentative sample are all admitted by Morley himself, and whilst the author undoubtedly had the best of intentions, his argument presented in this form ultimately reinforces its own determinism, and taken out of the author's own careful hands appears as a set of 'facts' in textbooks: Men like documentaries. Women like love stories. That's how it is. Given that many of our diarists rejected the premise of a question which merely *asked* about sex differences, we are pleased to be able to say that there is empirical support for academics who might want to write about gender in more sophisticated terms (Ang and Hermes 1996).

Having said that, cultures do not change overnight, and some of the elements detected by Morley and Gray were present in our study. For example, although there were not so many cases where the woman in a heterosexual couple had to suffer the imposed TV choices of her undemocratic male partner – there being 11 per cent of households where the man 'usually' decided what to watch – the 1990s solution was sometimes that the woman had to leave the comfortable main viewing room and watch on a less-preferred TV set elsewhere. We did find that although men were not usually making viewing decisions without consulting other viewers, they did tend to make sure the remote control was to hand. Nevertheless, whilst men seemed to enjoy wielding this symbol of power and control, they still generally consulted others about what to watch – a point which should remind researchers that the responses to survey-style questions like 'Who usually operates the remote control?' should be interpreted with some caution: the person who does the button-pushing is not *necessarily* forcing other viewers, against their will, to suffer their devilish selections.

We also found that some female and male diarists were critical of the representation of gender on television, particularly in relation to women, whom it was felt broadcasters required to be young and good-looking. The way in which daytime TV addressed its audience was also considered to be nauseating: female and male viewers alike insisted that they did not want to be treated like housewives of little intelligence.

IDENTITY

People's individual identities are clearly touched by the media in very gentle ways: whilst the ways in which people see themselves and others may be subtly influenced by many different television elements, this is not something which we would be able to trace in a study of this kind. (This also illustrates how short-sighted those studies are which aspire to measure media 'effects' in one sitting.) Only where people chose to write about themselves in relation to specific TV programmes were we able to start to gather any insights into this subject, and the scope was limited. Our experience in this area mirrors that of Joke Hermes, who has written that doing her research on people's reading of women's magazines was like throwing dice, which would usually land with rather dismissive or practical answers to her questions; but 'while they were rolling, an occasional glimpse showed other sides of the dice', revealing flashes of ways in which the media might be connected to the respondent's thinking about identity (1995: 143).

Only with the elderly did we feel we could make some general comments about a group identity and its association with media use (although at the same time we had to note that the over-60s were a diverse set of individuals – not really a group at all – and that becoming 'elderly' is not something that suddenly occurs a year after a 59th birthday). Older viewers were grateful for the 'virtual mobility' which television gave them – showing them interesting and unusual parts of the world – and we found them to be well able to operate their videos and other equipment. We argued that older people's preference for 'light', 'gentle' and often nostalgic TV programmes could be accounted for in terms of the psychological needs of those people adjusting to the fact that they are in the later stages of life. Whilst it is easy for young people to argue that the elderly are 'hiding' from the 'real world', we suggested that it is reasonable that older people might want to protect themselves from its excesses. On the other hand, we do not want to be deterministic: it might be cruel to take your grandparents to see the package of violence, sex and swearing that is *Species II*, but there is a possibility that they might enjoy it. After all, someone had to.

Identity was more clearly marked in another sense, as people stamped their *own* identities *upon* technologies. It was clear that once video entered people's homes, for example, a range of meanings were assigned to it, and in chapter six we saw people making creative use of this technology, 'customising' its functions so that it was of use to them. We have also seen that television itself, of course, comes to take on a wide range of uses and meanings when put into the human context of a household.

SEDUCTION

Television was seen as *seductive*, in a range of ways, by our diarists. Those with time on their hands, such as the retired, seemed to view television slightly warily, conscious that if they were not 'careful' their days might be taken over by the allure of TV. Correspondingly, there was a aversion to daytime TV, not merely because of the common view that the programmes were no good, but also because watching television in the daytime was seen as a kind of moral weakness which such respondents did not want to give in to. A culturally imbibed work ethic meant that most diarists felt they should be doing something 'more useful' in the daytime, and daytime TV-viewing was associated with periods of illness – although in their later years the elderly would often 'allow' themselves to watch more.

Our respondents reported feelings of guilt, like adulterers, when they had allowed TV to seduce them into watching more than they had intended to spend. The video cassette recorder, which we found diarists of all ages were well able to use, was partly a tool to regain control over TV's seductive tendencies. By organising their own viewing through timeshifting and storing programmes, viewers were able to seize some sense of power.

Some control over TV-overload was also maintained by the way in which programming seemed to be divided into three types: *favourite* programmes which were always watched, or else would ideally be taped; other programmes which would be *routinely* watched but which would not be listed as favourites – the news and teatime soaps were particularly likely to be in this category; and other shows which would be watched because they happened to be on, looked engaging enough, and there was time to see them.

A FRAGMENTED AUDIENCE?

We have repeatedly emphasised that our diarists, and 'the audience' in general – that being almost everybody – are a diverse bunch, but they still have a lot in common. The idea of the 'fragmented audience' has been a popular way of considering changes in the reception of television, following from the changing face of broadcasting, for some time now. But we found little evidence of it. In the minority of households equipped with satellite or cable TV, there was some evidence that those who watched the sports channels were not doing so with the happy participation of other household members, but in general 'new' channels like Sky One, Sky News, UK Gold and movie channels, were treated as conventional broadcasters (as opposed to special-interest 'narrowcasters') and watched by families and households who were as more or less united as they ever had been around the TV set.

It could be said that our respondents' prolific use of their video machines had created a more fragmented audience, as programmes of particular interest to one person were timeshifted away for exclusive viewing. But at the same time, this was often done to enable the viewer to participate in the shared experience of watching something with broader appeal during mainstream viewing time, in the company of their family or friends, which rather counteracts the previous point. So whilst it remains possible, and perhaps likely, that television audiences will become more fragmented in the future, it is worth noting from this study not only the particular point that British audiences refused to fragment much in the first half of the 1990s, but the more general and important finding that people's social impulses will most likely mean that they will not become fragmented, isolated viewers to the extent that some have predicted.

REFLECTIONS ON WRITING DIARIES AND THE RESEARCH PROCESS

At the end of this study, in 1996, some respondents used some of the space in their fifteenth and final diary to comment on the process of producing these texts themselves. Some of these remarks noted the length of time that had passed, and the number of things that had happened to the respondent since they had joined the project – such as this one:

> I've just thought – I have been in contact with you since I got 'A' level results – left home – went to university – got a degree – got married! If you'd kept going – I might have been able to fill in the parents' question-naire!!
>
> (23-year-old female housing association support worker)

Some of the comments reflected the fact that the study had prompted the respondents to be reflexive about their television viewing practices, in a way which they suggested they were not usually:

> I have enjoyed writing these diaries because it has made me stop and think about something which everyday I just take for granted and don't spend much time thinking about.
>
> (15-year-old schoolboy)

> This study has affected my attitude to TV as it necessitates my examining subjective perspectives as subjective rather than allowing me to assume that my views are much the same as millions of others.
>
> (62-year-old retired disabled man)

In a sense this is a problem for our study, if people had switched to an 'analytical mode' which did not reflect their everyday approach to life in general, or television in particular. At the same time, asking people to reflect honestly upon a topic is not a bad thing, and is common to all research methods which ask things of their subjects. It is the feeling of those people who worked on this project that the respondents were being 'true' in their diaries, and if the research prompted the diarists to be more thoughtful or critical about their own behaviours and attitudes, they were nevertheless reporting 'how it was for them', as it were. (The possible exception to this would be the people who were self-conscious about the *amount* of television which they watched, as we will discuss below.) Whilst we are aware that as researchers we cannot take everything that is said at face value, it is worth considering this elderly woman's discussion of this subject:

> I have always tried to answer diary questions honestly. I am aware of my prejudices but I don't think flabby answers and wishy washy criticisms are of much use to Audience Study. It is important to me that the impression of criticism should not be interpreted as ammunition for controlling what producers put on screen. I feel that every producer should be constantly reminded of the powerful effect of their work. They should always be encouraged to feel responsible for what they do. As a viewer I am very grateful to them for all the effort they put in – even when I dislike the results.
>
> (78-year-old retired woman)

Whilst this woman seems to have been well aware that her words were going to be studied, and might even have an impact upon broadcasters, others professed to be less confident about the power of their writings:

> If I realised these studies were going to be used as 'historical documents' I'd have taken the time to write a bit neater and cut the stupid comments out! (Hope they have amused you though!) I wonder at the end of all this what sort of person I have come across as? Hmm...
>
> (21-year-old male accounts assistant)

> I have enjoyed 5 years of the diaries and hope I have been of some help and not just a 'moaning minnie'.
>
> (72-year-old retired female teacher)

Ellen Seiter noticed in her study about audiences and soap operas that certain respondents did not want to present themselves as 'too familiar with television' (1994: 392). Seiter suggests that it was the presence of academics in the interview that influenced this reluctance of her subjects to appear as 'telly addicts'. Two retired men emphasised the ways in which they were busy with other leisure activities, and that unlike other soap opera fans (women in particular) they had better things to do than sit around all day watching television. Seiter discusses the fact that, as 'a researcher', her presence might have inhibited respondents' discussion of television consumption practices. She notes: 'The social identities of academic researchers and the social identities of our TV viewing subjects are not only different, they are differently valued' (1994: 395). For Seiter, academics may wish to research TV audiences, to access 'the other', but they should not assume that they can 'be this other audience' (ibid.).

In our study, because of the nature of the diary format, respondents were able to reflect on television and everyday life uninterrupted and unprompted by researchers. This ensured that respondents offered their own accounts of what happened to them and their television viewing over a five-year period: they defined what was or was not important about their daily routine, or about issues such as gender or media violence. However, the fact that respondents knew they were writing for an academic study almost certainly did have some influence on how they constructed their responses. There were some diarists who clearly did not wish to be perceived as 'heavy' television viewers, despite the fact that television seemed to occupy an important part in their daily lives. This says something about the nature of academic research, which by its very nature cannot help but suggest a certain 'superior' or 'expert' approach to the study of the media (even the name of the kind of study upon which the present study was based – 'mass observation' – suggests an elite gathering information on the masses, which is ironic since the approach was actually one of the first to give respondents their own voice). The respondents' caution also says something about the enduring myth that watching television is bad for you, which we will discuss next.

TELEVISION CONSUMERS: CONSUMED BY TELEVISION?

We discussed in chapter five the fact that television means a great deal to people, and that respondents often thought of television as a kind of companion or even friend; this friendship had its ups and downs, but it was clear that despite sometimes feeling guilty or unhappy about the amount and type of television that may be watched, people on the whole did not want to be without it. The fact that so many diarists wrote about their feelings of guilt in relation to television suggests that a certain self-consciousness about watching 'too much' television is common, and perhaps incorporates a feeling that watching a lot of TV is rather unhealthy. We saw that the more television people watched, the more they were likely to feel guilty for not doing other things, such as household chores, homework, or socialising, or any number of other things that people don't do if they're watching television. If we looked at the responses about TV guilt in isolation, it would be easy to form the impression that the British public is fundamentally uncomfortable with watching television, and is somewhat annoyed that TV has come to settle so easily into their living rooms and everyday lives. However, taking into account the context in which these responses were written, and looking at how much pleasure people get from watching television – even when they only have daytime TV for company – we can see that these respondents are well able to 'cope' with whatever guilt their viewing may bring, and in fact would be most reluctant to part with their TVs.

We should note that this study also showed respondents *regulating* their own levels of television viewing. This point was made in chapter nine on media violence and self-regulation, but this is something that needs considering in relation to television consumption practices overall. Young adults, unemployed people, parents, retired couples, all regulate their television viewing. The fact that many respondents took the time to examine TV schedules and plan their viewing in advance would suggest that taking a controlled or regulated approach to their television viewing is something that people rather enjoy. Far from fulfilling the stereotype that people are glued to the TV set, we found that our respondents were leading busy lives, and when they did find the time to watch television, they thought that TV was a useful means to relax, interact with others, and keep up to date with the 'real' world of current affairs as well as the fictional worlds of their favourite soap characters, detectives and starship captains. Certainly, some diarists could be classified as 'heavy' television viewers, but this category does little to help us understand why people may choose to watch a great deal of television, and how they regulate their television viewing. It ignores their choices, their fluctuating levels of attention at different times, and their reasons for viewing different types of programme, as well as failing to recognise the hobbies, activities and social interaction that go on in front of the TV. One of our findings in relation to levels of television viewing is that people who are suffering from long-term illness or disability use television as a means to aid recovery. Television does not involve a great deal of physical exertion, but it does offer mental stimulus, and this is why news and current affairs programmes and quiz shows are favoured by people in the older age bracket who were feeling the physical and psychological strains of later life. The point here is that categorising people as 'heavy' or 'light' viewers is not helpful in understanding how and why television is integrated into the domestic space. Viewers regulate their own television consumption according to their changing work and home lives, and furthermore the audience themselves are the first to be critical of watching 'too much' television. Viewers are perfectly capable of choosing other media, such as the video, radio, or magazines for entertainment; and if this is not satisfactory, viewers are very capable of doing other things entirely.

In general, we feel that the method of this study was a good one, and indeed the data it produced – the three and a half million words about everyday life and television written by the diarists – is far from being 'finished' with; inevitably, in this one book we have only been able to pick up a selection of the themes which emerged. It would have been better if the sample had been more representative, as the young and ethnic minorities were under-represented, and it is likely that the sample was overly middle class. The only other problem is the sheer scale of the project: whilst on the one hand the methodology is good because it hands over a lot of the control to the respondents themselves, who can write what they like (in common with the theme of taking the primary voice away from researchers and towards their 'subjects', as highlighted in Gauntlett 1997, and Hill 1997), at the same time there is so *much* data that the researchers end up imposing frames and filters on the mass of diary texts in order to be able to say *anything* about them in one book of less than multivolume proportions. The diaries were full of fascinating accounts of everyday life, and built up to make moving stories of some individuals' struggles through difficult times, and most of those lengthy individual stories do not appear in this book, which would have been more anecdotally rich but more sociologically weak if we had filled up its pages with a selection of a few of these 'nice stories'.

Nevertheless, we hope that we have shown the audience being thoughtful, critical and creative consumers of broadcast television, aware of and somewhat cautious about its place in their everyday lives. We also hope that we have been able to communicate a flavour of the variously funny, tragic, complex, anxious and happy turns of their reflections on life as they have lived it, and that we have been able to learn something from our diarists without doing them an injustice.

Note

1   Ann Gray (1992: 160–1) produces similar charts of gendered polarities, but here their impact is slightly less offensive, though somewhat more depressing, as the dichotomies are directly taken from the arguments of the women themselves – who felt that the 'female' behaviours and genres were inferior to the 'male' ones.

Appendix
Further methodological details

Dealing with the data

Several early attempts were made by the authors and Rob Turnock, our research assistant, to capture and encode Tracking Study data in a consumable form, with varying degrees of success. A recurrent problem was that such attempts often separated the data from the context in which it had been written. For example, some data had been entered onto computer throughout the study period, using SPSS (the Statistical Package for the Social Sciences), but this statistical program is inevitably best able to analyse numerical and numerically coded data. The vast bulk of qualitative data could not be inputted using this package, and this meant that we had to consider alternatives. NUDIST is a common computer software program used by qualitative researchers which helps the researcher to code material (see, for example, Richards and Richards 1994). However, the amount of written data in this study meant that we did not have the time, or the inclination, to ask our researcher to input three and half million words into the computer. An attempt was made to trawl through the diaries for each respondent and write a summary of each diary, but this proved rather too laborious. A summary/template sheet was then created on the basis of key diary questions over the five-year period. The key questions were identified on the basis of important personal and viewing data recorded at the beginning and at the end of the study period. Added to this were other thematic questions which related to issues such as gender, or violence. This data was recorded onto a summary sheet, which provided relevant data in a raw (and therefore 'true' to the diaries) form while at the same time providing a portrait of each respondent, and an insight into their lives and viewing behaviour. A reasonably simple database package, Filemaker Pro, was adopted; although designed for keeping commercial records and mailing lists, the package was useful for storing both numerical and textual data. Search functions could be performed on the basis of categories or fields, and could be used to conduct word or title searches in fields containing vast quantities of textual, qualitative data. At the end of the data-entry stage, our research assistant had inputted well over half a million words. Even so, this electronic store of quotes and information often served just as a prompt to go back to the original set of diaries written by a respondent, and get at the richer material in the old-fashioned way.

There is always a question of what to do with the text in a qualitative research project (Richards and Richards 1994), and from the above account it can be seen that we wanted to ensure that we could look at all of the evidence in the diaries in order to validate claims that we wished to make about television and everyday life. In a large project such as this one, the coding process can make the data seem, to use a phrase by Richards and Richards, 'distant and dead' (1994: 151). The Filemaker software enabled us to ensure that segments of information could be read by the researchers, but these parts always remained within the context of the diarists' lives. Working within a grounded theory tradition enabled us to get a sense of the larger picture, and we were able to explore ideas and verify claims that emerged from this data. At all times we therefore had a first-hand sense of the 'lived in' nature of respondents' everyday lives and how this intersected with television viewing practices.[1]

Geographical distribution of the diarists

Tables A1 and A2 show the broad range of areas which the diarists came from. Table A1 shows the type of residential area: inner city life is perhaps under-represented, but a majority of the diarists do live in towns and cities, with more rural populations also having a voice. Table A2 shows that the diarists were well spread across Britain.

Table A1 Type of area lived in by diarists

Type of area	Tracking Study diarists' homes
Rural	9.0%
Village	17.5%
Small town	28.0%
Large town	15.5%
City suburb	23.0%
Inner city	6.5%
Other	9.0%

Table A2 Geographical distribution of sample by ITV region, 1991

ITV region[a]	Tracking Study diarists
Thames/LWT	12.8%
Yorkshire	12.0%
Central	11.6%
HTV	10.0%
Granada	9.8%
Tyne Tees	9.4%
Anglia	9.0%
STV	7.6%
TVS	7.0%
TSW	3.5%
Grampian	2.6%
Ulster	2.2%
Border	1.7%
Channel	0.2%
Ireland and Saudi Arabia	0.4%

Note

[a] In the franchise auction of 1992, Thames was replaced by Carlton as franchise holder for London (weekdays), TVS was replaced by Meridian for the South East, and TSW's South West franchise was taken by Westcountry Television.

Note

1   We are very grateful for Rob Turnock's comments and insights with regard to data collection and data inputting, many of which have been incorporated here.

References

Allat, Patricia and Yeandle, Susan (1992) *Youth Unemployment and the Family: Voices of Disordered Times*, London: Routledge.

Anderson, Digby and Mosbacher, Michael (1997) 'Sex-mad, silly and selfish', *Guardian: Media*, 24 November 1997, pp. 4–5. (See also Ahmed, Kamal (1997) 'Sex, sex, and a bit of fashion on the side', *Guardian*, 24 November 1997, p. 7.)

Ang, Ien (1985) *Watching Dallas: Soap Opera and the Melodramatic Imagination*, translated by Della Couling, London: Methuen.

Ang, Ien (1991) *Desperately Seeking the Audience*, London: Routledge.

Ang, Ien (1996) *Living Room Wars: Rethinking Media Audiences for a Postmodern World*, London: Routledge.

Ang, Ien and Hermes, Joke (1996) 'Gender and/in Media Consumption', in Ien Ang (ed.) *Living Room Wars: Rethinking Media Audiences for a Postmodern World*, London: Routledge.

Atkin, C. and Gantz, W. (1978) 'Tele-news and Political Socialization', *Public Opinion Quarterly* 42: 183–97.

Baker, Meredith and Elias, Peter (1991) 'Youth Unemployment and Work Histories', in S. Dex (ed.) *Life and Work History Analyses: Qualitative and Quantitative Developments*, London: Routledge.

Bandura, A., Ross, D. and Ross, S. A. (1963) 'Imitation of Film-Mediated Aggressive Models', *Journal of Personality and Social Psychology* 66: 3–11.

Barker, Martin (ed.) (1984) *The Video Nasties: Freedom and Censorship in the Media*, London: Pluto Press.

Barker, Martin and Petley, Julian (eds) (1997) *Ill Effects: The Media/Violence Debate*, London: Routledge.

Barratt, Jim (1995) 'Moral Minorities', *Sight and Sound*, 'Forbidden Cinema' Supplement, 22 (6): 22–3.

Barwise, P. and Ehrenberg, A. (1988) *Television and Its Audience*, London: Sage.

Baszanger, Isabelle and Dodier, Nicolas (1997) 'Ethnography: Relating the Part to the Whole', in D. Silverman (ed.) *Qualitative Research: Theory, Method and Practice*, London: Sage.

BBC (1979) *The People's Activities and Use of Time*, London: BBC Data Publications.

Bellaby, Paul (1991) 'Histories of Sickness: Making Use of Multiple Accounts of the Same Process', in Shirley Dex (ed.) *Life and Work History Analyses: Qualitative and Quantitative Developments*, London: Routledge.

Belson, William (1978) *Television Violence and the Adolescent Boy*, Farnborough, England: Saxon House.

Bower, Robin (1992) 'Media Education as an Essential Ingredient in Issue-Based Environmental Education', in Manuel Alvarado and Oliver Boyd-Barrett (eds) *Media Education: An Introduction*, London: British Film Institute.

Bromley, Michael (1998) 'The "Tabloiding" of Britain: "Quality" Newspapers in the 1990s', in H. Stephenson and M. Bromley (eds) *Sex, Lies and Democracy: The Press and the Public*, London: Addison Wesley Longman.

Brooks, Ann (1997) *Postfeminisms: Feminism, Cultural Theory and Cultural Forms*, London: Routledge.

Brunsdon, Charlotte (1997) *Screen Tastes: Soap Opera to Satellite Dishes*, London: Routledge.

Brunsdon, Charlotte and Morley, David (1978) *Everyday Television: 'Nationwide'*, London: British Film Institute.

Bryce, Jennifer (1987) 'Family Time and Television Use', in Tom Linlof (ed.) *Natural Audiences*, Norwood, New Jersey: Ablex.

BSC (1993) *Broadcasting Complaints Council Complaints Bulletin* (May), p. 2.

BSC (1996) *Young People and the Media: Research Working Paper 13*, London: Broadcasting Standards Commission.

BSC (1997) *Regulating for Changing Values*, Research Working Paper 1, London: Broadcasting Standards Commission.

BSC (1998) *Annual Review 1997–8*, London: Broadcasting Standards Commission.

Buckingham, David (1987) *Public Secrets: 'Eastenders' and Its Audience*, London: British Film Institute.

Buckingham, David (1993a) *Children Talking Television: The Making of Television Literacy*, London: Falmer Press.

Buckingham, David (ed.) (1993b) *Reading Audiences: Young People and the Media*, Manchester, England: Manchester University Press.

Buckingham, David (1993c) 'Boys' Talk: Television and the Policing of Masculinity', in David Buckingham (ed.) *Reading Audiences: Young People and the Media*, Manchester, England: Manchester University Press.

Buckingham, David (1996) *Moving Images: Understanding Children's Emotional Responses to Television*, Manchester, England: Manchester University Press.

Buckingham, David and Allerton, Mark (1996) *A Review of Research on Children's 'Negative' Emotional Responses to Television*, Research Working Paper 12, London: Broadcasting Standards Council.

Butler, Judith (1990) *Gender Trouble: Feminism and the Subversion of Identity*, London: Routledge.

Cairns, E. (1984) 'Tele News as a Source of Knowledge about the Violence for Children in Ireland: A Test of the Knowledge-Gap Hypothesis' *Current Psychological Research and Reviews* 3: 32–8.

Chambers, Sue, Karet, Nicki and Samson, Neil (1998) *Cartoon Crazy? Children's Perceptions of 'Action' Cartoons*, London: ITC.

Clarke, Jeremy (1998) 'I Was Alf Garnett's Love Child', *Independent: Thursday Review*, 30 July 1998, pp. 1 and 8.

Cohan, Steven and Hark, Ina Rae (1993) *Screening the Male: Exploring Masculinities in the Hollywood Cinema*, London: Routledge.

Cohen, Stanley (1972) *Folk Devils and Moral Panics: The Creation of the Mods and Rockers*, London: MacGibbon and Kee.

Coleman, Peter (1990) 'Adjustment in Later Life', in John Bond and Peter Coleman (eds) *Ageing in Society: An Introduction to Social Gerontology*, London: Sage.

Coleman, Peter (1991) 'Ageing and Life History: The Meaning of Reminiscence in Late Life', in Shirley Dex (ed.) *Life and Work History Analyses: Qualitative and Quantitative Developments*, London: Routledge.

Cornell, Paul (1998) 'We Are Time's Champions', interview with Dave Owen, *Doctor Who Magazine* 267 (July 1998): 46–51.

Corner, John (1995) *Television Form and Public Address*, London: Arnold.

Corner, John, Richardson, Kay and Fenton, Natalie (1990) *Nuclear Reactions: Form and Response in 'Public Issue' Television*, London: John Libbey Media.

Cubitt, Sean (1991) *Timeshift: On Video Culture*, London: Routledge.

Cubitt, Sean (1993) Videography: Video Media as Art and Culture, London: Macmillan.

Cumberbatch, Guy and Howitt, Dennis (1989) *A Measure of Uncertainty: The Effects of the Mass Media*, London: John Libbey.

Curran, James and Seaton, Jean (1997) *Power without Responsibility: The Press and Broadcasting in Britain*, 5th edition, London: Routledge.

Dahlgren, Peter (1988) 'What's the Meaning of This? Viewers' Plural Sense-Making of TV News', *Media Culture and Society* 10 (3): 285–301.

Davies, Máire Messenger (1989) *Television is Good for Your Kids*, London: Hilary Shipman.

Dayan, D. and Katz, E. (1992) *Media Events*, Cambridge, Massachusetts: Harvard University Press.

Day-Lewis, Sean (1989) *One Day in the Life of Television*, London: Grafton Books.

Demo, David, H. and Ganong, Lawrence, H. (1994) 'Divorce', in Patrick C. McKenry and Sharon J. Price (eds) *Families and Change: Coping with Stressful Events*, London: Sage.

Dewar, Kate (1992) '"Nature Park": A Project with Media Education Focus', in Manuel Alvarado and Oliver Boyd-Barrett (eds) *Media Education: An Introduction*, London: British Film Institute.

Dex, Shirley (1991) 'Life and Work History Analyses', in Shirley Dex (ed.) *Life and Work History Analyses: Qualitative and Quantitative Developments*, London: Routledge.

Dinsmore, Uma (1998) 'Chaos, Order and Plastic Boxes: The Significance of Videotapes for the People Who Collect Them', in Christine Geraghty and David Lusted (eds) *The Television Studies Book*, London: Arnold.

Dowmunt, Tony (1980) *Video with Young People*, London: Inter-Action Inprint.

Durkin, Kevin (1985) *Television, Sex Roles and Children: A Developmental Social Psychological Account*, Milton Keynes, England: Open University Press.

Edwards, Tim (1997) *Men in the Mirror: Men's Fashion, Masculinity and Consumer Society*, London: Cassell.

Emerson, Adrian (1993) *Teaching Media in the Primary School*, London: Cassell.

Erikson, Erik (1950) *Childhood and Society*, Harmondsworth, England: Penguin (1965 edition).

Finn, C. (1992) 'TV Addiction? An Evaluation of Four Competing Media Use Models', *Journalism Quarterly* 69: 422–35.

Fiske, John (1992) 'Popularity and the Politics of Information', in P. Dahlgren and C. Sparks (eds) *Journalism and Popular Culture*, London: Sage.

Frazer, Elizabeth (1987) 'Teenage Girls Reading *Jackie*', *Media, Culture and Society* 9: 407–25.

French, Karl (ed.) (1996) *Screen Violence*, London: Bloomsbury.

Friedan, Betty (1963) *The Feminine Mystique*, London: Penguin.

Gallagher, M (1980) *Unequal Opportunities: The Case of Women and the Media*, Paris: UNESCO.

Gaudoin, Tina (1997) 'Nothing But Sex, Clothes and Boyfriends?', *Times*, 24 November 1997, p. 19.

Gauntlett, David (1995) *Moving Experiences: Understanding Television's Influences and Effects*, London: John Libbey.

Gauntlett, David (1997) *Video Critical: Children, the Environment and Media Power*, Luton, England: John Libbey Media.

Gauntlett, David (1998) 'Ten Things Wrong with the "Effects Model" ', in Roger Dickinson, Ramaswani Harindranath and Olga Linné (eds) *Approaches to Audiences*, London: Arnold. (Also on the internet at www.leeds.ac.uk/ics/david.htm)

Gauntlett, David (forthcoming) *Media, Gender and Identity: A New Introduction*, London: Routledge.

Geraghty, Christine (1991) *Women and Soap Opera: A Study of Prime-Time Soaps*, Cambridge: Polity Press.

Gerbner, George, Gross, Larry, Morgan, Michael and Signorielli, Nancy (1980) 'The "Mainstreaming" of America: Violence Profile No. 11', *Journal of Communication* 30 (3):10–29.

Gerbner, George, Gross, Larry, Morgan, Michael and Signorielli, Nancy (1986) 'Living with Television: The Dynamics of the Cultivation Process', in Jennings Bryant and Dolf Zillmann (eds) *Perspectives on Media Effects*, Hillsdale, New Jersey: Lawrence Erlbaum Associates.

Gillespie, Marie (1995) *Television, Ethnicity, and Cultural Change*, London: Routledge.

Glaser, B. G. and Strauss, A. L. (1967) *The Discovery of Grounded Theory: Strategies for Qualitative Research*, Chicago: Aldine.

Glasgow University Media Group (1976) *Bad News*, London: Routledge and Kegan Paul.

Glasgow University Media Group (1980) *More Bad News*, London: Routledge and Kegan Paul.

Gledhill, Christine (1997) 'Genre and Gender: The Case of Soap Opera', in Stuart Hall (ed.) *Representation: Cultural Representations and Signifying Practices*, London: Sage.

Goodwin, Andrew (1993) 'Riding with Ambulances: Television and Its Uses', *Sight and Sound* 3 (1): 26–8.

Gray, Ann (1987) 'Behind Closed Doors: Video Recorders in the Home', in Helen Baehr and Gillian Dyer (eds) *Boxed In: Women and Television*, London: Pandora.

Gray, Ann (1992) *Video Playtime: The Gendering of a Leisure Technology*, London: Routledge.

Gunter, B. and Winstone, P. (1993) *Television: The Public's View*, London: John Libbey.

Gunter, Barrie (1987) *Television and the Fear of Crime*, London: John Libbey.

Gunter, Barrie (1995) *Television and Gender Representation*, London: John Libbey.

Gunter, Barrie (1997) *Measuring Bias on Television*, Luton, England: John Libbey Media.

Gunter, Barrie and Wober, Mallory (1988) *Violence on Television: What the Viewers Think*, London: John Libbey.

Gunter, Barrie and McAleer, Jill, L. (1990) *Children and Television: The One Eyed Monster?*, London: Routledge.

Haddon, Leslie and Silverstone, Roger (1996) *Information and Communication Technologies and the Young Elderly: A Report on the ESRC/PICT Study of the Household and Information and Communication Technologies*, Brighton, England: University of Sussex, Science Policy Research Unit.

Hall, Edward T. (1973) *The silent language*, New York: Anchor Press.

Halloran, J. D., Brown, R. L. and Chaney, D. C. (1970) *Television and Delinquency*, Leicester, England: Leicester University Press.

Harding, Thomas (1997) *The Video Activist Handbook*, London: Pluto Press.

Hargrave, Andrea Millwood (1993) *Violence in Factual Television*, London: John Libbey.

Hargrave, Andrea Millwood (1998) *Bad Language: What Are the Limits?*, London: Broadcasting Standards Commission.

Harris, C. C. and the Redundancy and Unemployment Group (1987) *Redundancy and Recession*, Oxford: Basil Blackwell.

Hartley, John (1982) *Understanding News*, London: Methuen.

Hermes, Joke (1995) *Reading Women's Magazines*, Cambridge: Polity Press.

Hevey, David (1992) *The Creatures Time Forgot: Photography and Disability Imagery*, London: Routledge.

Hill, Annette (1997) *Shocking Entertainment: Viewer Response to Violent Movies*, Luton, England: John Libbey Media.

Hill, Annette (forthcoming) *Natural Born Killer: Risk and Media Violence*, Luton, England: John Libbey Media.

Hill, M. S. (1988) 'Marital Stability and Spouses' Shared Time: A Multidisciplinary Hypothesis', *Journal of Family Issues* 9: 427–51.

Himmelweit, H. T., Vince, P. and Oppenheim, A. N. (1958) *Television and the Child*, Oxford: Oxford University Press.

Hobson, Dorothy (1980) 'Housewives and the Mass Media', in S. Hall, D. Hobson, A. Lowe and P. Willis (eds) *Culture, Media, Language: Working Papers in Cultural Studies 1972–79*, London: Hutchinson.

Hobson, Dorothy (1982) *Crossroads: The Drama of a Soap Opera*, London: Methuen.

Hodge, Bob and Tripp, David (1986) *Television and Children: A Semiotic Approach*, Cambridge: Polity Press.

Humm, Peter (1998) 'Real TV: Camcorders, Access and Authenticity', in Christine Geraghty and David Lusted (eds) *The Television Studies Book*, London: Arnold.

ITC (1997) *Television: The Public's View*, London: ITC Research.

ITC (1998) *Programme Complaints and Interventions*, London: Independent Television Commission.

Jensen, Klaus Bruhn (1986) *Making Sense of the News: Towards a Theory and an Empirical Model of Reception for the Study of Mass Communication*, Viborg, Denmark: Aarhus University Press.

Joint Industry Group (1997) *Violence on Television Pilot Study*, London: Andrew Irving Associates.

Joint Working Party (1998) *Violence and the Viewer: Report on the Joint Working Party on Violence and Television*, London: BBC, BCS and ITC Publication.

Kantor, David and Lehr, William (1975) *Inside the Family*, San Francisco: Jossey-Bass.

Keighron, Peter (1993) 'Video Diaries: What's Up Doc?', *Sight and Sound* 3 (10): 24–5.

Kieran, Matthew, Morrison, David and Svennevig, Michael (1997) *Regulating for Changing Values*, London: Broadcasting Standards Commission.

Kitzinger, Jenny (1990) 'Audience Understandings of AIDS Media Messages: A Discussion of Methods', *Sociology of Health and Illness* 12: 319–35.

Kitzinger, Jenny (1993) 'Understanding AIDS: Researching Audience Perceptions of Acquired Immune Deficiency Syndrome', in John Eldridge (ed.) *Getting the Message: News, Truth and Power*, London: Routledge.

Kramer, Jerry Lee (1995) 'Bachelor Farmer and Spinsters: Gay and Lesbian Identities and Communities in Rural North Dakota', in David Bell and Gill Valentine (eds) *Mapping Desire: Geographies of Sexualities*, London: Routledge.

Kubey, Robert and Csikszentmihalyi, Mihaly (1991) *Television and the Quality of Life: How Viewing Shapes Everyday Experience*, Hillsdale, New Jersey: Lawrence Erlbaum Associates.

Langer, John (1998) *Tabloid Television: Popular Journalism and the 'Other News'*, London: Routledge.

Lax, Stephen (1997) *Beyond the Horizon: Communications Technologies – Past, Present and Future*, Luton, England: John Libbey Media.

Livingstone, Sonia (1990) *Making Sense of Television: The Psychology of Audience Interpretation*, Oxford: Pergamon.

Lull, James (1980) 'The Social Uses of Television', *Human Communication Research* 6 (3): 197–209.

Lull, James (1982) 'How Families Select Television Programmes: A Mass Observational Study', *Journal of Broadcasting and Electronic Media* 26 (4): 801–11.

Lull, James (1990) *Inside Family Viewing: Ethnographic Research on Television Audiences*, London: Routledge.

Macdonald, Myra (1995) *Representing Women: Myths of Femininity in the Popular Media*, London: Arnold.

Mackay, Hugh (1997) 'Consuming Communication Technologies at Home', in Hugh Mackay (ed.) *Consumption and Everyday Life*, London: Sage.

McKenry, Patrick C. and Price, Sharon J. (eds) (1994) *Families and Change: Coping with Stressful Events*, London: Sage.

McQuail, Denis (1997) *Audience Analysis*, London: Sage.

McRobbie, Angela (1991) *Feminism and Youth Culture: From Jackie to Just Seventeen*, London: Macmillan.

McRobbie, Angela (1994) *Postmodernism and Popular Culture*, London: Routledge.

McRobbie, Angela (1997) 'More! New Sexualities in Girls' and Women's Magazines', in Angela McRobbie (ed.) *Back to Reality? Social Experience and Cultural Studies*, Manchester, England: Manchester University Press.

Midwinter, Eric (1991) *Out of Focus: Old Age, the Press and Broadcasting*, London: Centre for Policy on Ageing.

Miller, David (1994) *Don't Mention the War*, London: Pluto Press.

Moores, Shaun (1993) Interpreting Audiences: The Ethnography of Media Consumption, London: Sage.

Moores, Shaun (1996) *Satellite Television and Everyday Life: Articulating Technology*, Luton, England: John Libbey Media.

Morgan, Michael and Signorielli, Nancy (eds) (1990) *Cultivation Analysis: New Directions in Media Effects Research*, London: Sage.

Morley, David (1980) *The 'Nationwide' Audience*, London: British Film Institute.

Morley, David (1986) *Family Television: Cultural Power and Domestic Television*, London: Comedia.

Morley, David (1992) *Television, Audiences and Cultural Studies*, London: Routledge.

Mort, Frank (1996) *Cultures of Consumption: Masculinities and Social Space in Late Twentieth-Century Britain*, London: Routledge.

Mullan, Bob (1997) *Consuming Television: Television and Its Audience*, Oxford: Blackwell.

Newburn, Tim (1992) *Permission and Regulation: Law and Morals in Post-War Britain*, London: Routledge.

Nickols, Sharon Y. (1994) 'Work/Family Stresses' in Patrick C. McKenry and Sharon J. Price (eds) *Families and Change: Coping with Stressful Events*, London: Sage.

Nixon, Sean (1996) *Hard Looks: Masculinities, Spectatorship and Contemporary Consumption*, London: UCL.

Nixon, Sean (1997) 'Exhibiting Masculinity', in Stuart Hall (ed.) *Representation: Cultural Representations and Signifying Practices*, London: Sage.

O'Hagan, Simon (1998) 'Seven Is Still a Magic Number', *Independent on Sunday: Review*, 19 July 1998, pp. 21–2.

Office for National Statistics (1997a) *Living in Britain: Results from the 1995 General Household Survey*, London: Stationery Office.

Office for National Statistics (1997b) *Family Spending: A Report on the 1996–97 Family Expenditure Survey*, London: Stationery Office.

Office for National Statistics (1998) *Annual Abstract of Statistics 1998 (No. 134)* London: Stationery Office.

Palmer, Patricia (1986) *The Lively Audience: A Study of Children around the TV Set*, Sydney: Allen and Unwin.

Palmer, Patricia (1988) 'The Social Nature of Children's Television Viewing', in P. Drummond and R. Paterson (eds) *Television and Its Audience: International Research Perspectives*, London: British Film Institute.

Petrie, Duncan and Willis, Janet (1995) *Television and the Household*, London: British Film Institute.

Phillipson, Chris (1990) 'The Sociology of Retirement', in John Bond and Peter Coleman (eds) *Ageing in Society: An Introduction to Social Gerontology*, London: Sage.

Philo, Greg (1990) *Seeing and Believing: The influence of Television*, London: Routledge.

Philo, Greg (ed.) (1996) *Media and Mental Distress*, London: Addison Wesley Longman.

Pitkin, D. S. (1985) *The House that Giacomo Built*. Cambridge: Cambridge University Press.

Pointon, Ann and Davies, Chris (eds) (1997) *Framed: Interrogating Disability in the Media*, London: BFI Publishing.

Postman, Neil (1982) *The Disappearance of Childhood*, New York: Delacorte.

Postman, Neil (1987) *Amusing Ourselves to Death*, London: Methuen.

Rabbitt, P. M. A (1984) 'Investigating the Grey Areas', *Times Higher Education Supplement*, 1 June 1984, p. 14.

Radway, Janice (1984) *Reading the Romance*, Chapel Hill: University of North Carolina Press.

Richards, Lyn and Richards, Tom (1994) 'From Filing Cabinet to Computer', in A. Bryman and G. Burgess (eds) *Analyzing Qualitative Data*, London: Routledge.

Roe, Keith (1994) 'Media Use and Social Mobility', in K. E. Rosengren (ed.) *Media Effects and Beyond: Culture, Socialization and Lifestyles*, London: Routledge.

Rogge, Jan-Uwe (1991) 'The Media in Everyday Family Life: Some Biographical and Typological Aspects', in E. Seiter, H. Borchers, G. Kreutzner and E. Warth (eds) *Remote Control: Television, Audiences and Cultural Power*, London: Routledge.

Rogge, Jan-Uwe and Jensen, Jensen (1988) 'Everyday Life and Television in West Germany: An Empathetic-Interpretive Perspective on the Family as System', in James Lull (ed.) *World Families Watch Television*, London: Sage.

Rosengren, K. E. and Windahl, S. (1989) *Media Matter: TV Use in Childhood and Adolescence*, Norwood, New Jersey: Ablex.

Rosenthal, Leslie (1991) 'Unemployment Incidence following Redundancy: The Value of Longitudinal Approaches', in Shirley Dex, (ed.) (1991) *Life and Work History Analyses: Qualitative and Quantitative Developments*, London: Routledge.

Sarland, Lucy (1991) ' "...Different, but not better...": A Primary Video Project', *Multicultural Teaching* 9 (2): 28–34.

Scannell, Paddy (1988) 'Radio Times: The Temporal Arrangements of Broadcasting in the Modern World', in P. Drummond and R. Paterson (eds) *Television and Its Audience: International Research Perspectives*, London: British Film Institute.

Scannell, Paddy and Cardif, David (1991) *A Social History of British Broadcasting: Serving the Nation, Vol 1: 1922–1939*, Oxford: Basil Blackwell.

Schlesinger, Philip (1978) *Putting 'Reality' Together: BBC News*, London: Methuen.

Schlesinger, Phillip, Dobash, R. Emerson, Dobash, Russell P. and Weaver, C. Kay (1992) *Women Viewing Violence*, London: British Film Institute.

Seiter, Ellen (1994) 'Making Distinctions in TV Audience Research: Case Study of a Troubling Interview', in H. Newcombe (ed.) *Television: The Critical View*, 5th edition, New York: Oxford University Press.

Silverstone, Roger (1994) *Television and Everyday Life*, London: Routledge.

Silvey, Robert (1974) *Who's Listening? The Story of BBC Audience Research*, London: George Allen and Unwin.

Skeggs, Beverley (1997) *Formations of Class and Gender: Becoming Respectable*, London: Sage.

Smith, David James (1994) *The Sleep of Reason*, London: Century.

Smith, R. (1986) 'Television Addiction', in J. Bryant and D. Zillman (eds) *Perspectives on Media Effects*, Hillsdale, New Jersey: Lawrence Erlbaum Associates.

Social Trends (1991) *Social Trends 21*, London: Central Statistical Office/HMSO.

Social Trends (1996) *Social Trends 26*, London: Office for National Statistics/HMSO.

Social Trends (1997) *Social Trends 27*, London: Office for National Statistics/HMSO.

Social Trends (1998) *Social Trends 28*, London: Office for National Statistics/HMSO.

Steiner, G. (1963) *The People Look at Television*, New York: Knopf.

Strauss, A. L. (1987) *Qualitative Analysis for Social Scientists*, Cambridge: Cambridge University Press.

Tasker, Yvonne (1993) *Spectacular Bodies: Gender, Genre and the Action Cinema*, London: Routledge.

Thomas, Lyn (1997) 'In Love with Inspector Morse: Feminist Subculture and Quality Television', in Charlotte Brunsdon, Julie D'Acci and Lynn Spigel (eds) *Feminist Television Criticism: A Reader*, Oxford: Oxford University Press. (Originally published in *Feminist Review* 51 (Autumn 1995): 1–25.)

Tuchman, Gaye (1978) 'Introduction: The Symbolic Annihilation of Women by the Mass Media', in Gaye Tuchman, Arlene Kaplan Daniels and James Benet (eds) *Hearth and Home: Images of Women and the Media*, New York: Oxford University Press.

Tulloch, John (1989) 'Approaching the Audience: The Elderly', in Ellen Seiter, Hans Borchers, Gabriele Kreutzner and Eva-Maria Warth (eds) *Remote Control: Television, Audiences, and Cultural Power*, London: Routledge.

Urwin, Sarah (1990) 'Transitions in the Youth Debate: A Critique', in H. Corr and L. Jamieson (eds) *Politics of Everyday Life: Continuity and Change in Work and the Family*, London: Macmillan.

Van Evra, Judith (1990) *Television and Child Development*, Hillsdale, New Jersey: Lawrence Erlbaum Associates.

Van Zoonen, Liesbet (1994) *Feminist Media Studies*, London: Sage.

Walker, James R. and Bellamy, Robert V. (1996) *Television and the Remote Control: Grazing on a Vast Wasteland*, New York: Guildford Press.

Whelehan, Imelda (1995) *Modern Feminist Thought: From the Second Wave to 'Post-Feminism'*, Edinburgh: Edinburgh University Press.

Willis, Janet (1995) 'Staying in Touch: Television and the Over-Seventies', in Duncan Petrie and Janet Willis (eds) *Television and the Household: Reports from the BFI's Audience Tracking Study*, London: BFI Publishing.

Wilson, Patricia, and Pahl, Ray (1988) 'The Changing Sociological Construct of the Family', *The Sociological Review* 30 (2): 233–72.

Wood, Julian (1993) 'Repeatable Pleasures: Notes on Young People's Use of Video', in David Buckingham (ed.) *Reading Audiences: Young People and the Media*, Manchester, England: Manchester University Press.

Wood Bliese, Nancy (1986) 'Media in the Rocking Chair: Media Uses and Functions Among the Elderly', in Gary Gumpert and Robert Cathcart (eds) *Inter/Media: Inter-Personal Communication in a Media World*, New York: Oxford University Press.

Woodward, Kathryn (1997) 'Concepts of Identity and Difference', in Kathryn Woodward (ed.) *Identity and Difference*, London: Sage.

Worcester, Robert, M. (1998) 'Demographics and Values: What the British Public Reads and What It Thinks about Its Newspapers', in H. Stephenson and M. Bromley (eds) *Sex, Lies and Democracy: The Press and the Public*, London: Addison Wesley Longman.

Wright, David W., Nelson, Brian S. and Georgen, Kathleen E. (1994) 'Marital Problems', in Patrick C. McKenry and Sharon J. Price (eds) *Families and Change: Coping with Stressful Events*, London: Sage.

Index